To Sarah + Ale;

Jah Rastafari

Volume 2

The Babylon System

ONELOVE!!

Tchandela

www.jahlove.co.uk

www.Jahlovepublishing.com

e-mails: info@jahlovepublishing.com

tchandela@yahoo.co.uk

SOON COME

ISBN - 9780955861697

To my Great Brother, Friend, Guide and Spiritual Preceptor,

Rasta Field Marshal, General Thunder, Torpedo, Jah Mice

To Our Sublime Ancestors and Predecessors:

Leonard Percival Howell, Marcus Mosiah Garvey, Robert Hinds,

Prince Emmanuel

His Sublime, Imperial Majesty, Emperor Haille Selassie I

~

To

My Mother, Mrs. Eunice O'Connor

Kaya Amarava O'Connor

Noah Abaka

And to all our Children of Tomorrow

I have used male pronouns in most cases in this book. This in no way is intended to reflect a bias in terms of the sexes, but merely for the sake of expediency. Please freely assume the alternative when necessary. Whatever mistakes the reader might find in this volume are solely my responsibility. As we're all human and imperfect in our grasp at truth and reality, I ask for your forbearance.

Jah Bless

*The **Za-Yan** that can be described in word or form is not the **eternal** Za-Yan.*

-The Golden Path of Jah Rastafari -

'I hear the words of the Rastaman say, *"Babylon your throne gone down, gone down. Babylon your throne gone down"*.

Then I hear the words of a Higher Man say, *"Babylon your throne gone down, gone down, Babylon your throne gone down"*.
And then I hear the angel with the **seven seals** singing, *"Babylon your throne gone down, gone down. Babylon your throne fall down"*.

-Bob Marley & the Wailers-

The denial of Truth leads to destruction and ruin, and the envying of your brother leads through the gates of Hell.

-The Golden Path of Jah Rastafari -

"No matter the influences of time, space or dimensions, **I AND I** *will continuously and* **consciously** *incarnate and* **re-incarnate** *in creation, by the* **Divine Will** *of the Most High,* **Jah Rastafari,** *to free human beings from the* **entanglement** *and* **corruption** *of the* **Babylon System**. *I AND I will keep on fighting until* **Babylon fall"**.

- Vows of the Rasta Fire warrior-

- The Golden Path of Jah Rastafari -

*Be very careful of the idea of a beginning. A beginning, like an ending, is always strewn with the seeds of treachery – **perception** and **definition**. As concepts, they limit the search for possibilities that could bring us closer to truth. The **Hegelian dialectic** of Eurocentric philosophy must be seen for its narrow emphasis. That which **precedes** and as a consequence, **give birth** to these terms must be the primary object of our enquiries.*

*Essentially, there was never a beginning, as human beings understand it; therefore there could never be an end. The **Eternal Body of Truth** that is **Jah Rastafari** is beyond all concepts of duality we know and understand. **Jah Rastafari** is the **Eternal Field of Potentiality** from which all forms and multiplicity arise continually and ceaselessly; the begin-less and the endless, beyond all known qualities and definitions, and which cannot be perceived or defined from a point of ignorance but only from the platform of clarity born of unswerving devotion to **Truth**. Truth transcends the **erroneous conceptions** of time, space and dimensionality, and more so, the dictates of man.*

-The Golden Path of Jah Rastafari –

The difficulty for us as human beings in developing and transmitting knowledge lies mostly in our inability to process necessary information in ways that can be readily understood and used by the majority of people. In this regard, the verbal human language forms we are used to are very limited because we have never learned to utilize the full range of our multifaceted, *multidimensional* sensory perceptions adequately. Language is not just about speaking words but the utilizing of a whole range of other subtle sensory faculties to express our thoughts, emotions and actions. The very fact that we exist as human beings in fleshy bodies is in itself a *form of language*. In religious or spiritual terms one might even venture to say that creation in its entirety is God's *divine language*; the *Word* of God made *manifest*. Our entire being is actually a language that the *mind/soul* uses to express itself through time, space and dimension. Verbal language presents specific limitations in this regard, therefore our concept of what is limited are only constrained by the way we use language and consequently, our knowledge of its function.

There might be times when we want to say something but we don't know how to say it, or we can't seem to find the appropriate type of language with which to say it. The limitation in the end lies in the manner in which we understand the possibilities of our mind's functionality. Even if we augment our physical biology with material technology such as prescribed by Euro/American *Transhumanist* philosophy, we would still be unable to use verbal language alone to articulate our thought processes adequately.

There is however, a language that transcends verbalization. It's not a new language; it's just that most times we seem to forget that it exists. During the turmoil of our daily lives running around in this system of fear and illusions which characterizes the Babylon System, our minds and senses are bombarded with '*sensory viruses*' that infect our thought processes and therefore our very perception of ourselves as human beings. A thought is a form of language as much as a feeling (emotion) or a word. Some languages are not recognized as such because of the nature of their manifestation, which at times causes confusion and misunderstanding. And some languages, such as Latin, died many centuries ago but are still given prominence by a few, not because it has inherent relevance to people these days, but because it represents *certain values* and *loyalties to specific causes*.

In Jamaica, our particular cultural verbal language form, the Jamaican Oral Tradition, (JOT – which is commonly referred to as patois), embedded in our Reggae Music and culture, has taken flight across the world, developing, growing and expanding positive vibrations everywhere. In Japan, USA, Latin America, Africa, UK, France, Belgium, Germany, Switzerland, Italy, Asia and so on the language of Reggae Music and Rastafari can be heard loudly, protesting, pleading and inciting truth vibrations. Rasta Reggae Music or *Consciousness Music* (as some of us refer to it) has ignited a world-wide language of unity and the principles of divine ONELOVE. It's one of the most important *carrier waves* of Rastafarian culture.

The language of the ONELOVE that we use to navigate our pathway through existent nature is the most simple, natural and profound language form. It's the most instinctive and enlightening method to create and maintain rational perspectives in all areas of our lives on earth. The language of the ONELOVE can never die because it's eternal. It existed before creation and indeed is the very language of the *Supreme Creative Power* we Rastafarians know as *Jah Rastafari*, the eternally established, living embodiment of what human beings refer to as *God*. In essence we are the very embodiment of God's language; '*the word manifest as flesh*'.

*"We are not divided; we're all one family, one in hope and justice, one in charity. **We are not divided, we're all one family.**"*

- The Sublime, Brother Leonard Percival Howell -

*" I am convinced that the children we are teaching today, will become vanguards and guardians to our freedom tomorrow and better citizens to defend our democracy, and to ensure that generations to come will learn from the **Holocaust of slavery, and keep the flame of remembrance burning**. Help them to understand more about the past, so that our history **NEVER** repeats itself, and that we can create a better future for **the whole human race.**"*

- The Sublime, Brother Leonard Percival Howell -

Countless brave *Rasta Fire Warriors* have fallen on the battlefield of life, fighting for our liberation from the tyranny of illusion and the prison of mental and spiritual conceptions spawned by erroneous perceptions of truth. And countless more will rise up to do the same again tomorrow. The fight for human dignity and freedom of self expression in creation is the cornerstone of our existence as Rastafarians, not lofty religious doctrines or cotton-candy ideals; only the plain and simple right for each being to express itself in the manner it chooses and that is beneficial to the *Greater Good* of all.

Among the first and most esteemed of our Rastafarian brethren, manifested the works and deeds of our *Sublime Prophet and Teacher, Brother Leonard Percival Howell*. In the tradition of the true Rasta Fire Warrior, Brother Howell walked the *Golden Path of Jah Rastafari* to progressive and fulfilling *Livity*. His contributions to the works of Rastafari is a magnificent and shining achievement that most people in the world (including Jamaica) have never heard about, yet is one of the *keys* to true Rasta knowledge and understanding.

Like our *Sublime Elder, Marcus Mosiah Garvey,* Brother Howell left Jamaica for the USA during the stirring times of the 1920's. *'The spurt of the Pan-African movement enticed him to find his way by ship to* ***New York City,*** *and to search through its boroughs to discover the epicenter of the black civil rights movement, Harlem'.*

When he went to New York he found the intensity of racial oppression against black people was far more than he had imagined. The Sublime, Marcus Mosiah Garvey also expressed the same sentiments when he arrived in New York at an earlier time, citing that ***'slavery was bad in Jamaica but in America it seemed to have cut through the souls of our people'.*** After personal encounters of racism, bigotry and white hatred in America, Brother Howell made his vow to spend the rest of his life fighting against all human oppression.

Brother Howell lit the fire of radicalism and righteousness and began to preach his message of mental and physical emancipation of the black man in America and the West Indies. His firm stance and eloquent message gained the attention of many influential thinkers on matters of race and civil liberties at that time. Upon his return to Jamaica in 1932 he felt an overwhelming ***'urge to share his wealth of knowledge with his kinsman'.*** The ***Pan-Africanist*** movement of the ***UNIA*** (United Negro Improvement Association) formed by The Sublime, Marcus Mosiah Garvey was by then a permanent fixture in Jamaican society, garnering support among the poor and disenfranchised black majority (who continued to suffer under the yoke of British colonial oppression). Brother Howell at some stage during his sojourn in the USA became aware of the ascension to the throne of Ethiopia of the ***Negus Tafari*** who was crowned Emperor in November 1930. This great event was a momentous occasion for black people world-wide who at that time were severely oppressed by racism. Ethiopia was the only African country that successfully resisted colonization by Europeans and boasted a proud and ancient history of monarchy that stretched back thousands of years to biblical times. The newly crowned emperor became the shining symbol of hope for many black people, especially in the African Diaspora. His impressive titles created much speculation as European envoys and nobilities attending his investiture bowed low before this black emperor. His Imperial Majesty Haille Selassie I was the direct descendent of the ancient union between the biblical King Solomon and the Queen of Sheba, and the 225th king of the ***Solomonic*** royal dynasty of Ethiopia. Among his titles on accession to the throne of Ethiopia were; ***King of all earthly kings, Lord of all earthly lords, Conquering Lion of the tribe of Judah, Power of the Trinity, Defender of Faith, Elect of God, Light of the World.*** Brother Howell found his calling in the expression of the emperor as the ***living link*** to black people's great ancient historical past. He formulated a doctrine and began spreading word of the manifest virtues of the great ***King of Kings***. Several quotations and prophecies from the Christian bible were garnered to support the emerging ideology of His Imperial Majesty's status as a *divine incarnation.*

It's also important to be cognizant of other elements in the formulation of early Rasta thinking, particularly the traditional aspects of African spiritual systems that embellished the philosophical body of the *black churches* and religious *revivalist movements* in Jamaica during the struggles for freedom against slavery and British colonial oppression.

In Jamaica, Brother Howell lost no time in mobilizing the sentiments of a developing *Rastas consciousness* into a credible socio/political force for change in a society that was still British colonial property. The history of Jamaican culture and particularly Rasta culture is indebted to Brother Howell and many other stalwart brethren of faith who, against the oppressive tyranny of the white supremacy system in Jamaica, forged a conscious path to the dismantling of the *mind control* influences of what was now termed *The Babylon System.* During the early years of Rastafarian development, the British colonial government perceived the emergent *Rasta Movement* as being composed of *'sixty thousand lawless and mentally deficient men whose only aim was the destruction of civilized government and society'.* The idea that black African Jamaican people could seek to be *repatriated* back to their ancestral homeland, (which was then labeled by whites as the *'Dark Continent of Africa'*) must therefore, according to the racist government, stem from *'criminal behavior'* or worse still, *'deranged minds'.*

The early Rasta movement was consequently labeled a *'terrorist organization'* and steps were taken by the British colonial authority to utterly destroy its progress. Brother Howell along with other leaders such as the *Sublime, Brother Robert Hinds* was duly arrested on trumped up charges and imprisoned in 1934. After his release from prison Brother Howell and his brethren raised enough money to acquire land and create resources with which to develop the emerging philosophy of Rastafari. He bought 500 acres of land in *Sligoville*, Spanish Town, and named the space *Pinnacle.*

Writing on the *Leonard P. Howell Foundation website,* his daughter *Catherine Howell* gives a description of Pinnacle and its founding principles:

*"Despite the fact that Howell became **the most persecuted man in the history of Jamaica**, he must be credited for purchasing over 500 acres of Land at Sligoville, in St. Catherine which became known as **Pinnacle**. It quickly became the center of the Rastafarian Movement, the first free slave, self sufficient and economically*

*empowered African village in Jamaica which at that time was a tremendous **historical** move.*

Many generations of former African slaves, in the thousands, came from rural and urban Jamaica to settle on the land and made their vision a reality. They lived a natural way of life, in harmony with the universe, showed love and peace to all race and color, lived in unity worked collectively, upheld culture, heritage, freedom and justice,

Many who were farmers planted organic food, others who were skilled in arts and craft made household items. In addition, herbal medicine, roots, tonics and other produce were made and sold to the local government, private and public sectors. Howell became the most successful teacher of Rastafari doctrine. He enjoined black people to be proud of heritage and culture, to have their own money and Banks; be self-motivated, strong self-sufficient, where black owned economies would emerge and to hold high the value of education. Furthermore, he preached to show respect, love and honor'.

This is essentially what the Rastafarian movement in Jamaica set out to achieve many decades ago; the establishment of the precepts of pure **Livity** and the pursuit of the natural and ideal life of peace, justice and Compassionate **ONELOVE** for all human beings. Along the way the colonial government labeled Rastafarians as a *'threat'* to society simply for the fact that we avowed to remove ourselves from the *slave mind control program* of the evil and destructive *Babylon System*. Perhaps this same scenario might sound *familiar* to some people who are reading these words right now. When some people fight for their natural human rights and freedoms, the label *terrorism* is generally used to vilify them in the eyes of those who are the *keepers* and *maintainers* of the Babylon System.

Brother Howell's pronounced allegiance to *H.I.M Haille Selassie I, Emperor of Ethiopia* led to the Jamaican colonial government voicing concerns regarding his *'implicit allegiance to a foreign King'*, as recorded in a report by a member of the Jamaica Secret Service. His condemnation of the Christian Church led to fears by the authorities of insurrection and revolt by the poor black masses if he was not dealt with once and for all.

The continuous persecution of Rastafarians in Jamaica by the British colonial state culminated in 1954 in a major joint police/military operation against the movement. Under orders from *Alexander Bustamante,* (a Jamaican servant of the British colonial regime), and on special advisement from the government of Britain, a battalion of soldiers, police and the Jamaica Secret Service executed a pre-emptive raid on The Pinnacle and completely destroyed the village, farms, homes, and schools that had been constructed, leaving thousands homeless. Brother Howell was once again arrested on charges of sedition and conspiracy to overthrow the British colonial regime in Jamaica.

The British colonial authorities, fearful of the independence of the black Jamaican masses and the *'brazen challenge'* that Rastas posed to its authority, harassed the Pinnacle commune, beating, killing and imprisoning hundreds of Rastafarians. In other important Rasta communities across the island such as *Back O' Wall* in Kingston and *Coral Gardens* in *Montego Bay* the same brutal repression was enforced against peaceful Rastafarians. The dreadlocks of many Rastas were forcibly chopped off with knives and machetes and the communities were brutally beaten and dispersed at the point of the gun. This most shameful episode in Jamaican history has always been quietly hidden away and many people around the world nowadays who wear dreadlock hair, the *Red, Gold* and *Green* Rasta standards and listen to Rasta Reggae music would not have even heard of the terrible struggles that Rastafarians had to endure against the evil Babylon System in Jamaica. Our Sublime Brother and Teacher, Howell was again arrested, beaten and illegally imprisoned in a mental asylum by the colonial government in order to crush the movement of Rastafari. Each and every Rastafarian walking the earth today is a living testament to the abject failure of the *Babylon System* to destroy us and our hopes and aspirations that one day the entire human race will gain its freedom from tyranny and oppression here on earth. **Jah Rastafari.**

In Jamaica, many people are still ignorant of these very important issues. The horrendous treatment of the Rastafarians of Jamaica parallels that of other communities of people around the world who are even today still fighting for their natural freedoms of human self expression. The atrocities against peaceful Rastafarians have never truly been addressed by the authorities of Jamaica and even today there is a struggle by our *Talawa* Rasta brethren to reclaim the *blessed land* of *Pinnacle* from the government so that we may continue our development as free human beings in peace, freedom and compassionate ONELOVE.

From its humble beginnings, Rastafari has become a world wide movement that has gained the respect, support and admiration of millions of people around the world yet, to the puzzlement of observers, has no centrally organized core. *Rastafarian Houses* such as the *Bobo Ashanti*, founded by *The Sublime, Prophet Elder, Prince Emanuel*, the *Ethiopian World Federation, Twelve Tribes* and others have blazed the trail of Rasta consciousness across the earth for decades, citing the awareness of peace, Livity and the ONELOVE to the nations of the world. The *governments* of the Babylon

System are always *terrified* of people taking control of their own lives and living according to the dictates of real human values and understanding. If people turn their backs on the Babylon System and face the *Pure Light* of *Eternal Truth* that *Jah Rastafari* represents, then it cannot exist because it is a complete fraud; an illusion that can rapidly fade away in the astonishingly beautiful radiance of the *free human spirit*.

Mystery Babylon

Kette drum, *Kette Drum, mek mi hear the sound*
Beat the Kette Drum and mek we burn down Rome.
Get a Drum, Kette Drum, mek mi hear the sound
Shake the tambourine and mek old Pope drown.
*When the Kette beat, the **Beast** get defeat,*
And people [dancing] in the street

-Kette Drum- Beenie Man & Determine-

Rastafari is a system of ***earthical*** and ***spiritual*** philosophy developed in Jamaica as a reaction to the destructive power of human slavery and oppression imposed on black African peoples by white Europeans. The roots of Rastafari has been watered by the suffering of African peoples who were ***kidnapped*** and taken as slaves to the *New World* to languish under the most severe forms of oppression know to human beings for four hundred years. This evil system of human ***mind control, slavery, dehumanization*** and ***destruction*** for material ***profit*** encapsulates what we Rastas of Jamaica call the ***Babylon System*** and which still exists today across the world in the 21st century. It's this system of oppression that is now manifesting overtly as a global *New World Order* fascistic dictatorship that will engulf the entire world in the very near future.

When we speak of systems, it's necessary to understand that the term can be applied to almost anything we care to think of. A system basically can mean a set of interacting or interdependent parts, components or ***structures*** that form an ***integrated*** whole; the comprehension and rationalization of a given ***operation;*** a method or way of action or thought that results in a coherent process.

For instance, in an office we have filing systems; ways of keeping things in order. Or perhaps the political system which explains the manner in which politics is pursued by politicians and how a country is governed by a government. A computer functions as an *'integrated'* system; all its parts working together to form a coherent pattern of operation. At home, parents usually have a system of dealing with the children after school such as doing their homework before watching TV or brushing their teeth before going to bed at night and so on. Our lives operate as multi-faceted systems. We're born, we grow up, we become old and we die; that in itself is a system which

20

operates efficiently and continuously.

The Babylon System functions very much like any other system. It has a definable structure, a clear agenda, is continuous in its manner of operation and has a definite *goal*. It's an incredible structure that has the ability and flexibility to grow intelligently, organically, multiply and extend itself beyond boundaries or borders. Most importantly, the Babylon System is *invisible* unless your senses are trained to see it. Always when people see it in operating for the first time, they are astonished that such an incredible thing could exist in the world and they were completely unaware of it.

The Babylon System is all around us, inside our minds and in every decision we make about our lives. It's a system of *psychology* and *perception* that has locked our minds inside a *mental* and *spiritual prison*. That's why we see the world and ourselves in the way we do. Its aim is to make us suspend our cognitive, rational and imaginative mental processes and be completely absorbed in the illusions of a false version of life; its invisible nature is its key defense strategy. *You can't affect something that you don't know exist*.

The Babylon System incorporates a specific *'science'* of mind control, which is the knowledge and ability to remove from a human being his or her natural, rational, cognitive senses and *replace* or *reroute* them through a false *mental program* that allows complete obedience and control over the individual. This state of slavery was imposed upon black Jamaicans and African peoples in general for *four hundred years*. Collectively as a people we fought courageously against the Babylon System and through our hard efforts, and that of some *conscious* white *brethren* in Britain and America, attained a degree of freedom from it. We are still fighting even now in the 21st century to free ourselves completely from *this very great evil*. In addition to this we have been able to ascertain that white *Euro/American* peoples have also equally been enslaved by the same mind control programs of the Babylon System. In recent times some have begun to wake up to *specific aspects* of this reality. This is the battlefield upon which the *Rasta Fire Warriors* of Jah Rastafari consciously incarnate and re-incarnate to take up the struggle so that all beings will become free from this destructive illusion of mental and spiritual slavery.

The mind control program of the Babylon System is the cause of the insane, pathological behavior exhibited within all human societies across the world. In every nation there is a structure generated to undermine the natural positive impulses of human beings through the established political states, religions and educational structures that mislead human beings into *false versions of reality*.

The Babylon System was consciously created in the world for the purpose of enslaving the minds and souls of human beings. It's controlled and directed by small *'elite'* groups of human beings allied to negative *multidimensional forces* that spans time, space and dimensional structures. The reality of our situation as human beings on earth is far more surprising than we can really imagine.

The systemic abuse of masses of human beings by a small powerful elite is not a new thing but in fact the hallmark of most human civilizations across the world. History, as it's written, is a clear and unambiguous testament to this principle. In fact, what is known as *history* is but a *mind control* structure put in place to prevent real understanding of the senseless and evil phenomenon that has been inflicted upon the *human race* by those who style themselves conquerors, kings, queens, superiors and leaders. The poor and wretched of this earth have been deliberately kept in the bondage of darkness and ignorance for untold ages by these elite groups of *policy makers* and *rulers* whom we refer to nowadays broadly as the *Illuminati*.

When we analyze history, we see with heart-breaking clarity the chilling, calculating web of *deception* that has kept the majority of human beings on earth in *slavery* for thousands of years. This situation has now intensified to the point where the entire human population will soon be *micro-chipped* like animals, thus making us easier to control at the touch of a button. This is the future for all human beings living on the earth and will certainly become our reality, if we don't wake up and tear down the walls of the Babylon System. A micro-chipped population ruled by the iron fists of cruel, calculating and thoroughly evil *overlords* is the actual future waiting for us all.

The Babylon System is not a *'natural'* phenomenon but in part a reflection of our ability as conscious beings to utilize the energies of our minds to create thoughts and concepts that manifest as exterior phenomenon. It's a byproduct of *erroneous conceptions* which has been *deliberately stimulated* in the consciousness of human beings over a vast period of time by very negative forces situated mostly beyond our five sense reality paradigm. This mind control program traps us into thinking, believing and behaving in a completely false mode of living.

The term *consensus reality* has been coined to express the nature of how we as sentient beings collectively can agree (*subliminally* and largely *unconsciously*) on set formulas to understand and function in the world. This is one of the main mind control programs of the Babylon System. The prevailing structure of negative politics, economics, war, racism and general destructive mode of living that all human beings have been subjected to throughout recorded history is a clear manifestation of this principle.

The consensus reality in which we now live is what everyone *thinks* is *real*, therefore there's a common (mostly unconscious) agreement amongst the majority. For example, the sky is blue, water is wet, I am black and you are white, politics is real, school educates our children, marriage brings happiness, history is exactly how we're told, war brings peace, Bin Laden blew up the Twin Towers and so forth. This common agreement by most of us (whether conscious or unconsciously) becomes the accepted norm of any given social structure; conventions that set the laws by which we operate. These laws, or ways of accepting and believing what we are told, is consciously and covertly stimulated by media, politicians, the church, education establishments, scientists and so on, and often becoming habitual, enduring, unquestioned and thus exhibits various degrees of resistance to any kind of alterations or changes. This consensus reality illusion is intended to serve the purpose of making human beings compliant and governable within social structures. We are told by our *'jailors'* that the only other option left open to us is *chaos*.

If the consensus reality that the majority subscribe to sometimes become shaky or under attack by something that does not fit into the accepted paradigm, then the *agents* of the Babylon System, (what George Orwell referred to as the *'thought police'*) the media, teachers, police, soldiers, paramilitary, parking attendants, university lecturers, scientists, employers, politicians and, unwittingly, even the next door neighbor, reinforces, by any means necessary, the illusions of the system. In fact we ourselves reinforce the control program within our minds because the Babylon System imperative makes us believe that if we *go against the grain* we are mad, stupid, inconsiderate to other peoples feelings or just plain *crazy*.

Within the larger consensus reality that most human beings subscribe to, we have what's called *'mindsets'*. A mindset is basically groups or sub-groups, (usually referred to as *sub-cultures*) formed of individuals who are *'like-minded'* in their perception of the illusion. A mindset can also, (given specific impetus), create its own variation of a consensus reality that functions within the *orbit* of the larger consensus and, if given time and enough energy, can become a part of the larger consensus reality, (if it can add to the bigger illusion in a desirable way). Black people all share in a specific consensus reality simply by accepting the idea that we're black and whites do the same on account of their physical appearances, languages and cultures and so on. For instance, in Jamaica when you buy a pair of *Clark's* shoes you are functioning as part of a consensus reality because Clark's shoes are *supposed* to be stylish and an indicator that you have enough money to afford a pair. It supposedly gives you *class* and *street-cred*. No one knows who first said that was true, people just believe it and act upon that impulse of irrational belief. Even the poorest person in the ghetto will spend their last dollar on a pair of Clark's instead of buying something that's more needed, (even though Clark's shoes are not essentially any better than cheaper versions). Jamaicans on a cultural level at times epitomizes consensus reality living to extremes. There are several reasons for this, chief of which is the experience of *slavery,* which was a common reality for all our predecessors here in Jamaica.

From some of the earliest known civilizations on earth we can discern the development of the Babylon System and chart its devastating impact on our cultures, especially nowadays in an age of widespread access to information and technology. Ancient Sumer, Egypt, Greece, Rome, Byzantium and so on were all *slave societies*; in fact most human civilizations that we know of and their grand achievements have all been tainted with the negative influences of the Babylon System. This is no mere accident but a deliberately designed phenomenon for specific reasons that will very soon impact upon the human race in the most unbelievable ways.

---

*We are too used to using our **five gross senses** to validate our understanding of reality. What happens when something occurs and persists **outside** of our normal sensory experiences? What happens when we attempt to articulate this by using the forms of languages we have become accustomed to?*

*These are among some of the principle questions that one will encounter upon the **Golden Path of Jah Rastafari**. Analyse the meaning of the words **sense** and **non-sense**. Understand fully their implications in regard to the mind control programs of the **Babylon System**.*

-The Golden Path of Jah Rastafari-

In order to clearly understand the terrible nature of the Babylon System and its operations, it's best to observe it in an analytic manner using what I refer to as the **analytic mode** of **conscious observation** during a process of reflective or contemplative meditations. This requires one to engage the mind in a process of **mental quiescence**; a state of mind that's relaxed, quiet, calm and peaceful yet completely alert and able to analyse diverse sets of information rapidly, in rational and coherent order, thus gaining deep and valuable insight into a thought, a process or thing. This can be done at anytime; while doing your shopping, looking after the children, being at work, sitting on the bus or train or just sitting quietly and thinking things over in your mind. Part of the process of analytic observation involves being able to **de-construct** by firm analysis any given set of information that appears to and moves through the mind. One is then able to analyse **sensory data** and **thoughts-forms** critically, without colouring that information unnecessarily with one's own personal feelings. One should remember the subtle difference between **subjective** and **personal**. Usually there are many people who seem to have an erroneous conception of what we mean by these terms. This is beneficial when we wish to understand the mechanisms behind and within any situation, and can create clear and precise perception of anything in material nature and beyond.

The analytic mode is an essential component in the structure of the **Fire-Meditation,** which is s state of consciousness and awareness that assists the mind to penetrate the illusions of the Babylon System and **see** with complete clarity its illusory nature in opposition to the structure and nature of true reality. Great insights into all spheres of

25

life, physical, mental and spiritual can be attained by this method of mental training and is invaluable in all that one does. Eminent Jamaican Rastaman such as **Rasta Field Marshal, Torpedo Jah Mice**, (whom I've had the greatest fortune to know and walk with for many years), exhibit great proficiency in this method of mental perception and is able to discern information about things that many people might find difficult to comprehend.

The act of observation isn't just about using our eyes or the other basic senses of the physical body but a much more subtle form of **perception** that includes our faculties of **memory, imagination, intellect, intuition, logic, analytic reason**, and **judgement**. When one has de-constructed a set of information in the mind, and lay bare all its components, the next step in analytic observation is to then relate the results of ones perceptions to the **personal aspect** of knowledge accumulation; the **actual process** of understanding and **digesting** information. There is no such thing as **objectivity** in reality. Everything is **subjective** because the very manifestation of the universe itself is **part of the real and actual nature of our being**. We are not separate from creation; we are intrinsic parts of it, from the pre-atomic, subatomic, atomic, molecular, cellular and energetic and so on. Our perception of creation and ourselves are inextricably intertwined, so therefore nothing can really be objective or separated from our perceptions, no matter how big or small.

The precepts of Jah Rastafari teach us that materially and spiritually the very '**act of observation**' affects the process of that which one is trying to observe. In other words, if you're looking at something and thinking about it, (or more to the point, mindfully concentrating on it with full awareness), your mind is affecting that thing's nature in relation to your being in time, space and dimensionality in some way, no matter how briefly or even if one is not cognisant of this process. The human mind has the amazing ability to consciously manifest, manipulate and shape matter by thought alone. This is basically the way that '**mental technology**' works through the vehicle of **sense consciousness**. This ability is a natural part of our functioning as human beings and is crucial in understanding the functional capabilities and weaknesses inherent in the Babylon System and the great strengths that we possess as sentient beings in creation. All that we observe and understand ultimately is derivative of higher mental processes.

*In order to gain real knowledge of human beings origin, function and purpose on earth, we must challenge and completely dismantle the erroneous and misleading assumptions of **academic history** as taught by racist Euro/American scholars and historians. Their views are prejudiced as a natural course of their lack of real knowledge and obvious fears concerning their own origins as a **segment** of the human family. This is a direct result of the workings of the **Babylon System** and its **mind control programs**, and is designed to prevent the black and the white and all other branches of the human family from realizing their true potential as created beings within **Jah** creation. Compassionate Unity in **ONELOVE** between all the different branches of humanity is the goal of Rasta. Compassionate Unity is the only way for humanity to defeat the nilistic forces of evil that threatens to subvert our evolutionary path within the **Creation Field**. But let it be known that unity must be a '**common consensus**' born of true knowledge and realization of our purpose as created beings in existent nature.*

-The Golden Path of Jah Rastafari-

Usually if we're trying to understand a phenomenon or that which causes a phenomenon we start by tracing its point of origin in space and time. The scientists, anthropologists and archaeologists of Babylon use this principle to establish what they believe to be a chronology of our beginning as sentient beings on earth and so on. However, there are some things that we cannot decipher by going directly back to their points of origin because the fact of their being cannot be substantiated by the faculties we use to perceive and rationalize them. We must remember that there are many things we cannot perceive with our physical senses but which are very real in other ways. In that case, we perhaps could employ a system called '**back engineering**'. This means that when we are confronted with a phenomenon we don't understand or can't rationalize, we start (from the point of observation) by breaking it apart methodically according to our system of logic and reasoning; analyzing the various parts until we arrive at the most likely conclusion as to its origin and meaning. For example, if we saw a car for the first time and didn't know how it functioned, the most likely way of understanding it completely would be to take it apart and try to put it back together again. Then, to reach full comprehension we would have to drive it and experience its various motions. This is the type of methodology that Euro/American scientists use in their various experimentations such as the **Big Bang**

Theory, the quest to rationalize a *Unified Field Theory* and so forth.

The ages old question of our origins as human beings on earth seems to have frustrated this method of inquiry. Most of the world's prestigious thinkers have applied this method to developing theories of our evolution as a species without any real definitive conclusion. This misunderstanding of our origins and our purpose has contributed to terrible wars, hatred and unmentionable cruelty throughout our recorded history and continue to do so even today in the 21st century. Many have come claiming to be messiahs, prophets, tyrants, mystics, teachers and demagogues who have some special insight or revelation into the truth of our origin and purpose and so on, only to lead ignorant masses into the damning precipice of human folly. I believe the reasons for this failure to understand our true nature as sentient beings is indicative of our lack of understanding of the real issues involved when dealing with our human origins and development on earth due to the negative and destructive influences of the mind control programs of the Babylon System.

What if our perception of the knowledge we *think* we possess is completely wrong? *What if there was no beginning, as we understand it*? Many of us are afraid of even thinking of this scenario because such questions fall completely outside our programmed *dualistic mode* of perception. The long *'human trauma'* we label *civilization* could be likened to an unsettling circus of the absurd when real insight of these issues dawn upon our minds.

When we analyze these things clearly and consciously, we can discern several key components that make up the *systems* of our perception of human existence. Perhaps one of the ways in which we can approach this issue is to look at it in different perspective such as *'rhythms of information'* that culminates in specific *'cycles of knowledge'* manifesting through space, time and dimension using our bodies and consciousness faculties as *'vehicles'* and *'carrier waves'* to manifest awareness of phenomenal being.

Phenomenon arises in the form of composite energetic structures, as a direct result of the actions of the mind, consciousness and our *soul* energy functioning within creation (time/space dimensions). This process is uniformly and eternally directed by the *Supreme Power* that is *The Eternal Field of Potentiality* designate, *Jah Rastafari,* which we refer to as *The Creator* or *God.* All forms and life expressions are the embodiment of the *Supreme Unity* in eternal *mystic* action. *Jah Rastafari* is the *Eternal Originator* of this principle and is completely transcendent to all phenomena; being the cause and the controller of all phenomenal appearances – the multi-versal structures, universes, stars and planets and all energetic life-forms that furnish the Creation Field that we observe with our gross senses as time, space and dimensions.

Through constant analysis using the *analytic mode* of conscious observation, one can clearly see this process working fluidly and perfectly. There is really no mystery in creation if one simply applies the mental processes to understanding in the correct manner.

The *Creation Field* of space, time and dimensions is the subtle phenomenal expression of the will of the Supreme, Jah Rastafari and is expressed as the universal *Demiurge* energy in ancient knowledge systems. The idea of the Demiurge in European Platonic philosophy alludes to an *'entitized'* concept of the creative force of the Supreme that *'externalized'* and *fashioned* the structures for existent nature and all life-forms. This concept was outlined in Plato's writing *Timeus* (c.360B.C) and informed all subsequent concepts that expanded upon this primary idea in later European philosophy. The Demiurge in Platonic thought is equated with the *Nous*, an intelligence faculty of the Godhead and incorporates the *Logos,* which is the active essence of the divine that functions through the *Demiurgic energy array*. The origin of all these concepts can clearly be found in the most ancient African spiritual systems that deals with the creation of the universe from the Primordial Field of Potentiality, designated as the *Nun*. This original African thought became the fuel for all Greek learning and theorizing that came after, as we shall explore in depth later on.

Reality is a truly inconceivable state without borders, restraints or boundaries, as opposed to the *phenomenal* representations of space, time and dimensionality; these are all symptoms of temporary phenomenon and its limitations which is a direct result of the actions of mind and consciousness within the boundaries of the Creation Field. The energetic nature of the Creation Field allows almost infinite varieties of energies to interact and create the various phenomena we perceive as *materialism*.

When we ascribe the term illusion to phenomenal expressions we need to understand that all materialism is in the end but a *projection* in a similar way that we might sit inside a theatre or cinema and watch a movie being projected onto a white screen. The movie appears real with people running around on the screen but in actuality we know that it's being projected by someone operating a piece of machinery in the background. For instance, when we watch a great action movie such as Star Wars or Avatar we become absorbed in the excitement and realism of the special effects that appears quite real. For the duration of the movie we have to *suspend* our *rational* senses so that we can enjoy the *illusion* that is presented to us. All phenomena have a beginning and an end; true *reality* is *beyond* concepts of beginnings and endings. It's the calm that cannot be disturbed by the vibrations of materialism, the Abode of Truth and Eternal Peace and the Highest Region of being that we refer to as *Za-Yan*.

Za-Yan encompasses the blessed state of spiritual being beyond all phenomenal appearances that we are presently *acquainted* with and is utterly and completely *transcendent* to the illusory Babylon System. It's the culmination of the Golden Path of Jah Rastafari *in this phase of existent nature* and the opening of the *gateway* to the *higher reality of our divine Creator, Jah Rastafari.* When one has walked the Golden Path of Jah Rastafari through a perfect meditation in true *Livity,* the end of the journey on earth is rewarded with the most perfect wisdom, joy and divine ONELOVE. It's from this highest point of spiritual realization that one is *raised up* to the enlightening grace of *Jah Rastafari,* the *Shatterer of Illusions.* Za-Yan cannot be described in words because it's a state of transcendent existence beyond materialism and the entropic corruption of the Babylon System. In terms of human evolution therefore, Za-Yan is the transcendent state of spiritual realization that all beings are destined to reach beyond the states of bodily incarnations in the *'physical'* realms. Although all states of existences within the Creation Field are based on phenomenal expressions, there are various states that are less or more developed in terms of life-form expression, experiences and motivation.

The universe we know is but one of *numerous universes* that manifests by the divine will of the Creator, and by that same will it is sustained through its various cycles of *being* and *non-being.* All material energies manifest from the *Formless Nature* by the *Superior Will* of the Creator, Jah Rastafari, through the *agency* of the Creation Field. The energies that make up materialism, universes, stars, planets and organic compounds that create life-forms were (and are continuously) *designed* before *becoming* to interact in precise measures and details. Euro/American science teaches the theory of a *Big Bang* that created the universe in a single explosion without being able to explain the real nature of such an occurrence. At present they are trying to find these answers by using high technology telescopes and particle accelerators such as the *Large Hadron Collider* to test their many theories.

Jah Rastafari suffuses existent nature as the *Limitless Field of Potentiality* which gives rise to the Creation Field of material nature and individuated perception we call *mind* and its attendant subtle structures – *soul/spirit, consciousness* and *physical being.* Mind, through its nature, operates in tandem with the *soul/spirit* matrix, which acts as a nexus for the consciousness faculty we perceive as *intelligence.* The soul/spirit matrix is *our personalized energetic link with The Creator.* In actuality, there's no real *separation* between mind and consciousness as consciousness is merely a *'technological expression'* of mind *extended* into various *mediums* of *action* and *cognizance.* Material biological being is established when mind/spirit *merges* with the realm of the *formed,* which is an expression of the energies of the Creation Field. The energies we *perceive as space/time dimensionality* exist in relation to this *action, interaction* and *reaction* because that is the nature of the creative force and the action of mind as awareness *continuously extending itself into being*.

Structured materialism, as we perceive it, mostly isn't real in the ***true sense of being objectively outside our minds*** but merely a magnificent phenomenal display of the Creator's abilities to form and un-form matter through the ***vehicle*** of what we perceive as our ***minds*** and ***consciousness faculties***. The concept of ***real*** is limited by our lack of understanding about these energetic displays of the Creator and the irrational fear projected by the consciousness faculty we call the ***ego***. If we all knew the truth consciously, perhaps none of us would want to remain here in the Babylon System of illusions because ultimately we would all prefer to live in true reality where there's no suffering, anxieties or death.

There are many phenomenal realms or dimensions of being, of which the earthly plane and our three dimensions are but a part. Many ancient spiritual traditions of the world eloquently explain the nature of the human being as a ***traveler*** through the dimensions of existence, (what has been referred to in some spiritual philosophies as the ***transmigration of souls***). The guiding principle for understanding this process is ***Livity***; ethical existence that teaches us the various essential lessons along the journey of our lives. Tradition explains that we are all born into the world; we live out our lives and at some point we have to die. We (our soul/mind/consciousness/being) then spend some time in an after death realm (the experience of which we inadvertently ***'create'*** ourselves, mentally and energetically due to our material perceptions and attachment for ***sensuous*** existence). At some time thereafter we emerge again (***reincarnate***) from the realms of the ***spiritual*** dimensions back into the world of the flesh. Some of us reincarnate on other worlds in space and time. This can happen a few times or many hundreds, thousands or maybe even millions of times, depending on the state of Livity we find ourselves in during our lifetimes here on earth or elsewhere. Almost all life-forms go through this process of graduated development which takes a great deal of time (in our way of understanding time).

During the period in the after death state, (which is really existence in another '***mental dimension***', stimulated by the perception we develop while living on earth), the lessons we learned in our lives are ***digested*** and ***contextualized*** so that we have an understanding of the nature of our existence on a multi-dimensional cosmic level. Some people take longer to adjust to these situations when they die more than others. It all depends on how much we learn and the nature of our thoughts and actions while we are living in the world of the ***flesh***. Knowledge isn't just about accumulating information, it's a ***living energy*** that's at the heart of our evolutionary experiences as sentient beings and is vital to our development as much as physical food is to our bodies.

It must be understood that the states beyond life on earth are just as *'real'* mentally and spiritually in their dynamics because all states of being are determined by the state of mind that sentient beings express within the domain of the Creation Field. So, one can find oneself in a *heaven* or *hell* situation, which ultimately depends on personal understanding. It's really about the nature of mind and its ability to *shape* the energy matrix of the Creation Field to fulfill a *desire* or *potential*. This is a necessary determinative to our evolutionary process through the multi-versal and multidimensional systems of existence. One might conjecture that, 'what use is evolution if we're all aspects of the same divine energy of creation' and so forth? Or perhaps even, 'If the Creator is omniscient, why then does it need expression through creation?' and so forth. What we do know is that the acts of creation and the processes by which the Creator expresses its manifold energies are really of a completely *superior order* and that using our present unbalanced senses of cognition many of us just cannot fathom the subtleties and intricacies of this issue in the most beneficial manner. The only way to understand these things is to enlighten our minds to the very basic steps that allow us to see with clarity the structures that can assist us in our mental and spiritual elevation to a higher platform of perception beyond the ordinary gross five senses. This can best be approached from understanding the precepts of *Livity* and the eternal Law of the *ONELOVE*. From this point we can perceive the greater workings of the Divine Will within us and then be in a position to make informed judgments, should we choose to do so. The *conscious* cultivation of spiritual humility in the quest for the correct knowledge base is specifically designed to lead our minds to deeper insights of these principles.

As stated in the previous volume *Jah Rastafari, Visions of Faith*, people generally find it impossible to think of something that has no beginning or end. Even when referring to God as the Creator we usually, somewhere in our minds, try to envision a beginning to God and creation as a whole. We refer to God in the masculine, as the *Alpha* and *Omega*, the beginning and the end, (and indeed, the Renaissance painter Michelangelo once painted a picture of god as an old white man with a grey beard flying through the sky, which many people probably believed was an actual depiction of God).

Many ancient cultures clearly believed with conviction that the creator of human beings possessed physical human characteristics such as arms legs, heads and so on and very human traits such as emotions – anger, lust, greed, jealousy, pride and hate. In fact ancient historical documents invariably portrayed the mythological Gods as human like *'super men'*, (similar to comic book characters such as *X-Men*, *Superman* and *Spiderman* found in our modern cultures today).

A beginning and an end is a very human invention. They appear to wrap things up neat and tidy. When something out of the ordinary occurs in our daily lives we all feel some sense of apprehension or consternation. We abhor chaos. The Babylon System tell us that one plus one *must* equal two and nothing else will suffice because that is the rule we have learnt, accepted and added to our erroneous systems of beliefs.

---

*From the **Unformed** and **Unmade Field of Potentiality** flows the **Creation Field** as a matrix of subtle energy that gives birth to the **Ifa Wave**, (the **tripartite** resonance wave) that stimulates the formation of what we view as **matter**, **time**, **space** and **dimensional** structures. The Field of Potentiality is the birth-pool from which all possibilities emerge; the Creation Field, the multi-verse and space time continuums, shape, form, being and all sentient life expressions.*

*The Mind/Soul/Spirit matrix uses this **field-energy** as the vehicle for sensory perception and a **gateway to enter into being**. Local consciousness is stimulated by the presence of mind interacting within the matrix of the Creation Field and its attendant energies, which assists in the perception of '**exterior**' realities. All is perception. Nothing in this universe is of what could be termed the **real**. **We entered here from the domain of the real**. We are at play delightfully in the astonishing garden of Our Creator's **wondrous dream**.*

-The Golden Path of Jah Rastafari-

When we speak of an illusion, we are talking about a phenomenon that *appears* real to our *senses* yet has no reality at all. We see this in the performance of stage magicians and illusionists who use tricks of light and sleight of hand techniques to fool an audience into believing that they are able to do impossible things. People usually marvel at tricks performed by illusionists such as the American David Blaine, who *seem* to suspend the laws of our accepted perception of reality. We all know these are illusions but we always seem to desperately want to believe in something other than the mundane existence we live in. We *want* to believe in magic, and it's that *wanting to believe* that allows illusions to manifest in our lives in what appears at times as very real events and situations. We *suspend* our logical and rational mental faculties in order to comprehend or fit the incredible into some frame of reference that our minds can accept. This involves one of the most important faculties of the mind – the mental process we call *imagination*. By wanting to believe, we give our consent or allow ourselves to believe in a given thing or situation by actively imagining in our minds the *possibility* of such and such a thing occurring.

The imagination is one of the major keys to understanding the operations of the Babylon System because it's that area of our senses that's most affected by the mind control program. Our natural imaginative faculty allow us to **create** and **project** thoughts, ideas, and pictures and so on in our minds. *This process is one of the most crucial ways in which we **interpret** the phenomenon of existent nature and create structures for learning and being.* Without our imagination we wouldn't be able to exist as free thinking beings.

Thoughts arise in our minds as subtle energy vibrations that our consciousness perceives. This process stimulates sensations and pictorial representations in our brains. We order these into a framework or a '***program***' that dictates our **emotional responses** and **actions** in the world. This program in fact forms part of very intricate and subtle effects of much larger structures that Euro/American science is presently (and very excitedly) referring to as the ***holographic theory*** of existence.

A hologram is a program that interacts with our '***brain computer***' and sensory faculties – taste, sight, hearing, feeling and smell, to present a three dimensional ***sensory experience***. It's usually made in a dark room or space with laser/light beams. One of the reasons why we see space as black is that a holographic structure such as the universe uses various energies such as light and dark and an array of ***sub-quantum mediums*** to manifest its presence within the **context** of our consciousness faculties. This works in tandem with the quantum forces of the Creation Field through the agency of the ***Ifa Wave*** that manifests a coherent structure which impacts upon our senses and subtle mental perceptions. Space is not infinite, as we would believe; it's just that our present mode of perception is not yet developed to understand the true nature of the interaction of the energies of the Creation Field and its impact upon our sensory faculties. ***In actuality, what you <u>see</u> with the physical eyes isn't necessarily what's there.*** In the near future science will come to the realization of these very important phenomenons.

It must be understood clearly that we do not actually ***live*** in a hologram, as Euro/American science is trying to portray nowadays. This is a very clever and calculated illusion created by the Babylon System to fool human beings into believing that the basic five senses alone are capable of creating our total experiences of sentience and what we call material existence. Essentially, what Euro/American science is trying to explain is this basic principle:

The human five senses operate by the movement of ***electrical impulses*** through our sensory faculties to our ***brain computer*** which decodes these signals and translates them ***inside the brain*** as coherent and rational conceptions of a physical ***exterior world***. The external world in the manner that we perceive it, does not really exist separate from ourselves, but is really a '***construct***' inside our brain computer. Our bodies naturally are also parts of this dynamic; therefore we are *imagining* ourselves (in our brain computers) as existing in bodies in an exterior world. When we *see* with our eyes we are actually decoding the effects of electrical impulses that manifest within the brain computer as *sensory data,* and that goes for all our other senses and so on. In this regard, there is really no *exterior world in the way we perceive it,* as no light can enter the *enclosed brain*, (except through the eyes). Therefore the images we observe when we see with our eyes are actually formed *inside* the brain and not in any exterior world. In tandem with this principle is the realization that on the *quantum level* particles behave in the most extraordinary ways when being observed in any experiment; they cease to exist as definable forces when scientists try to *measure* or *quantify* their *objective reality*. In fact, it has been realized that quantum particles exist in very *indefinite* states of time, space and *locality*. The question of measurement and locality brings up a host of conundrums that defy our dualistic perception. It has also been realized that a particle can exist in two different quantum states *simultaneously*. In extension therefore, *the particles that make up our physical reality – bodies, plants, animals, earth, stars, universe and so on –potentially exist in other places at the same time as existing in the locality we perceive them*.

Although this is a *logical* framework and a very interesting concept, it's only a small part of the story and therefore can be quite misleading. When we apply the *Fire Meditation* to penetrate this issue we are able to discern far more complex principles at work.

What the theory of holographic existence observes is merely a basic interpretation of a set of structures and information formulated through our five sense technological apparatus that assists the *mind* in its navigation through the energies of the *Creation Field,* that is the multi-versal and multi-dimensional space / time reality. The Creation Field is not an illusory manifestation but is formed of subtle energies that are non-physical. It's the *medium* that allows the *collapsing* and *translation* of *Ifa Waves* into what Euro/American science calls quantum forces – *subtle dynamic structures,* so that our minds can *link* with and become established in phenomenal nature. There are many more senses that human beings are able to use apart from the five gross senses. For example, within the African tradition the Babalawo/Shaman or 'Seerman' are able to utilize at least *twenty four different sensory faculties* apart from the basic five senses of perception to operate as a human being in space and time. Of course this has never been observed or tested *'scientifically'* by Euro/American scientists and would no doubt be counted as invalid by that establishment, but is a proven fact time and time again to those who have access to this knowledge.

When the mind/spirit separates from the body in death or *out of the body experiences,* (*OBE*), we are still able to perceive five sense realities just the same but it's very difficult to interact in them without a physical body. If we are able to *perceive* five sense realities *without a physical body*, then in actuality what is referred to as holographic theory must be extended into areas that takes cognisance of wider *physical* and *metaphysical* relationships because sensory being is not just dependent upon the basis five senses alone (or even a biological vessel) to manifest. Throughout African spiritual cultures (in African and the Diaspora) this has been proven time and time again.

Essentially, the five senses are but parts of wider *extended subtle senses* which we use to experience time, space and dimensions and do not explain the whole picture of our existence as sentient beings. Indeed, if we existed exclusively as *holographic projections,* how can we then explain the universe, which seemingly *preceded* all life-forms and therefore our cognition of its actuality? And what exactly is *being* if everything is but a projection of forces and fields? Where is the projector of this holographic phenomenon *located*? And indeed, more importantly, *what* is the projector of it?

There is an interesting concept formulated by religions such as Buddhism and various New Age cults which states that everything is *void* and ultimately *emptiness* or *nothingness*, which in many ways allude to the concept of a holographic reality where all forms are but phantasmagoria. The problem is that using such words as void, empty and nothingness simply does not explain very much at all because we end up using *words* to explain concepts and aspects of phenomenon and being that cannot really be rationalized by words alone. This conundrum tend to confuse many people into believing that life ultimately is a kind of pointless, random nothingness that cannot be really understood and therefore perhaps has no real meaning. People sometimes latch onto the words of scientists and spiritual gurus and such like in a sense of desperation when they are fed these conflicting, and indeed, mind controlling ideas without any firm basis in reality.

Essentially, we do exist *partially* in what could be loosely termed a holographic space/time reality but the structure of this is *infinitely more complex* than we are being led to believe by Euro/American scientific theory. The multi-versal and multi-dimensional Creation Field is the *background* to the interactive scenario that was developed as a means for sentience to explore various possibilities of being. Although the 'hologram' is in *one sense* a type of *simulation,* we link with it on the level of the *collective mind* and experience *individuated awareness/consciousness* through it and so on. This in no way means that existence isn't real; it means we are part of vast structures that we are only just beginning to become aware of in this present time/space. It also implies that the *meaning* of the word *real,* as we understand it, has been *'doctored'* to give people the wrong view of truth. This knowledge, although quite exotic for some, isn't new; it's just that we are seeing it through the *prism* of our present civilization in the manner that Euro/American scientists present it to us publicly.

The mind does not exist solely in the grey matter of the brain but *expresses* itself through the quantum fields of our individuated experiences. In essence, mind/soul operates from a transcendent point of awareness and is only *linked* to our physical experiences through sub-quantum energies stimulated by the *dynamics* of the Creation Field. Mind in its real essence is perpetually *situated* in the *Unformed Nature*, the *Eternal Field of Potentiality*, which is the province of the *Supreme Being*, **Jah Rastafari**, *The Creator* of all life, forms and phenomenon, and uses a complex array of mental technologies, (multi-dimensional consciousness, spirit/soul) to assume awareness and expression as *subjective being*. In a sense, mind uses body as a form of *portal* through which to manifest in physical reality.

When we dream and experience sensory perceptions, we are using another part of our extended senses. Precognition, telepathy, clairvoyance, *laying-of-hands* healing and a whole host of other sensory faculties clearly expresses a wider conception of consciousness on levels that transcends the basic five senses and the theory of holograms.

Within the African tradition of spiritual knowledge, the western theory of holographic reality takes on a very different kind of meaning. Essentially, what appears to be the impersonal manifestation of creation (holographic reality) is actually a manifestation of the *unique, mystical, personal* and *efficacious energy* of *The Creator*. The Creator, although distinct from the created, imbues creation with its limitless array of energies. Everything posses this potent energy, even what appears to be inert matter. That is why within the African tradition a stone, a seashell, a feather, a mountain, a river, a tree and even a handful of earth is believed to possess varying degrees of *divine potency* and *dynamism*. The idea of an *impersonal inert energy* that pervades creation is a misunderstanding due to the confusion of the *ego* sensory faculty inherent in human beings and the mis-education given by many western educational institutions. The desperation by some western thinkers to rationalize and order the universe into a little box that they can put a lid on only amount to erroneous perceptions of this subtle but overwhelmingly important knowledge.

The *transcendent* mystic nature of reality cannot be understood or rationalized from the point of perception dictated by the ego but can only be approached through the application of profound reasoning and genuine insight.

In order to understand these principles clearly, we have to suspend the false knowledge that the Babylon System has put into our minds. We have to then go back to the ancient knowledge of our earthly Ancestors that explains these things in clear and unambiguous terms. It must be understood that the principles of holographic reality are now being used to further *specific agendas* that would allow the controllers of the Babylon System to divest us of our innate spiritual powers and to create uncertainty and delusions in the minds of those who are not able to grasp the fundamental issues behind these ideas.

The so-called *'objective'* intellectual can only approach these things *theoretically*, it's primarily the conscious imaginative faculty that we use to observe and make sense of our perception of reality. And conversely, it's our imagination (or lack of it at times) that has become the principle avenue to control and confine our minds in the illusions of the Babylon System here on earth.

*"The white man's **doctrine** [of **mind control**] has forced the black man to forsake silver and gold and seek heaven after death. It has brought us to live in **disgrace** and to die in **dishonor**".*

-**The Sublime, Brother Leonard Howell**-

Most of us these days are familiar with the way a computer works. A set of coded instructions called a **program** or **software** is inserted into the hard drive, which is part of the *'physical body'* of the computer. These instruct the computer in its operations and enable it to function and process information as an **integrated** piece of equipment. The computer will function continuously until the program is corrupted, changed or no longer has a specific use. This is essentially the same idea as **the slave mind control program** that was used on black African people in Jamaica and the African Diaspora for four hundred years to destroy our cultures, enslave us and reprogram us to function as **biological robots**. Significantly this same program was used on the masses of white Euro/American peoples, the Chinese peoples and also the Indian/Asian peoples since ancient times here on earth. It's the same program that's still in use today, albeit modified to suit the changing nature of the societies we now live in.

Despite the slickness and sophistication of a computer, the program it uses is actually just a set of logic based, coded instructions transmitted as electronic impulses that can be altered and readjusted at any given moment. Anyone can learn how to do this. There are many **subsidiary programs** that create various details which assist this primary process in a coherent and logical manner.

Every piece of technology we use today functions by using programs that we don't see with our naked eyes; cars, traffic lights, cell phones, TVs, light switches, washing machines, toys and so on. In fact, without these numerous programs to operate our societies, we wouldn't be able to function together socially in the way we do presently.

The main programs that run the Babylon System are embedded in the three powers of civilizations – **church, state** and **academia**. These *'programs'* dominate all social structures on earth. Within these are **embedded** more sophisticated **sub-programs** and *sub-routines* that create the cohesion necessary for the **Babylon System** to function smoothly and efficiently: ***politics, economics, educational complex, industrial complex and military complex.*** The church structure operates on different ***sub-routines*:** ***Gods, Devils, Holy Scriptures, morality (sex, sin and guilt complexes) and reward (heaven and hell complexes).*** Academia operates on the structures of ***knowledge accumulation, knowledge manipulation*** and ***dissemination.*** When we understand these sub-structures and sub-programs, how they function and their effects upon our minds, we can clearly see how the Babylon System has been able to create the ***false reality*** in which we exist.

*It's very important to understand that words are **conceptions** that convey ideas, which form in our minds. Words do not explain what things are in essence, but allude to what we have been **taught** they should mean. We use words as tools to navigate through our material existence. We give power to them via the process of our imaginative sensory faculty. Verbal language, in a sense, can really be seen as a form of **'sympathetic magic'**.*

-The Golden Path of Jah Rastafari -

The **Babylon System** is the mother of all programs used to create what appears as a coherent social structure and extends far beyond our usual senses of perception. It's one of the most sophisticated **programs** ever designed and functions on principles not unlike all the other low level programs we're familiar with. This primary program stimulates us to act according to its basic rules of compliance, thus all human civilizations are created according to the guidelines laid down by the protocols of the Babylon System.

The most astonishing thing is that this program has become the very basis of our existence on earth for countless thousands of years without us even being aware of its existence. It has been running our lives for so long that most of us wouldn't know how to live without it because its **operational parameters** transcend our conscious understanding. That's essentially the **key** to its success and continuous function. If we all understood it we can affect it at will and it would cease to function in the way it does. Our **ignorance** is its **strength**.

The **Babylon System** is responsible for the destruction and death that affects us all, wherever we are in the world, no matter our nationality or skin colour. One of the most important pieces of knowledge we can discern about the program that the Babylon System uses is that it isn't a **physical** thing. We cannot see it, touch it, smell or taste it, yet it creates the rules by which we function as human beings in the world. However, with the right **mental training** such as the **analytic mode** of the **Fire Meditation** we can perceive it very clearly and understand how it functions, how it affects us and how we can free ourselves from its insidious and destructive control.

Within the tradition of Rastafari there are clear and precise methods by which we can recognize the operations of the Babylon System and formulate effective measures to engage it and free ourselves from its deadly poisons. In fact, Rastas have been one of the main groups of people who for decades have been trying to wake up the world to these terrible dangers.

In our present time frame one of the main operating programs of the Babylon System is *racism;* the systemic abuse and dehumanization of *melanized* peoples of earth through the process of the *white supremacy mind control program* that dominates the planet and which has been instituted by an *elite group of Europeans.* It's this elite group of whites that's commonly referred to as the *controllers* or *Illuminati.* The most important point about this however, is that this small group actually owes no allegiance at all to their racial background as white people. Essentially, they believe that they're elevated far above the common masses of whites and have no qualms whatsoever about killing millions of their fellow white people in order to reach their goals, as the numerous wars, (World War I, World War II, Vietnam, Iraq, Afghanistan), genocides and environmental destruction across the world clearly shows.

The Illuminati elite are what has been referred to in so-called *'conspiracy theories'* as the *shadow government*, the manipulators behind major world events and the architects of the *New World Order global dictatorship* that's being established on earth right now. Ultimately, this shadowy group are controlled in their deadly, paranoid endeavours by negative, discarnate extra-dimensional entities that are setting the human race up for total mental and spiritual enslavement. The Illuminati cabal have been *bred*, through specific human bloodlines over many generations to become the *management team* of earth and to assist in bringing the world to a point of chaos so that their New World Order can become established after our present civilization is destroyed. Wars, earthquakes, Tsunamis, devastation of resources, plagues, civil wars, famine are mostly engineered to bring the world to its knees and into the clutches of these negative powers.

The governments that we *think* we elect are merely fronts for the manipulation of the shadow government behind the scenes. Political, monetary, economic and social policies are dictated to national governments who dispense the local laws that govern our societies. The prime ministers such as *David Cameron* and *Nick Clegg* of Britain and presidents *Obama, Putin* and others are all controlled through this *secret* network of subterfuge and Machiavellian tactics. Absolutely no election is free or fair but simply exercises in subterfuge and manipulation of the masses. Politicians are almost always corrupt in their pursuit of elected office. Elections are always manipulated to put key Illuminati stooges and puppets into office.

Through the science of *psychology*, a system of *mind control* has been put in place to subvert our perception of reality and the true potential of human life in the world. This structure dictates the way we understand how we function as human beings, individually and collectively. It outlines principles and laws that are used to define the reasons for our various behavioral patterns and so on. Psychology and its practice as we understand it today is purely an invention by European cultures. The word psychology is derived from *Latin*, an ancient European language that has been dead for centuries and which is used only in the realms of white *academia* and *Roman Catholicism,* (which says a great deal in terms of the mind control programs of the Babylon System).

Psychology is supposedly the science of studying the operations of the *mind*. For Euro/Americans it's largely an abstract theorem that does not take into account many deep and subtle nuances in the way the human psyche operates. When we understand the real nature of mind then our perception of psychology takes on a very new and more interesting perspective.

According to the beliefs of Sigmund Freud, the renowned psychoanalyst, the human psyche is comprised of three elements, the *Id, ego* and *super-ego*, the three mental structures that operate within our consciousness faculties. This corresponds exactly to the ancient African perspective of the intellect, *Ka*, the sensitive soul, *Ba* and the vegetative soul, *Sed* from which these ideas filtered into western philosophical thought through the ancient Greek philosophers who conducted their theoretical studies in ancient Africa.

Instinctual behavior is commanded by the *'id'*, the *organized realistic* part of the psyche is the *'ego'* and the *critical* and *moralizing* part is the *'super-ego'*. This understanding was developed by Freud into a speculative framework which attempted to *objectify* his analysis of the workings of the human mind. The knowledge of Rastafari shows clearly that the ego is *one* element in the make up of human beings consciousness faculties. It is not divided into three separate aspects but acts in accordance with the principles of mind on a *multi-dimensional level*. This perspective of knowledge concerning the ego and sensory faculties are not new but a reflection of the methods used to understand, manipulate and divide the human being mentally and to create *false dichotomies* and assumptions that ultimately act as *neutralizing agents* for the mind. Importantly, these ideas were refined during the period of enslavement of black Africans, which is explicit in the principles of the *Willie Lynch slave making mind control programs*. For four hundred years black African peoples were subjected to the most sordid, indecent, horrific, invasive, negative and destructive techniques of mental conditioning by the power crazed white Euro/American elite. The effectiveness of mind control programs are self evident in the *social/cultural and mental dysfunction* of black African people and communities across the world even today in the 21st century.

From the point of view of Rastafari, psychology, as it's presently understood, could never be a science of understanding the mind, as mind actually transcends all human sciences that we know. Psychology is the attempt to rationalize human behavioral patterns that are stimulated by the *psychosis* we label *egocentrism*. It analyzes the conflicting tendencies of dualism which is an effect of the ego mind control program and attempts to rationalize pathways through these. Mind in its pure essence cannot be analyzed from the point of view of the ego or dualism as it completely transcends these concepts. An African understands psychology very differently from a European and an Indian differently from a Chinese and so on. Culture is extremely important when we approach psychology but the common denominator must be our perception of our humanity that binds us together as a sentient race on earth.

The Euro/American institutional practice of psychiatry has become the standard for dealing with all mental behavioral problems that affects us, regardless of our 'racial' background. Most internationally recognized text books on this subject are written by white Euro/Americans who invoke the *'scriptures'* of Freud, Jung and other eminent so-called white *'experts'*. Student psychologists therefore end up studying theories that are completely inconsistent with most human social behavior. It's taken for granted that health professionals who administer treatment for *mental disorders* to patients have a real grasp of the fundamental principles that govern the mental processes of all human beings. Unfortunately it's abundantly clear that our understanding of the field of *Euro/American psychiatry* has never been able to adequately, (much less honestly) dissect the rationale behind human behavior effectively. It analyzes specific behavioral patterns or traits that correlate with certain specific *perceptions* of human activities. This allows us to form *opinions* about the operation of human *consciousness perceptions* and the effects on human relationships to *certain degrees*. As I've stated before, an opinion is not a fact but a conclusion drawn from a process of reasoning which ultimately is based largely on flawed perception of reality due to our mental *imprisonment* within the illusory Babylon System. It is this flawed method of analysis that we humans have been using to understand ourselves and our development on earth. Some people call it *reason* and try to defend it with the most illogical arguments one could possibly imagine.

The theories of the founding fathers of Euro/American psychiatry and neuroscience revolutionized white cultural perception of *mental health* yet failed to tackle the deeper aspects of the real issues that psychology and psychiatry should really address – the **roots of erroneous consciousness perceptions (egoism)** in human beings and the resultant unprogressive behavioral patterns that we exhibit. Similar to the Euro/American philosophers, the psychologists and psychiatrists have been addressing what is in effect a symptom of **white cultural neurosis** within the bounds of the **white consensus reality**, which is a by-product of the mind control programming of the **Babylon System**.

Because of the mind control program and its effects, (citing the white supremacy program across the world), the norms of addressing and treating **white neurosis** has become the accepted method to diagnose **'mental illnesses'** in all other **'racial'** groups on earth, regardless of culture. The mental problems that affect the black man in his own natural environments are very different from those that affect the Chinese man or the Indian man for that matter. Culture, biology and a host of related factors are important in understanding these things. **The Fire Meditation** clearly implies also that **mind** functions with noticeable variations according to the nature of the structure of the **biological vessel** it links with while it operates within the bounds of a particular **consensus reality** paradigm. A black person and a white person, although both being human equally, function on varying different levels because the minds that operate within their respective biological matrices are also **affected** by the dominating consensus reality paradigm they subscribe to. Culture, nurture and environment all play a great part in this process. This also affects the operation of DNA and its role in human evolutionary processes.

White psychologists in our western societies seem to have very little clues as to the reasons why there is such a prevalence of Blacks in **'mental health care'** institutions in Euro/American societies. This glaring problem has been garnered by some influential groups of white **'racial scientists'** to forward their programs of **eugenics** and the systematic destruction of the black cultural presence on planet earth through the agencies of the Babylon System. What we do know from research conducted by many white **'racial scientists'** is that there's deliberately false and indeed scurrilous information bandied around in white scientific journals such as **Nature, Scientific America, New Scientist Magazine** and the like, that attempts to justify inequality between so-called races on earth in terms of genetics and human developmental processes. Prominent contributors to this argument such as, **Arthur P. Jensen**, a **white racist scientist**, (and most certainly a member of the Transhumanist/eugenics circle) supposedly researching theories of human intelligence has, over the years, continued to spout the most transparent ramblings about what he believes to be **'black inferior intelligence'** and **'white superior intelligence'** as though such ideas can be divorced from their obvious deficiencies. Most whites who read this brain-washing nonsense passed off as **'scientific research'** no doubt automatically subscribe to these completely false notions simply because it's dressed up between the covers of so-called *reputable scientific journals*. Young, impressionable students might read this racist propaganda, believing it to be pertinent discourse and consequently formulate biased opinions without ever knowing the real facts of these issues. When we analyze the nature of the private bodies (such as the *Pioneer Fund Inc.* in the USA) that fund these researches in so-called *'human intelligence factors'* and the companies that publishes these journals, we can get a real glimpse of how aspects of the white supremacy mind control program operate from a *media disinformation* perspective. This situation is one of the keys to understanding our social conditions on earth at present. Consensus reality programs are subtle parts of the Babylon System that assists in the mental confinement of individuals and groups within societies. Human behavioral sciences have been developed by Euro/Americans as means of enslaving the masses of people on earth through actions and lifestyles imposed by nebulous entities that we really know almost nothing about.

The ultimate agenda of *social scientists/mind controllers* is to neutralize groups of dissenters or radicals in society (whether black or white) who might pose a threat to the continued functioning of the Babylon System. It's imperative to our very survival as free human beings to commit the time and effort to raise within our communities behavioral scientists and social engineers that can guide our people toward *group successes beyond the Babylon System's mind control programs.*

Self preservation is one of the most important laws of *Livity* and necessitates the mastering of tools that are applicable for whatever task that will allow the individual and consequently the human race as a whole to survive and live in freedom. That is why we must study the *origins* of the various *psychological systems* such as *Motivational Research,* how they came into being and what their effects are in our lives. Motivational research is described as:

'a systematic and scientific analysis of the forces influencing people and populations so as to control the making of their decisions. This can be applied in advertising, marketing, politics, economics and war'.

At the end of the beginning of the 20th century, a Russian scientist named *Ivan Pavlov* (1849-1936), discovered what is called the *conditioned reflexes* in a dog for which he received the Nobel Prize for medicine in1904. The famous experiment is called the *Pavlov's Dog experiment* which basically entails a bell being rung just before a dog is presented with a piece of meat. Whenever the meat is presented to the dog the animal salivates in anticipation of a tasty meal. If the *bell* is rung *before* the meat is given to the dog, the animal reacts by turning to orient itself to the *direction* from which the *sound* comes. If the bell is rung repeatedly and immediately after the meat is given to the dog, after a certain number of times, simply ringing the bell provokes salivation in the animal, which prepares its digestive system to receive the meat. The bell then becomes a signal for the *meat* that will come after it is rung. Whenever the bell is rung at any time after, the dog reacts, salivating in anticipation of getting a meal. A stimulus that has nothing to do with feeding has created this reaction in the animal. The mere sound of the bell has *reconditioned* the dog *mentality* to equate the *sound* with *food*, even though it cannot see any physical evidence of it. Just the sound of the bell alone then becomes capable of *inducing* salivation in the dog. Anyone can try this experiment with their dog and the result will be the same. Motivational Research uses these types of principles on human beings (among many other complex forms) to get us to *comply* unquestionably with the authority of the Babylon system. Most times we do things and we are not quite sure why, we simply comply with a particular situation, *unconsciously*.

We drink *Coca Cola* and Lucozade because the adverts on TV and magazines tell us it's cool to do so, although these things are very bad for our bodies. We buy the latest cell phone, iPod and computers because the adverts tell us they are the latest fashion accessories and we would not be *sexy* and *cool* if we didn't have them. We wear Prada, Nike, Reebok, and Versace because the fashion magazines and our favorite pop stars or Hip-Hop stars are wearing these things; plus, these *'labels'* supposedly give us something called *'status'*. We watch the latest movies with our favorite Hollywood movie stars in them because everyone else does the same thing and we want to be part of what's going on. We never question our motivations because we're simply, like Pavlov's Dog, being manipulated to behave as our *controllers* want us to. We are manipulated subliminally every moment of our lives and are completely unable to see the direction from which the manipulators are functioning. This is how the Babylon System really functions but on a much grander and more complex and detailed level. We've *all* become Pavlov Dogs running around senselessly in a never ending maze we call real life. This mind control technique began in the USA around the 1930s when *social scientists*, *economists* and the corrupt *banking elite* joined forces to develop new methods of selling products and ideas to the masses, thus creating what we now call the *'consumer culture'*. This was a necessary ploy to entrench people further into cycles of *debt*, which drives the bankers' profits up and maintain their strangle hold over the world economy and resources. Behavioral scientists are the *Gestapo* of the Illuminati and its New World Order; they search for ways to reinforce the mind control programs within our minds by using the most subtle inflections in language and the manipulation of common social perception.

Motivational Research incorporates another aspect of mind control labeled *Compliance Gaining* which was conceived in the late 1960's as a result of studies and research by two social scientists, **Gerald Marwell** and **David Schmitt.** In 1967, Marwell and Schmitt produced a series of compliance-gaining *tactics* surrounding the idea of getting a teenager to study. This can be applied to virtually any scenario within any social situation; the results will be the same. The tactics, sixteen in all, are as follows:

Promise: *If you comply, I will reward you*. Offer an incentive to get compliance.

Threat: *If you do not comply, I will punish you.* Threaten to take something away if the person does not do what you want.

Liking: *Act friendly and helpful to get the person in a "good frame of mind" so they comply with your requests.* For example, you try to be as friendly and pleasant as possible to put Dick in a good mood before asking him to study.

Aversive stimulation: *Continuously **punish** the person, making cessation contingent on compliance.* For example, you tell Dick he may not use the car until he studies more.

Debt: *You must comply with my demands because you owe me for past favors.* For example, you point out that you have sacrificed and saved to pay for John's education and that he owes it to you to get good enough grades to get into a good college.

Moral appeal: *You are immoral if you do not comply*. You tell Dick that it is morally wrong for anyone not to get as good grades as possible and that he should study more

Altruism: *I need your compliance very badly, so do it for me*. For example, you tell Dick that you really want very badly for him to get into a good college and that you wish he would study more as a personal favor to you.

Esteem (positive): *People you value will think better of you if you comply*. For example, you tell Dick that the whole family will be very proud of him if he gets good grades.

Esteem (negative): *People you value will think the worse of you if you do not comply.* For example, you tell Dick that the whole family will be very disappointed in him if he gets poor grades.

Expertise (positive): *If you comply, you will be rewarded because of the "nature of things."* For example, you tell Dick that if he gets good grades he be able to get into college and get a good job.

Expertise (negative): If you do not comply, you will be punished because of the "nature of things." For example, you tell Dick that if he does not get good grades he will not be able to get into college or get a good job.

Pre-giving: Reward the person before requesting compliance. For example, raise Dick's allowance and tell him you now expect him to study.

Self-feeling (positive): You will feel better about yourself if you comply. For example, you tell Dick that he will feel proud if he gets himself to study more.

Self-feeling (negative): You will feel worse about yourself if you do not comply. For example, you tell Dick that he will feel ashamed of himself if he gets bad grades.

Altercasting (positive): A person with "good" qualities would comply. For example, you tell Dick that because he is a mature and intelligent person he naturally will want to study more and get good grades.

Altercasting (negative): Only a person with "bad" qualities would not comply. For example, you tell Dick that he should study because only someone very childish does not study.

In 1967 Marwell and Schmitt conducted experimental research using the sixteen compliance gaining tactics and identified five basic compliance-gaining strategies: *Rewarding activity, Punishing activity, Expertise, Activation of impersonal commitments, and Activation of personal commitments*.

Another element of compliance-gaining was created in the early 1960's, as *French* and *Raven* were researching the concepts of *power, legitimacy*, and *politeness.* They identified five influential aspects associated with power, which help to illustrate elements of the study of compliance. The fives *bases of power* are as follows:

Reward Power: A person with reward power has control over some valued resource (e.g., promotions and raises).

Coercive Power: A person with coercive power has the ability to inflict punishments (e.g., fire you.)

Expert Power: Expert power is based on what a person knows (e.g., you may do what a doctor tells you to do because he or she knows more about medicine that you do).

Legitimate Power: Legitimate power is based on formal rank or position (e.g., you obey someone's commands because he or she is the vice president in the company for which you work).

Referent Power: People have referent power when the person they are trying to influence wants to be like them (e.g., a mentor often has this type of power).

Another mind control technique that's used to brain-wash people into submission is called the ***Delphi Technique.*** This is a very important method as it is extremely effective in gaining the compliance of individuals who would not normally succumb to mind control easily. This was developed by the ***RAND Corporation*** for the ***US Department of Defense*** as a ***psychological warfare weapon*** in the 1950s and 1960s. The Delphi Technique is specially formulated to affect groups and to gain group or community consensus. This is done by dividing a group of people, picking out the ones that might cause a problem, isolating them and gaining their compliance before putting them back into the group. Whether common consensus is reached the group *'controller'* is able to put forward an idea that everyone will eventually agree with, (whether or not they understood the process that drove them to agreeing). This is used widely in politics and the media these days. When we hear about this poll or that poll that's been conducted to gauge a group or community reaction to government policies or environmental issues, invariably, if you know what to look for, you will be able to identify the Delphi Technique behind it.

A specialized use of this technique was developed for teachers in schools and colleges, the ***Alinsky Method***.

*The setting or group is, however, immaterial. The point is that people in groups tend to share a certain knowledge base and display certain identifiable characteristics (known as **group dynamics**). This allows for a special application of a basic technique. The '**change agent**' or '**facilitator**' or what we will term the **'controller'**. The controller goes through the motions of acting as an organizer, getting each person in the target group to elicit expression of their concerns about a program, project, or policy in question. The 'controller' listens attentively, forms '**task forces**', '**urges everyone to make lists**', and so on. While she is doing this, the facilitator learns something about each member of the target group. He/she identifies the 'leaders', the 'loud mouths', as well as those who frequently turn sides during the argument the '**weak or noncommittal**'.*

These techniques have been used in schools for many years to weed out *'trouble makers'* from the *'bright kids'* and in the work place by bosses to get rid of *'troublesome workers'* who might want a pay rise or **union rights** and so on. Many black children going to school in Euro/American societies have been severely attacked and manipulated by these despicable methods of mind control. The so-called under achievement of black children in Euro/American societies is an indication of the workings of the institutional mind control programs deliberately set in gear to continually undermine the educational progress of blacks.

The **controller's** job really is to play *'devil's advocate'* by using the *'divide and conquer'* techniques, manipulating one group opinion against the other and so on. This is accomplished by manipulating those who do not understand the dynamics of what's really going on to appear *'silly, ridiculous, unknowledgeable, and inarticulate'* and so on. The **controller** cleverly and quietly agitates certain members of the group to become **angry**, thereby *forcing tensions to accelerate*. The **controller** is well trained in **psychological manipulation** and is able to predict the reactions of each group member expertly. Those who oppose aspects of the policy or program will be removed or closed out from the group.

The Delphi Technique has been used in black communities in the USA and increasingly in countries like Jamaica very effectively. It's very effective with teachers, school children, and community groups. Many black people rarely, if ever, know that they are being manipulated. If they do suspect this is happening, they do not know how to end the process. The desired result is for group **polarization**, and for the controller to become accepted as a member of the group and group process. He/she will then throw the desired idea on the table and ask for opinions during discussion. Very soon his/her associates from the divided group begin to adopt the idea as if it were their own, and pressure the entire group to accept the proposition. This particular technique has been used often in industrial disputes between **management** and **unions** to dissolve **workers strikes** and gain compliance in lowering wages, redundancies and so on.

More recent mind control programs such as the **Nudge Theory** as postulated by academics **Richard Thaler** and **Cass Sunstein** attempts to *'use the leverage of the state to make us all improve our social behaviour'*. This was recently adopted by the **Barack Obama** administration in the USA and the **David Cameron/Nick Clegg** administration in the UK and is being used at **all levels of government** to move specific policies to preset conclusions, (particularly in the UK, policies to do with the integration of Britain into the **European Federation** of the **New World Order**). When you encounter the chair person of a meeting who is supposed to be neutral yet has a vested interest in steering the meeting towards a specific conclusion you will usually see these techniques in operation. In Britain there are specific people in government, media and the business sector who are well versed in these techniques and who use them daily to gain our compliance on various levels.

There are effective ways to *disable* all mind control programs providing you are aware that you are being affected and the manner in which they affect you. With all compliance based mind control programs, it's important to always remain *centered* and *focused* in your own mind. Always try to resist *anger* at all times; it is among the greatest detriments to mental clarity. Be calm and reflective on everything that is being said or asked of you. The best way to counter mental intrusion and manipulation is to employ the *Analytic Mode* of perception through the *Fire Meditation*. Be completely alert and *observant* even of things that do not appear to have a bearing on what is happening. Ask as many questions as you feel are necessary, (this can give you more time to gather your thoughts and to formulate your response to a particular position taken by the 'controller'). Don't be over emotional just try to be alert and listen attentively. Interrupt the proceedings and pin point any *inaccuracies* you come across immediately. Do not agree to anything. Go away and think about what your response should be. These things usually throw off the 'controllers' and break down their pattern of aggressive mind control. Smile. Be pleasant and courteous at all times; moderate your voice so as not to come across as being loud and aggressive. Particularly as black people, the aggressive posture is always used as an excuse by the police and law enforcers of the Babylon System to brutalize us.

Recently in Britain, researchers have uncovered another shadowy organization functioning discretely under the cover of local governments and public institutions called *'Common Purpose'*. The British researcher and activist *Brian Gerrish* has been exposing this organization over the past several years and has unearthed a wealth of information about their covert and insidious activities in British society. There are many informative videos on YouTube that explains the depths of Common Purpose and its programs of deception. Common Purpose is a so-called *'political charity'* organization that uses *'Behavioral Modification'* to entrap young people in its strange and dubious programs. According to current research:

Common Purpose (CP) is a Charity, based in Great Britain, which creates 'Future Leaders' of society. CP selects individuals and 'trains' them to learn how society works, who 'pulls the levers of power' and how CP 'graduates' can use this knowledge to lead 'Outside Authority'.
Children, teenagers and adults have their prejudices removed. Graduates are 'empowered' to become 'Leaders' and work in 'partnership' with other CP

graduates. CP claims to have trained some 30,000 adult graduates in UK and changed the lives of some 80,000 people, including schoolchildren and young people.

*But evidence shows that Common Purpose is rather more than a Charity 'empowering' people and communities'. In fact, CP is an elitist pro-EU political organization helping to **replace democracy** in the UK, and worldwide, with CP chosen **'elite' leaders**. In truth, their hidden networks and political objectives are undermining and destroying our democratic society and are threatening 'free will' in adults, teenagers and children. Their work is funded by public money and big business, including international banks.*

*It is important for researchers to realize that the majority of Common Purpose 'graduates' are **victims**, who have little if any understanding of the wider role of Common Purpose within UK society, nor of its connections to higher government and the European Union. Drawn into CP training by a **flattering invitation**, or **selected** by their company or organization, this recruitment is normally carried out by a previously trained CP person - now recruiting for the cause. Candidates are screened and selected (or rejected) by CP Advisory Board members in their area.*

*Both candidates and 'trained graduates' will have no real understanding of Common Purpose's wider role to help achieve a political and social paradigm shift in the UK. The real objective would appear to be to replace our traditional UK democracy with the new regime of the **EU superstate**.*

*By blurring the boundaries between people, professions, public and private sectors, responsibility and accountability, CP encourages graduates to believe that as new selected leaders, CP graduates can work together, **outside of the established political and social structures**, to achieve this paradigm shift or **CHANGE**. The so called "Leading Outside Authority". In doing so, the allegiance of the individual becomes re-framed' on CP colleagues and their NETWORK.*

These are just some of the many ways in which the Babylon System functions in our societies and the world in general. Unless we are astute enough to be able to question the very foundations of our social reality, we will be easily fooled into giving over our freedoms to the mind control systems that order our lives.

"Whoever controls the volume of money in our country is absolute master of all industry and commerce...and when you realize that the entire system is very easily controlled, one way or another, by a few powerful men at the top, you will not have to be told how periods of inflation and depression originate".

President James A. Garfield (The 20th President of the United States who lasted only one hundred days) speaking two weeks before he was assassinated in1881.

One of the best ways to understand the Babylon System is to analyze the numerous sub-programs that are used to manipulate us into oblivious states of ignorance. *Money* is one of these main sub-programs. Most of us spend our entire lives in pursuit of it. We try to acquire as much of it as possible in the vain belief that possessing vast quantities of it will make our lives better and more fulfilled. We lie, cheat, beg, borrow, steal and *kill* for it every day, and even though we might amass billions of it, our lives are still impoverished on the real levels that matter. We're still very ignorant of the *real value* of life. No matter how much money we have it has never been able to stop us from getting sick and it cannot prevent us from facing the inevitability of death. And we certainly cannot take it with us when we leave this world.

The most important thing to realize is that *money is not real* and has no *intrinsic value* whatsoever. It's a tool of exploitation to control us mentally and physically and to lock us down into the Babylon System permanently. The little pieces of papers and coins that jingle around in our pockets have been responsible for some of the most destructive behaviors by apparently sane and rational human beings throughout known history.

What is money, really? Money is a medium that facilitates the *exchange of goods and services* within society. Because the money we use has no *real* or *intrinsic value* it's referred to as *'fiat money'*. Fiat money is basically *'fake money'* and has no value as a *physical commodity*; it's only valuable because *governments declare it to be legal tender*. This means that it must be accepted by all in society as a form of payment within the national borders of a specific country for 'all goods, services and public and private debts'.

The money supply of a country is usually held to consist of what we call *currency*. Currencies are banknotes and coins we refer to as *'deposit money'*. Deposit money is held in checking accounts and savings accounts within the banking structure. This money is *intangible* and exists only in the form of various *bank records* and *figures on a computer screen* which accounts for the larger part of the money supply rather than physical currency.

When you go to a bank to get a loan, the money is not inside the bank in a vault; it's *created out of thin air* at the touch of a button on a computer. All money is made in a factory and sent to the bank where you receive it as physical currency. The author *Andrew Carrington* explains in his important volume, *The Synagogue of Satan*:

Let's say for example the amount of money in circulation in a given country is £5,000,000, and a central bank is set up and prints another £15,000,000 and releases that out into the economy through loans and so on, then this will naturally reduce the value of the initial £5,000,000 that was in circulation before the bank was formed. This is because the initial £5,000,000 that was 100% of the economy is now only 25% of the economy. It will also give the bank control of 75% of the money in circulation with the £15,000,000 they sent out into the economy. This causes inflation which is simply the reduction in worth of money borne by the common person, due to the economy being flooded with too much money, an economy which the Central Bank are responsible for. As the common person's money is worth less, he has to go to the bank to get a loan to help run his business etc, and when the Central Bank are satisfied there are enough people with debt out there, the bank will tighten the supply of money by not offering loans. This is stage two of the plan.
Stage three, is the bankers sitting back and waiting for the people in debt to them to go bankrupt, allowing the bank to then seize from them real wealth, businesses and property etc, for pennies on the pound. Inflation never affects a central bank, in fact they are the only group who can benefit from it, as if they are ever short of money they can simply print more...

The *Bank of England*, the *Bundesbank* of Germany the *Federal Reserve* of the USA and all other banks are really *private institutions* owned and run by various networks of *private cooperations* which in turn are *subsidiaries* of the *Illuminati power structure*, not the legally elected governments of nations. Those who make, distribute and control the money that runs our societies are not the governments and therefore are ultimately not accountable to anyone but their own private interests.

Private cooperations such as the *Federal Reserve* through their various companies, chop down trees, pulp them into paper, make money out of the paper and *loan* it to governments at a rate of *'interest'*. We go to work in order to get this *'piece of paper'* so that we can buy food, goods and services. The government has to repay the loans they *'borrow'* back to the Central Banks *plus* whatever percentage of *interest* that has accrued on them. The interest that the government pays back to the bank is not real or physical money and ultimately has to be *created by the bank itself at the touch of a button*. And so, the cycle of borrowing and debt continues, holding governments and the populations of the world to *ransom*, indefinitely.

A bank can withhold money, thus causing inflation which generally dictates the developments in our societies, economically, politically and socially. The money manipulators create elaborate *monetary policies* in order to disguise from the public the manner in which they manipulate and control our lives through a complete *illusion*. The banks and their shadowy owners are ultimately the arbiters of how society functions, not governments. *John D. Rockefeller* one of the elite Illuminati once said:

"Give me control of a country's money supply and I don't care who makes its laws".

When we understand how we have been controlled by this illusion of money, it sheds a new light on why our lives have become so poor and desperate. It's worth pointing out that internet videos such as the *Zeitgeist* series sheds a great deal of light on this subject and is compulsory viewing, (you can view these on YouTube). For a more in-depth understanding of how this system works, type in Zeitgeist on your internet browser and watch.

Walking through *Brixton Market* in *South London*, one of the most obvious things you will observe is the fact that almost all the people selling *African/Caribbean foods* such as yams, bananas, mangoes and so on and various products such as *wigs, weave-on, cosmetics, clothing*, *'fried chicken shops'* and anything else that black people buy, are not black people. Do the same in downtown *Kingston* or *Montego Bay*, *Jamaica* and you will observe a very similar pattern, (except for the natural foodstuff grown on the island); all the major retail and wholesale outlets that cater to the majority of the people there, (the predominantly black African majority) are controlled by those who are not black/African Jamaicans. Take a walk in Africa, lets say, down town *Dakar, (Senegal), Nairobi,(Kenya), Cape Town, (South Africa)* and many other places and you will observe quite similar situations. In the USA it's very much the same. The economic plight of black peoples across the world is a very telling point when it comes to understanding the nature of the white supremacy mind control programs and the New World Order conspiracy. Black people are not in a position to be assertive economically anywhere in the world, *and never will be,* no matter how hard they try. That's one of the main rules of the *'game'*. Usually, a few *'token blacks'* are put in positions of *'semi-authority'* as a means of fooling the majority of people (both black and white) into believing that black people are being given real opportunities. This is what's called the *'Black showcasing'* method of mind control to give a false impression that black people are gaining some real power in societies. A tiny handful of blacks such as rappers *Jay-Z, Puff Daddy, Oprah Winfrey, Barack Obama* and the like are given a degree of prominence to keep the majority of blacks believing that it might be possible for them to *'make it'* one day. Behind the scenes, black African peoples of planet earth are being annihilated like flies.

Illustrative of these issues is the willful social and economic destruction of *Jamaica* during the 1970s by the then USA regime, by proxy of the *CIA* and the *International Monetary Fund* (*IMF*). Most poor/working class Jamaican people don't understand the reasons why they are economically and socially deprived.

The Jamaican Prime Minister, Michael Manley of the People's National Party (PNP), during his tenure as leader of the nation, developed significant programs for social and fiscal reforms that attempted to avoid the traps of a debt driven social developmental programs imposed by the draconian IMF. During Manley's time in power the country experienced waves of progressive reforms and significant growth in many areas. Education became free and accessible for the poor majority coupled with land reform and working policies. The ban on *Marxist* and *Black Power* literature, (upheld by previous JLP governments) was also lifted, enabling a welcomed development of intellectual debate on the nature and direction of nationalistic imperatives. Important to his socialist agenda many foreign-owned companies such as electricity, telephone and bus companies were nationalized. Major strategic assets such as bauxite (aluminum ore) were targeted by Manley for *renationalization*. The 1970s was a time of deep and widespread politicization of Jamaican society and the country '*backed Michael Manley's refusal to adhere to the repressive [fiscal adjustment] terms demanded by the IMF' for governmental development loans.* He announced to a cheering crowd of 35,000 Jamaicans at the National Stadium in the capital Kingston, *"We [Jamaicans] are not for sale"*. According to Caribbean scholar *Fitzroy Ambursley*:

"At that time, Manley was recognized as the Socialist International's most important representative in the so-called Third World".

This was a test case – for both the IMF and what could be termed the *anti-imperialist* movement of socialist thinkers at that time throughout the Caribbean and South America. The proposed IMF structural adjustment program for Jamaica was to be a model for *neo-liberalism* and *global debt negotiations* throughout the Third World.

The battle between Jamaica and the IMF has been noted by Caribbean and progressive historians as a turning point in the fight by developing nations against the enforced system of economic slavery and tyranny by international *big-business* cartels. In January of 1974, Manley's government announced a plan to radically overhaul the system of tax breaks and incentives offered to US and Canadian bauxite companies based in Jamaica. *He annulled all previous agreements and imposed a production levy on all bauxite mined or processed in Jamaica.*

This move by Manley provoked the wrath of the USA and those in the business sector who in the past had a free reign in dictating the relationship between big business and the Jamaican government – *a massive, and now well-documented, destabilization program followed.* Threats were leveled against the Manley government by the international big business cartels. Aluminum and bauxite processing were rapidly shifted to other locations. The levy imposed on bauxite mining and processing was contested by the bauxite companies in terms of its legality and they duly filed actions with the World Bank's international centre for the settlement of investment disputes. Local business leaders (most of whom were foreigners) became vocally opposed to government fiscal policies that sought to impose realistic tax structures. Many poor Jamaicans began to experience lay-offs and rising commodity price increases created the foundations for an inflationary spiral that saw wages fell dramatically. The inflow of foreign capital also plummeted, while at the same time the CIA became actively involved with stirring up local political rivalries that created major social unrest across the country. For the first time in its history Jamaica experienced massive social destabilization on all levels as what can only be described as a *terror campaign* was unleashed by the CIA against Manley's government. Affiliates and notorious thugs of the Jamaica Labour Party (JLP) were suddenly in possession of *high caliber weapons* and running gun battles and wholesale slaughter brought the programs of social reforms and development to an abrupt halt. Many thousands of innocent Jamaican people were killed in the turmoil that ensued without ever realizing the real extended nature of the conspiracy to overturn the legally elected government of Jamaica.

Although Manley's government tried to regroup in the face of enormous opposition by the USA he was ousted from power in 1980 by the CIA backed JLP Labour Party headed by *Edward Seaga*. Manley's socioeconomic reforms proved no match for the power of the globalist capitalist power-bloc that championed his downfall and deliberately wrecked the economy of Jamaica. The ending of Manley's eight years in power saw *'average income of the poor fell by at least 25 percent and the cost of living rose 320 percent higher'*. The social democracy experiment in Jamaica was dealt a heavy blow by the imperialist agenda of the global capitalist cartel. It is worth noting that at the end of Seaga and the JLP Labour Party's two terms in office,

'Jamaica had paid out a total of £443 million to its foreign creditors, including £176 million to the IMF'. The country's foreign debt had grown to a staggering £2.2 billion, among the highest per capita in the world at that time'.

Over the years in Jamaica we have seen an erosion of civil liberties (most people living in very socially deprived situations think that we now live in what is effectively a *police state*). Social welfare programs have been cut back drastically and the standard of living for the poor *black majority* have never recovered from this assault on the state by the USA. The continuing situation of gun violence and widespread poverty among the masses of poor black Jamaicans is indicative of the hostile forces that still (even after four hundred years) keep our people in slavery. Jamaica today, like most developing countries, suffers from the intransigence of corrupt and inept political leadership compounded by moral and social degradation that has impoverished the nation. The appallingly inadequate education system continues to breed generations of Jamaicans to develop servile mentalities and infantile perceptions of reality.

What occurred in Jamaica has happened in many other countries in the developing world; Africa (the *Congo*, Rwanda, Zimbabwe, and so on), South America and South East Asia, and is indicative of the *Illuminati* conspiratorial policies that keep billions of people impoverished and disenfranchised from real decision making in how the world is governed.

*Nelson Mandela was once labelled a **terrorist** and locked up in prison for twenty seven years by the **white supremacists** because he fought like a Great Lion against the destructive, racist Babylon System for the freedom of black African peoples. Later, the same **duplicitous**, serpentine Babylon System heaped upon him the honours of a king, (while setting traps to diminish his **potency** and **power**).*
*We would do well to remember that the squalid ghettos of **Soweto** and **Johannesburg** are still **festering** wounds in the body of our **Sacred Mother Africa**. Oppression by proxy is still oppression. **We have now seen the puppet master's sweaty little hands behind the shabby curtain of illusion.***

*The Babylon System invokes the mind control program of what it calls morality to prevent its disguise from falling away. As **Mumia Abu-Jamal** outlined; it was considered moral to **enslave** and **oppress** millions of black peoples for four hundred years; it was considered moral to violently **steal** the very earth from beneath the Native American Nations; it was considered moral to drop **atomic bombs** on innocent populations; it was considered moral to **plunder** the earth, **destroy** the rainforests and **poison** the oceans for **profit,** and it is considered moral to implement **war** and **aggression** for the sake of white supremacy expediency. Naked lies, deceit, duplicity, horror and evil cannot be misconstrued as morality.*
*Our Freedom as human beings inevitably must transcend the mind control program that the Babylon System defines as **'morality'**. **True Freedom cannot be called into question or be held to ransom**.*

-The Golden Path of Jah Rastafari -

The eminent African American psychiatrist **Dr. Francis Cress Welsing** outlined in her substantially weighty body of work over a number of years the need for a **Unified Field Theory** of psychiatry that takes into account the **essential** element of **racism**, (which is described as the **White Supremacy Mind Control Program),** as a necessary means to understanding the human condition on earth within the context of what we Rastas refer to as the **Babylon System**. Dr. Cress Welsing's seminal work, **The Isis**

Papers-The Keys to the Colours, has undoubtedly become one of the most important, controversial and in-depth analysis of racism ever undertaken on a *scientific* level. Her thorough and informed understanding of these issues lays bare some very essential points that we need to understand in order to grasp the dire nature of our predicament as human beings here on earth. *The Isis Papers* (*the Keys to the Colours*) has been dismissed (naturally) by the *enforcers* and *gate-keepers* of the Babylon System in the world media, yet remains unchallenged in its integrity and power since its publication.

Racism is the system of awareness, thought, action, emotional responses, whether consciously or unconsciously determined in the minds of persons who classify themselves as *'white'*. The goal of racism as an *'operating system'* is the complete white domination over the majority peoples of our planet, (whom whites have classified as *'non-white'* – black, brown, red and yellow) in order to ensure *white genetic dominance* on earth. *One tenth* of the peoples on earth classify themselves as white and *nine tenth* of the peoples on earth are black, brown, red and yellow, according to the classification imposed by whites. This is essentially the dynamics that created slavery, apartheid and segregation in human societies.

This is the actual reality of the world we live in today, whether we wish to acknowledge it or not. Racism or white supremacy is one of the most important factors in human existence and I believe the reasons for this is more far reaching than we ever suspected. It's intrinsically involved with our very beginnings as human beings on earth and spells dire portents for the future to come.

The overwhelming majority of the people on earth are genetically dominant in terms of the genetic factor called *melanin*. Melanin is what gives human beings their varied skin tones; black, brown, red and yellow. Black Africans possess the highest concentration of melanin in any group of human beings. Whites also possess melanin but in very reduced quantities. Black, brown, red and yellow peoples are genetically dominant in terms of melanin and whites are genetically recessive. This is basic scientific knowledge which anyone can learn about. The state of genetic recessivness is the condition called *albinism*.

In *scientific theory* therefore, white skin is a state of albinism, (and this is a definition that white Euro/American scientists themselves recognize). The word albino or albinism refers to a group of *inherited* genetic conditions. People with albinism have little or no pigment in the eyes, skin, and hair; (in some cases in the eyes alone). They have inherited from their parents an *altered* copy of a gene that does not function normally. The altered gene does not allow the body to make the usual amounts of *melanin* pigment. As a consequence whites are most prone to sunburns and usually

62

suffer from *vitamin D* deficiency and so on. The deficiency syndrome of albinism affects people from all races. The parents of most children with albinism have normal hair and eye color for their ethnic background, and do not usually have a family history of albinism.

In order to gain a better insight into this, let's take a brief look at the science that elucidates these points. *Melanin* is a dark compound that acts as a *photo-protective pigment* in the skin. One role of the melanin pigment is to *absorb ultraviolet light* (*UV*) that comes from the sun so that the skin is not damaged by radiation and heat. Sun exposure normally produces a tan in most white people, which is an increase in melanin pigmentation. Most people with *albinism* have very small amounts of melanin pigment in their skin and as a result their skin is sensitive to sun light, which culminates in sun burn. The skin behaves normal even if there is no melanin present.

Melanin pigment is important in other areas of the body, such as the *brain, muscles, eye* and major organs such as the liver, but science has not ascertained its function in these areas yet. It is also present in the *retina* and the area of the retina called the fovea does not develop correctly if melanin pigment is not present during development. The nerve connections between the *retina* and the *brain* are also dysfunctional if melanin pigment is not present in the retina during development. The iris has melanin pigment and this makes it opaque to light, (no light goes through an opaque iris). Iris pigment in albinism is reduced, and the iris is translucent to light, but it can develop and function normally.

Melanin is formed in a cell called the *melanocyte* which is found in the skin, hair follicles and certain organs. There are several steps in the process of converting the amino acid *tyrosine* to melanin pigment. In the *melanin pathway*, two types of melanin are formed: black-brown *eumelanin* and red-yellow *pheomelanin*.

Tyrosinase is the major enzyme involved in the formation of melanin pigment and is responsible for converting *tyrosine* to **DOPA** and then to *dopaquinone.* The dopaquinone then forms black-brown *eumelanin* or red-yellow *pheomelanin*. The tyrosinase enzyme is made by the tyrosinase *gene* on chromosome 11, and alterations or *mutations* of this gene can produce one type of albinism because the tyrosinase enzyme made by the altered gene does not work correctly.

There are two additional enzymes called *tyrosinase-related protein 1* or **DHICA oxidase** and tyrosinase-related protein 2 or *dopachrome tautomerase* which are important in the formation of eumelanin pigment. Alterations of the DHICA oxidase gene are associated with a loss of function of this enzyme and this also produces a type of albinism.

Three other genes make proteins that are also involved in melanin pigment formation and albinism, but the exact role of these proteins is not understood by geneticists at present.

That's the basic science, so to speak. It's very easy for anyone to understand. You don't have to possess knowledge of genetic science, just an inquiring mind. The *'big words'* and phrases you encounter while reading these things are just *'scientific terminologies' deliberately designed to compartmentalize* and *hide knowledge* from the masses. This can be overcome by having a good medical dictionary when reading and by having conversations with other people on these issues.

I have outlined this process because it's very important to have some grasp of the basic science behind something as pronounced as skin colour, which appears so mysterious to human beings and causes so many problems in our societies. In fact, recent genetic data has outlined that all human beings in the remote past were actually various shades of brown. That was the standard model before the processes of genetic mutation was stimulated (whether naturally or *'artificially'*) to create a differentiation in the human species. It's been estimated by some geneticists that the Caucasoid (white) group of humans only transformed into their present state roughly some 15,000 to12,000 BC.

What can be discerned is that melanin is very much involved with enzymatic action, the creation and absorption of proteins, the *'vitality'* of human *DNA* and the general health and cohesion of the biological structure. The purpose of melanin also appears to infer something to do with the catalytic conversion of light energy into *'nutrients'* for the body. Recent research has also theorized on the *libido enhancing* effects of melanin and ongoing research has been looking at interesting correlations between melanin and human perception also.

Melanin is one of the ingredients for the incredible phenomenon we recognize as *racism* on our planet right now. If a human being has no melanin and he or she breeds with a melanized human being then the offspring will always be born with melanin. White Europeans realized the mechanisms of this process during their encounter with melanized humans; racism was developed partly as a reaction to the fear that white is *genetically recessive*, which means that if whites bred wholesale with other human beings, in time the white race could potentially become completely melanized. The *white supremacy mind control program* was therefore instituted in the minds of the white minority on earth as a means of white *genetic survival*. The development that we see in artificial *white breeding technology* over the years clearly informs this view and impacts dramatically on the nature of the future to come.

There is much more about this subject that needs to be researched by science as the implications of this knowledge can add greatly to positive human development. The point is that the colour of a person's skin is vastly important and there are many things that we are not aware of when it concerns our most basic humanity.

The essential element is the fact that melanin actually prevents various forms of radiation from harming the skin while absorbing *light* into the biological system and storing and converting it to *specific and unique forms of energy*. The bio-molecular process of light absorption by the body is not fully understood by science at this present time in the 21st century, but the fact that human bodies can absorb, store, utilize and (we are just finding out now) *produce* light in various ways through melanin pigmentation, (on what would appear to be a wide spectrum) presents staggering implications on many levels. What we can therefore discern is a process by which light is separated and transformed from its basic wavelengths and *bonds* with a human body on a molecular level, thus imparting some form of *'energy*, and *information'* to the body on a bio-molecular level. Someone once coined the phrase *'living light'* to express this process of light interaction within the human body.

Within Rasta tradition, light is a manifestation of the subtle *fire element* within creation and like the other elements of Air, Water and Earth is vital to our existence. This knowledge when understood in its proper context can radically alter our perception and development on earth. For black peoples, the colour of *'black skin'* is far more important than we could have ever realized. Research in the various fields of knowledge could begin to throw up incredible patterns that might elucidate the reasons why blacks have black skins (and not just because we have been supposedly *cursed* by some wrathful biblical patriarch and so on).

All colours of the visible spectrum when mixed together become black. The observable universe appears totally black, yet contains all the stars, galaxies and light in existence and so on. The point is that the term black has been applied in our modern cultures in very negative ways because of the mind control programs of the Babylon System to defraud us of our natural human rights. And of course the word white, (as used by some people), implies positive and good things and so forth). According to the popular internet dictionary *Wikipedia:*

*'The sensory perception of light plays a central role in spirituality (vision, enlightenment etc). The presence of light as opposed to its absence (darkness) is a common **Western** metaphor of good and evil, knowledge and ignorance, and similar concepts'.*

Looking at these issues from the analytic perspective of the *Rasta Fire Meditation* we can glean important aspects of a fundamental knowledge that can open our minds to a more far reaching perception of ourselves as black peoples. Light is one of the main basic generative energies of the universal structure. It has many functions beyond the formation of the *bio-energy fields* that binds our material perceptions to the observable space/time continuum. It's also a means of connecting us to specific higher vibrational frequencies. The skin is the largest organ of the human body; if we are able to absorb photons of light into our biological matrix (cells and DNA structures) and utilize this process to develop conscious and holistic awareness of our position and purpose in time and space, then having so-called *'black skin'* appears to be a most positive thing. This statement is in no way intended to imply anything as ridiculous and vain as some racists would have it, but that this process which occurs at a greater rate within the biological matrix of humans with higher amounts of melanin, does warrant open and conscious investigation as to its implications. Light isn't just radiation, it's a specific and significant form of energy that can be *absorbed* by the cells of the body and used as a type of *'food'*. The fact that black/brown peoples inhabit the zones of the earth that are most prevalent in sunlight does have interesting implications where human evolutionary processes are concerned. It's really no accident that the human race began in Africa which is invariably a hot climate.

There's much discussion nowadays about melanin and its physical and metaphysical relationship with light radiation. Ongoing research attests to the paradigm that black African peoples were the first human beings on planet earth. Information directly received from the analytic mode clearly shows that the nature of the earth environment dictates the state of life-forms that evolve in the most *productive* ways – specific climatic and environmental conditions that are most likely to promote life along the *path of least resistance*, (what I refer to as the *PLR model* of human evolution). Euro/American Darwinian science contends and maintains the theory of *'competition'* and *'survival of the fittest'* as the tenets that govern evolutionary systems, but I propose the PLR to be a far more pragmatic model for human development and specifically human evolution that would reach its *maximum impact and potential on multi-dimensional levels*. The PLR model dictates cooperation rather than competition to be the most effective means in the development of successful and productive evolutionary systems in higher lifeforms.

The Euro/American scientific community is at present, probing this knowledge, albeit tentatively. But I would surmise that *'conscious'* scientists would ultimately be the ones to pursue any real and useful research in this area. The *consciousness transforming* work of the African American surgeon and holistic teacher *Dr. Jewel Pookrum* has charted astounding research into the relationships between the function of melanin, the holistic nature of consciousness and our spiritual relationships on a cosmic/multidimensional level and is *essential* reading. Her videos are also essential viewing in order to grasp the fundamental knowledge of these issues.

*"If you do not understand **racism** – **white supremacy** – everything else that you <u>think</u> you understand will only confuse you. White supremacy is a system set up and maintained by people who classify themselves as **white** and who believe that the entire universe should be dominated by people who classify themselves as white. And all of the activities of people that **they classify** as **non-white** will be subject to them, by them for their satisfaction, forever. It's the most powerful political concept ever thought of; that you can go all over the universe and one criteria alone, regardless of language or anything else, defines you. If you are a non-white person you are subject to this process. **This is what racism and white supremacy ultimately means".***

- Dr. Neely Fuller Jr, (Psychologist) -

Since the concept of evolutionary science was formed with the publication of Darwin's theories, an odious undercurrent of racism has informed the relationship between black and white peoples. This became solidified in the ***mind control doctrine*** of '***white racial superiority'*** and '***black racial inferiority'*** in Euro/American academia and society. Black African peoples have suffered intolerably because of this. In fact, the philosophy of white racial superiority seems to have been elevated to the position of a *religion* among its proponents. It's a system that is controlled and defended with left-handed politics, rapacious economic policies, science, racist academia and a frightening array of ***high-tech weapons systems*** and ***atomic bombs***.

Having run out of justifications for the atrocities committed against large swathes of the human race, the racist elements in white academia have latched on to what they believe to be their penultimate hope for maintaining the illusion of white racial dominance – the so-called question of human *intelligence*; (no doubt their military/industrial complex is standing by should this argument atrophy in time and bear no fruit, as it is destined to do).

In recent years these racists have been disseminating a noxious tirade of jaw-dropping nonsense that has fueled the debate in white society about what they call '***white superior intelligence'***. I dealt briefly with writings such as the ***Bell Curve*** (in the first volume, Jah Rastafari – Visions of Faith) which I heartily recommend everyone to at least browse through. The amusement of volumes such as Bell Curve and other similar publications is only tempered by the sober realization that most white people who read these books actually *believe* their transparent little *'theorizing'*. This spurious doctrine is filtered out to the masses of whites in all social classes world-wide in order to garner their support in the white supremacy conspiracy. Many white people in general (wherever one may go in the world) seem believe (whether consciously or subconsciously) in some sort of *'white superior genius'*. They have been brainwashed with the racial poison for so long, that they have no recourse but to believe it.

The consciousness expanding work of eminent people such as, **Dr. Neely Fuller Jr., Dr. Francis Cress Welsing and Dr. Jewel Pookrum** amongst many others, outlines the astonishing depths of the white supremacy mind control program that threatens to annihilate black peoples on planet earth. Dr. Cress Welsing explains that:

I have for a long time looked at the problem of Black people as being related to ***racism***, *which is* ***White supremacy***. *Those words are synonymous—meaning* ***global behavioral system*** *for* ***white genetic survival*** *on the planet.*

In other words, the white population on the planet is a tiny ***minority***, ***less than one-tenth of the people on the planet***. *They are genetic recessive in terms of skin coloration—meaning, white can be genetically [submerged]. White plus Black equals Colored. White plus Brown equals Colored. White plus Yellow equals Colored. So, the white minority is aware; I would say they have been aware since they circumnavigated the globe, that they were a minority. White males having sexual relations with non-white women found out that the children conceived by those women all look like the mothers, meaning the white was [submerged].*

I say that this is the fundamental motivation of people who classify themselves as white, whether it is conscious and/or subconsciously determined. In other words: what the ***'white collective'*** *is doing on the planet is engaging in behaviors—in economics, education, entertainment, labor, law, politics, religion, sex and more—in order for them to survive on the planet, by any means necessary.*
*When people are consciously and/or subconsciously on course for their genetic survival—meaning that they're found genetically vulnerable to other people who can cause their genetic annihilation—**then the practice of genocide is a logical outcome from this.***

As I see what is happening on the Continent of Africa and other places where there are non-white people—even if we just look at the AIDS-HIV epidemic—this is something that is ***killing tens of millions of Non-White people***. *I don't think that an intelligent and aware Black person—any aware person—is not thinking that*

68

*HIV/AIDS is something that just spontaneously occurred in nature... **This is biological warfare until proven otherwise**. I would say that it is used against non-white populations—as **Dr. Neely Fuller** used the term, **'population tailoring'**— to kill certain numbers of non-white people on the planet.*

The **Cress Welsing Theory** is one of the most controversial and important analysis of the white supremacy mind control program ever conducted and is a vital tool to understanding the dynamics of the Babylon System and its aims. History, in the manner that it is taught in educational institutions, is a clear indicator of the white supremacy agenda and its overt and covert modes of operation.

White supremacy is therefore, to all intents and purposes, a **definable historically based, institutional system of exploitation and oppression of continents, nations and peoples of color by white peoples and nations of Europe for the purpose of maintaining and defending a system of wealth, power, advantages and privilege and genetic heritage, by whatever means necessary.**

Black African slavery, colonialism, apartheid, Nazism and Aryanism, were among the most visible, **structured** manifestations of this phenomenon.

Structural racism, in the context of the white supremacy mind control program, is the legalization and social/cultural legitimization of patterns of behavior – institutional, historical, cultural, and interpersonal – that consistently gives advantages to people who consider themselves **white**, and which automatically produces corresponding and cumulative **adverse effects** and **outcomes** for people who are considered to be **non-white**. It's a system based on hierarchy, inequity, preferential treatment, privilege and power for white people at the expense of Black, Asian, Latino, Native American, Arab and other racial groups of the world.

This phenomenon encompasses all human interactions and all aspects of society - politics, economics, history, culture and our entire social fabric. All other forms of racism, whether institutional, interpersonal, internalized and so on emerge from this primary body of structural racism.

Some obvious manifestations of structural racism are: **inequalities in access to opportunities, socio- economic/political policy implementation, impacts and outcomes, whether consciously or unconsciously created** in social dynamics and people/group interactions. Structural racism in the raw sense involves the **reinforcing effects** of **multiple institutions** social and cultural, past and present that continually produces new and varying forms of racism to fit constantly changing perceptions and perspectives and to maintain the mind control program indefinitely. Racial prejudice, xenophobia, internal fear of racial violence and so on internalize and individualize the operating system of racism thus **tying the minds of whites into the common white**

69

racial consensus reality paradigm. One of the most obvious parts to this mind control program is the fact that white Euro/American nations have hijacked the *'war market'* and have become the biggest *manufacturers* and *distributors* of *destructive weapons* on planet earth. They completely control the means of making war on all levels, and through this process *control* the economic and political power of the world.

Racism therefore is a means developed by white nations and peoples to remove *power* from other peoples of the world whom they have classified as non-white. Power can be perceived in many ways but essentially *it's the ability – the means and motivation – to define a perceived reality and to convince others that it's also their definition as well.* This is essentially the grease that turns the wheels that drives the mind control program of white supremacy and the Babylon System in general. White political, cultural, economic and military domination of the world is a clear and precise explanation of this truth. The oppression and destruction of black peoples in Africa and the African Diaspora is the result of this mind control program.

A crucial part of this is the application of another subsidiary program we refer to as *scientific racism* as a means of reinforcing the mind control program of racism in whites. Scientific racism is a very clever way of upholding and propagating the doctrine of racism so that it appears as though it's justified by the laws of *science* and *nature*. This is essentially what the insidious Bell Curve book and so-called *'research'* carried out by various closeted racists attempted to do. They try to gain respectability from whites by covering their tracks with what they classify as *intellectualism*.

White supremacy is among the greatest impediments to human progress because it allows the most dangerous fantasies of a small minority to subvert and overturn the *natural and most productive evolutionary pathway* of the entire human species on earth.

Media such as television are among the greatest weapons in the arsenal of the Babylon System. It's a mind control tool to subjugate the masses of black people and to coerce whites into believing in a false version of reality. It's one of the greatest methods of mass mind control ever invented. In every African and Caribbean country the images shown on TV gives the impression that the world is ruled, maintained and dominated by *ingenious* white people. This medium is used to insinuate the *white consensus reality paradigm* into the minds of all blacks wherever they might be in the world. Consequently, black cultures imitate the *'cultural norms'* of whites and continually aspire to emulate the conventions of the *white world-view*.

*Pacifism is the belief that violence, war, and the taking of **human** lives are unacceptable ways of resolving disputes. Within the structure of the Babylon System the philosophy of Pacifism will always defeat itself in its undertaking. It's an unworkable idea given our predicament of **racism** and the **white supremacy** dominated world. We must firstly look at those who created this philosophy and their motives for doing so. Warmongers are the first to speak of Pacifism while at the same time engaging in constant **aggression and war** against others. We must redefine the word Pacifism in the context of evolving human developmental paradigms. The so-called **morality** that underpins the philosophy of Pacifism is merely a **mind control tool** created by the Babylon System to weaken and divert the resolve for true freedom into dead-end dogma and meaningless intellectual gymnastics.*

*There is no such thing as **passive resistance** against the aggression of an enemy that is **obviously** trying to **kill** you. The term was created by the Babylon System as a defence mechanism in the case of attack by the **true moral forces** inherent in human beings. The Babylon System will not tolerate anything that attempts to resist its progress, least of all Pacifism. It will always change the rules of the game to suit its purpose. **Peace** and **resistance** are **opposing forces**. Peaceful resistance has never worked against the Babylon System; the endless list of humanity's 'peaceful martyrs' who have (throughout the ages) given their lives to the cause of human freedom on earth speaks **eloquently** of Pacifism.*

-The Golden Path of Jah Rastafari -

Most **Rap** and **Hip-Hop** music are specifically designed to destroy black people's will to challenge the **New World Order**. In recent times we can clearly see the dramatic influences of the Illuminati agenda within African American society through the creation of specific genres of popular music and consumer culture. During the 1980s and throughout the 1990sAfrican American culture was targeted by the mind control program of the Illuminati. The reason behind this was the continuation and (projected) growth in the early 1980s of black radicalism in American society and the need to prevent blacks from **galvanizing** and inciting violence and uprising against the Babylon System – (white youth culture has always been heavily influenced by black popular culture and radicalism).

The remnants of the **Black Panther Party** of the 1960s, having been dismantled and eradicated effectively by the Illuminati agenda, in many ways looked to the black Muslims of American for aspiration – the **Nation of Islam** headed by **The Honorable Minister, Louis Farrakhan**. One of the primary aims of the Black Panther Party was to take the Civil Rights movement to the centre of the struggle for black American *'independence'*. No longer was the goal an abstention by police from brutalizing blacks but a wider and more condensed ideology that would enable the grassroots of the movement to acquire real degrees of *political power*. The ideology behind such a move cited the gains of the previous two decades as being below the benchmark for black social development and progress in America. African Americans were no longer just talking about power sharing with whites but the need for a separate and *autonomous* state for themselves *within the boundaries* of the United States of America. The last thing the Babylon System wanted then was regiments of black males with AK47s and rocket propelled grenade launchers dictating terms of power sharing in America. The memory of the black soldiers of the **UNIA** on American soil, established by the Sublime, Marcus Mosiah Garvey in Harlem during the 1920s was an inspiration to the Black Panthers of the 1960s and a clear reminder to the Babylon System of the possible portents of unchecked *black radicalism*. During the 1960s and 1970s other radical nationalist groups such as the Provisional Irish Republican Army (IRA) in Britain and Ireland, The Palestinian Liberation Army (PLO), Basque separatists of Spain (ETTA) and others were busy fomenting revolutionary activism that caused much problems for the Illuminati led Babylon System. The Illuminati and their affiliates had to find ways and means to curtail and destroy these potentially destabilizing situations at all costs. We do know that during the stirring times of the early 1980s the **AIDS** epidemic came to prominence, affecting amounts of African Americans, disproportionately. The sudden arrival of *crack cocaine* and other forms of highly addictive narcotics in the black communities across the nation assisted the destruction of black radicalism on American soil. We do know for a fact also that *elements within the CIA* have been implicitly involved with the procuring of drugs from South America and depositing them into black communities in the USA to destabilize black people's efforts at civil disobedience during those times.

The 1980s saw gun crimes increased dramatically in New York, Los Angeles and many of the urban centers with high black populations. *It is a fact that black peoples do not make guns*. The phrase *'black-on-black-violence'* was first coined by the racist white media as a way of entrenching the stereotype of black people being *violent* and *aggressive*. One should note carefully that crimes perpetrated by *whites on whites* are never labeled as *'white-on-white-violence'*. This is another clear indicator of the mechanics of the Babylon System's mind control programs.

During those times, we see the extended policies of wide ranging *'political'* assaults on radical black countries such as *Jamaica*, which has always been an influential mark upon black cultures around the world. As mentioned already, the shadowy conspiracies of the *CIA* in the Caribbean markedly influenced the fall of the Manley government in Jamaica in the late 1970s and the attempted assassination of *Bob Marley* at his home during that time. Bob Marley, being a great *revolutionary* Rasta prophet to many black and white youths, represented very grave dangers to the Babylon System. Having access to vast sums of money, economic clout, the support of masses of the worlds blacks and disenfranchised and a radical agenda for upliftment of the poor masses, he presented all sorts of complications and headaches for the Babylon System. The cold-blooded murder of other great Rasta prophets such as *Peter Tosh* by agents of the Babylon System in Jamaica only highlight the extents to which the controllers will go in their attempts to snuff out the light of human freedom. It has been stated clearly that at the time of his murder, Tosh was about to procure a radio station through which he would be able to set an agenda for social awakening in Jamaica. It is obvious that the last thing the system wanted was an astute revolutionary Rastaman of his caliber in charge of such a powerful media that would reach a wide audience.

Music has always been at the heart of black culture and black musical forms have played a significant role in white music development and hence white popular culture on a whole. During the late 1980s the development of musical forms such as *'Gangsta Rap'* dominated black music globally, coupled with what was referred to as *'Slackness'* music, which came out of *Jamaica* at the same time. Jamaican musical culture (*dancehall*) has been a significant influence on black American musical forms (Rap, Hip-Hop, R&B and so on) and to some degree also, vice versa. Some black thinkers, commentators and academics place these issues at the heart of the *slide* from an optimistic view of black cultural development (at the end of the 1970s) to one of apathy, self loathing, despair and self-destruction through drug and gun culture fostered upon our culture by the Babylon Systems powerful mind control programs. The glorification of the gun, self denigration (referring to each other in negative terms such as *'Niggas'* and *'dogs'* and our women as *'whores'* and *'bitches'* have been effective tools in the mind control programs of the Babylon System. How could any proud and intelligent black man find it acceptable to refer to and be referred to as dog or Nigger? These forms of behaviour and expressions become embedded within our *cultural psyche* and assist in the removal of the self esteem of black people, not just in America but internationally. Blacks in other countries, (Caribbean, continental Africa, Australasia and so forth) then begin to *identify* with and use these terms within their local cultures without understanding the implications of the wider issue. Slackness and Gangsta Rap (along with the baser elements of Hip-Hop) are sponsored by the largely white owned *'popular culture establishment'* (record companies, producers and so on) and are used as tools to subjugate, compartmentalize and distort the *reality* of black culture, to black people and white youth who idolize black culture and musical art forms. It's a quite basic mind control program but we as a people seem to fall for it, continuously.

In the last ten years or so there has been a concerted *attack* on Reggae Music and *Jamaican culture* in general by the agents and *social engineers* of the Babylon System. This has been instigated by what we are led to believe are gay lobby groups in the UK and the USA who are campaigning for gay civil rights in Jamaica. Most of us are probably familiar with the arguments leveled at the behaviour and lyrics propagated by specific dancehall singers such as *Beenie Man, Sizzla, Capleton, Elephant Man, Ninja Man* and many others who call for the burning of homosexuals and lesbians and so on. Jamaicans are very familiar with these things and tend to take such lyrics and sentiments in their stride. The point is that these sentiments, as expressed in Dancehall music, are not taken literally by most progressive Jamaicans but are reflections of the deeply held moral views entrenched by the *Christian religious authorities* of the country. The words of the Bible are believed by the majority of Jamaicans to be the revealed truth of God, therefore its authority cannot really be questioned or reinterpreted. The Bible says that homosexuality is wrong, and if the Bible is the word of God then the word of God cannot be wrong. This is really the core of the argument. Modern societies have evolved to take into consideration the differences in human personal self-expression in whatever form that might appear. The sexual nature of human beings has always been a source of contention in whatever society one exist, and homosexuality is but part of human self-expression, whether one agrees with it or not on a personal level. It's obvious that there are many gay people who lead very normal and productive lives, contributing greatly to society in various ways. The rights and wrongs of people's personal choices in sexual matters is firstly an issue for each individual to make their own enquiries into, and society to debate and to draw conclusions that would assist greater understanding. The so-called *norms* of one society are not necessarily the same for others and these things must be taken into consideration also. But equally, and most importantly, the rights of each human being to express his or her own personal nature, positively and constructively, must be protected, (providing those rights are not detrimental to the evolutionary advancement of the greater whole). We might disagree with the way some people choose to live their lives but according to the universal principles of *Livity*, freedom of positive self expression is a vital part of human existence. Positive self expression can only be understood through the *moral principles* dictated by the universal *Law of ONELOVE*. Within the parameters of the Laws of Livity we have the principle, '*do not kill*' or '*kill not that which you cannot create*'. No man can *create* life; therefore, to kill our brothers and sisters because of their personal sexual expression (simply because we disagree with it) is complete ignorance and disregard for the *Laws of*

74

Livity and the eternal principles of Jah Rastafari. Tolerance and wider understanding are the only means by which peaceful situations can be cultivated so that our society can develop for the greater benefit of all its members.

This situation has been deliberately *aggravated* by people *outside* of Jamaica who are pursuing their own agenda of cultural dislocation and destabilization. Certainly we're not going to violently abuse or kill our youth if they choose to express what they feel is *instinctive* and *intrinsic* to their nature as free human beings. We will however, assist and educate them and ourselves as to the real extended nature of life and that the sexual expression of a human being does not ultimately dictate whether a person is good or bad, in the same way that the colour of a person's skin does not dictate whether or not a person is good or bad. The problem with this issue is that some are trying to use it to attack our Jamaican culture for ulterior reasons and that must not be allowed. The aggressive promotion of homosexuality in white Euro/American countries is another part of the mind control program used by the Babylon System to further its agenda of *social manipulation and population control*. Ultimately, the Babylon System does not in any way care about homosexual people, only that they can be used as *'political leverage'* in whatever situation the conspirators care to engineer.

The uncompromising revolutionary power of Reggae music is self evident and has become an *iron thorn* in the side of the Babylon System. Our music is a vehicle of self expression for us as a people and cannot be compromised by the attacks of the Babylon System. We do however need to evolve our perception of issues that are very relevant to our development as human beings.

It has been called to attention that so-called black music superstars such as *Jay-Z, Beyonce, Kanye West* and *Rhianna* and so on have been *indoctrinated* at a *very local level* into the Illuminati mind control agenda. Recent research clearly indicates the usage of various *occult symbolisms* in their hypnotic stage performances, (the Luciferic eye and pyramid and the *Baphomet* demonic symbol), videos and clothing and fashion labels such as *Rocca Wear* and *G-Unit*. These people have proven to be seminally influential among young blacks and without doubt represent grave dangers to the conscious development of our culture on many levels. A quick browse through the internet (*YouTube*) should illustrate these points; type in Jay-Z, Illuminati and so on in your browser to assess these issues for yourselves. The Illuminati will always use any and all means to indoctrinate the masses into compliance with its evil agenda.

Another (of the numerous) calculated assault on black culture has been the elevation of black American ghetto street-talk to the form of a generally accepted idiom. The term *Ebonics* was used during the 1990s to categorize this supposedly new black language of the streets in America. Using Ebonics we can ascertain some of its fundamental principles quickly:

Wicked means *good*

Sick means *amazing*

Psycho means *strong* and *brave*

Bitch, *whore* means *woman*

Dog means *man*,

Nigger means man and also is used as way of *greeting friends*

There are countless more examples. It's worth noting that no one has ever laid claim to being the one who created the term ebonics. The predominant idea behind this is that positive forms are always turned around and expressed in a negative manner, i.e. *good* means *bad*, *light* means *dark*, *hot* means *cold* and so on. The promotion of a separate language such as so-called ebonics is one of numerous ways to entangle the minds of black people in a quagmire of *self defeating contradictions* (an essential part of the mind control program). There's nothing empowering about creating a language that appeals to just a small, powerless underclass. This is clearly divisive and is intended to segregate people in order to control them more effectively. The information we seek that will liberate our minds is not *written* in so-called ebonics. This merely encourages negative, sloppy and degenerative thinking, which is exactly what the *controllers* of the Babylon System want us to do.

What have been referred to as national, Black language forms such as JOT (Jamaican Oral Tradition, commonly called patois) are invaluable cultural assets to our survival and development as a people and needs to be harnessed and promoted as positive tools to our upliftment. Although most Jamaicans use a form of Standard English in an official capacity, our *'true national language'* always takes precedence in all things. In fact, many Jamaican authors and intellectuals have in recent times placed great emphasis on our exquisitely expressive language as a means of personal and social empowerment. We can now read books written in JOT, which says a great deal about our sense of pride and confidence in our cultural development. In fact, the power of JOT has over the years cause much alarm in Euro/American countries on account of its popularity among the young, both black and white who cite it as being cool, stylish and expressive and so on.

*"We do not want word to go out that we want to **exterminate the Black populations**. If it ever occurs to any of their more **rebellious members**, there would be **grave consequences**"*

- Margaret Sanger, (former Director of Planned Parenthood, USA) -

An honest assessment of human history on earth will clearly and unambiguously outline the theories of Dr. Jewel Pookrum, Dr. Neely Fuller and Dr. Francis Cress Welsing as undoubtedly among the most pertinent enquiries into the destructiveness of racism and the white supremacy *mind control program* that threatens to annihilate black peoples from the face of the earth. Racism as an operating system is encoded into the minds of the white masses through deliberate policies of mind control that define the interaction of human beings on the premise of skin colour and cultural traits. The program works both ways by instilling an exaggerated sense of *'racial superiority'* in whites and a sense of *'racial inferiority'* in the minds of blacks.

One of the main aims of the New World Order is to annihilate at least ***eighty to ninety percent*** of Black African people world-wide within the next hundred to hundred and fifty years or so. The remaining few blacks will be confined to certain geographical areas of the planet where they will be used for *slave labour* and *genetic research material*.

Most white people who are totally ignorant of these things would think such an idea laughable or insane, but this is one of the principle chilling goals of those whom we refer to as *Illuminati*. The other side to this is the fact that the white population of the world will also be culled but most are completely unaware of the duplicitous and evil nature of the controllers of their societies. Poor, underprivileged and what is considered *genetically unfit whites* will all be annihilated alongside blacks, Hispanics, homosexuals, deviants and so on. These crucially important points impacts dramatically and astonishingly upon our quest to rationalize the reasons *why* and *how* the entire human race has been imprisoned within the Babylon System.

The architects of the New World Order are busy formulating subtle ways to kill as many Black people as possible using their knowledge of social and genetic science. They have already produced horrifying weapon systems labeled *'ethnic bombs'* that are capable of targeting specific racial groups:

*'Israel is working on an **'ethnically targeted'** biological weapon that would kill or harm **Arabs** but not **Jews**, according to Israeli military and western intelligence sources cited in a front-page report in the **London Sunday Times, November 15, 1998** (Israel Planning Ethnic Bomb as Saddam Caves In, by Uzi Mahnaimi and Marie Colvin).*

*In developing this 'ethno-bomb' Israeli scientists are trying to exploit medical advances by identifying distinctive **genes** carried by some Arabs, and then create a **genetically modified bacterium or virus**. The goal is to use the ability of viruses and certain bacteria to alter the DNA inside the host's living cells. The scientists are trying to engineer deadly micro-organisms that attack only those bearing the distinctive   genes.*

The so-called *'ethnic bomb'* is a reality right now and poses one of the greatest threats to black people's continued existence on planet earth. This is only part and parcel of wide ranging programs being implemented to kill as many *'undesirable'* people as possible. The infamous American racist and eugenicist **Margaret Sanger** (1883-1966) was the founder of **Planned Parenthood**, an odious, fascist New World Order organization that was created to find ways to cull the African American population through forced sterilization, birth control and *any other means available*.

In her autobiography, Sanger admitted her entire life's purpose was to promote birth control. Not only did she establish the research organization that financed *the contraceptive pill*, she contributed toward the work of the German doctor who developed the *IUD*. Sanger believed that, for the purpose of white racial *'purification'*, some couples should be rewarded who chose sterilization, while others should be required to submit applications to have a child. One of her favorite sayings was;

"More children from the fit, less from the unfit - that is the chief aim of birth control"

The goal of eugenicists is to *'prevent the multiplication bad stocks'*, wrote Dr. Ernst Rudin in the April 1933 **Birth Control Review**. Another article exhorted Americans to *'restrict the propagation of those physically, mentally and socially inadequate'*.

These individuals were part of the *scientific technocracy* that instituted programs to *'ethnically cleanse'* the human race. In the final analysis, according to the principles upon which the Babylon System is based, the ethnic cleansing of humanity can only mean one thing – *the complete and systematic destruction of the black race on planet earth*.

The appalling moral degradation of our societies is largely a reflection of these policies. The active promotion of *sexualism* in our schools among children as young as five years old, and society's overt sexual depravities being promoted as suitable lifestyle choices for human beings are all parts of a systematic plan to erode the traditional family unit so that people can be easier to control. When the emotional and moral bonds that holds a family together breaks down, each member of that family becomes easy victim to the predation of the Babylon System.

In the past three decades *Jamaica* has been targeted by specific groups of *social engineer ideologues* in order to destabilize any radical elements and keep the black majority poor and ineffectual. Our country has long been a challenging force for the New World Order criminals and any which way they can destroy our society they will. The sudden growth of sexual and moral degradation in Jamaican society is a testament to this principle: sex clubs, brothels, prostitution of both males and females, child sexual molestation and the growing AIDS epidemic are all set to erode and annihilate traditional Jamaican society. A large part of the plan is to allow the natural sexual instincts of human beings to have free reign. This is a very subtle part of the mind control program and needs to be understood. The sexual energy of humans is an incredibly powerful thing and a great deal of research has gone into devising strategies that will enable populations and groups of people to be controlled purely on a *psychosexual* level. We learn from a most telling article that:

'One of Sanger's greatest influences, sexologist/eugenicist *Dr. Havelock Ellis (with whom she had an affair, leading to her divorce from her first husband), urged **mandatory sterilization of the poor as a prerequisite to receiving any public aid**. Ellis believed that **any kind of sex was acceptable, as long as it hurt no one**'*.

Sanger, being merely a shadow of a true woman, once expressed that: *"A woman's physical satisfaction was more important than any marriage vow"*. This woman's ultimate intention in life was to find the most effective ways to exterminate all black people in the world. She admitted, however, that it might be necessary on occasion to employ a few, *"for appearance sake"*.

Planned Parenthood is one of the most evil organizations on earth and black people need to urgently become aware of these things. The blood of millions of our aborted babies cries out from the sewers of our cities because of our continued ignorance about these crucially important matters. The issue of abortion is a very contentious one and has been hijacked by these groups of racist and eugenicists as a means of implementing covert programs to kill as many black babies as possible. In a report by journalist Dan Glaister for the British *Guardian* newspaper Saturday October 1, 2005 (in Los Angeles):

'*A leading Republican crusader on moral values declared that one way to reduce the crime rate in the US would be to 'abort black babies'. Speaking on his daily radio show, William Bennett, education secretary under Ronald Reagan and drugs czar under the first George Bush, said:*

"If you wanted to reduce crime, you could, if that were your sole purpose; you could abort every black baby in this country, and your crime rate would go down."

"There's no question this is on all our minds. What I do on our radio show is talk about things that white people are thinking ... we don't hesitate to talk about things that are touchy. We can't say this is an area of American life [and] public policy that we're not allowed to talk about - race and crime".

Bennett once served as chairman of the National Endowment for the Humanities under Reagan from 1981-85, and as *Secretary of Education* from 1985-88. He became *'drug czar'* under the first *President Bush* in 1989. Further research into Bennett's background reveals some of the most shocking and truly disturbing aspects to his character.

These are just a few of the individuals who are continuously planning the destruction of black peoples by peddling our children drugs, guns and negativity as a means to kill as many of us as possible.

The prevalence of charity organizations, *NGOs* and *AID* groups in Africa and South America should be cause for great alarm among indigenous peoples. These organizations are not always there to help poor people but to gather information on the best ways to carry out their genocidal programs and to dispense toxic medicines to kill as many people as possible. Wherever certain NGOs and AID groups go you find shortly thereafter *political strife*, *civil wars*, *disease*, environmental devastation and death among local people. In 1972 the *World Health Organization* (WHO) funded by the *Illuminati/ Rothschild Foundation* undertook massive *small pox vaccination* programs across Africa. These vaccines were laced with the genetically engineered *HIV/AIDS* virus and millions of African children were infected. The explosion of AIDS in Africa during the early 1980s was deliberately calculated and instigated by the *Rothschild* Illuminati *population reduction campaign* to rid the world of black African peoples.

In recent times, *Microsoft* co-founder, multi-billionaire *Bill Gates*, has been trekking across Africa handing out money to any country who would implement programs of *population control* under the disguise of his charitable foundation. The concerns of such notable public figures for poor Africans are always an indicator of the real agenda which is sowing the seeds for Africa's destruction – *population reduction*, or more precisely, the *calculated genocide of black African peoples*. Bill Gates is merely another front man for the various Illuminati sponsored population reduction programs in so-called third world countries. People such as Madonna and various Hollywood movie actors such as Angela Jolie, George Clooney and rock musicians such as Bono, Sting and the like who act as champions of the poor and dispossessed ends up merely as an absurd and farcical pantomime of Illuminati controlled *robots* who have no real clue as to what is going on in the world. These people are used to front issues and gain public support for the population reduction programs of the New World Order.

The perennial malaria epidemics that sweep across Africa can therefore be seen in a new light. In a report in the *Independent Newspaper* (UK) 22 October 2010 we learn that:

*Scientists have found that **Anopheles gambiae** (a species of malaria carrying mosquito), which is responsible for about half of the **500 million** new cases of malaria each year, has split into two genetically different strains that are on their way to becoming two distinct species...Out of the 500 million people infected **at least 2 million will die each year from the disease**...*

That's what is essentially meant by *'Silent Weapons for Secret Wars'*. The engineering of diseases that kill vast amounts of people and *wars* that creates *refugee crises*, which inevitably lead to recurring *famines* and the *starvation and death of millions of black Africans*. In his crucially important work, Dr. Neely Fuller explains these awful and unspeakable policies as *'population tailoring'*. The mysterious outbreaks of various deadly diseases in Africa such as the *Ebola* virus, cholera and meningitis that kill millions of black people must be seen it its proper context as *covert racial war and genocide* perpetrated by the white supremacy collective. The recent so-called pandemic of *'swine flu'* (H1N1) that created huge panic across the world is indicative of the policies of scaremongering and manipulation that the globalist New World Order factions are carrying out on ignorant and unsuspecting populations.

Recently, it has come to light through the efforts of the *Wikileaks* organization that US pharmaceutical companies such as *Pfizer*, for years have been clandestinely operating in Africa testing unsafe drugs on African children; drugs that are considered unsafe for white Euro/American children. For anyone, whether black or white, who believe these things are fiction or a joke, *please do your research*. If we do not stand up now and stake our claim to life on earth, we will be swept away in the coming storm.

During the 1960s, Planned Parenthood and its affiliated organizations became part of (and indeed inspired largely) what was termed the *sexual revolution* that occurred in Euro/American countries. The deliberately overt *sexualization* of society has been passed off cleverly as *sexual liberation.* The development of *Feminism* was a calculated part of this program that supposedly set out to *'empower'* women. This we all know now was merely a mechanism within the mind control program devised by *'social scientists'* of the Babylon System to create specific tensions within society and to have greater leverage in manipulating masses of white people. The birth of the *contraceptive Pill* happened during these times. The words *Feminism,* *'sexual liberation'* and *contraceptive pill* became synonymous and were cleverly *tied together* and used in the Illuminati controlled media to give the impression of a seamless development and exploration of human sexual culture.

What was called the sexual liberation movement is a key factor in the erosion of the structure of the family unit by promoting *'varied lifestyle choices'* under the guise of what has been termed *sexual freedom* – (note the word freedom). The rate of abortion during the 1970s, 1980s, and 1990s soared dramatically along with horrendous sexual crimes against women and children, pornography, prostitution and an international *sex industry* that is ranked among the biggest grossing industries in the world all came out of the so-called sexual liberation movement. Never before in the known history of the world has human sexuality been so exploited for profit on such a large scale. One has to question how the social and psychological dynamics that created the sexual liberation movement ultimately ended up *'giving birth'* to the world-wide *sex industry* and who benefits from this. The increasingly visible *sexual slavery* and *desecration* of women (*the child-bearers of humanity*) and the horrific sexual exploitation of children (*the future of the human race*) says a great deal about the psycho-dynamics of the mind control program that actively encourages human beings to *corrupt and destroy the very elements that brings life into the world and sustain it*. The *Sexual Mind Control tool* operates by engendering within the minds of people who are ignorant of the mechanisms of sex and human emotional faculties a sense of helplessness in the midst of powerful instinctual energies. Ultimately one need to ask, why would the New World Order controllers want to kill black peoples primarily? The answers will prove to be among the most challenging insights into the Babylon System and its *predatory demonic* inter-dimensional connections.

Beginnings

'And now I am become death, the destroyer of worlds'

-John Oppenheimer, *one of the principle creators of the atomic bomb quoting from the Hindu holy book, the* **Bhagavad-Gita,** *after witnessing the testing of the first atomic bomb -*

After World War II, the Illuminati secret society made a concerted effort to unite and consolidate their power structure on earth. In fact, the last two major world wars (1914 - 1918 and 1939 - 1945) in which millions of poor white Europeans massacred each other was a cynical ploy to coerce Euro/American nations into compliance with the ultimate white supremacy agenda. The controllers of the Babylon System coldly calculated the loss of millions of their fellow whites along with Africans, Asians and Indians as *collateral damage* in order to climb upon their rotting corpses to power. This has been the general trend for centuries in Europe wherein a small white elite, owing allegiance to specific *bloodlines* and *powers* has continuously created mind control programs of war and mayhem as tools to take control of the minds of the white masses and enslave them. Hitler and his Nazis failed in their evil mission to racialize the world and dominate it through hate and fear, (or so it seemed). In fact, the very powers that were behind Hitler have succeeded beyond their wildest dreams. Many of Hitler's *scientists* and *eugenicists,* instead of being tried for war crimes against humanity, were secretly transported to America after World War Two (*Project Paperclip*) to continue their research in massive top-secret bases underneath the *Nevada Desert* and elsewhere. The horrific scientific data collected by German Nazis scientists who inhumanely experimented upon concentration camp victims were used to advance various fields of scientific research by *American* and *British* scientists after World War II. The leap in American weapons and space technology over the subsequent decades was clearly due to *German Nazi* research scientists of the *Third Reich*.

There is a great deal more about this odious system of oppression that threatens the survival of the human race here on earth. *Use the internet while you still can*. Search out and read books and magazines that deals with these crucial issues. It's imperative for us to take responsibility for our thoughts and actions and not be swayed by the corrupting designs of the Babylon System.

Curiously these days, some people think that things are getting better where race relations are concerned. Fifty years ago it would have been unthinkable that a person like *Barak Obama* could become a minister in government or even hold an eminent position such as the presidency of the United States of America and so on. However, for black people the world over the scenario couldn't be more different. If we take a look at the predicament of black African cultures in the twenty first century, we can clearly see that the overriding facts of the depopulation agenda of the Illuminati are self evident. From Darfur in the Sudan, Ethiopia, Kenya, South Africa, Zimbabwe, Congo, Rwanda, Sierra Leon, Ivory Coast and right throughout the continent, no African country is unaffected. Any opposition or resistance to the Illuminati agenda in Africa is quickly and quietly crushed by the serpentine organizations of the Babylon System. Exceptions to the rule are few and far between.

These days more and more black people are becoming acutely aware of the genocidal plans and actions of the racist mad men that control Euro/American societies and indeed the world, (politically, economically and militarily) but feel completely powerless to effect any change. Black people invariably feel powerless in the face of such overwhelming *military might* held over the earth by the Euro/American hegemony. The testament to this is the fact that Euro/American nations spend *trillions* of dollars and *billions* of pounds maintaining huge arsenals of nuclear weapons and funding research into many forms of secretive *exotic weapon systems*. The military power of white nations is intended to *psychologically,* and when necessary, *physically subjugate* and prevent any form of real resistance to the white supremacy agenda of a New World Order. The mind control program of racism is so effective that the slightest effort to understand it requires a radical shift in perception.

White Europeans are as much slaves as blacks, Indians, Chinese and so on but mostly are unable to see this reality because they have been so severely affected by the mind control programs of the Babylon System. We do know, however, that the controllers of the Babylon System are not really concerned about the racial background of people in the end, only that we all comply with their designs, by any means necessary.

For approximately one and a half millennia the white British nation has been subjected to some of the most *ferocious* assaults of the Babylon System without fully comprehending this dire state of affairs. The various ancient tribal nations of England, Scotland and Wales were ruthlessly conquered and subjugated by the *Roman occupation* that instituted draconian measures on the entire population as a means of corralling them into the Roman Empire, not really as citizens but as slaves. The valiant uprisings against the Roman occupation, instigated by native Celtic rulers such as *Queen Boudicca* and others, were viciously crushed by Rome's legions. Subsequent *bloodline* elite of kings, queens and nobility (endorsed and controlled by the conniving *priesthood* of the Roman Catholic Papacy) throughout the ages have continued the same traditions of manipulation and enslavement upon the population of Britain without abate. In schools we learn about such triumphant figures as William the Conqueror who ruthlessly subjugated the native peoples of Britain and instituted *feudal systems* of control. Medieval English kings such as Richard II, enforced their tyrannical reign through the blood and suffering of the British people for centuries. After a massive peasant's revolt during his reign, he callously and vehemently scolded his poor and wretched subjects who dared to rise up against his *'god-given right to rule'*:

*"God omnipotent, is mustering in his clouds on our behalf, **armies of pestilence and they shall strike your children yet unborn and unbegot, that dare lift your vassal hands** against my head and threat the glory of my precious crown…You **wretches, detestable on land or sea, you will seek equality with lords and are unworthy to live**. Give this message to your colleagues - rustics you were and rustics you are still. **You will remain in bondage, not as before, but incomparably harsher. For as long as we live we will strive to suppress you and your misery will be an example for posterity**. However, we will spare your lives if you remain faithful; choose now which course you want to follow".*

It's these ruthless tyrants that are still lauded in Britain as *'great historical figures'*. The system of *serfdom/slavery* from which the British populations suffered over the last one and a half thousand years has never been questioned by naïve and sycophantic historians, nor has it truly ended but simply *transformed* with time to consolidate some of the most covert and devious aspects of the Babylon System. In fact, Britain has clearly been one of the principle *experimental fields* for the Babylon System over the centuries. In our times, the ruling elite have compromised the nation's economic productivity and therefore its wealth by dispensing the main industrial/manufacturing bases such as the *steel, car manufacturing, textile, oil and gas and coal industries* and so on, to foreign multinational companies, who dictate the pace of economic growth. This process divests the independent nation state of its assets and its national identity as a productive and socially cohesive entity. This process is designed to create a path for the unification of the nation states of Europe into a larger supranational entity, the *European Union, (EU)*, a structure that was created to foster the ambitions of a *Federal United States of Europe* within the global governing body of the **New World Order**.

The British peoples have become so controlled and subjugated by the Babylon System for so long that any dissenting voice is quietened or ignored instantly. A gangrenous apathy seems to have eaten away at the heart of any meaningful resistance by whites to the Babylon System mind control programs, overturning their natural, rational mental processes in order to gain their compliance in the *mental subversion program of racism*. History clearly demonstrates that the white *ruling elite bloodline* have always treated the white *working classes* (*serfs*) with complete and utter contempt. Numerous attacks against the despotic feudal system of Medieval Britain by the peasantry and its leaders such as *Watt Tyler* in the *Peasant Rebellions*, (1381), have become the faintest background props to the pomp and glamorous pageantry of 'noble' Kings and queens and fictitious knights in shining armour. In fact, it's not beyond the bounds of possibility that an historical incident such as the Great Fire of London in 1666 could have been a deliberate attempt at clearing out masses of unwanted poor and destitute peasants who had infested the city, so that it could be redeveloped afterwards.

The British peoples have been brainwashed for so long that they've completely forgotten the truth of their real history, subscribing only to erroneous perceptions of nationhood spun to them daily by an aggressive, mind controlling media and supported by a mind numbing education system. Until this very day, the British peoples still remain a cowed and conquered nation, constantly monitored by millions of CCTV cameras and a frighteningly hostile bureaucratic system that is clearly designed to confuse, intimidate, manipulate and keep them imprisoned in the white supremacy consensus reality. The white working classes have been completely disenfranchised and the middle classes have been corralled into effete compliance, while the ruling elite diligently prepare the nation for the *coup de grace*. The appalling mind control program that our present British society suffers under is designed to elicit specific reactions from the discontented poor who are not able to articulate their plight consciously. Reactionary forces within society will no doubt set the ferment for unrests and outright public rebellion (particularly the young people of the *'internet generation'* who feel a nebulous sense of disenfranchisement and alienation). This will set the scene for the final showdown that will usher in the New World Order of tyranny, which will inevitably come to us all, if we don't wake up quickly from this nightmare.

Most black people are now aware that the shackles of colonialism and slavery were removed from our hands and feet and reinforced inside our minds. *Mental slavery,* (our oppressors found out through tried and tested methods) is a far more effective and long lasting solution than physical slavery. *With the right know how, one can enslave a human being and he or she would not even suspect that they have been enslaved.* One can extend this principle to a society and even an entire *planet* and the system would hold its integrity. Slavery is ignorance of our true state of being. Ultimately the question must be asked, *"How did this all begin?"*

Mind control programs are very subtle, using complex and sometimes simple symbols and verbal and gestural languages. A **symbol** *(pictorial, slogan or word) can be planted within the psyche of an individual or a nation. That individual or nation will respond to the symbol when prompted to do so by a specific agency; in war and peace, in sex, and economics. This is the essence of the consensus reality paradigm that governs the Babylon System...*

One of the most efficient mind control structures that the Babylon System uses is symbols reinforced with slogans - in advertising, art, literature, history, science and all areas of human activity. The **psyche** *is the primary theatre of war in this fight to free the human race from oppression and slavery. A single word or an* **'innocent looking'** *sign can* **imprison you or kill you**. *The same can also* **free** *you or even bestow* **life**. *Never underestimate the power of a symbol; it can move the mind of man to unfathomable extremes.*

-The Golden Path of Jah Rastafari -

Euro/American science tells us that life on earth began through a series of random processes without any actual forethought or deliberate design intended – *an 'accident'* – and that *all life* is the result of this arbitrary accidental process. Enormous data has been presented by palaeontologists and evolutionary scientists to substantiate the idea of a gradual incremental progression of life-forms on earth from inert matter to complex life forms. *Darwinian science* has championed this model as the zenith of human knowledge concerning this subject matter.

But what we have also come to understand is the equally enormous data that has been unearthed and presented to substantiate other startling aspects to the origins of human beings on planet earth. In the published volume *Forbidden Archaeology* by *Michael Cremo* and *Richard L. Thompson* is outlined compelling information that boldly arrests the theories and assertions of Darwinian science. Across the world thousands of artifacts have been found that are so old that they completely contradict the idea that human beings are relatively recent arrivals on earth. All the major scientific institutions have chosen to ignore what is tantamount to the biggest *heresy* in human history. From a very revealing article on the subject by *Will Hart*, an American journalist, book author, nature photographer and documentary filmmaker, we can glean some insight into this:

'In 1996, the American television station, NBC, broadcast a special program called **The Mysterious Origins of Man**, *which featured material from Michael Cremo's book. The reaction from the scientific community went off the Richter scale. NBC was deluged with letters from irate scientists who called the producer 'a fraud' and the whole program 'a hoax'.*

But the scientists went further than this; a lot further. In an extremely unconscionable sequence of bizarre moves, they tried to **force NBC not to rebroadcast** *the popular program, but that effort failed. Then they took the most radical step of all: they presented their case to the* **federal government and requested the Federal Communications Commission to step in and bar NBC from airing the program again***'.*

This is just one of the ways in which real knowledge is *filtered* and kept away from the general public. Everything that we were taught and our children are being taught in schools, colleges and universities today is controlled by the *'thought police'* of the **Babylon System**.

Grooved Sphere from South Africa

A metallic sphere from South Africa with three parallel grooves around its equator. The sphere was found in a **Precambrian** mineral deposit, said to be dated at around *2.8 billion years old*. [p. 813, *Forbidden Archeology*] (photo courtesy of Roelf Marx).

Reck's Skeleton

The first significant African discovery related to human origins occurred in 1913 when Professor Hans Reck, of Berlin University, found a human skeleton in the upper part of Bed II at Olduvai Gorge, Tanzania. Modern dating methods give a late Early Pleistocene date of around *1.15 million years* for this site. Reck said, *"The bed in which the human remains were found....showed no sign of disturbance".*

The skeleton was distorted by compression from the weight of substantial accumulation of sediment in the overlying strata. W. O. Dietrich, writing in 1933, stated that this feature of the skeleton argued against it being a recent, shallow burial. George Grant MacCurdy, a leading anthropologist from Yale University, considered Reck's discovery to be genuine. [pp. 630-631, *Forbidden Archeology*]

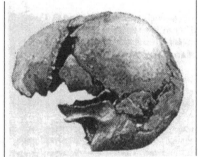

Castenedolo Skull

This anatomically modern human skull (Sergi 1884, plate 1) was found in 1880 at Castenedolo, Italy. The stratum from which it was taken is assigned to the Astian stage of the Pliocene (*Oakley* 1980, p. 46). According to modern authorities (*Harland* et al, 1982, p. 110), the Astian belongs to the Middle Pliocene, which would give the skull an age of *3-4 million years.* [p. 424, *Forbidden Archeology*]

Mortar and Pestle from Table Mountain, South Africa

This mortar and pestle were found by J.H. Neale in **Tertiary** deposits dating back some *33 to 55 million years old.* On August 2, 1890, J.H. Neale signed the following statement about his discoveries:

In 1877 Mr. J.H. Neale was superintendent of the Montezuma Tunnel Company, and ran the Montezuma tunnel into the gravel underlying the lava of Table Mountain, Tuolumne County....At a distance of between 1400 and 1500 feet from the mouth of the tunnel, or between 200 and 300 feet beyond the edge of the solid lava, Mr. Neale saw several spear-heads of some dark rock and nearly one foot in length. On exploring further, he himself found a small mortar three or four inches in diameter and of irregular shape. This was discovered within a foot or two of the spear-heads. He then found a large well-formed pestle and mortar.

...Mr. Neale declares that it is utterly impossible that these relics could have reached the position in which they were found excepting at the time the gravel was deposited, and before the lava cap formed. There was not the slightest trace of any disturbance of the mass or of any natural fissure into it by which access could have been obtained either there or in the neighborhood.

Grooved spheres, South Africa

These spheres found in rock strata dating *2.3 **billion years old*** and are just a few samples of the ***enormous*** data concerning archaeological discoveries across the world in every continent; from Africa, Japan, South America, China, India, North America, Europe and Asia which clearly shows that human beings on earth are far older than we have been told by academia. Scientists - archaeologists, geologists, anthropologists and some historians are all aware of these things but a systematic, impenetrable wall of conspiratorial silence has removed this knowledge from the public domain.

If these things are indeed true, (which by all accounts they appear to be, given the overwhelming data that has been presented), then the history of human origins on planet earth that we have been taught is an obvious and deliberate *lie*.

According to this new paradigm human origins on earth go back much further in time than we have been told. In all probability the earth is far older than the Euro/American scientists tell us. There have been many prehistoric and antediluvian civilizations on earth going back hundreds of thousands and possibly even millions of years. This indeed makes nonsense of the commonly accepted viewpoint of Darwinian evolutionary theories.

Much of the anomalies in our development as a species can be answered by shifting our perceptions to a new angle. Research has indicated that ancient human beings at some stage in prehistoric times coexisted alongside various populations of primates, Neanderthals, Cro-Magnon and so on. Why have we been misled about our origins on earth? Who or what created this ***falsification*** of human history and, most importantly, who benefits from our ignorance of this knowledge?

---

*Now the **Ethiopians [Africans]** were the first of all men. The **Egyptians** are **colonists** sent out by the Ethiopians. **Osiris** having been the leader of the colony, gathered together a great army, with the intention of visiting all the inhabited earth and teaching the race of men how to cultivate ... for he supposed that if he made men give up their savagery and adopt a gentle manner of life he would receive immortal honors.*

*-**Diodorus of Sicily, author of Bibliotheca Historica, who wrote between 60 to 30 BC-***

For us to see clearly how the Babylon System and its operators have enslaved the human race, we must first look at the very beginnings of human *history* and *culture*. This is an extremely delicate matter as the treacherous nature of the mind control program is rooted deep within the cultural psyche of each 'racial' group of human beings and consequently the entire species. Let's look at some of the main ideas propagated by the Babylon System regarding the origins of life on earth. This can be easily understood by applying our minds to comprehending the basic scientific words and phrases that abound throughout the official explanations given by Euro/American academia. A good dictionary is always useful when reading in order to understand the meaning of unfamiliar words.

There are two main schools of thought regarding the origin of life on earth proposed by Euro/American scientists. One suggests that *organic compounds* may have *arrived on Earth from space on board comets and meteorites*, while the other argues for a *terrestrial origin*. It's *believed* by Euro/American scientists that life on earth arose roughly around *4 billion years ago*.

In the crucible of the early Earth, a molecule (or perhaps something else – no one has adequately explained what), somehow *developed* the ability to make copies of itself– what's called a *replicator*. The original nature of this replicator molecule is *unknown*, as scientists believe that it has long been superseded by the present replicator, *DNA*. It's *theorized* that in first making copies of itself, this replicator, DNA, did not always perform accurately. Errors in the replicating process appeared from time to time.

When an error affected or destroyed the copying ability of the molecule, there could be no more copies; therefore that particular line of development would *mutate* or die out. A *mutation* potentially could have made the molecule replicate faster or better. Mutated strains, in theory, could become more successful at *adaptation* and *propagation*. What caused errors to appear in this process have never been adequately explained also.

It's assumed that *competition for resources* among the more resilient strains of replicators and the less able ones might have enhanced the mutated strains capacity to exploit the situation. Different models have been put forward to explain *how* a replicator could have developed. Different replicators have been posited, including *organic* chemicals such as *proteins*, *nucleic acids*, *phospholipids*, *quantum systems* and so on. There's currently no method of determining which of these models, if any, closely fits the origin of life on Earth.

Thermal energy from lightning, volcanoes, electromagnetic, ultraviolet and various forms of radiation may have helped to drive chemical reactions within the primeval soup of organic elements on the early earth, producing more *complex molecules* from simple compounds such as methane and ammonia.

As the quality of this organic soup *diversified,* different molecules could have reacted with one another. The presence of certain molecular *combinations* may have become catalysts that sped up chemical reactions. All this is believed to have continued for a very long time, (billions of years) with reactions occurring more or less at random, *until by chance* a new molecule arose - the *replicator*. This had the bizarre property of promoting the chemical reactions which produced a *copy of itself,* and evolution, (according to this model), became the result of this process. At some point in time, it is believed that DNA was formed and *took over* the function of the replicator. All known life use DNA as their replicator, in an almost identical manner, (some *viruses* and *prions* are the only exception to this rule).

This process, after billions of years (we are told by Euro/American scientists), eventually gave rise to single celled organisms; bacterial life-forms, algae and complex higher life-forms such as marine creatures, land based animals and eventually, intelligent *human beings*.
According to Darwinian evolutionary science, the first fossil evidence for sentient life on earth goes back some *2 billion years*. The first apes and monkeys are supposed to appear about *40 to 50 million years ago*. The first ape-men, (Australopithecus) appeared roughly about *4 million years ago,* closely followed by other ape-men such as Homo habilis, Neanderthal man and the later Cro-Magnon man.

The first human beings of modern type *(Homo sapiens)* appeared only ***100,000 or perhaps 200,000 years ago in Africa***, (depending on which body of scientific research one chooses to believe). Human civilization, according to Euro/American scientists, is approximately 7,000 years old (starting with ***Sumer*** in Mesopotamia). These are the basic tools and mechanisms used to structure the commonly accepted knowledge of what some believe to be the reality of the human presence on planet earth.

It must be noted that all of the above data, albeit very intelligently laid out by very intelligent Euro/American scientists, are ***theories***, not ***facts***. Might, could have, maybes, and much supposition litter the explanations of these scientific theories concerning human origins. These lofty ideas have never been proven by anyone to be the ***absolute truth***. The pictorial representations we form in our minds when we read or analyze this information often lead us to believe in a coherent and plausible linear process of development, *(**evolution**)*. We are taught these things in schools, colleges and universities as pertinent framework for understanding the basis for life on earth. We use theories such as these to make sense of our existence; due to what seems a lack of concrete evidence or anything else to the contrary.

We all desperately want to believe in a linear process of knowledge. If we look closer at these theories we come to realise that they have never been substantiated as plausible by any authority ***outside of the Euro/American system of education.*** This is an extremely important point because on further scrutiny we come to realize that what we have been taught as facts about human origins and development on earth has been constructed exclusively by white Euro/American *'scientific consensus'*, informed by ***their points of view of science, culture, knowledge gathering, experimentation and experience***. The theory of evolution, in all its grandeur, is actually one of the ***lynchpins*** in the ***consensus reality*** mind control program that locks our minds collectively and solidly into the illusions of the Babylon System.

Ongoing archaeological research in the ***Sahara Desert*** and ***southern and central Africa*** is at present revealing staggering evidence of what will prove to be the oldest known human civilizations ever discovered so far. There are many African spiritual wise men/shamans that have always alluded to extremely ancient civilizations buried beneath the Sahara desert sands and the savannahs and jungles of Africa. Much informative work by genetic scientists over the past decades have outlined some very relevant theories concerning the populating of the earth by small groups of African ***migrants*** in very remote prehistoric times:

*The high **heterozygosis** levels, high STRP variance, and high **haplotype**-diversity levels within and between **African populations** compared with populations from all* *other geographic regions suggest that African populations have an **older population** **history** and have maintained both a **large effective population size and high levels of** **population subdivision [genetic diversity]**. These results are consistent with results of studies of other STRP haplotype systems which suggest that African populations (a) **may have expanded in size earlier than have non-African populations and (b) have** **maintained a larger effective population size.**

*Africans have many more **region-specific haplotypes**, and in general, non-Africans have a **subset** of the haplotypes present in Africa. Compared with African populations, the non-African populations have **less haplotype diversity**, **more-extensive LD**, and a similar pattern of haplotype variation across geographic regions (**e.g., Asia, Europe,** **Oceania, and the Americas**). These results are consistent with both an appreciable **founder effect** associated with **migration out of Africa** and a recent shared common ancestry of non-African populations that has been followed by rapid population ex-pansion. In addition, there is no indication that non-African populations have descended from multiple migrations from different source populations in Africa; rather, the shared pattern of variation among geographically diverse non-African populations supports previous findings that indicates that **all non-African** **populations have descended from a single source population**, most likely from **northeastern Africa.**

According to these models that are being developed by some Euro/American genetic researchers, African peoples over many hundreds of thousands of years migrated in successive waves to populate the earth, shifting through various stages of '**genetic** **mutations'** to **diversify** into the branches of humanity we know today; **Oriental,** **Asian, Caucasian** and the various sub-sets and admixtures:

*African populations have high levels of **haplotype diversity within and between** **populations, relative to non-Africans**, and have **highly divergent patterns of LD**. Non-African populations have both a subset of the haplotype diversity present in Africa **and a distinct pattern of LD**. The pattern of haplotype variation and LD observed at the **PLAT locus** suggests a recent common ancestry of non-African populations, from a small population originating in **eastern Africa**. These data indicate that, throughout much of modern human history, Africa has maintained both a large effective population size and a high level of population substructure. Additionally, **Papua New Guinean** and **Micronesian** populations have **rare** **haplotypes** observed otherwise **only in African populations, suggesting ancient gene-** **flow from Africa into Papua New Guinea, as well as gene-flow between Melanesian** **and Micronesian [Asian and Oriental populations].**

[My emphasis]

*...Both the total number of haplotypes and haplotype diversity are greatest in **African populations**, lower in **Middle Eastern**, **European**, and **Asian** populations, and lowest in **Pacific Island** populations of [the **Americas**].*

There are many more haplotypes specific to African populations than to non-African populations. *In general, non-African populations have a subset of the haplotype diversity observed in Africa. This pattern of variation is consistent with results from the CD4.*

In addition, African populations have highly divergent patterns of haplotype variation, whereas the non-African populations share a more similar pattern of haplotype variation. *However, **genetic drift** has resulted in some divergent haplotype distributions in isolated populations from all regions of the world.*

[My emphasis]

In essence therefore, the human race is actually just one race, genetically, with **subdivisions**. It's interesting to note that ***non-African*** populations appear to have more ***uniform*** haplotype patterns which might allude to very ***'specific conditions'*** that allowed the development of the various ***branches*** of humanity:

*Two measures of population subdivision that are particularly useful for highly variable STRP systems are DSW, which takes into account the stepwise-mutation process of STRPs (Shriver et al. 1995), and a likelihood-ratio test—DLR—described by Paetkau et al. (1997). Values for both DSW and DLR are lowest for the Oceanic populations and are highest for the African populations. These results demonstrate considerably higher **haplotype heterogeneity** among **African populations** than among populations from **Europe** and the **Middle East, Asia, Oceania**, or the **Americas.***
*Alu haplotype systems are highly informative for reconstructing **historical migration** and **population-differentiation** events, as demonstrated by the PCA plot of population-clustering based on haplotype-frequency variation. **These results are consistent with anthropological knowledge** [and] suggests a __recent__ and **primary subdivision** between **African and non-African populations**, high levels of divergence among African populations, and a recent shared common ancestry of non-African populations, **from a population of human beings originating in Africa.***

[My emphasis]

Various earth environmental challenges such as solar radiation and the impact of melanin played a significant role in these processes. The striking genetic changes instigated by our DNA array over time are only now being unraveled. We should note that the atmospheric conditions we're experiencing on earth now were very different in prehistoric epochs. The electromagnetic and gravitational fields of the earth, the atmospheric density and composition of gases, soil conditions, plant and animal life have not always been stable throughout the many millions of years of our development. Fluctuating radiation patterns, 'Ice Ages' and so on have all contributed to the process of life-form evolution on earth and human beings naturally have always been in the thick of it.

With this analysis we can clearly see that the fallacy of racism is but one of the greatest tragedies that have befallen the human race and is a direct result of the **Babylon System** and its mind control programming. Presently, cutting edge genetic science coupled with archaeological and anthropological evidence gives clear proof that Africans were the **primary root race** (Homo sapiens) generated on the planet earth. Some in the scientific fraternities of Euro/American academia and various fields of research choose to ignore or disguise the results of these findings because they are still unable to stomach the startling implications in the results that appear. How could these findings be explained to a world that has been so brainwashed to believe that racism is a valid part of human life on earth and that black Africans are little more than upright apes ? The appalling racist views and egocentrism of many within **some sections** of the scientific fraternity, provides the stumbling block to greater understanding of whom and what we are as a sentient species on earth. Every group wants to claim superiority or primacy over the others. It's the old egocentric mind control program that we find so hard to disengage ourselves from. Although humanity has been affected by various **'external forces'** over hundreds of thousands of years, ultimately there is only **one race** of human beings on earth, but if we can be fooled into thinking that our regional differences constitutes separate races then the **'controllers'** of the Babylon System can easily divide and conquer us.

Over the past three centuries some white racist scientists have been trying to prove their theory of white racial superiority by using what might seem like very clever and intelligent arguments, stimulated by their personal research into questions of human intelligence. This has culminated in hard edged, forceful attempts at trying to prove once and for all what they fervently believe is evidence of some sort of **'white genius'**. The line of reasoning against what the white supremacists term **'race deniers'**, (people who don't agree with their racist arguments), although framed with the latest breathtaking research in genetic science, are disappointingly bland and on closer scrutiny, without any merit whatsoever. Their arguments are generally laced with an unhealthy dose of paranoia and childish name calling. Racist scientists like to blame so-called **'Leftists'** who they believe have an avowed interest in denying the realities of white **'racial superiority'**. In an internet article titled **Frequently Asked Questions about Biological Races among Humans** these issues are outlined:

Leftists are vastly overrepresented among race deniers. Leftists tend to have a strong interest in social engineering and are therefore averse to factors that limit the prospects of social engineering. Leftists will stick to their worldview even if doing so causes more harm than accepting that their worldview is mistaken and subsequently changing it and their behaviors. Genetically-based differences between populations limit the extent of social engineering that is feasible, easily explaining why so many leftists loathe the concept of biological races in humans.

And of course, when all else fails, paranoid vitriol is called to the fore:

Malicious Jews *have a strong interest in undermining the welfare of non-Jews, especially whites. Malicious Jews have been at the forefront of race denial in academia, and the reason is obvious. By convincing others that there are no genetic differences between populations with respect to behavior, talent, personality distributions, aptitude, creativity, acquisition of culture and other features relevant to social existence, opposition to replacement immigration can be reduced, and replacement immigration is surely an excellent way to harm the cultural and genetic interests of a population.*

This kind of tirade by supposedly intelligent men can be found everywhere in articles, books and especially on the internet in forums and chat rooms. The end result of these arguments is once again a clear indicator to the realities behind this transparent little ideology:

Western civilization, particularly America, **is reeling under the impact of massive Third World immigration, minority handouts, affirmative action and a high frequency of crimes on the part of numerous non-European ethnic groups**. *The people promoting this have not only made no attempts to examine whether the Third World* **masses possess the same** **<u>aptitude as whites</u>** *and* **whether they can be made to <u>behave like whites</u>**, *but also have attempted to sabotage attempts to answer these questions [of white racial superiority] and persisted with their policies in spite of evidence that decades of affirmative action has not reduced the need for affirmative action for American blacks in the slightest amount, reduced the aptitude/performance gap between whites and blacks,* **made non-Europeans behave like Europeans...in short make the non-Western populations Western apart from looks**.

[My emphasis]

This same mind control program of so-called '**scientific racism**' was famously used by Hitler and his notorious cabal of Nazi scientists to determine that the Jews (and everyone else that were not *Aryan*) were sub-human vermin and that it was perfectly logical and acceptable to exterminate them in the most callous and inhuman ways possible. Other tyrants such as Mussolini, Pol Pot, and Mao Tse Tung and so on, used similarly outrageous arguments in their time to commit the most appalling genocide against millions of defenseless human beings. There are countless examples of this in our long and troubled history on earth.

The ancient history of Africa should be as important to the white man and the black man in equal measure, for the history of one group is intrinsic to the history of the others. There are really no special privileges or vain glorious sentiments that can be attached to this fact; it just happens to be one of those things.

Recent discoveries by researchers *Michael Tellinger*, (author of *Adam's Calender*), *Johan Heine* and various interested scientists have unearthed the most astonishing evidence to substantiate a clear African origin of human civilizations on planet earth – vast, monumental ruins of *prehistoric civilizations* that stretch from southern Africa right across the continent are now being unearthed. These ruins of African *cities* and continent-wide civilizations have been estimated to be *no less than 200,000 years old,* and arguably much older, (bearing in mind that officially we're told that civilization began in Mesopotamia a mere *5,000* years B.C). The incredible prehistoric civilizations of Africa now being unearthed, challenges *everything* we've ever believed about human *genesis* and development on earth by bringing to light the real hidden dimensions of our existence here over vast periods of time.

*Why would scientists try to hide the truth and avoid any test of their hypothesis [concerning the beginnings of human civilization]? Their motivations are equally transparent. If it can be proved that the Egyptians did not build the Great Pyramid in 2,500 BC **using primitive methods**, or if the **Sphinx** can be dated to [at least] **9,000 BC, the whole house of cards comes tumbling down**. Orthodox views of cultural evolution are based upon a chronology of civilization having started in Sumer no earlier than 4,000 to 5,000BC. The theory does not permit **an advanced civilization [in Africa]** to have existed prior to that time. End of discussion. Archaeology and history lose their meaning without a fixed timeline as a point of reference.*

[My emphasis]

Will Hart - Extracted from Nexus Magazine, Volume 9, Number 3 (April-May 2002)

All across southern Africa can be found the very visible traces of thousands of ancient ruins that up until now have not been properly explored or excavated by archaeologists. These ruins and monuments, according to researchers Michael Tellinger and Johan Heine, represent the oldest known structures of human civilizations on earth to date. Scattered across incredibly huge distances stretching into **Zimbabwe, Botswana, Namibia, Kenya and Mozambique**, the remains of the world's oldest man made structures (including huge unexcavated **pyramid** shaped mounds) have created a stirring controversy in the field of archaeology.

According to Tellinger's research on an important series of ruins what he has dubbed **Adam's calendar** a huge prehistoric calendar monument that is now being referred to (perhaps more appropriately) as the **'African Stonehenge'**:

*"[This monument]...links to the countless other stone ruins in southern Africa and suggests that these ruins are much older than we thought. The complex that links Waterval Boven, Machadodorp, Carolina and Dullstroom covers an area larger than modern-day Johannesburg and has emerged as **the largest and most mysterious ancient city on earth**. The discovery of petroglyphs of **winged discs** and carved*

101

*dolerite statues of giant birds, some resembling the **hawk-headed god Horus**, suggests that the prototype **Sumerian** and **Egyptian** civilizations had their **origins** in southern Africa thousands of years before they emerged in the north ".*

[My emphasis]

Although the prehistoric ruins of the earliest known human civilizations exist in Africa for all to see right now, it's worth noting that no *official* scientific or archaeological body in Euro/America seem interested in rushing to excavate these sites. In fact, there has been a clear and concerted effort to conceal and *hush-up* these finding as much as possible because of their utterly shocking and incendiary implications. *All history books will now have to be rewritten. Everything we know about human origins on earth will have to be radically overhauled.*

The *'Adam's calendar'* site is situated on the edge of the Transvaal Escarpment, which consists of Black Reef Quartzite that's rich in gold, but the monolithic stones that form the calendar are all dolerite (some of which weigh over five tons) were brought from a kilometer away from the site. Johan says that the central monolith was carved with such precision as to allow the setting sun to cast a shadow on what is called the *'flat calendar stone'*. After measuring the site (drawing upon his expertise in aeronautical science and navigation, he concluded that the circular structure was in alignment with the cardinal points, the equinoxes and solstices. He also realized that the north/south, east/west alignment was out by 3 degrees, 17 minutes and 43 seconds. This meant that the structure had to be *at least 25,000 years old*, based on archaeoastronomic calculations relating to the 26,000 years cycle of the *precessional wobble*. Further geological studies over a six year period have elucidated a further date of *75,000* years old. More recent research has delivered dated exceeding *100,000 years old.* Retired archaeology professor *Revil Mason* has estimated the numbers of ruins in southern Africa stretching across a wide expanse is in excess of some *100,000 archaeological sites,* (all, I might add, as yet unexplored).

Tellinger exposes some more mind-blowing details to this study:

These findings poses huge problems for archaeologists, anthropologists and historians because the accepted history of this part of the planet does not place, at any time in our past, anywhere near enough people here to have built these numbers of structures.

It gets even more complex when you realize that these were not just isolated structures left behind by migrating hunter-gathers. The true reality hits you when you take in the magnitude and expanse of these settlements and witness the staggering numbers of ancient terraces that surrounds these settlements which covers over 450,000 square kilometers and possibly much more.

Another astounding feature of the ancient sites is what has been defined as a network of *roads* that links all these settlements. Tellinger further explains:

*The picture gets even more complicated when you observe the **ancient roads** that linked these settlements together. We have traced the network of roads that can still be seen stretching to a distance of about 500 kilometers. In their original state they would have covered **thousands of kilometers**. The position of the roads suggests that this network once ran continuously from the coast of **Mozambique** to **Botswana** and possibly beyond... just the visible pieces of the original roads would have required over 500 million stones, each weighing between 10 and 15 kilograms to construct. If we assume that the roads make up only 2 percent of the ancient settlements, the number of stones required to build the entire city/settlements becomes **unthinkable**. The other issue we need to deal with is the need for roads since it is assumed that the **wheel** only arrived in this part of the world with the Portuguese explorers in the 1500s.*

The enormous implications of this study cannot really be understated. These monumental prehistoric ruins of Africa, when analyzed properly, will change forever our view of ourselves as human beings on earth and the unrecorded contributions that African peoples have made to human development and civilization on earth. The obvious intellectual and professional cowardice expressed by most Euro/American archaeologists, when confronted by this very important issue, is most telling indeed.

*The discovery of an ancient calendar in Mexico connected to the African **Olmec** civilization dating back to 3,113 B.C, the date given for the beginning of an advanced culture in Mexico, has actually **shocked** many historians and archeologists. In fact, reports point out that the Mexican authorities were **"embarrassed"** by the findings because they placed Olmec civilization at about 1,200 years B.C. The discovery of the calendar pushes the dates back to 3,113B.C –*

(ancientamerica.com)

The fact that we can observe a wide distribution of **technically advanced** cave paintings, rock and terrestrial art across the world clearly indicate that ancient human culture once cultivated an **intellectual/spiritual** dimension that seems out of **synchronization** with the data of human development that Euro/American archaeology furnishes us with. The numerous cave and rock paintings in diverse places such as Australia, South America, France, Italy and all across Africa speaks of ancient wars and devastation that preceded the fall of very ancient prehistoric civilizations. Also, the fact that most rock/cave paintings exists in the manner that they do points to the idea that the people who created them did so not purely for the sake of creating *'art'* but specifically to **transfer a code of knowledge**. As opposed to the archaeological premise that these were just ritualized works of art, we can deduce from the various oral and mythological traditions in Africa that there was a conscious and deliberate structuring of information that relates various aspects of human cultural knowledge that spanned vast periods of time. The remarkable and obvious similarities between the various cultures around the world in art, mythology, language, spiritual systems, occultism, initiations, architecture and astronomical knowledge certainly points to the existence of **world-wide** ancient cultures that once existed on earth and had clear connections with each other linguistically, racially and culturally.

In every continent we find megalithic structures – temples and pyramids that defy all pertinent conventional archaeological explanation. The technical expertise required to create these structures cannot possibly be explained using present archaeological models. In fact the huge populations of people required to carry out such intricate and monolithic works weren't supposed to have existed so far back in time, according to present conventions.

What can be termed the **Proto-Saharan** civilization, (the ancient civilization that once existed in and around the Sahara region of Africa) is alluded to in the vast range of mythological systems of coded knowledge passed down over many thousands of years in most African cultures, (secret societies, cults and Mystery Systems). New thinking in archaeology is now piecing together a clear outline of an **Early Global Civilization** on earth. One of the things that one notices in almost all the literature that deals with this issue is the **absence** of pertinent theories that put Africa at the **centre** of this paradigm. Most white Euro/American authors unfortunately are still affected by the racial mind control program that blinds them to some of the most **obvious** clues to this enigma. Archaeological evidence and studies in linguistics have clearly shown that there was also an **early global language system** that spread outward from Africa, to the Levant, Mesopotamia, India, China and South America. Linguists are now piecing together an astonishing array of data that attests to these things. It has always been my summation that all languages on earth (from Chinese to Indo European) can be traced back to a **proto-language** once used by Africans in Africa throughout prehistoric times during the Early Global Civilization. The ancient migration routes of the early **Africoids** gives clear indications about the ways in which this language dispersed and changed over time to become the '**local/regional dialects**' we recognize today as distinctly different and separate national languages.

The paradigm of the Ancient Global African Civilization follows that a global civilization once existed that began on the African continent and which operated through a distinct **global language system**, (in some sense similar to the civilization we are experiencing now in our time). Hand in hand with a common global language, we can also discern a common **religious/spiritual system** that can be detected in the echoes of all the known world religious systems – Hinduism, Buddhism, Islam, Christianity and all the ancient spiritual systems of Egypt, Kush, Sumer, Greece, Rome and Babylon and so on.

In recent years a great body of information has surfaced to give credence to the rapidly developing knowledge that African peoples of the ancient Early Global Civilization migrated across the world and founded the first noted civilizations. Much has been put forward to support the now widening evidence that the ancient **Olmec** (or

Olman) culture of *Mexico* (the precursor to the *Mayan* culture) was indeed largely of African origin. Thousands of artifacts point to an influx of black Africoid peoples into South America over an undetermined period of time. The research is still ongoing but we can glean important aspects of the current state of the debate surrounding this new paradigm of the development of human civilizations on earth. *Clyde Winter* one of the foremost researchers on the Olmec question states:

*The Mayans were not the first to occupy the **Yucatan** and **Gulf** regions of Mexico. It is evident from Maya traditions and the artifacts recovered from many ancient Mexican sites that a different race lived in Maya-land before the Mayan speakers settled that region. The Pacific area was early colonized by Olmec people in middle pre-classic times. The linguistic evidence suggests that [possibly] around 1200 B.C., a new linguistic group arrived in the Gulf region of Mexico.*

This early group that arrived in Mexico appeared with a ready made culture and all the trappings of a well established civilization. Researchers have found that significant amounts of Mayan people have genetic markers that point **unmistakably** to an **African genetic origin**. According to researcher **Paul Manansala**:

*Mestizos in Mayan or nearby areas show significant African admixture. The East Coast had extensive admixture according to a recent study byLisker et al. (**Genetic Structure in Mesoamerica, Human Biology, June 1996**). The following percentages of African ancestry were found among East coast populations:*

Paraiso - 21.7%

El Carmen - 28.4%

Veracruz - 25.6%

Saladero - 30.2%

Tamiahua - 40.5%

Among Indian groups, the Chontal have 5% and the Cora 8% African admixture. According to Crawford et al., the mestizo population of Saltillo has 15.8% African ancestry, while Tlaxcala has 8% and Cuanalan 18.1%.

The Olmecs built their civilization in the region of the current states of *Veracruz* and *Tabasco*. Now here again are the percentages of African ancestry according to Lisker

106

et al.:

Paraiso - 21.7%

El Carmen - 28.4%

Veracruz - 25.6%

Saladero - 30.2%

Tamiahua - 40.5%

Paraiso is in Tabasco and Veracruz is in the state of Veracruz. Tamiahua is in northern Veracruz. These areas were the first places in Mexico settled by the Olmecs. I'm not sure about Saladero and El Carmen.

Going by the vast amount of data furnished by many researchers, anthropologists and linguists, there is overwhelming proof for a pre-Columbian stratum of black Africans who developed the first civilizations of South America that we know of to date. The numerous artifacts such as the large stone carvings of *Africoids*, coupled with pertinent *skeletal* information is unveiling an aspect of history that has been deliberately and consistently hidden from the world. The Mayans themselves said that they received their civilization from very ancient peoples who came before them. Of course, (as expected), some racist commentators have poured scorn on these findings citing that if there were blacks in South America in ancient times then they most likely would have been slaves brought there from elsewhere. Logically, as a rule, *slaves do not make monumental sculptures dedicated to their glory*, nor do they leave countless *thousands of artifacts lying around*. And most of all, slaves could not possibly bequeath their *language, religion, rituals* and *civil structures* to a ruling class of overlords. There's absolutely no precedent for this scenario in history whatsoever. Another noted researcher into the Olmec question is *Dr. Andrei Wiercinski*, who is the Head of the Department of Anthropology at Warsaw University. His extensive scientific studies of *skeletal* remains from several Olmec sites brought him to specific conclusions:

*13.5 percent of the skeletons from Tlatilco were of **Africans** and 4.5 percent of the skeletons from Cerro were of Africans. **Black African people made up a considerable segment of the Olmec population**... the percentage of **Africans** among these skeletal remains was 26.9 percent at Tlatilco and 9.1 percent of the **crania** from Cerr de las Mesas were of **African origin**.*

Analysis of the Olmec language by Clyde Winter has brought to light astounding relationships between the ancient *Mende* language of West Africa and the *Olmec* system of writing:

From the archeological evidence gathered both in ***West Africa*** *and* ***Meso-America****, there is reason to believe that the* ***Africans*** *who founded or influenced the Olmec civilization came from West Africa. Not only do the colossal Olmec stone heads resemble Black Africans from the Ghana area, but the ancient* ***religious practices*** *of the Olmec priests was similar to that of the West Africans, which included shamanism, the study of the Venus complex which was part of the traditions of the Olmecs as well as the* ***Ono*** *and* ***Dogon*** *People of West Africa.* ***The language connection is of significant importance, since it has been found out through decipherment of the Olmec script that the ancient Olmecs spoke the Mende language and wrote in the Mende script...***

Astonishingly, the Olmecs were not the only African civilization found in the Americas. In a volume entitled *The Black Nations of America* written by I. Rafinesque (1783 - 1840), some of these black nations are mentioned such as the *Washitaw* of Louisiana, the *Guale* and *Jamassee* of the South-eastern U.S and the Black Californians of *California* and the *South-Western U.S*. These black American nations existed for thousands of years in the Americas before the coming of Columbus and his gang. The Olmec language has certain pronounced linguistic characteristics that are recognizable also in the ancient *Chinese* language of the *Xia* or *Xi* people; very different civilizations on different continents that shares similar linguistic traits. The Xia civilization of China is important in this regard as there is also a clear correlation with the movement of continental Africans to south East Asia in very ancient times.

African Horse Drawn vehicle, Tasili N'Jer, North Africa, (Sahara) at a time when the wheel wasn't supposed to have been invented. 8,000 to 10,000B.C

Egyptian tomb painting depicting ancient Africans from the Kushite Empire

Ancient Pyramid fields and Temples in Kush (Sudan, East Africa)

Ancient colossal African Olmec sculpture in Mexico

Kerr Maya Vase *- The Chama Vase clearly shows people of African origin in poses similar to ancient* ***Kushite*** *and* ***Egyptian*** *art forms.*

109

The ancient *Xi* (or *Xia*) peoples of China were also very much related to black African peoples genetically and culturally. It's noted that the ancient mystical scientific system of divination, **The Ifa Oracle,** as practiced by the Yoruba, Igbo, Bambara, Dogon and most other African peoples has unique parallels with the Chinese divination system, the *I-Ching*, although the African Ifa Oracle is far older, more extensive and detailed than the I-Ching. Recent data suggests that there are definite genetic correlations between Chinese and Africans that alludes to an ancient stratum of blacks that once existed in mainland China *before* its later populations of Mongoloids arrived:

An international study has found that the Chinese people originated not from **'Peking Man'** *in northern China, but from early humans in* **East Africa** *who moved through* **South Asia** *to* **China** *some* **100,000 years ago**, *Hong Kong's* **Ming Pao** *daily reported yesterday in a finding that confirms the* **'single origin'** *theory in anthropology. 'A research team led by Jin Li of Fudan University in Shanghai has found that modern humans evolved from a single origin, not multiple origins as some experts believe.*
In China, school textbooks teach that the Chinese race evolved from 'Peking Man', based on a theory that humans in Europe and Asia evolved from local species. But Jin and his fellow researchers found that early humans belonged to different species, of which only the **East African** *species developed into modern humans'.*

These ancient *'migrations'* by Africans to China were, in all likelihood, from the Early Global Civilization that flourished and extended itself outward from the African continent and began its expansion around 70,000 B.C. According to some researchers, blacks still existed in China in early historical times:

African *skeletons dating to the early periods of Southern Chinese history have been found in Shangdong, Jiantung, Sichuan, Yunnan, Pearl River delta and Jiangxi especially at the initial sites of Chingliengang (Ch'ing-lien-kang) and Mazhiabang (Ma chia-pang) phases. The Chingliengang culture is often referred to as the Ta-wen-k'ou (Dawenkou) culture of North China. The presence of African skeletal remains at Dawenkou sites make it clear that Africans were still in the* **North** *in addition to* **South China**. *The* **Dawenkou** *culture predates the* **Lung-shan** *culture which is associated with the* **Xia** *civilization.*

Further research in recent years has thrown astonishing light on this issue:

*In Chinese literature the ancient Blacks of China were called **Li-Min**, **Kunlung**, **Ch'iang (Qiang)**, **Yi** and **Yueh**. The founders of the **Xia** Dynasty and the **Shang** Dynasties were **Africoids**. These blacks were called **Yueh** and **Qiang**. The modern Chinese are descendants of the **Zhou**. The second Shang Dynasty (situated at Anyang) was founded by the **Yin**. As a result this dynasty is called **Shang-Yin**. The Yin or **Oceanic Mongoloid** type is associated with the Austronesian speakers. The Austronesian or Oceanic Mongoloid types were called Yin, Feng, Yen, Zhiu Yi and Lun Yi.*

At a later stage (possibly around 2,500 B.C) there appeared very small groups of **Aryan** (Caucasian) people who migrated into **northern** China. These bands, perhaps fleeing war or famine in the Caucuses, entered northern China and developed settlements that appeared to have lasted a short time. Upon discovery of the remains of these small groups, white archaeologists immediately jumped up triumphantly in anticipation of some proof of a great ancient white civilization anterior to Chinese civilization. We do know that there was no lasting impression by these groups of Caucasians upon later Chinese culture as no archeological evidence points to this. Ongoing research will, in the future, clarify this situation.

*About 1,100 B.C, migrants from northern China predominated by **Mongoloids** called Chou, invaded the Shang Kingdoms and described the Shang as **'black and oily skinned'**. During that period many of the **Black Shang** migrated to **Southern China**, **Indo-China** and the **Pacific Islands**. Others, it is theorized, went to the Americas...*

One would suppose, given the state of racism in our world presently, the last thing some Chinese would want to hear is that black Africans at some time in the distant past existed in China and very likely set precedents for **'civilizing factors'** there. This though, is only the very tip of the iceberg. All across south East Asia can be found the presence of ancient Africans. In Vietnam, the Philippines, Taiwan, Papua New Guinea, Solomon Isles, Malaysia, the list goes on. Archaeologists and those in the various scientific fraternities know this but consistently hide these facts from the world. The incredible evidence is truly staggering should one choose to look for it.

One of the most hotly debated issues for the past three hundred years or so is the ancient Egyptian question. Many white Euro/American researchers have tried for centuries to counter the idea that the true ancient Egyptian peoples were a black African race. The magnificent achievements of black African civilizations have never been accepted by white academia, because in accepting them whites believe they would have to acquiesce to being somehow *'inferior'* to blacks on all sorts of levels. This infantile behavior by white academia has prevented real scholarly debate and development of knowledge in the world. Although the ancient Egyptians left us all the proof we could possibly need to draw our conclusions, a staunch racist element in white academia stubbornly cling to a meager hope that they can hide the facts of history.

It's abundantly clear that ancient Egyptian civilization developed from migrating waves of black Africans who moved through successive cultural stages from the **Sahara** and the southern regions of what is now known as **Sudan**, (ancient **Kush/Nubia**) and **Ethiopia** and the borders of **Uganda** and **Kenya**. These peoples converged and in time their efforts at social development culminated in what we know as ancient **Kamet (or Kemet)** – ancient Egyptian civilization. A recent informative study by a research scientist, **C. Fox**, outlines the genetic relationship between ancient Kushites/Nubians and other continental Africans:

mtDNA analysis in ancient Nubians supports the existence of gene flow between sub-Sahara and North Africa in the Nile valley:

*The Hpal (np3,592) mitochondrial DNA marker is a selectively neutral mutation that is very common in sub-Saharan **Africa** and is almost absent in North African and European populations. It has been screened in a **Meroitic** sample from ancient **Nubia** through PCR amplification and posterior enzyme digestion, to evaluate the sub-Saharan genetic influences in this population. From 29 individuals analyzed, only 15 yield positive amplifications, four of them (26·7%) displaying the sub-Saharan African marker. Hpa I (np3,592) marker is present in the sub-Saharan populations at a frequency of 68·7 on average. Thus, the frequency of genes from this area in the Meroitic Nubian population can be estimated at around 39% (with a confidence interval from 22% to 55%). The frequency obtained fits in a south-north decreasing gradient of Hpa I (np3,592) along the African continent. Results suggest that* *morphological changes observed historically in the Nubian populations are more likely to be due to the existence of **south-north gene flow through the Nile Valley than to in-situ evolution.***

The civilization that existed in and around the Sahara was dominated by Mende speakers who migrated from that region after the final collapse of the Ancient Global Civilization roughly some 15,000 to 12,000B.C and pushed south-west towards West Africa and eastwards towards the Nile region. Other groups from the very ancient **southern** African civilizations pushed **north** and **north- east** through the central African areas, developing various settlements along the way. These movements created the foundations for larger and more stable social structures that culminated firstly in the establishment of **Ta-Seti,** in Central Sudan, about 12,000 to 10,000 BC or earlier. Ta-Seti was called the **Land of the Bow** by the Egyptians because its peoples (the Anu and Kushite confederacies) in ancient times were the world's most expert marksmen with the bow and arrow and renowned warriors. In 2001, **Time Magazine** ran an article that detailed the discovery of fine glass work, pottery and various artifacts that dated to about 8,000 BC. The article was entitled; '**Nubian [Kushite] Civilization is the World's Oldest':**

*It has been discovered that one of the world's most ancient **observatories** was found at **Ta-Seti** which was the **parent** civilization that gave birth to Egypt when Africans from there moved into the middle part of Egypt and began to build settled communities as early as 10,000 BC. The Delta region of Egypt was still swampy and covered with water at that time. **In fact, there were large areas of water very close to where the pyramids were built**.*

*A **cultural renaissance** occurred in Ta-Seti about 10,000 BC during the era of **Leo**, when **a new enlightenment** was occurring and the first steps in building began to take shape there. Pyramids were not built but giant, **circular monuments** and **star observation sites** were being built.*

The Ta-Seti civilization and the now unknown civilizations of the Sahara and southern Africa were the **precursors** to dynastic Egyptian civilization, and the ancient Egyptians themselves recognized this paradigm most clearly. In fact, the place name **'Egypt'** was not known in ancient times as the correct name for it was **Kemet (Kamet)**, the name ancient Egyptians used for their civilization which approximates in meaning to the **'black land or soil'**. Some scholars have translated the term to mean '**land of blacks**' and so on. The term Egypt is derived from the much later Greco/Roman period.

The development of prehistoric and ancient African civilizations is now being explored by few outside the realms of academia as the implications of ancient black Africans being the torch-bearers of some of the greatest innovations in human history has systematically been distorted by outright racist research and publications such as *National Geographic Magazine.* In 2008 (February) this magazine published an article entitled *'The Black Pharaohs'* by a researcher named Robert Draper. This article in its entirety was written (presumably) with the intent on shedding some light on an aspect of history that has been deliberately concealed for a very long time by white academia. Needless to say, on scrutiny, the published article lay bare the essential ignorance and indeed downright complicity in the continuing whitewashing of ancient black African civilizations. Fortunately these days many informed African scholars, academics and people in general have taken huge interest in these historical deceptions and are now combating the white academic mind control programs. The popular online forum, *Ta-Nefer Ankh website* has published much informative articles on these issues in response to the constant acclamation by racist writers and researchers on the Egyptian racial question:

Here again African people are confronted with the racial pathology exhibited by another bastion of ***white racism*** *and the* ***myth of 'white supremacy'****. In spite of the overabundance of facts and documentation that proves beyond any doubt that the* ***Kemetians*** *(ancient Egyptians), like their* ***Nubian*** *(Kushite) relatives, were* ***Black Africans,*** *the pathology of white racists apparently will not allow them to accept reality, so instead they persist at propounding a* ***contrived*** *myth of* ***'white created ancient civilizations'*** *as though it were history. This contrivance reappears frequently, as if it were a person suffering with the hiccups. Nevertheless, we find it important to address these episodes of 'psychopathic-hiccups' as they occur.*

National Geographic is circulated on the basis of it being a *reputable* publication that deals *objectively* with history and culture yet at the same time consistently produces *what appear to be completely erroneous* documentation about black history and culture. The consistency in their erroneous views can therefore be logically assessed as contrivance in disseminating to its readers false versions of history. In using such silly headlines as *'The Black Pharaohs'* people might erroneously believe that somehow the ancient black African pharaohs of Egypt just happened by some strange twist of fate to have perched themselves precariously on somebody else's chair. The brief periods in history when Egypt was not ruled by *'black pharaohs'* were the interregnums that saw the collapse of institutions as a result of socio/political programs that resulted in the influx of huge amounts of foreigners into Egyptian territories. This situation inevitably created periods of social destabilizing that resulted in the usurpation of the pharaohnic throne by various Semitic/Asiatic elements over time.

Until the conquest of Lower Egypt (the eastern delta areas) by the **Hyksos**, (who were a confederation of /Semitic/Asiatic speakers), Egypt was predominantly a **black African** society. *Despite the countless thousands of books and documentation produced about ancient Egyptian culture, absolutely no proof whatsoever has been shown that any other groups of human beings but black Africans built and maintained the ancient civilization of Egypt from its inception.*

The final conquest of Egypt by **Arab Muslims** in the 7th and 8th millennium A.D largely replaced the indigenous black Africans with a broad Arabic/Muslim (Semitic/Asiatic) population which we now refer to *'culturally'* as Egyptians. This process of **Arabization** and **Muslimification** of black African territories is still continuing presently across several African countries to the point where **African** lands such as **Libya, Tunisia, Morocco, Algeria, Mauritania** and others are being casually and, quite astonishingly, referred to nowadays as a non-entity called the *'Middle East'*.

The head of Egyptian antiquities in Cairo, Professor Hawass has stated that he doesn't believe the ancient Egyptians were black Africans. *We certainly know they weren't Arabs*; nor were they Caucasians or Indians, Chinese, Aboriginals or Eskimos. There are no other *'races'* of human beings on earth that we know of, therefore one might come to the very erroneous conclusions that the ancient Egyptians were some discrete *'other race'* that somehow miraculously *vanished into thin air* after *'throwing down'* one of the greatest periods of human history. The connivance and stunningly ignorant attitudes of Hawass and others who subscribe to the white supremacy fraternity that hold black people's cultural heritage hostage to racist fantasies beggars belief. Arabs could never hold claim to the grandeur of ancient Egypt as their own making because we all know from clear historical evidence that Arabs were systematically conquered, subjugated and enslaved by ancient Egyptians wherever they met them. We know also that ancient Egyptian's conquered some of the Mediterranean islands and *sowed the seeds* for later Greek civilizations. This the Greeks themselves readily (if not graciously) admitted to in their numerous historical volumes that they bequeathed to posterity.

The first people to inhabit what came to be known as Egypt were the **Anu** people who migrated down the Nile Valley from the Sudan/Ethiopia regions of the African continent (the Great Ta-Seti). We do know these people were black Africans who conquered and occupied not just the areas of southern Egypt (Upper Nubia) but much of the areas of eastern Libya and the regions of Sinai, (current archeological research is uncovering much evidence to clarify these issues). The Anu was a confederation of peoples and tribes that over an as yet undetermined period of time migrated from central and southern Africa.

The French Egyptologist *Abbe Émile Amélineau* (1850-1916) was among the first archaeologists to have discovered the tombs of some of the most important early kings of Egypt such as *Ka, Den* and *Djet*. He has also been credited with the discovery of the first migratory waves of the Anu peoples and their primary contribution to what we know as ancient Egyptian civilization. Through his exhaustive studies he was able to throw significant light on the first *black race* that occupied Kemet (Egypt). He outlined the paradigm of their progress down the Nile valley, establishing the cities of *Esneh, Erment, Qouch* and *Heliopolis* and the structure of ancient Egyptian religion epitomized in the worshipping of the great Gods – *Osiris, Horus, Isis, Hermes* – who all belonged to the '*old race*' of the *black Anu*. It's Amélineau's contention that:

*If **Osiris** was of **Nubian [Kushite] origin**, although born at Thebes, it would be easy to understand why the struggle between **Set** and **Horus** took place in **Nubia[Kush].** In any case, it is striking that the goddess **Isis**, according to the legend, has precisely the **same skin color that Nubians always have**, and that the god **Osiris** has what seems to be an **ethnic epithet indicating his Nubian origin. Apparently this observation has never been made before.***

Amélineau further states:

*To this people [**the Anu**] we can attribute, **without fear of error**, the most ancient Egyptian books, **The Book of the Dead** and the **Texts of the Pyramids**, [and]consequently, all the myths or religious teachings... and almost all the **philosophical systems** then known and still called Egyptian.*

The overwhelming evidence that clarifies the beginnings of ancient Egyptian civilization as the endeavors of purely black African peoples leaves no shadow of doubt except for those who, for their own perverse reasons, cannot seem to accept the clear historical data that the very people themselves left behind. Researcher, *Boyce Renseberger*, further elaborates on the issue:

*Evidence of the **oldest recognizable monarchy** in human history, **preceding the rise of the earliest Egyptian kings by several generations**, has been discovered in artifacts from ancient **Nubia (Kush)** in Africa.*
*The discovery is expected to stimulate a new appraisal of the origins of civilization in Africa, raising the question of to what extent **later Egyptian culture** may have derived its advanced political structure from the **Nubians**. The various **symbols** of Nubian royalty that have been found are the same as those associated, in later times, with*

Egyptian kings.
The new findings suggest that the ancient Nubians may have reached this stage of
*political development as long ago as **3,300 B.C.**, **several generations before the***
earliest documented Egyptian king.

A particular artifact of interest for quite some time among archaeologists is what's
called the **Qustul incense burner**, a fragment of pottery found in a royal cemetery in
Nubia by **Professor Keith C. Seele** of the University of Chicago. The significance of
the artifact, which had been in storage at the university's Oriental Institute, was not
fully appreciated until **Dr. Bruce Williams**, a research associate, began to study it:

On the incense burner, which was broken and had to be pieced together, was a
depiction of a palace façade, a crowned king sitting on a throne in a boat, a royal
*standard before the king and, hovering above the king, the falcon god Horus. **Most of***
the images are commonly associated with kingship in later Egyptian traditions.
The portion of the incense burner bearing the body of the king is missing but scholars
are agreed that the presence of the crown in a form well known from dynastic Egypt
*and the god **Horus** are **irrefutable evidence** that the complete image was that of a*
king.

In ancient times the black Africans of Egypt always looked to the **south** from whence
their ancestors came for the maintenance of their spiritual and cultural heritage. On
occasions when the cultural and spiritual traditions became diluted and corrupted by
foreign interruption such as the Hyksos (Semitic/Asiatic) invaders, Egypt was always
revitalized from its original birthplace in the south. Throughout Egypt's long history
its formidable army was always staffed by Nubian/Kushite generals and soldiers who
were renowned and feared throughout the ancient world for their bravery and martial
skills.

As to the question of what could be perceived as the ethnic diversity of the ruling elite
of ancient Egypt, it's uncertain how a Semitic/Asiatic infusion came to be present
within the royal bloodlines of the later rulers, but we do know from documentation by
the ancient Egyptians and sources such as **biblical texts** that wars, famine and the
quest for knowledge drove many Semitic, Asiatic and in later times, small groups of
Caucasoid peoples into Egypt, which was then the archetype of the first **cosmopolitan**
society. Trade, alliances, political marriages and the royal harem system have always
been factors that profoundly affected the racial make-up of ancient Egyptian society
and to some degrees, specific royal dynasties. From the **proto-dynastic** times through
to dynasties 1 to 13, the black African element from Nubia/Kush (the founding Anu
peoples of the south) clearly **dominated** ancient Egyptian civilization and its ruling

elite of royalty, ruling class and specifically the *priesthood*.

During the *second intermediate period* of Egyptian civilization, somehow (no one seem quite sure of the dynamics) a foreign Semitic/Asiatic alliance appeared to have conquered parts of Lower Egypt from and established what has been referred to as the *Hyksos* dynasty. Many details have come to light about these foreign usurpers who became the kings of the 15th dynasty, and certainly we do know that the nature of Egyptian civilization changed markedly from that time. Foreign immigration of Asiatic, Semitic (Phoenicians) and small numbers of Caucasoid peoples from the Mediterranean area (Ionian/Dorian and related Hellenic tribes) flooded into the Egyptian territories of the Nile Delta during the period when Hyksos rule was instituted, providing a steady stream of mercenaries and fortune seekers. Egypt was at that time divided and warring factions of native Egyptian nobility seeking political ascendency, sided with various foreign influences and factions. Astute scholars such as *Martin Bernal* (author of *Black Athena*) have shown clear correlations between the Hyksos invasion and usurpation of pharaohnic power and the proliferation of peoples from the Levant and the Mediterranean at that time, which affected the balance of power in a disunited Egypt. The Hyksos invasion and rule of ancient black Egypt, the establishment of the ancient Israelite/Jewish nation, and the rise of *Phoenician*, *Greek* and later Roman civilizations have some profoundly interesting bearing on the larger picture of ancient black Egypt's prodigious influence and ultimate *legacy* to world civilization.

Noticeably, the fight to reestablish the ancient order and rid Egypt of the foreign Hyksos bloodline came from the south, (Kush/Nubia) during that time of foreign occupation. Under the revolutionary leadership of *Ahmose*, '*Prince of the South*', who mustered a formidable army of Kushite warriors, the foreign element was expelled from Egypt in a war of liberation, after which we then see the rise of the renowned *Golden Age* of the *18th dynasty*, ruled once again by the traditional black African Egyptians. The same process of reestablishing the authenticity of Egyptian culture after periods of foreign invasion and usurpation of the pharaohnic throne occurred again at the later stages of the 24th dynasty and the period of chaos that ensued before the establishing of the noted 25th dynasty under the leadership of the great pharaohs of the ancient Kushite/Nubian empire – *Meriamon-Piankhi*, *Taharqa* and their successors. During the reign of the Kushite/Nubian pharaohs over a united Egypt the ancient philosophical, cultural and spiritual traditions were restored to their *rightful order*. The eminent Egyptologist, *W.M. Flinders Petrie* in his renowned volume, *A History of Egypt*, states:

*"That the kings of **Napata** [Nubia/Kush] represented **the old civilization of Upper Egypt** is clear; and were actually **descended from the high priests of Amen (Amun)**,*

*who were the rightful successors of the XVIIIth and XIXth dynasties. So far, then, as **hereditary rights** go, **they were the true kings of Egypt**, rather than the **mob of Libyan chiefs** who had filtered into the Delta, and who tried to domineer over the Nile valley from that no-man's land".*

An important stela discovered in 1862 by the famed archaeologist **George Reisner** in the temple of **Amun** at **Gebel Barkal**, (present day **Sudan**) gives some remarkable insight into this time. The stela (known as **Piankhi's Victory Stela**) commemorates this illustrious Kushite pharaoh's campaign northward from Nubia to Egypt to put an end to the disunity of the empire caused by foreign invasion and usurpation of Egyptian sovereign power. He marched into Egypt and took the warring factions by storm, crushing dissent and **reestablishing** the ancient order of traditional Egyptian civilization. Some interesting and revealing personality traits have been cited in **Piankhi's** now famous victory stela:

He sought to avoid bloodshed; he forgave his enemies and made special devotions to the gods of the cities and towns that fell under his might.

Despite his victories, Piankhi certainly expressed no interest in consolidating his personal rule over a reunited empire. He installed a revitalized system of government through his royal house in Egypt, lavishly restored the ancient temples, laid down the order of societal development and subsequently withdrew to **Napata** (the ancient Nubian/Kushite capital city in Sudan) from where his rule extended over his vast empire.

The pharaohs of the 25th dynasty later went to war against the Asiatic/Semitic powers of Asia Minor, the Persians, and were eventually overwhelmed by that force. They retired to Kush/Nubia where they held their borders and continued to cultivate their civilization long after Egyptian civilization disintegrated in the hands of its foreign Persian rulers. The end of the 25th dynasty was, to all intents and purposes, the end of ancient Egyptian civilization. Subsequent conquerors such as Alexander of Macedonia created (through his general Ptolemy) the line of rulers under the foreign Greeks, the **Ptolemy** dynasties who ruled as self-styled pharaohs. These usurpers lorded over what was left of the embers of Egypt until it was finally extinguished by the Romans and swept away by the Arabs later on.

Black African Egypt has always presented something of a dilemma in 'western' historiography. Most white Euro/American historians have always tried to maintain the stubborn and futile notion of some sort of **'romantic white Egypt'** having existed in ancient times. To do this they had to ignore great masterpieces on *'Egyptian history written by other white historians who did not support this point of view, such as* **Gerald Massey's** *great classic,* **Ancient Egypt, The Light of the World***, (1907) and*

119

*his other works, **A Book of the Beginnings** and **The Natural Genesis**. Other neglected works by white writers are **Politics, Intercourse, and Trade of the Carthaginians, Ethiopians, Egyptians**, by **A.H.L. Heeren** (1833), and **Ruins of Empires**, by **Count Volney** (1787)'.*

Many Euro/American scholars and archaeologists continue to peddle the myth of a white Egypt as a way of trying to disenfranchise black Africans from their rightful cultural legacy by attempting to *'hype up'* the Hyksos invasion of the 15th dynasty as something that significantly and permanently changed the racial/cultural make-up of Egypt in ancient times. Of course, nothing could be further from the truth. A tiny handful of Egyptian mummies from dynastic times, when studied by some researchers seem to have what has been termed *'Caucasian hair'*, thus the paradigm of a white Egypt ruled by whites appear to be validated by some. The mummies of Ramses the Great and Queen Hatshepsut appear to be examples of this. It's in the realms of possibility that these rulers could have been partly descended from the Hyksos *bloodline* that once ruled sections of Egypt. In fact, many black Africans from East Africa do have straight or wavy *'Caucasian looking'* hair even today. Unfortunately for those white scholars and researchers who have excitedly set their beliefs on the *'hair theory'* the evidence of genetic science and pertinent anthropological studies (and the recorded history of the very people themselves – the ancient African Egyptians/Kushites/Nubians) – validates the facts beyond any shadow of doubt. Essentially, what we are confronted with is the struggle by white academia to *come to terms with* what **Black** and **African** really mean in the ideology of *race*. The people who created ancient Egyptian civilization were, absolutely without question, *genetically* black African peoples.

The *hijacking* and *subversion* of ancient black African cultures by the white supremacy mind control program is a crucial part of the puzzle to understanding the nature of the Babylon System. This is very much at the heart of the program – its *conception*, *development* and *aims* and its impact upon our future on earth in some rather astonishing ways.

There is always a pedantic, persistent unwillingness by Euro/American archaeologists to continue the work of uncovering the thousands of known sites in Sudan, East Africa in general and the Sahara region of North Africa that will undoubtedly drive home the facts that ancient black African peoples were the light bearers of the world's first great historical civilizations; not to mention the rest of Africa where literally many thousands of sprawling, monolithic ancient sites are known of but have been left completely undisturbed, (the argument being a *lack of funding* by world academic institutions for archaeological excavations). One archaeologist, *Professor Fabrizio Mori*, discovered in 1958 in the Libyan region of the Sahara the *mummified* remains of a black African child that attests to the fact that this process of burying the dead existed in other regions of Africa outside of Egypt and, most importantly, at a date that clearly **preceded** Egyptian civilization by far:

*Uan Muhuggiag is a place in the central Libyan Sahara and the name of the mummy of a small boy found there in 1958 by. The mummy displays a **highly sophisticated** mummification technique, and at around **5,500 years old is older than any comparable Ancient Egyptian mummy**. The culture that produced the mummy ... occupied much of North Africa, at a time when the Sahara was a **savannah**. Possible links with later Egyptian culture have also been found, including the representation in rock art of dog-headed human figures (resembling Anubis), and a type of pottery decoration later found in the **southern Nile valley**.*

Egyptology as a discipline was developed at the same time as the *African slave trade* and the *European colonial system*. It was during this period that Egypt was literally taken out of Africa, *academically*. How else could Euro/American scholars, historians and society in general, justify the criminality of slavery while at the same time admiring the vast glory of ancient *black Egypt*? The solution to the problem was a rather simple (and curiously schizophrenic) one: firstly, deny completely that black Africans had created ancient Egyptian civilization and secondly (and rather disturbingly) assign ancient Egyptian civilization to a non-existent *'white race'*. To this effect, *Hollywood* has been the most useful tool in this conspiracy.

These enquiries into the ancient past of black African peoples are crucial to greater understanding of how the mind control program of the Babylon System has completely subverted real knowledge of the *true root of human genesis* on earth. Most white Euro/American people would not even dream that these things could have any degree of truth in them. In fact, many positively refuse to even look at this kind of data for fear that it could completely upset their accepted and cozy view of history and human cultural development. These things are extremely important whether one is black, white or any other 'racial' group. It's our history, collectively, and needs to be known, understood and shared positively.

Once more, space does not permit me to expand in greater depth but I urge the reader to research these issues at leisure. The extensive evidence is absolutely *profound* and will radically change the view of everything we have ever learned about human origins and civilization on earth. Suffice to say that this knowledge is widespread in the realms of white Euro/American academia but has been fiercely hidden by those who know the truth of it. The important point to this is that black African history has always been systematically denied, altered and in most cases destroyed deliberately so that white society and its very recent achievements can be lauded triumphantly as the most important contributing factors to human development on earth. This is an outright lie as we all now know, and is clearly and unmistakably a key ingredient in the mind control program of the *Babylon System*.

There is a great deal of mysteries surrounding specific details of the genesis of the various branches of human beings from their original African root. If we look at the cultural developmental processes of white Europeans we find that they seemed to have appeared out of a Neolithic cultural phase that was much more prologue than continental Africans. Very little has been pieced together that gives a clear and credible picture of any *Caucasoid civilization* that *predates* the older African/Asiatic cultures. We are usually led to believe that Caucasoids emerged suddenly as the *Aryans* out of the steppes of Russia and in no time at all, miraculously conquered continental Europe, Iran and India with powerful armies and superior weapons technology around 2,500 BC. But when we look at the *heartland* of what is supposed to be Caucasoid territories in Europe, the complete absence of developed civilizations on par with the older Africoid/Asiatic civilizations presents a very telling picture. Some of the oldest remnants of civilization in Europe such as *Stonehenge* has always presented enormous problems for archaeologists as these have never been proven to be the work of *'indigenous'* Aryan cultures. The culture that built that monument is still, strangely, unknown. How could the Aryan groups, supposedly coming out of the harsh wasteland of an *Ice Age,* have risen to cultural prominence so rapidly and conquered such vast territories across Europe and Asia unaided when they apparently had no effective *centralized* civil structures to speak of? The *Harrapan* civilizations of India were far older and superior in every way to the *small disunited tribal groups* of Aryans who were supposed to have invaded those territories. The enormous manpower needed in terms of armies, planning, weaponry and logistics was completely beyond the scope of such small groups who were far busier trying to find food to live on and defending themselves from constant intertribal bloodletting. How could these apparently unsophisticated Aryan cultures be the cultivators of *Vedic* literature and culture when they were, in all manner of speaking, an uncultured barbarian rabble *without writing*? The question of Aryan writing is a most troubling one on account of its obvious absence. Archaeologists have not found any remnants of burned or destroyed cities at the levels that would be expected had there been a serious and effective *invasion* of Indian civilizations in the distant past. These important questions shed necessary light on the great *myth* of Aryanism that suffuses white Euro/American culture even today. The mind control program of racism prevents rational comprehension of these issues by many whites who have been completely brainwashed into believing in some kind of seamless, innate white racial superiority. Some recent interesting studies have shone fascinating light on the issue of Caucasoid development over time:

*The **'white European phenotype'** as we know it today did not come into existence until after 12,000 years ago. **Before that, European Caucasians resembled Arabs.** For instance, a 24,000 year old Cro-Magnon European shows DNA similarities to Near-East Arabs. A 23,000 year old Italian Cro-Magnon sample genetically resembles modern Middle Easterners from Palestine, Syria, Yemen and Iran.*
*The original **proto-Asians** came out of Africa 65,000 years ago... The original [**proto**] **Caucasians** [Cro-Magnon] came out of Africa about 40-45,000 years ago.*

*The early genesis of the Caucasoid race [seems to] involve a large **injection** of Asian genes from **Mongolia**, Siberia and **East Turkestan**... (Bowcock 1991).*
*These proto-East Asians probably looked something like **Aborigines** or possibly **Ainu [Anu-Sudanese/Nubian]**. Modern Near-East Asians do not appear until about **9,000 years ago**. Before that, all Asians looked like Aborigines, Melanesians, or Ainu (Anu)... So both modern Whites and modern East Asians only go back 10,000 to 12,000 years. **All humans had darker skins before then.** What birthed lighter skin? **The glaciers.***

*The other 1/3 of the line was an early African, possibly a **Khoisan** or **Bushman** type, but maybe a proto-Caucasian African... Out of the proto-African and proto-Asian 'mixture' was birthed the proto-Caucasian.*
***Caucasians** are closer to **Blacks** than any other group since they were the last to split from them. (Bowcock 1991),*

[My emphasis]

The findings of genetic science have revolutionized our way of thinking about ourselves as human beings on earth. However, there are other very *interesting* areas of exploration that geneticists and anthropologists have not taken into consideration. The specific details of how the varieties of human beings came to be on earth are still a hotbed of controversy. According to theory, the conditions for human genetic *mutation* can readily be understood by present models of genetic evolutionary science. But what can be detected behind the reams of *'facts and figures'* and the latest research is a disquietingly unknown factor that noticeably disturbs the palatability of the *'primeval soup'*. The selective breeding processes that created the different varieties of human beings we know today are most likely to be brought about by *'specifically designed'* and *'controlled means'*.

These radical issues, although highly emotive for all sorts of reasons, throws up huge questions and are very important in the light of the known facts of the Babylon System's mind control programs, and must be dealt with consciously, devoid of petty racism and dogma that leaves us in the blind alley of 'nowhere'.

What can be aptly described as the *cult* of Aryanism was created in the eighteenth century by groups of white Europeans influenced by the so-called 'Enlightenment' movement formed by small groups of European thinkers. This was in response to the discovery by whites on their journeys around the world that *all* the great ancient civilizations they encountered were created by people of other so-called races; Black Africans, Asian/Indian, Chinese and Amerindians. Apart from ancient Greece and Rome (which were relative latecomers in terms of anciency), no other ancient 'great white civilizations' have ever been recorded. If whites were *innately* superior to all other groups of humans then naturally they had to have been the first branch of the human race to create the first great civilization on earth. According to white European thinkers who subscribed to the ideals of the *'white racial genius'*, there just had to be some other very ancient white civilization that *preceded* all other ancient civilizations of other races, otherwise the transparent tenets of white racial and cultural superiority could not be upheld; hence, the frantic quest by the *Romantics* of the eighteenth century to *mythologize* and embellish the achievements of the ancient minority Aryan groups. To this effect various European thinkers of the so-called Enlightenment period concocted a strangely melancholic mythology that attempted to explain a paradigm of a superior ancient white Aryan culture. The story of Atlantis was garnered to support this view but as we shall see this holds some rather interesting clues to these enigmas.

The Out of Africa Theory states that human beings evolved from a pre-human hominid to become Homo sapiens roughly 200,000 to 100,000 years or so and that every human being on earth stems from these early humans. But recent findings in southern Africa attests to the paradigm that even at that remote time, Homo sapiens were already living in highly organized civilized communities.

According to ancient esoteric African systems of knowledge and Mystery Teachings held by most tribes, some human beings did not originate on planet earth at all but came here from more than one planetary and star systems, namely Mars, Sirius and Orion and possibly also the Vega constellation, perhaps millions of years ago. The *Igbo* peoples of Nigeria maintain the tradition that:

'Our earliest Ancestors came to earth in very remote times in ships made of light called Ufo'.

The word Ufo is an ancient Igbo word that literally, (and somewhat astonishingly), means what it says; a ship made of light that moves through *space*.
In fact, the word *Zulu* means people who came from *'beyond the sky'* meaning space.
One of the most important African spiritualists, the renowned Zulu shaman, *Credo Mutwa*, explains:

*"...The people of Rwanda, the **Hutu**, as well as the **Watusi** people, state, (and they are not the only people in Africa who state this), that their very oldest ancestors were a race of beings that they called the **Imanujela**, which means 'the Lords who have come'. And some tribes in West Africa, such as the **Bambara** people, also say the same thing. They say that they came from the sky, many, many generations ago, a race of highly advanced and fearsome creatures, which looked like men, and they call them **Zishwezi**. The word Zishwezi means the dival or the glidal-creatures that can glide down from the sky or glide through water. Everybody has heard about the **Dogon** people in Western Africa who all say that they were given culture by the Nommo, their Ancestors who came from the stars. The Dogon people are but one of many, many peoples in Africa who claim that their tribe or their king were first founded by the supernatural race of creatures that came from the sky. The Zulu people are famous as a warrior people; the people to whom King Shaka Zulu, of the last century, belonged. When you ask a South African white anthropologist what the name of Zulu means, he*

will say it means 'the sky' (laughter), and therefore the Zulu call themselves 'people of the sky'. That, sir, is nonsense. In the Zulu language, our name for the sky, the blue sky, is sibakabaka. Our name for inter-planetary space, however, is izulu and the weduzulu, which means inter-planetary space, the dark sky that you see with stars in it every night, also has to do with traveling, sir. The Zulu word for traveling at random, like a nomad or a gypsy, is izula. Now, you can see that the Zulu people in South Africa were aware of the fact that you can travel through space. Not through the sky like a bird, but you can travel through space..".

Incidentally, the Zulu word **Imanujela** (which means the Lords who have come) and the word **Immanuel** another name for Jesus the messiah (which means **the Lord is with us**) seems similar linguistically and is most likely to have the same root connection as **all** earth languages are related to an ancient **proto-language** spoken by ancient Africans. According to Zulu spiritual traditions and secret knowledge, many black people once lived on the planet **Mars** and were part of a planetary civilization there some millions of years ago. Due to massive conflict involving warring factions, that civilization was destroyed. Some of the survivors went underground to escape the fall out of radioactivity and planetary destabilization, while the rest escaped in massive starships that took them to the **Sirius** and **Orion** star systems. The **Asteroid Belt** is the remains of another planet that used to exist somewhere between mars and Jupiter, which was destroyed in prehistoric times.

The Dogon people of Mali became famous for possessing what seems an inexplicable knowledge of cosmology and data concerning advance scientific structures:

*The Dogon of Mali are clear and explicit on the exact star system, which is their original homeland: the **Sirius** star system. The Dogon dwell in a mountainous terrain near the border of Mali and Upper Volta in West Africa. They revealed some of their cosmological science through their interaction with two French anthropologists: Marcel Griaule and Germaine Dieterlen. Most of Griaule and Dieterlen's work has been translated into English in the two books, **Conversations with Ogotemmeli** and **The Pale Fox**. The Dogon have been the center of anthropological debate for some time, for they have astonishing knowledge of the Sirius star system that western scientists were able to confirm only by using high powered telescopes.*

*The Dogon say that the first eight Ancestors (the **Nommo**, amphibious beings who were like a cross between dolphins and humans) traveled from Sirius to Earth in various ships some large and round and other **pyramidal-shaped** called the **Kora-Na**. Beyond carrying the Unum (progenitors) of humanity, the Kora-Na also contained the seeds of eight 'celestial grains' - **millet, black rice, chickpea, teff, sorghum,***

wheat/kamut, brown rice, maize, and gungun /pidgeon pea. *The Dogon say that the Kora-Na contained all of the materials, information and science humanity would need for making Earth's environment compatible and conducive for human existence.*

In recent years some Euro/American researchers have made it their sole mission to find ways to discredit the Dogon cosmogony. Credo Mutwa elaborates further interesting details concerning the African genesis of human beings on earth:

'Originally our people lived on Mars and created a great civilization there. A great war occurred that decimated that ancient civilization and caused the survivors to flee the planet in the belly of a giant metal ship...'

The vessel that carried humans from the Sirius star system to earth was said to be a large **egg shaped star-ship**. After the Nommo brought humans to earth in the large starship was sent back out into space. Curiously when we look at the images of **Iaeuptus** one of the moons of Saturn, there is a striking similarity to some of the ancient **grooved spheres** found in southern Africa. Recent theories seem to indicate that this **'moon'** of Saturn may well be a **hollow structure**.

Many African mythological systems explicitly tell us that some humans did not originate on earth but came here (or were **placed here**) from other places **beyond the stars**:

The **Maasai** peoples of east Africa states that: *'the Gods sent some of their children to earth. They came from above the clouds and brought **plants** and **animals** with them.*

The **Jaluo** (East Africa): *'Apodho came down to earth accompanied by his wife, bringing with him all **cultural assets**'.*

The **Madi-Moru**: *'The first people lived in the Heavens. Until that connection was cut, there was a lot of traffic from the Heavens to Earth'.*

The **Ganda** (of Lake Victoria): *'The primal women came from the Heavens'.*

The **Nyoro**: *'When God established the Earth, he sent the first human couple down from the Heavens'.*

The **Kivu-Pygmies**: *'Our ancestors fell from the Heavens'.*

The **Kuluwe**: *'The first humans came from the Sky, arriving with **seed**, rake, axe and tools'.*

The **Bena-Lulua**: '*God sent four of his sons to earth*'.

The **Ashanti**: '*Seven people created by God climbed down to earth. After conceiving other people, they returned to the Heavens*'.

The **Ziba**: '*God Rugaba travels upwards to the heavens and then **through the darkness***'.

The **Nandi**: '*God Tororut lives in the heavens. He looks like a human but has wings that can cause lightning*'.

Why would so many black African tribes say categorically that their Ancestors came to earth from somewhere else? The probability that *some* human beings originated on Mars and elsewhere in *interstellar space* might not be as far-fetched as most people might believe. It's also known that there are massive, ancient structures on the far side of the moon and recent data from the various probes sent to Mars has brought to light what appear to be very ancient structures that are artificially made.
The prolific writer/researcher Zechariah , in his many volumes that deals with the genesis of human civilization on earth, charts an interesting story of what he believes to be clear evidence of man's *creation* by groups of extraterrestrial beings called the **Annunaki** who were once worshipped as *'gods'* by early humans. This paradigm has caused much controversy over the years and has been gaining growing support in some quarters. It has opened a new avenue from which to view our origins as a species and expands upon the materials of myth and legends that we find throughout all human cultures on earth.

Atlantis and Lemuria – A Paradigm For Understanding Human Origins

(Genesis of the Babylon System)

Many civilizations have arisen and fallen on the earth over countless thousands and even million of years, although we do not know the historical details of this consciously. The earth and its system of planets go through tumultuous changes throughout the epochs. Our notion of the ages of human beings upon the earth is ***woefully miscalculated****. Man's present attempt at civilization is but a single link in the chain of our long and prodigious evolution as a species in this* ***dimension****.*

-The Golden Path of Jah Rastafari -

As far as the ***unofficial*** archaeological records are concerned, what can be clearly deciphered is a diverse and solid stratum of prehistoric civilizations that spanned the continent of Africa ***before*** the commonly accepted dates for the formation of human civilizations. In order to understand this paradigm, we need to analyze the history of some of the earliest African civilizations we know of to date. A crucial part of this is the many thousands of terrestrial art, rock paintings and artifacts found all over Africa depicting black African peoples living and operating in highly structured, settled ***prehistoric*** communities. These were not just some type of hunter gathering cultures as we are usually led to believe but among the first ***farming*** and ***mining*** communities on earth. The first depictions of horse drawn ***vehicles*** with wheels are to be found at in the Sahara and can be dated to the time of the prehistoric civilization there. These rock art tell an astonishing story of human beings prehistoric past and the involvement and interaction with what are obviously ***non-terrestrial humanoid entities***. We are usually told that the various otherworldly shapes and forms of *'**gods**, **monsters** and **spirit beings'** were shamanic chimera induced by hallucinogenic drugs. From this inadequate analysis it might appear that our ancestors of the early Global Civilizations were all hooked on drugs for thousands of years continuously, for all over the world in every human culture we find the same remarkable phenomenon.

At the end of the last Ice Age, the ancient civilization centered in and around the Sahara expanded outwards due to suddenly encroaching desertification that precipitated massive upheavals and conflicts. According to the ancient Egyptian historian, Manetho, the *'gods'* rule over the earth lasted up until some 36,000 years B.C, after which men established their own rule over kingdoms. The ancient Sumerians also spoke of a time when the gods departed and *'kingship was then lowered to earth'*. We can deduce through archaeological research that around this time there was a marked jump in the development of an early human group known as *Cro-Magnon* man (approximately35, 000 to 40,000 B.C) and a *decline* in the Neanderthal groups in Europe and Asia. Genetic archaeology states clearly that Cro-Magnon and Neanderthals existed during the same time frame along side Homo sapiens and consequently all these groups must have been affiliated with each other (in whatever capacity). It has also been inferred that some Homo sapiens could have interbred with some Neanderthals and Cro-Magnons. Clearer details are not known as yet. But what can be deduced is that remnants of these strains of ancient humans existed up until what could be comparatively recent times (20,000 years ago) after which they completely disappeared from the earth. It has been widely accepted that Neanderthals were a species unknown in Africa and found only in climates (Europe and parts of Asia) that were suited to *cold-adapted* creatures:

It appears incorrect, based on present research and known fossil finds, to refer to any fossil outside Europe or Western and Central Asia as a true Neanderthal. True Neanderthals had a known range that possibly extended as far east as the Altai Mountains, but not farther to the east or south, and apparently not into Africa. At any rate, in Africa the land immediately south of the Neanderthal range was possessed by modern Homo sapiens since at least 160,000 years before the present.

According to the ancient African knowledge system, human beings have been living on earth as *Homo sapiens for many hundreds of thousands of years,* and growing evidence suggests perhaps millions of years. Certainly, many artifacts have been found in Africa and diverse places to substantiate this. There has been many ages followed by cataclysms that have destroyed prehistoric civilizations on earth. The mythology of *Atlantis* and *Lemuria (Mu)* are constant themes that tentatively open avenues to this paradigm. The existence of these civilizations in ancient times, according to many researchers, appears consistent with oceanographic findings of significant land masses that have sunk in the *Atlantic* and *Pacific* oceans, (the reputed geographical locations of these ancient civilizations).

From the various researches carried out over the last two centuries and the wealth of information gathered from the African knowledge system, it's deduced that the early Lemurian civilization was dominated by the first wave of human beings that were *seeded* on the earth by what I have referred to as the *Higher Hierarchies* of *spiritual intelligences*, (the *Orishas* in the West African Tradition), that are involved with the

Ancient artefact depicting a Grey Alien found in Neolithic deposits in Bosnia, Eastern Europe.

coordinating of the life experiences of sentience in the **Creation Field**, (the multiverse and multidimensional systems). The seeding of the early humans, (which I refer to as **Africoids**) occurred not just on a physical level but also on a multidimensional, (metaphysical/spiritual) level. The term Africoid designates the original species of human beings (Homo sapiens) that were seeded on earth in Africa. There had to be specific modes of compatibility with the physical **ecosystem** and the actual *'spiritual body'* of the planet before our planetary system could be seeded with specific types of life-forms. The African tradition gives many clues to the nature of these Higher Hierarchies at the time of human seeding on earth.

The Orishas (divine energies) manifests as what could be loosely termed **trans-dimensional** intelligences. They transcend all physical and human racial characteristics and can manifest in various **energy forms** at specific times in our dimensional frequency, (this happens usually at certain **junctions** in human development or particular points of crisis). The Higher Hierarchy is linked to the **spiritual matrix** of human **Ancestral** spiritual forces that exist on a multidimensional level (specifically 4th through to 9th dimensions) and, in an extended sense, **supervise** on local levels human lines of **incarnations** on earth. The Orishas essentially regulated the spiritual development of the human species in its **primary** manifestation on earth.

Going by the ancient African Tradition, humans were seeded by this process and allowed to develop **organically in harmony with the earth environment** towards **specific set goals**. There was also a clear mental/spiritual **linkage point** with all sentient life-forms on earth in terms of **empathy** and **telepathy** among the early Africoid human communities. Africans were once able to communicate openly and telepathically with the natural flora and fauna within the earth environment. This was a natural part of our functioning as human beings. Our DNA holds the key to these processes which can be activated at will through specific forms of meditations and mental conditioning/training (which in essence is what could be referred to as mind/soul *frequency modulation*).

The physical characteristics of Africans – **melanin** based and specific phenotype (thick lips, brown skin, dense musculature, wide nostrils and woolly hair) – are not just native to earth but also other planetary systems in our galaxy, notably the **Sirius**, and **Vegan** star systems. Earth Africans are essentially not really that unique in physical appearance but *related* to many varieties of *'black/brown/red skin humanoids'* that inhabit our galaxy. The specifics of African *phenotype* we see today on earth are purely incidental to our particular type of planetary habitation. We are but a small reflection of the many different varieties of what we generically term humans in our universe.

The first developmental stages of early humans were centered on the African continent stretching from the Sahara across to Eastern and Southern Africa. A second *seeding* occurred much later in Lemuria/Mu in what is now the Pacific Ocean. The terminology seeding does not necessarily imply actual physical creation but more a *transplantation* from one place (or in some cases, space/time) to another. The Africoid is the *genetic template* that was set by the Higher Hierarchy Orishas from which all the different branches of human beings were produced. The *original Africoids* on earth did not all have what we term *'black skin'* at all but a more pronounced *'reddish brown'* shade through to a *'brownish yellow'*. The term *'black race'* in the true sense is really a *misnomer* as early humans did not perceive themselves in the way that we do today racially. The variety of so-called blacks we see nowadays occurred as a gradual process of our development and *acclimatization* to *solar/cosmic radiation*, constantly fluctuating *biospheric conditions* here on earth and the reciprocal dynamics instigated by our *DNA* over hundreds of thousands of years. Incidentally, one may notice that most African babies are born with light reddish brown, sometimes quite pale, almost Caucasian type skins and only become a darker brown after about three weeks old.

The sun is a very important factor in the functioning of our DNA. Our connection with it is crucial as it facilitates a range of processes on physical/mental/spiritual levels. Early humans did not *'worship'* the sun as some might believe; they had an *organic connection* with it that facilitated a *holistic* dynamic which promoted the development of life and the articulation of *spiritual consciousness*. Our DNA array responds to our earth acclimatizing over long periods of time by activating the necessary *linkage points* (what has been referred to as *non-coding* DNA) between specific *proteins*, *enzymes* and *melanocytes,* creating noticeable physical changes in the *phenotype* and *skin*. As explained in above chapters, the functioning of melanin produces the colour variations *black-brown* and *red-yellow*, which gives the five different variations of the Africoid species, *blue-black* (as in certain tribes of Sudan and Uganda) to pale *white* northern Europeans. The *natural Caucasian* strain having developed at a later stage has the least amount of melanin. Melanin is specifically involved with the developmental processes of human beings on many levels not just physically. It is involved with the production of hormones and various bio-chemical reactions and the utilizing of *electromagnetic* energy that correlates with spiritual perception and consciousness articulation on a multi-dimensional level. *Africans, Native*

Amerindians, Asians and *Caucasians* are all from the same *original* genetic *'stock'* of Africoids seeded on earth despite phenotype variations. What could be termed the *original Caucasian* strain also had a more noticeably pronounced *melanin based* skin colouration. The *specific sections* (*hybridized-genotype*) of the pale northern European group, (what is referred to as *Aryan*), is incidental to the later *genetic manipulations* of the alien predatory factions that were on earth in ancient times.

The correlation between Africoid genetics and the earliest Homo sapiens in the Pacific/Australasia occurred during the development of the first Ancient Global Civilization in Africa and its eastern colony, Lemuria. The beginning of the Lemurian colony can be dated to approximately 100,000 - 80,000 B.C. During this time, several groups of extraterrestrials and interdimensionals (specifically the Reptilian/Nordic faction) appeared on earth with the implicit intent on capitalizing on the abundant, robust genetic variability of the developing human race. According to the author *David Icke*:

*Ancient legends and accounts say that the highly advanced cultures of **Atlantis** and **Lemuria** were inspired by knowledge brought by **extraterrestrial races** from many parts of the galaxy and other **dimensions** of the universe... The three main physical forms [of beings] from planets and stars like Orion, Sirius, the Pleiades, Mars and others appear to have been the **white race** or the **'blue-eyed blonds'**, a **reptilian race** of various expressions and the so-called **Greys**. There was also **the advanced black race** and another, which, according to those who claim to have been abducted by non-human entities, has an **insect-like** form.*

A very noticeable aspect of humanity's various mythological stories is the very obvious prevalence of *serpent motifs* and *Reptilian humanoid* beings that were venerated as god-like creatures and who imparted knowledge to human beings. The biblical book of *Genesis* details the famous incident in which Adam and Eve were tempted by a *talking serpent-being* to disobey 'god' and eat from the *'tree of knowledge of good and evil'*. Throughout the world in all cultures the serpent-men have been the predominant feature in most religious or mystery systems. The ancient Egyptians, Indians, Native Americans, Aztecs, Toltecs, Incas, Mayans and Chinese, all venerated the *wise* serpents and many cultures explicitly stated that the serpent-men were the progenitors of their civilizations. One of the main features of these serpent-men was their ability to *shape-shift* or change form from a Reptilian aspect to that of a human being; the Mayan god Quetzalcoatl, (the feathered serpent), the Nagas of Indian mythology, the Chinese Dragon kings and so on are all related concepts that explains this underlying phenomenon in human cultures. Absolutely no rational reason has ever been given why human beings should hold the serpent in such veneration, awe and fear except a deep subconscious knowledge that pertains to a *greater truth*.

During what I refer to as the *Age of Intervention*, (approximately 100,000 to 25,000 years ago), a faction of Nordic/Reptilian extraterrestrial and inter-dimensional appeared on earth and presented themselves to humans as god-like beings from the stars. They exhibited great intelligence, power and what appeared as *'magical technology'*, while at the same time pursuing a clandestine agenda of manipulation of the human population. The interaction between humans and these Reptilian/Nordic aliens created new dynamics in terms of spiritual understanding. Humanity was given a new concept of whom and what they were in relation to the universe and the Creator.

Some existing groups of *primate humans*, Neanderthals and the later *'hybrid'* Cro-Magnon Man became principle parts of the genetic experiments of the Reptilian/Nordic faction:

Genetic evidence suggests *'interbreeding'* *between Neanderthals and Homo sapiens (anatomically modern humans) took place between roughly 80,000 and 50,000 years ago in the Middle East, resulting in 1to 4% of the genome of people from Eurasia [Europe and Asia]having been contributed by Neanderthals...*

Early modern human skeletal remains with *'Neanderthal traits'* *were found in Lagar Velho (Portugal), dated to 24,500 years ago and controversially interpreted as indications of extensively* *admixed* *populations...*

The main Africoid gene-line (Homo sapiens) along with the alien Reptilian and Nordic gene-line was inserted into these experimental groups to facilitate their development into variant gene-lines. The Neanderthal and Cro-Magnon gene-lines were used as templates for further developments and it appears that *specific sub-groups* of the genetically altered strain of Caucasoids (what has been referred to as the *Aryans* - cold adapted humans) that appeared around 15,000 to 12,000 years ago in Europe are derived from these later gene-lines with further admixtures of the original Africoid gene-line and a pronounced Nordic/Reptilian infusion. These were the *prime groups* of genetically created *Homo sapiens hybrids*. It must be understood clearly that not all Caucasoids are from this particular strain, only that a small, *specific experimental sub-group* were created with these genetic traits. It is this ancient genetically altered sub-group of human/alien *hybrid bloodline* that can be traced directly to the *Illuminati bloodlines* in our present time. Caucasian groups such as early Celtic peoples have specific genetic markers and distinct blood grouping that shows a developmental lineage that stems straight from an ancient African source.

There are what could be called *Master-Control genes* that can be turned *on* and *off like switches* and which are able to send *signals* to an array of *non-coding DNA* that regulate specific combinations of relevant proteins, assisting in the *tuning frequencies* of DNA structures that build life-forms. Science is now trying to understand these principles in-depth. The apparent complexity of life-forms is dictated by the combinations of genes, electromagnetic frequencies and their *vibrational modalities*. By *tuning* specific combinations of DNA array, an organism can be radically altered or entirely new species created. This is in essence a large part of what creates life-form diversity in an evolutionary sense and can also happen naturally with rapid spontaneity through the rhythmic and harmonic vibration of cosmic radiation, earth's biospheric and electromagnetic energy fields and so on. The developmental processes of life-forms on earth after successive periods of *extinctions* over the ages allude clearly to these principles at work.

The Nordic and Reptilian aliens are essentially inter-stellar and inter-dimensional species who have been at war for many aeons in parts of our galaxy and inter-dimensional space/time. For various reasons, some factions of Reptilians and Nordics created alliances on both sides to pursue far reaching agendas. I once again refer the reader to the prodigious work of British author, David Icke and many others who have elucidated a clear paradigm for this scenario. The work of the renowned African spiritualist *Credo Mutwa* is very important in regards to this knowledge also.

At some time in our linear past, a *Grey alien* faction became involved in the process of human manipulation and genetic experimentation. *And here now is an essential key*. It must be explained that the Greys joined this scenario at a particular *junction* in our *linear* past by the manipulation of *timelines*. Analysis firmly states that the Greys entered the agenda from a *divergent future timeline*. This might appear somewhat difficult to comprehend but I will elucidate as we progress. They are able to *slide* through time and effect specific changes in the past. It appears that they are also genetically Reptilian/human base in origin with an *Insectoid* infusion. Essentially, the Grey life-forms are based in a *future timeline* but through their *time-sliding* capabilities they figure largely in our human past. An alliance of sorts was formed by the Reptilians, Nordics and Greys giving the Greys *access* to the hybridization breeding program. The Grey's primary interest is the development of specific multigenerational gene-lines for their own use while assisting (to some degrees) in the overall agenda of the Reptilian/Nordic program. The small group of Caucasoid Reptilian/Nordic hybrids referred to as *Aryans* (created from the splicing of genes from a primate ancestor, Homo sapiens and the Reptilian/Nordics)have been the main line of study and manipulation by the Greys for thousand of years and the black

Africans, Native Americans and Indians/Asians have been predominantly affected by the Reptilians. A specific group of human related beings from the *Sirius* star system has also been very active in Africa over many thousands of years.

The Reptilian/Nordic alliance, over time, infiltrated early human societies by posing as benign *'gods'* who might assist human development. Through this process the human race was *hijacked* and led along a path that saw the new *human-hybrid bloodlines* of the Reptilian and Nordic factions assuming positions of authority and power in human affairs. It is these human/alien hybrids that have been referred to in the Old Testament of the bible as the *Nephilim* and the *'sons of the gods'*. Atlantis was established roughly some 50,000 years B.C as a major civilization, not for Homo sapiens, but solely for the Reptilian/Nordics experimentations and their hybrid creations. Human/alien alliances were formed and through widespread subterfuge on the part of the new *hybridized race* (which manifested predominantly as Caucasoids due to Reptilian/Nordic DNA insertion) and their alien *'gods'*, early humans began to *gravitate away* from the original paradigm of development set by the ancient trans-dimensional *Higher Hierarchy Orishas*. The Orishas do not intervene directly in the development of humans on earth but impart specific *multi-dimensional matrices* of information that manifests as *'psychic codes'* and *spiritual inspiration* to guide the developmental processes of sentience. If the situation on earth becomes completely out of control then *'agents'* of the Orishas are usually *incarnated* at specific junctions to realign humanity back with the original purpose of the program – prophets, messiahs and so on. The respect of the freewill of sentient beings is one of the hallmarks of higher spiritual forces.

The creation of the Reptilian/Nordic/human hybrid bloodlines in ancient times developed new dynamics such as *racism,* which was a calculated tool used by the Nordic/Reptilian factions to keep their *hybrid gene-pool* from being *contaminated* or *diluted* through interbreeding with the original Africoid species. This negative interaction between human groups, psychologically and physically created sub-divisions or *cultures* – inferiority and superiority complexes and so on; those who were paler skinned Reptilian/Nordic hybrids later became elevated above the browns, blacks, yellows and red skins during the late Atlantean times (20,000 to 15,000 B.C). All Africoids (black, brown, red, yellow are genetically dominant in terms of the *photosynthetic factor, melanin*). As ascertained, melanin is a crucial component in our ability to function on a *psycho/spiritual* level within the earth environment. In fact, if we trace a line through history we see the constant racial confrontation between blacks, browns, reds and the Aryan groups over periods of time in all cultures across the world.

Whatever the causes of the Fall of Atlantis around 13,000 to 12,000 B.C it's certain that the warring Reptilians and Nordics were deeply involved in the process. The fact that these beings became *noticeably absent* from the earth at a time of *global cataclysm* points to the likelihood of some type of intervention by other *non-human agency* – namely the Higher Hierarchy Orishas. The Reptilians/Nordics would not have *willingly* given up their activities on earth (which they obviously gave much energy to) unless more advanced and powerful intelligences became involved in what was occurring here at that time. Since Atlantean times, small groups of Nordics/Reptilians have periodically returned to earth at brief intervals to adjust specific aspects of their genetic programs. The Greys, due to their time sliding capabilities, have always been able to continuously *monitor* their selected experimental groups of human hybrids over extended periods of time. It is very possible that those who were called the *Watchers* in biblical scriptures were actually the Grey alien faction.

The details of the fall of Lemuria and Atlantis are not really known but much has been inferred about those incidents. *Tectonic plate shift*, earth *'pole reversal'* and the use of *exotic weapon systems* by the various warring factions of extraterrestrials might be contributing factors to Lemuria's destruction. The survivors of the Lemurian event migrated to Australia, Papua New Guinea, New Zealand, China, Philippines and the various islands in the Pacific. The destruction of Atlantis happened much later after Lemuria's.

Some of the survivors of the fall migrated, (or more likely were *taken* by Reptilian/Nordics), to the Americas (north and south) and areas of Africa (specifically West Africa). Others gradually joined colonies in Asia Minor, southern Europe and Sumer. The Sumer colonies were principally founded by the Reptilian/Nordic groups referred to as Annunaki. The *hybridized bloodlines* of the Reptilian/Nordic faction of extraterrestrials, *embedded* among the remnants of *human populations* after the fall of the Ancient Global Civilization, migrated along these same routes as well. The hybrid bloodline manifested strongly in the rulers of ancient Sumer, the Hittite 'federation' and later Greece and of course, Rome. The infiltration into the Nile Delta by the *Hyksos* (Asiatic/Semitic hybrids) much later, introduced the hybrid bloodline into the *royal lineage* of dynastic Egypt.

According to David Icke's research, after the fall of the ancient Global Civilization:

*The reptilian bloodlines, **covertly operating** within human cultures, created many of the ancient **mystery schools** to hoard the knowledge of true history, and the esoteric and technological expertise of Atlantis and Lemuria and the post-cataclysmic world, especially the Sumer empire. **They also seized control of the mystery schools that were formed with a more enlightened agenda**...*

The fact that in Mexico we find the ancient African civilizations of the Olmecs, the anomaly of what are clear references by ancient Chinese writings and present genetic data to a black African stratum of civilization in ancient China and the Aboriginal Australasian cultures (Australia, Papua New Guinea and Micronesia) that relates directly to black Africans are undeniable clues to the structure and nature of the events of ancient human civilizations that spanned the globe. In prehistoric times Africoids lived in what were networks of global communities that traded and influenced each other in very remarkable ways. Genetic evidence giving clear relationships between Africoid populations in the diverse parts of the world attest to this paradigm:

Papua New Guinean and *Micronesian [including Australia] populations have rare haplotypes observed otherwise only in African populations, suggesting ancient gene-flow from Africa into Papua New Guinea, as well as gene-flow between Melanesian and Micronesian [Asian and Oriental] populations.*

[My emphasis]

When researchers speak of ancient *gene-flow* over periods of tens of thousands of years, one might get the erroneous impression that somehow genes by themselves have the extraordinary ability to get up and *'fly'* across continents unaided. *Gene-flow means that human beings got up, physically travelled by whatever means, interacted socially and culturally and, most importantly, had sexual intercourse with each other.* Any other means of genetic interaction between humans necessarily must involve specific forms of *'artificial breeding'*. Australian aboriginals are directly descended from Africans, we all know that. How, has never been convincingly explained:

The genetic survey, produced by a collaborative team led by scholars at Cambridge and Anglia Ruskin Universities, shows that Australia's aboriginal population sprang from the same tiny group of 'colonists', along with their New Guinean neighbours.

Academics analyzed the mitochondrial DNA (mtDNA) and Y chromosome DNA of Aboriginal Australians and Melanesians from New Guinea. This data was compared with the various DNA patterns associated with early humans. The research was an international effort, with researchers from Tartu in Estonia, Oxford, and Stanford in California all contributing key data and expertise. The results showed that both the Aborigines and Melanesians share the genetic features that have been linked to the 'exodus' of modern humans from Africa [about] 50,000 years ago.
[My emphasis]

The *exodus* across the Pacific however, wasn't really just from Africa but the land mass of what has been called Lemuria that African peoples once colonized in remote prehistoric times. The genetic similarities between Africans and Pacific Basin peoples infers a common heterogeneity that alludes to a functional framework of cultural relationships which could only be explained by *direct contact* and *influences* over a *vast* period of time. In prehistoric times, factions of Nordic/Reptilians 'gods' would have naturally *'moved'* groups of humans from Africa and other places for their own obscure purposes. The similarity in creation myths of many diverse cultures that speak of gods coming from the sky bringing the first human couple with *farming equipment* and *seeds* to create community in a specific geographical area clearly alludes to this principle. When we analyze the myths of most tribal communities across the world we are invariably presented with the same basic scenario: *gods (plural) came from the heavens (sky) in fiery ships/boats/chariots and made us what we are*.

Human beings on earth in the Early Global Civilizations certainly had wide-spread contact with various alien species and (we are coming round to realizing) *some* specific groups of humans were *genetically altered* by them in ways that are not readily perceptible to the casual observer. These aliens were what some of our ancestors referred to as *'the gods'*. I once more refer the reader to the prodigious work of renowned writer Zechariah Sittchin that alludes clearly to this scenario and is worth analyzing to get a wider grasp of the issues. His very pertinent theory, (although I am not in agreement with specific aspects of it), is based largely on the writings of ancient Sumerian civilization, the *Enuma Elish* and various cuneiform tablets and correlates with aspects of this principle in some interesting ways.

These ancient events outline the very *genesis* of the *Babylon System* on planet earth and the manipulations of what I have termed the *predators* – very sophisticated, highly advanced extraterrestrial and inter-dimensional life-forms. The Babylon System was created as a means to cloud the minds of human beings to the true state of affairs pertaining to our origins as a sentient race on earth. The Christian bible in some ways outlines many aspects of this forgotten human history. The book of Genesis clearly states:

And there were giants on the earth in those days. And when men began to multiply upon the face of the earth and daughters were born to them, 'the sons of the gods' saw that the daughters of men were fair and took unto themselves wives of them.

The 'sons of the gods' were the hybrid offspring (*Nephilim*) of the alien predatory forces, Nordic/Reptilian. The gods (aliens) and their strange hybrid progeny were always *regarded with awe, fear and suspicion.* We learn from the book of Enoch that the birth of Lamech's strange son, *Noah*, was cause for great consternation. Lamech's wife was grief stricken when she beheld the unsettling and unusual nature of her new born child:

I have begotten a strange son. *He is not like an ordinary human being, but looks like the children of* **the angels** *of heaven to me. His form is different and he is not like us…it does not seem to me that he is of me but of the angels…*

Behold, I thought then within my heart that **conception was due to the Watchers and the Holy Ones…and the Nephilim**…*and my heart was troubled within me because of this child.*

Lamech's father, **Methuselah**, then consulted the prophet Enoch about his strange grandchild. The latter says to the concerned grandfather:

This child who is born to you shall survive on the Earth, and his sons shall be saved with him. When all mankind who are on the earth die, he shall be safe. And this posterity shall beget on the earth giants, not spiritual, but carnal. Now therefore inform thy son Lamech that he who is born is his child in truth; and he shall call his name **Noah**, *for he shall be to you a survivor.*

It appears from these biblical texts that the prophet Noah was clearly a hybridized human/alien. Most people are familiar with the story of Noah and the flood. This event brought the Ancient Global Civilization to an end, after which the humans and the small groups of alien-hybrid survivors embedded in the population, slowly reestablished civilizations on earth. The tantalizing remnants of the knowledge of our ancient past became fiercely guarded secrets, nurtured by elite groups within human communities and the underground hybridized race of humans who later used this knowledge and information to undermine, oppress and control human societies through secret *sects, lodges* and *fraternities*. The faint memories of the times when the *'gods'* existed on earth among men became legends, myths and obscure mysteries that were enshrined in newly developed systems of power manipulation and control we refer to as *religions*.

Gods and Religions

We have come to slay false gods and serpents

-The Golden Path of Jah Rastafari-

The concept of gods and religions is perhaps the most ubiquitous aspect of our existence on earth. Most of us believe in some sort of celestial hierarchy that is responsible for everything that occurs. Although religion is one of the most important aspects of our existence in its true conception, its practice by many of the various churchical establishments has engendered a great degree of false hopes, apathy and unrealistic expectations for many. The rigid, dualistic structures of mainstream churchical establishments seem to leave very little room for real spiritual development. Within the accepted world religions, real spiritual and philosophical enquiries are at times stifled because from the outset we have to put on a mental straight jacket in order to understand the mechanisms that drive faith. We are usually told that only in first *believing* will we attain spiritual truth. The point is that people end up believing in all kinds of mindless rubbish that generates fear, uncertainty and the most horrendous forms of cruelty and inhumanity imaginable. Generally, if you are confronted by a man or woman who tells you to bow down and worship them as God, most sane people would just walk away knowing that that person must have lost their way to the mental hospital. Unfortunately, some people are gullible enough, naive or perhaps so needy spiritually that they end up believing mad men to be gods and prophets. A very important reason why religious institutions have declined is because there is a concerted effort by the Babylon System and its creators to destroy religion in the world. If people stop believing in religion then the void must naturally be filled with something else.

The spiritual impulse is strong in us and is an intrinsic part of our perception as created beings. It connects us to the origins of our true nature. By subverting the *original wisdom teachings* imparted to humanity by the higher *'spiritual hierarchies'* that supervise human earthly incarnations, and polarizing the manner in which they manifest, the predatory controllers of the Babylon System have trapped human beings in a never ending merry-go-round of illusions and feed from the negativity that that produces. All religious scriptures have been tainted in various ways by the manipulation of the alien predators and their hybrid creations.

After the so-called 'gods' physically vacated the earth in ancient times, their *'facilities'* and the areas they frequented became venerated as holy places and *temples* of worship – *the proverbial house of god*. Their hybrid/human bloodline decedents, having preserved remnants of ancient knowledge, created mysterious *cults* and *religions* that perpetuated the memory and deeds of their departed alien masters. The establishing of ruling elites or *'blue-bloods'*, and concepts such as the *'divine right of kings'* alludes to the idea that those who became the rulers were *sanctioned* by the gods who set up the institution of kingship and ruling elites in human society. Almost all ancient rulers claimed some form of kinship with the god's bloodline. Scriptures were written by newly established *priesthoods* to formally entrench the idea of god-worship and the concept of rewards and punishment (heaven and hell) became ways of coercing the masses into a system of fear, control and slavery.

In the biblical scriptures, The Jewish holy books and the Koran, (which are all clearly related books), everything is set from what we are told was a beginning. The bible states:

'In the beginning, God created the heavens and the earth...'

Straight away we can perceive a sense of limitation around our minds. There's no need to enquire further according to this sentence. That was the *beginning* according to *God's word,* (the scriptures), and for Christians, there's absolutely no reason to even look beyond that. We do know that the earth certainly wasn't created in seven days and could not possibly have been created before the rest of the universe.

Further on we read that God created man and woman (Adam and Eve) in his own image.

'Let us make man in our image and our likeness'

This statement completely contradicts the very idea of an eternal and omnipotent God who created stars, planets, life forms and other races of sentient beings in space and time, (who do not necessarily look like human beings or even function like us). If we are really talking about what I would term *real* God, then God's image and likeness does not necessarily mean a *physical* likeness.

There is an ancient tradition in the world, of divine saviours, messiahs and avatars that manifest at various times to save human beings from sin and evil. We read in the bible that Jesus Christ was born of a virgin (Mary) by a miraculous birth, taught noble truths, was persecuted, crucified on a cross and later rose from the dead. When we analyze historical data we also find that other Gods such as the ancient Egyptian God *Horus* was worshiped as being divine; ***God's only son who was crucified on a cross and rose from the dead.***

Horus was born of a miraculous conception and so was Jesus. The date ascribed to this is *December 25th*, (the winter solstice). In the case of Horus, the God Thoth came down to announce his birth just as the angel Gabriel did for Jesus. Three sages, or wise men, attended the child Horus at his birth as did three wise men for the infant Jesus and both births were heralded by a bright star, which we know to be the brightest star in the night sky, *Sirius.* Sirius has always held the most important place within Egyptian cosmology alongside the three stars of the *Orion constellation*, known in ancient times as the *'three kings'*. In fact the pyramids on the Giza plateau in Egypt are precisely aligned to the Sirius star system and the Orion constellation.

The infant Horus was carried out of Egypt to escape the wrath of the evil god, Typhon who wanted to kill him as was the infant Jesus carried *into Egypt* to escape the wrath of King Herod. Concerning the infant Jesus, the New Testament states the following prophecy:

"Out of Egypt have I called my son." (Matt. 2:15)

There are stories connected with Horus that is analogous to many stories found in the Old Testament. The hiding of the infant Horus in a marsh by his mother Isis undoubtedly parallels the story of the hiding of the infant *Moses* in a marsh by his mother. When Horus died, Isis implored Ra, the sun God, to restore him to life. Ra stopped in mid-heaven and sent down Thoth, the moon, to bring him back to life. (Incidentally, the stopping of the sun and moon by Isis recalls the story of the stopping of the sun and moon by *Joshua*). The parallels between ancient Egyptian religion and Christian religion are quite stark and there for all to see:

"Osiris, I am your son, come to glorify your soul, and to give you even more power." - Horus, (Book of the Great Awakening, Ch. 173)

"Now is the Son of Man glorified and God is glorified in him. If God is glorified in him, God will glorify the Son in himself, and will glorify him at once." - Jesus, (John 13:31-32)

The doctrine of the *Trinity, God the Father, God the Son and God the Holy Ghost* is found throughout ancient Egyptian religion and likewise the belief in *heaven* and *hell*, the existence of a *devil*, winged *angels*, spirits and saints, martyrs and virgins, intercessors in heaven, gods and demigods, and other elements of faith that we find throughout all modern religions. The *Ten Commandments* are of Egyptian origin and much of the *Psalms* of the bible can be easily traced back to their Egyptian sources, the Book of the Great Awakening (Egyptian Book of the Dead) and specifically writings purportedly created by the Egyptian pharaoh *Akhenaton*.

The ancient Romans also used to hold a festival on December 25th called *Dies Natalis Solis Invicti, 'the birthday of the unconquered sun'*. This was the date after the winter solstice, with the first detectable lengthening of daylight hours and was also the official birthday of the Roman God, *Sol Invictus* who was always portrayed with a *halo of sunrays* coming out from behind his head. We see the same expression in art that portrays Jesus and the saints. The title Sol Invictus was applied to a number of other solar deities before and during this period. The God, Sol Invictus, appears on imperial coinage from the time of *Emperor Septimius Severus* (193 – 211 A.D) onwards and was very much associated later with the Roman emperor *Constantine*.

The similarities between Christianity and other ancient religions and deities such as *Mithras,* the Roman *Sun God* who was worshipped across the Mediterranean, Europe and Asia Minor lends credence to the idea that much material was borrowed from various sources to create what ended up becoming the Christian religion we know today:

'In the ancient Zoroastrian religion of Persia, Mith-ra was the spirit or archangel of the sun and of fire. Mithraism evolved within Persian culture as a religion separate from Zoroastrianism. At some point this religion travelled to the eastern Roman Empire, where it underwent further changes to become a Roman religion. In the Roman offshoot, Mithra became Mithras'.

Like Jesus, Mithras' birthday was celebrated on the *December 25th*. He performed miracles, had followers, taught the mysteries of spiritual development and so on. The cross motif was also prevalent in all these religions; the *Egyptian ankh*, the *Christian cross* and the *Mithraic cross,* which is the intersecting circle of the *Zodiac* and the *celestial equator*.

Mithraism was an off shoot of even more older religions that developed out of older civilizations such as *Egypt, Babylon* and *Sumer*. It shares much with later Christianity, whose formal and orthodox creed was largely created to counter the growing influence of *Gnostic heresy* in the Levant by radical groups such as the

Essenes. The Christian founding fathers had to find *legitimate* and *publicly appealing* ways to interpret the newly created religion of Christianity and so adopted various ancient philosophies that suited their ambitions. It is quite possible that the man most likely responsible for the adaptation of mystery doctrines to the emergent Christian religion, (despite his reputation as an enemy of heretics), was *Paul*, the thirteenth apostle. Thus, Jesus was equated with an ancient philosophical term, the *Logos*, meaning the *Word*, (which was taken from Neo-Platonist philosophy and which was also ultimately derived from the ancient *Egyptian Mystery system*) and with the son of god, thereby becoming the *dying god of the mysteries* (much the same as previous gods – *Horus, Mithra, Tammuz, Osiris* and so on*)* whose births was celebrated every December (Christmas) and whose resurrection was celebrated every *Easter*. Analysis points to the idea that the apostle Paul was most likely a disaffected initiate of a sect or branch of Mystery school operated by such groups as the Gnostics who followed the ancient teachings of the Egyptian Mystery School. It's my assumption that his part in the formation and evangelizing of early Christian doctrine is indicative of this scenario.

The word Easter is a corruption of the name of the ancient Mother Goddess of Babylon, *Ishtar* or *Astarte* the queen of heaven and goddess of spring who was also worshipped as the Egyptian goddess *Isis*. The verb *'start'* in English means to *begin* or the *beginning* and is rooted in the name of this ancient Mother Goddess; (as I've always maintained, there was an *Ancient Global Language* rooted in Africa, and *all human spoken languages* are derivatives of this primary root language).

The son of Ishtar/Astarte was *Tammuz* the *Son of God*, saviour of mankind and so on, who died and was resurrected at spring time, which is the time *Easter* is celebrated:

...the great annual festival [Easter] is commemoration of the death and resurrection of Tammuz, which was celebrated by alternate weeping and rejoicing.

The celebration in ancient times of the death and resurrection of Tammuz, the Sun God, mirrors exactly the Easter sunrise services of Christianity today and is a continuation of that same pagan worship. I recall that as children growing up in Jamaica, on the morning of Good Friday, just before sunrise, we would break an egg in a glass of water in order to tell our future. As the sun rises upon the horizon, the white albumen would rise up and make shapes in the glass of water. This was supposed to give an indication of what ones future would hold in the coming year and so on. *Easter eggs* and the eating of *buns* with *crosses* inscribed on them are all pagan rituals that were incorporated into Christianity. This is the case throughout the Christian religion as a whole. For instance, when we look at the Ten Commandments we find astonishing parallels in the ancient *Egyptian Book of the Great Awakening*. We are all familiar with the biblical commandments but the more ancient Egyptian religious commandments appear without doubt to be the forerunner of these ideas. In the Egyptian Book of the Great Awakening, page one hundred and twenty five we read:

Behold, I am come unto thee O God, I have brought thee truth; I have done away with sin for thee. I have not sinned against anyone. I have not mistreated people. I have not done evil instead of righteousness . . .

I have not sinned against anyone. I have not mistreated people. I have not done evil instead of righteousness . . .

I have not reviled God.
I have not laid violent hands on an orphan.
I have not done what God abominates
I have not killed; I have not turned anyone over to a killer.
I have not caused anyone's suffering . . . I have not copulated (illicitly- adultery); I have not been unchaste.
I have not increased nor diminished the measure, I have not diminished the palm; I have not encroached upon the fields.
I have not added to the balance weights; I have not tempered with the plumb bob of the balance.
I have not taken milk from a child's mouth; I have not driven small cattle from their herbage.
I have not stopped (the flow of) water in its seasons; I have not built a dam against flowing water.
I have not quenched a fire in its time.

The Egyptian commandments are far more extensive than the ones we find in the bible. After four hundred years of supposed enslavement in Egypt, the Israelites had to forge a nation for themselves and no doubt plagiarized large chunks of Egyptian spiritual mystery systems. The patriarch *Moses*, according to the bible was, (like *Sargon* the 7th B.C Akkadian king), set in a basket of rushes, with bitumen cast onto a river as a new born babe to protect him from persecution. We are told that Moses grew up as an Egyptian noble and no doubt was taught a great deal about the Egyptian spiritual mystery systems. This knowledge he later adapted to create what became the Jewish religion and the ancient spiritual philosophy of Egypt later was woven into what became the Jewish holy books. Before the Israelite's journey to the *'promised land'* they had no set formula for strict religious worship; no temples, no laws, no formal writing, no books, no *Ark of the Covenant* and so on. These paraphernalia of worship were created by Moses (who was also an initiate of the Egyptian Mystery Teachings). The Jewish Kabala is derived from ancient Egyptian secret knowledge that deals with *ceremonial magic* and what I have referred to as *'multi-dimensional technological'* mediums.

Another very important aspect of this is the ancient knowledge of *astronomy* that was *inexplicably* prevalent throughout all the main spiritual systems of the world. How people of ancient and prehistoric times were able to monitor the precession of the equinoxes and chart the minutiae of the heavens *without* modern instruments has never been adequately explained at all. We can discern a core element of astronomical data that relates to the precession of the *equinox* and the rotation and movements of the various celestial bodies through the *Zodiac* in all systems. It might appear as though ancient peoples were very much absorbed in the mechanics of the stars and planets which formed a large part of their understanding of life, and contrary to popular thinking, knew far more about the science of astronomy than we might realize. This knowledge was structured as part of '*The Mysteries*', ancient bodies of knowledge handed down for thousands of years to selected individuals and groups through the process of initiations, obscure rites and *secret societies* and which was in turn extracted from older bodies of knowledge some of which *preceded* the manipulations of the ancient Reptilian/Nordic extraterrestrial predators and which was part of the *Ancient Global Religion* of prehistoric times.

Most human *spiritual systems* have a common *root* which I believe can be traced right back to an original source that predates the insidious hand of the predatory aliens on earth. After the seeding of the earth by what the African Mystery System call the Higher Hierarchy *Orishas*, human beings were endowed with a specific system of knowledge pertaining to our origins and purpose on earth. This spiritual system was corrupted by our interaction with the controlling and manipulative Reptilian/Nordic predators and their hybridized offspring who insinuated a new doctrine of *'god-worshiping'* that created a mind control program of spiritual ignorance and subservience to negative forces. According to the eminent African spiritualist Credo Mutwa, when the Reptilian/Nordics came to earth in prehistoric times, human's focus of spiritual understanding was very much earth centered. People believed that the God-energy was embodied within the physical and spiritual matrix of the earth and not in the sky or outer space. The predators told humans that they were the gods from the sky (heavens) who should be worshipped in exchange for knowledge and security. An important work by author, Michael Tsarion, entitled Atlantis, *Alien Visitation, and Genetic Manipulation* eloquently expands on this issue. He states:

The Negative Factors Still Operant In Human Cultures Springing From Our History As A Genetically Engineered, Subservient Race The First Factor - Background Of Conditioning to Subservience. The overwhelming evidence from the Sittchin paradigm demonstrates conclusively that we were genetically engineered by the Anunnaki and treated as slaves and then limited partners but always as subservient to them. The major ramification (Neil Freer: Breaking the Godspell) of the Sitchin explication is that "religion", as we have known it, is the transmutation of the Anunnaki-human relationship of master-subject servitude, of slavery and then limited, subservient partnership. The Anunnaki phased off this planet at the latest around 1250 B.C.

Since then, we have been going through phases of a traumatic transition to species maturity and independence. The major characteristic of this process has been the transmutation in all cultures of them, in particular Enlil/Jehovah in Western cult into a cosmic deity, commonly called "God" in the Judaeo-Christian tradition.

*Is this atheism? No, not as such. It simply is a long overdue correction of some local, intra-solar system politics, relatively rather pedestrian in cosmic perspective. **Garden variety atheist** can now be understood as an early sign of precocious species adolescent rebellion and questioning of the authority of the obviously all too humanoid characteristics of the particular local Nephilim 'god' of the Hebrew tribe and Christianity, Yahweh/Jehovah.*

The new paradigm, once the ancient, subservient godspell is dispelled, simply frees us to go one on one with the universe and to seek directly whatever unthinkable or thinkable ultimate principle is behind it.
In a later phase we have mythologized them into unreal beings and then, more "sophisticatedly" into psychological archetypes.

Only with cumulative evidence and restored history through modern scholarship have we now been enabled to grasp the true nature of our genetic creation, our traumatic transition, and the opportunity to emerge from species adolescence and amnesia into species maturity.

These issues although very contentious are of the utmost importance in our attempts at freeing our minds from the devious mind control programs of the Babylon System. What we have come to know as religion is but a facsimile of deeper insights into the creative principle that gave birth to existent nature.

"What is history but a fiction agreed upon?"

- Napoleon Bonaparte –

When we were small children our parents sent us off to school in order to socialize us in the conventions of *society*. Whatever colour skin we wear almost all of us have at some time or other gone through this process, (whether or not we agreed with what we were taught). From this point we perceived our place in the world in relation to everyone and everything else. Most of us grew up trusting the knowledge we gathered and many positively revel in the stability that this knowledge appear to imparted to them. So, with varying degrees of understanding we interact in the world with our fellow human beings in society.

History is written not by the majority of human beings but by a small selected elite in the fields of *academia*. When we read about historical events it's necessary to remember that we're viewing history from the perspective of those who write it. Unless you're actually there as a witness to events it's almost impossible to give a plausible narrative of the reality of any historical event, and even if you're present, the narrative is generally told from your own point of view. Objectivity is really impossible for almost all human beings. Ultimately what we term objectivity is itself subjective because the criteria we use to describe such terms are always formed from our own perspective of the consensus reality we subscribe to. The *experiencer* and that which is *experienced* is purely subjective on whatever level we care to see it. Psychology and human perception therefore defines history from this point.

There are ways in which we can approach history and historical events closer to actuality. This is not an easy thing because it can radically alter our accepted world view of what we believe to be real. So with this in mind, let's look at history within the *Babylon System*.

Throughout our *recorded* history the world has been governed by small tenacious elites of tyrants, despots, kings, queens, conquerors, priesthoods, and a *bloodline* of what has been termed *'blue blood'* nobility. This system of *hereditary* ruler-ship, for thousands of years has defrauded the masses of human beings on earth through a covert parasitic infestation of our perceptive faculties and powers of reasoning. History is the woeful mantra of their despotic reign, the sad story of human desecration by these demonic tyrants masquerading as Caesars, emperors and kings, prophets and Popes. Their monstrous deeds have been *enshrined* in the consciousness of the masses as great and unassailable historical facts. The European Czars and Kaisers, (corruptions of the word Caesar), Founding Fathers and Presidents; the great reformers and obsequious philosophers who became the paid henchmen of demagogues, have all conspired against the ignorant masses of humanity to defraud us of our inalienable human rights, freedoms and dignity. These cold and cruel despots have trampled with impunity upon the light of human civilization, masking their evil deeds in the sanctimony of pious words while ruthlessly slaughtering millions of innocent human beings at the altars of their macabre *gods*. History, we were told as school children, is a system of logical data that can be collated and verified by objective reasoning. That in itself is one of the greatest lies ever told to humanity.

From the times of the earliest known 'grand' civilizations mankind has been bound and chained to the cruel, bloody fantasies and ruthless ambitions of elite *bloodline* rulers. The ancient civilizations of the world such as Sumer, Babylon, Egypt, Assyria, Persia, Greece and Rome are all bywords for a thousand senseless tragedies upon the earth. But nowhere do we read about the faceless and nameless millions and perhaps billions of men, women and children who toiled and died in abject poverty, disease and endless slavery to build these magnificent civilizations: the Ziggurats and palaces, the temples and arenas and promenades of anciency. We are only left with the names of the rulers and the strange demonic gods they *fooled us into worshiping*. We glimpse in museums the tantalizing details of the opulence and undreamt luxuries that furnished the hallowed palaces and empires that arose from barbarism to glory in one or two dynasty of kings, only to totter and fall to the predation of greed, lust and avarice characterized by the ruthless, warped philosophy of *elite rulers* and their followers.

We were led to believe that the 'great' *Roman Empire* was an unparallel bearer of civilization and prosperity across the then known world; its culture, an impressive statements of civilization. We were never told that, in actual fact, ancient Rome was just one in a succession of feudal empires that set the format for human enslavement, desecration and destruction on unprecedented scales. The sadomasochistic tyrants labeled *Caesars* were purely bent on conquest and subjugation, *not social development of the masses*. They set alight the Mediterranean in their appalling madness without any real challenge. Prominent civilizations such as *Carthage* were laid to utter waste by the savage fury of Rome's legions, its people driven by the countless thousands like wild beasts into the Roman arenas to end up as mere *entertainment* for a ravenous and deranged Roman citizenry. ***It's in ancient Rome that we find the cold-bloodied slaughtering of human beings purely for mass entertainment*** first became the norm for any human civilization. The shabby remnant of the Coliseum in Rome nowadays should really be seen as nothing but the grim *gravestone* of countless thousands of victims of the Roman Empire, yet it's still viewed as something of a great tourist attraction by many who do not have the slightest clue as to what it really represents. The stench filled roads that once led to the heart of Imperial Rome were often decorated with the rotting corpses of innocent men, women and children, strung like macabre bunting upon crosses as a testament to a Caesar's power of utter destruction. The tyrannical megalomaniac rulers of empire to all intents and purposes, considered the general populations and the territories they conquered their personal possessions to be handed down as *dynastic property* to be squabbled over by their infantile, murderous progeny. The ancient Romans did not hide the fact that they held utter contempt for other human beings who did not subscribe to their awful psychopathic tendencies.

Their predecessors, the Greeks, although more inclined to philosophical pursuits were just as bent on conquest and subjugation of others. The Athenian city states that once flourished around the Mediterranean were just as brutal in their hunger for world domination and power as the later Romans, despite the romantic spin of eighteenth century European philosophers. Greece was a culture that gave rise to warlike nations such as *Sparta* who enforced some of the most barbaric and oppressive systems of slavery ever recorded upon their neighbors; worshiping *war* and *death as the highest ideals that human beings could aspire to – the apogee of human existence*. The despotic tyrant, *Alexander of Macedonia,* (son of an equally tyrannical father, Philip) has been labeled by ignorant and complicit historians as *'Alexander the Great'.* This completely psychotic and unconscionable man ravaged entire civilizations that dwarfed the achievements of ancient Greece. Proud Egypt fell like chaff before his raging storm. Assyria, Persia, the whole of Asia Minor and Babylon, all crumbled beneath his senseless brutality. The bounty of these civilizations was carted back to Greece to enrich the coffers of the nobility, and the knowledge and wisdom of the known world became the intoxicant of lauded Greek thinkers such as Aristotle and the rest who set the ferment for northern European civilization millennia later.

We are taught in history classes at schools, colleges and universities that these eminent Greek philosophers were original thinkers who somehow created the higher arts of philosophy, astronomy, and the sciences and so on, out of thin air. We now know that this *transparent lie* has been part of the brain washing technique used by the Euro/American intellectual elite to blind and defraud the world to the fact that *African peoples* were the fountainhead from which such knowledge sprang and blossomed into the first enquiries of what was termed the *Mysteries* by Greek thinkers who blatantly *plagiarized* this form of knowledge.

The Romans were not really thinkers but doers. Their intellectual achievements, albeit scant, were owed to the Greeks who came before them, who in turn had studied arduously at the feet of Africans. They did not build on it substantively but reveled complacently in their military might. Intellectualism became sparse side dressing to rampant debauchery and the reckless sloveness that is the outcome of that state of being.

The ancient Romans were really a sadistic, calculating *society of thugs* who derived their barbaric pleasures through war, bloodshed, conquest and enslavement of fellow human beings. The thin veneer of civility ascribed to Roman civilization is offset by the enormous savagery of its rulers and the incomprehensible ignorance and complicity of its citizenry. Factional infighting, monumental greed, the lust for unattainable power and a list of nameless evils heralded the demise of the Roman Empire. Even after Rome consumed itself upon the pyre of its iniquities other equally brutal regimes rose up to take its place and continue the tradition of mayhem across the known world. Most Euro/American historians appear incapable of assessing history in its raw uncompromising details.

The horror and dehumanization of human beings by ancient Roman civilization is always viewed through the convenient myopia of racist historians as the *'development of civilization'*. Indeed the present *New World Order* now manifesting in our time, when we look at it in detail, really began in ancient Greece and Rome. For the Caesars and their demented offspring complete *despotism and tyranny* was the end goal. It's no wonder that the *Fasces* symbol of the Roman Empire, and the eagle standard were adopted by Adolf Hitler and his Nazis, and successive generations of European ruling elite, as their emblem, (some of whom trace their blood-lineage back to ancient Rome and its bloody Caesars). Indeed, in the halls of Congress of the 'Imperial' United States of America the Fasces symbol can clearly be seen displayed and the eagle symbolism of America represents the same as the eagle standards of ancient Rome.

The Byzantium era of western civilization when so-called *'holy emperors'* and *'divine kings'* consolidated their political ascendancy with more bloodshed and mayhem, was certainly a continuation of the same old formula. Nothing changed only the faces and names of tyrants. The real tradition of the ruling elite throughout all ages has always been the preservation of their *bloodlines* at all costs, even the lives of those over whom they ruled.

The temporary halting of the decay of civilization culminated in the calculated gambit of the creation of what we have come to know as *Christianity*. Under the rule of

153

Constantine (another ruthless tyrant labeled *'the great'*) Christianity as a religion for the masses was formed, not out of a realization of a need for human beings to reach greater spiritual understanding, but of the desire for the ruling classes to hold onto their waning power. The teachings of the Jewish prophet/preacher *Yeshua*, (known as *Jesus the Christ*), was hijacked by unscrupulous groups of power hungry zealots and elevated above the pagan religions of the day. This was done in order to stabilize the precarious social situation in his empire as religious disputes and controversies have always been a major factor in causing socially destabilizing effects. As a Roman emperor Constantine wholly subscribed to the old pagan religion. While supposedly espousing *Christian values,* he still retained the old title of *Pontifex Maximus* or High Priest of the old pagan cults. The title of *Pontiff* as used by the *Popes* of the Roman Catholic Church today illustrates the line of continuity of this tradition of Roman emperors as Popes. Constantine was no more a Christian than Adolf Hitler, despite the clever spin by historians and the Catholic Church.

The *Dark Ages* that ensued the fall of the Roman and Byzantium empires was punctuated by more of the same barbarity. New conquerors such as the emperor *Charlemagne* rose up to continue the ancient tradition of conquest with the result being more bloodshed and suffering for the poor masses of human beings enthralled by the successful fiction of divine rulers and their lust for transitory glory. Charlemagne was one in a long line of bloodthirsty despots who sanctioned the torture and wholesale slaughter of countless thousands of poor white peoples across Europe who chose to hold onto their ancient spiritual traditions and refused to be brain-washed into the Babylon System of that time.

This then is essentially the real definition of what is called *history:* it is *the barbaric acts of criminal rulers, and the wanton enslavement and dehumanization of their fellow human beings*: Roman Caesars, Pharaohs, Constantine, Charlemagne, Otto *the great*, Genghis Khan, Attila the Hun, Richard *'the Lion Heart'*, Saladin, Louis XIV, Henry VIII, Elizabeth I, Vasco De Gama, Christopher Columbus, Henry the Navigator, Hernando Cortez, the *swineherd* Francisco Pizarro, El Cid, Peter *'the Great'*, Ivan *'the Terrible'*, Frederick *'the Great'*, Catherine *'the Great'*, Queen Victoria, Napoleon, Adolf Hitler, Stalin, Mao Tse Tung, Henry Kissinger, the Rockefeller family, Rothschild family, the Bush family; the list of these people is endless. We have always been led to believe that most of these people were among the great men and women who forged empires and brought civilization to the poor masses. The sycophantic complicity of so-called historians and scholars in this charade is damning to the extreme.

As mentioned, one of the telling facts about the elite rulers is their preoccupation with their *bloodline*. The British author *David Icke* explains these things clearly and concisely in his series of books that details the whole of this affair. I cannot express enough how important these books are and recommend them as necessary reading material for everyone who wish to understand the depth of this phenomena.

The distortion of history is a direct consequence of the workings of the mind control program of the Babylon System. This is no mere accident but a deliberate, systematic and calculated method of keeping real knowledge from the masses of human beings. Without real knowledge of whom and what we are, we are hopelessly lost in the illusions of the Babylon System. There can be no way to navigate ourselves back to reality. We live out our lives in meaningless pursuit of ephemeral dreams and incongruous perceptions of reality. We die in fear and uncertainty of whether there is a God or whether or not life has any real meaning at all. This wanton abuse of human life is packaged and fed to us by a cynical and calculating elite who glorify in their mediocrity and despotic crimes. Their *predatory* behaviour has very deep roots in our ancient past and is a dark omen of the future to come.

"God is dead"

- Fredrick Nietzsche -

The rise of Islam in the 7th century A.D is a key factor in the understanding of many issues that confronts us these days in the climate of what we are told is Islamic terrorism that threatens to destroy western civilization. The clash of religious ideology between **Christians** and **Muslims** over the past 1,200 years or so is a marker to far deeper and hidden aspects of the multi-dimensional agenda. In fact, if it wasn't for Islam's conquest and spreading of the knowledge of the ancient Mystery System to Europe, the stagnating times of the Dark Ages would have certainly been more prolonged.

After the death of Prophet Muhammad in 632 A.D, Islam was carried across the Levant and Asia Minor to solidify its position as the faith of millions. Disunited, nomadic tribal Arabs were forged into an effective **evangelical** force under the banner of Islam. The zealous Muslim armies commanded by competing warlords, Caliphs and Machiavellian ruling elites threatened the waning power of the **Byzantium Empire** (the last remnant of the **'glory'** that was Rome). Over the next two hundred years, the entire **'Middle East'** and **North Africa** fell to the armies of Islam, who duly converted the conquered masses to their religion. Through the successful conquests of the more ancient civilizations, the Arab ruling elite and their secret fraternities inadvertently became the **custodians** of the secret knowledge of the ancient Mystery System that was once the power of ancient great civilizations.

Between 710 – 711 A.D a **Moorish** (Arab and Black African Muslim confederation) crossed into Europe, conquered Spain and Portugal and threatened the autonomy of northern Europe. For the next 800 years, the Muslim confederacy imposed its rule throughout Spain and Portugal. Much of the knowledge of anciency preserved by the Muslim ruling elite filtered out into Europe gradually through contact between Islamic and Medieval European scholars. The city states of **Al-Andalus** and **Toledo** in Muslim Spain were important points for disseminating the ancient knowledge and for centuries became areas of contacts between hungry European scholars and their

Muslim *'teachers'*. The Moors of Islamic Spain prided themselves on being the repository of ancient knowledge systems such as *Algebra*, *Arithmetic*, *Alchemy* and so on, and the development of their society in Spain, conveyed vital and important knowledge northwards through Europe which ultimately added fuel to the fire of a new dawn that resulted in the birth of the European *Renaissance*. In fact the founding of the prestigious *Oxford University* in England over a thousand years ago was a direct result of this process of knowledge transference from seats of learning such as Toledo in Islamic Spain to England. The Renaissance period of European culture heralded the end of the Dark Age of chaos that followed the fall of the Roman Empire and the rebirth of methodic processes of learning and enquiry. The Renaissance was a result of the intellectual pursuits of artists and thinkers *directly sponsored* by the *ruling elite bloodlines* of Europe to search out and rediscovery the ancient knowledge systems of past civilizations.

The Renaissance saw the development of a new dynamic in learning and the acquisition of knowledge by the leaders of European society, (particularly the power structure of the Roman Catholic church and its armies of clergy). A broad spectrum *centralization of power* in the hands of the elite coupled with greater *social control* over the masses, economically and politically, saw church and state consolidating their power in coherent unison.

The Roman Catholic Church, (the progeny of the Roman/Byzantine Empire) gained its authority by forcefully and without apology by waging bloody wars that claimed the lives of millions of human beings in order to consolidate its position as *the only* organ through which human beings could gain spiritual salvation. *Final Warning: A History of the New World Order* by David Allen Rivera expands upon these issues greatly and is crucial reading in order to get a full account of the deceptions of the religious structures and their ultimate aims. This document can be downloaded from the internet presently and is vital reading.

The rediscovery by Europeans of the ancient knowledge system spurred them on to emulate the greatness of anciency; art, literature, philosophy and theology and for the first time since ancient Greece, a rigorous, speculative vision of the meaning of life beyond these principles. The iconic painters and writers such as Michelangelo, Titian, Da Vinci, Shakespeare, Blake and Dante and so on were among noted figures that symbolized this era of social and cultural development in Europe. The Renaissance over a period of two hundred years developed into a more dynamic reappraisal of culture and learning, manifesting at the end of the *Middle Ages* as the triumphant *'Age of Enlightenment'*.

The so-called Enlightenment (or Age of Reason) that mushroomed across Europe began somewhere in the eighteenth century, (no one seems quite sure when or how), and is reputed to be the time in history when the scholarly endeavors of the

Renaissance came together in Europe to create a wide ranging philosophical enquiry into the nature of man, life and existence. Ironically, this supposed Age of Enlightenment marked the most severe, brutal and damaging chapter in the history of *African* and *Indigenous Peoples* of the world; slavery and the conquest and wholesale slaughter and dehumanization of fellow human beings on a scale that made the ancient Roman's efforts seemed half-hearted. It's interesting to read the definition of the Age of Enlightenment as touted by the influential internet dictionary Wikipedia which *completely side step* enormous data that is vital to real understanding about this issue. Nowhere does it mention the inhumane atrocities of slavery that occurred during this so-called Enlightenment period. This is very telling when it comes to understanding how the mind control program works to subvert real knowledge and accurate historical information. The conquest and bloody colonization of the world by Europeans was at the *precise time* that lofty European philosophers such as *René Descartes* were strolling up the dizzyingly romantic *heights of reason*. According to some European scholars, the Enlightenment began after the discovery of the *new world* and consequently sowed the fertile breeding ground for the establishing of the *white supremacy mind control program* that has enslaved the world for the past several centuries.

One wonders, what could have inspired such new found developments in the powers of *reason* after the European voyages of discovery, (*Columbus, Vasco Da Gama* and so on) that found out that the world was *filled with brown peoples* who had created incredibly ancient cultures and monumental civilizations that dwarfed their thousand year of efforts? Suddenly, it appears that the all too brief Age of European Enlightenment and Reason collapsed into a rabid, envious frenzy to steal other people's gold and territory and, through virtue of guns and cannons, force untold millions of passive native peoples into dehumanizing slavery. This is a most crucial aspect of the whole affair of the Enlightenment period. We are led to believe that the Enlightenment was a time that gave birth to rational thinking, philosophical progress, the birth of democratic ideals through the *French Revolution*, the *American War of Independence*, the *Industrial Revolution,* a broad base *deistic* rational that allowed reformations in the religious structures and most importantly, a new approach to *science* as a tool for progressive social development. Darwinism, Marxism, (Communism), Capitalism, Democracy, economic policies that created private enterprise (cooperations – The East India Company) that *monopolized* commodities; all these factors came from the two centuries of struggle by Europe to define its present path as the dominating force in the world. While supposedly expressing ideals of freedom, justice and democracy in Europe and the Americas for themselves, white peoples got quite busy taking away the freedom of black and brown peoples around the world.

The European Enlightenment didn't really enlighten Europeans to anything at all except their own sense of fear as a *minority group* (in the newly discovered world), compounded by unbridled lust to manipulate, enslave and kill the people they encountered. In fact, the so-called Enlightenment brought down the dark suffocating shadow of slavery and colonization over the entire world and seeded a superficial culture of obsequious philosophers across Europe that created the justification for the *inhumanity* of slavery, the *criminality* of colonization and the wholesale *robbery* and *destruction* of other people's properties and possessions: *Voltaire, Fichte, Hegel, Hobbes, Descartes, Locke, Spinoza, Leibniz, Berkeley, Rousseau, Hume, Kant, Marx* and so on, all contributed to the direction of modern European culture as we know it now; (bearing in mind the origins of European philosophical thought – their predecessors, the Greeks).

The *dark side* to what we are told was the Enlightenment clearly has its roots in the emergence of the philosophy of *racism/white supremacy*, the development of the *New World Order* model for civilization and the ruling *Illuminati* organization as a coherent force in our world today. In fact the very word enlightenment in this regard is obviously linked to *Luciferian doctrine*; (Lucifer according to occultists being the bringer of the light, hence the *torch of Illumination* which became the hallmark of this period of European history). It was at exactly the same time that the European Enlightenment was established that the *Bavarian Illuminati* secret society was also formed by *Adam Weishaupt* and his sponsor *Amschel Rothschild* in *Germany*.

There has been a constant growing trend in Euro/American societies over the last three hundred years to question the validity of the Holy Bible and other spiritual scriptures as worthwhile tools to human/spiritual development. Consistently, in the media and academia, the term *Atheism* is used to describe a purely detached philosophical approach to understanding the spiritual nature of human beings on earth. Atheism basically means the absence of belief in God or the need for religion. Those who describe themselves as atheists believe that there could not be any *proof* of God and that man is but an animal that is a product of its environment, (Darwinian evolution theory). Another form of Atheism is *Agnosticism* which states the view that truth, such as the existence of God, can never be proven or disproved, therefore is unknowable and futile to ponder.

There appears to be many variations of Atheists and Agnostics, some certain of their belief, some not so sure but hanging on in there. The Atheist and Agnostic cite the word *proof* as the bedrock of their arguments. The problem is that such people, albeit being so very *intelligent* and highly *intellectual*, cannot seem to understand that they are using the basic senses of perception to comprehend something that is completely beyond their narrow framework of analysis. Their approach to such matters is firstly limited by their capacity to use their *imaginative sensory* faculties. It's worth pointing out that the trend in these dogmas as we understand it is entirely a white Euro/American invention. The concrete sticks and stones structure of European philosophy has bred these constructs that creates circular arguments, which usually end in mind-numbing apathy for most atheists and agnostics. It's this intellectual and spiritual *no-man's land* that is really the driving force behind the superficial glitz and glamour culture of our present western civilizations and speaks volumes of the manipulation of the *predatory forces* that have *infested* the consciousness of humanity.

The atheist and agnostic are propelled along their circular path in a stunning train of vanity that leaves no room for real dialogue. For them the magic word *objectivity* is the key to their type of *heaven*. Of course there is no such thing as objectivity but, to the atheist in particular, that is the greatest form of *heresy*.

These Euro/American philosophical ideas are based on the principles of *Darwinism*, which teaches us that human beings are, to all intents and purposes, just a collection of animals similar in many ways to apes and orangutans. The doctrine of Evolution was birthed from the trauma and turmoil of repeated cycles of social and spiritual confusion called the Enlightenment, as discussed above.

The thread of Atheism disguised as progressive philosophical discourse that runs throughout the works of most European philosophers of the so-called Enlightenment period is reflected and magnified in the works of more recent European writers such as *Richard Dawkins* who in recent years published with great media hype and fanfare his book entitled *The God Delusion* in which he continued the all too easy argument about the non-existence of God. He climbed the greasy pole of great acclaim by outlining what he believes to be four *'consciousness-raising'* messages:

'Atheists can be happy, balanced, moral, and intellectually fulfilled. Natural selection and similar scientific theories are superior to a "God hypothesis", which is merely the illusion of intelligent design, in explaining the living world and the cosmos. Children should not be labeled by their parents' religion. Terms like "Catholic child" or "Muslim child" should make people cringe. Atheists should be proud, not apologetic, because atheism is evidence of a healthy, independent mind'

What exactly could *mind* be independent of, he failed to elucidate. The spurious words *consciousness-raising* was applied to his work. In the world of people such as Dawkins, life and the understanding of certain human principles such as morality is whatever you want it to be. There is complete freedom to do anything and be whatever one want to be because there is no moral or spiritual imperative other than live and let live, or whatever else people want to think up. Astonishingly, his volume was reputed to have been a best seller in Euro/American societies under the heading of *non-fiction*. This is a most telling point.

I will add some interesting facts to this:

'*As of November 2007, the English version of The God Delusion had sold over 1.5 million copies and had been translated into 31 other languages. It was ranked number 2 on the Amazon.com bestsellers' list in November 2006. In early December 2006, it reached number 4 in the New York Times Hardcover Non-fiction Best Seller list after nine weeks on the list. It remained on the list for 51 weeks until 30 September 2007. It has attracted widespread commentary, with several books written in response*'.

It's quite bizarre how such an obvious work of fiction can be classed as *non-fiction* only by the *white media* establishment. The God Delusion is not remarkable or different in any way at all from other books in its genre, but it has been marketed extremely well by what appear to be very clever men.

Atheism could indeed be seen as a reaction against the *god-programming* of our ancient predators and in some sense, (psychologically), this has a degree of merit but in the wider context cannot be substantiated by pertinent enquiries into the nature of reality. The rejection of a God centered existence and the embracing of ideologies that supposedly allow human beings the freedom to explore life and do whatever they want in whatever way they choose, curiously mirrors *exactly* the philosophical basis of what is referred to as *Satanism*.

Satanism is the worshiping or adoration of what some people call *Satan* or the *Devil*, the adversary or opposition to *God* or *God consciousness* and the principle force or manifestation (spiritual/metaphysical) of illusion in existent nature. The cult of *Devil worshiping* seems to have evolved during ancient times on earth and has played a major role in the development of negative social and spiritual ideologies in some ancient societies.

Today, many people the world over are believers and followers of Lucifer/Satan/Devil. There are many churches of Satan in Euro/American societies and elsewhere. We learn from the words of *the current high priest of the Church of Satan, Anton Le Vey*, some intriguing details of principles and beliefs:

"*No religion has ever been based on man's **carnal needs and fleshly pursuits**...We're realists, we feel the greatest sin is self deceit. We believe in **selfishness, greed, and all the lustful desires that motivate man's natural feelings.***

*We feel **guilt** is a necessary thing. Instead of trying to free ourselves we turn all these things into useful tools. If you're going to be a **sinner,** then be the best sinner you can be".*

The core elements of the so-called European Enlightenment and atheistic doctrines are encapsulated in the statements made by this world renowned Satanist. He further explains:

*"Sexual freedom is very important to the satanic church. **A person should be free to indulge in any sexual fantasies they so desire"***

*"All religions are coming around to Satanism. We're in the very throes of a new **satanic age;** the evidence is all around us. All we have to do is look at it. There's a new title for Christians called **Christian Atheist.** The **Unitarian Church** is a form of atheism in evening clothes. **There are many people practicing Satanism who are Christians by day".***

These statements concisely expresses the ideologies that the occult controllers of the **Babylon System** use to confound and trap the minds of many weak, gullible and ignorant human beings in endless mind-numbing horror, soul destroying fantasies and illusions. The conundrum is never ending; it was designed that way. That is the nature of the Babylon System. **Humanism, Transhumanism, Atheism** and **Agnosticism,** all are isms and an ism ultimately represents a *schism*. These structures are clearly aligned with what has been termed the **New Age** movement which intends to destroy **Christianity** and **Islam** and all other religions and replace them with the doctrine of **Luciferianism,** thus ushering in what the Illuminati and their followers call a **New Satanic Age**.

---

*The concept of Utopia fabricated by Euro/American philosophers is a self defeating ideology; a pseudo-philosophical conundrum limited by concepts that have no definition in reality. Ultimately, **Freedom** and **Utopia** are opposing forces.*

*Utopia is a man-made concept. **Za-Yan** is true freedom. You cannot equate the two. A foolish man dreams of a man-made heaven while the wise dwell in Paradise.*

-The Golden Path of Jah Rastafari-

The ancient Greek writer Plato, in a piece of writing call the **Republic** (c. 380 BC), created the philosophical notion of the ideal social/political state that European thinkers later expanded into the ideology of **Utopianism**. According to Plato, his grandfather **Solon**, while studying in Africa at a prestigious seat of learning, was told by an Egyptian priest that there was once a great civilization called **Atlantis** that existed somewhere beyond the Pillars of Hercules, (possibly in the Atlantic Ocean, no one is quite sure of the details). Plato's Atlantis was supposed to have been a model of the utopian idealism extended by other Greek thinkers such as Socrates. In Plato's writings, **Timaeus** and **Critias** (c. 360 BC), the ancient civilization of Atlantis ended up being swallowed by the sea during a great cataclysm that struck the earth. The basic information Plato supplied in his writings was later embellished and extended by other commentators and authors over the centuries. Atlantis was later commandeered by notorious European romantic thinkers and pseudo-spiritualists such as **Madame Blavatsky,** and specifically Hitler and his notorious gangs of Nazis, as a symbol of some kind of fantastic ancient white utopia that once existed on earth. **Aryanism** and the doctrine of white supremacy formulated by the Nazis is a direct reaction to the fable of a white prehistoric homeland. German writer **Max Mueller** in an attempt at entrenching this **mental program** in the minds of the white masses further embellished this doctrine. Absolutely no proof has ever been furnished that Atlantis was an ancient white civilization predating all other civilizations. The real Atlantis (as I have alluded to above) is a far more complex issue that involves a multi-dimensional approach.

In the utopia of Euro/American conception, science is supreme, so the notion of eking out an existence from the hard earth becomes redundant. The Biblical story outlined in the book of Genesis in the Garden of Eden scenario seems to have informed many people's imagination of an original utopia that was destroyed by man's disobedience

163

of God.

In this scientific paradise human beings are attended by their ingenious *sentient machines*; a world ordered by a specific and commonly accepted view of reality. Euro/American writers have concocted much entertaining science fiction about these ideas; *A Brave New World* by Aldus Huxley, *1984,* by George Orwell, *The Time Machine* by H.G Wells and so on illustrates the point. British author/researcher Nigel Kerner elaborates on the prospect of a future utopia that is already in the making. He paraphrases scientist and futurologist *Michio Kaku*:

"By 2020 intelligence will be everywhere, practically in every object. Special sunglasses are already in development to act as screens that can download personal profiles of everyone we meet and provide a constant flow of information from the internet. A pill containing micro-technology when swallowed will diagnose us from inside our bodies. A technology now in development known as "tele-immersion" will allow us to meet others across the world in a virtual reality in which we see virtual images of ourselves and each other moving and talking in real time. Business conferences and family celebrations could all take place in a virtual world with the people involved thousands of miles away from each other. "Second Life" an online game offering life in a virtual world, has acquired five million subscribers in just five years. Kaku envisages that *"by 2020 there will be an entire 3D universe in cyberspace with virtual countries and governments, virtual schools and universities, virtual properties and stock markets and virtual families and friends. Virtual reality is going to be more and more like real reality."*
Kaku also points out that merging our minds with machines may sound like science fiction but it's already happening. Deep brain stimulation, inserting electric wires in the brain and attaching them to a brain pacemaker, is now used to cure conditions such as depression. Research is being conducted into computer chips that can store human memory when implanted in the brain. So far these technologies are only used for medical conditions, but Kaku predicts that in the future they may well be used to enhance intelligence with "thinking chips". He feels that although we might find all this off-putting at first, we may well get used to it when we realize the obvious advantages.
This is essentially the direction that Euro/American society is dragging the rest of the world, whether or not we want to go along. The future utopia is being strategized and implemented while the rest of the world, (particularly black/brown populations), suffer from *malnutrition, poverty, war, hunger*, and *disease.* This supposed high-tech utopia in the making is being touted as the answer to mankind's problems but when we analyze the data we find that *black African peoples of the world will certainly not be sharing in the new white utopia that's being created.*

Traditionally, African peoples held firmly to the principle of a purely spiritual perspective when considering the ideals of utopianism; *that progress towards a final material earthly utopia is not only impractical but downright suicidal*. According to the ancient knowledge system of African cultures, the material dimension (space/time) is not supposed to be a place of *finality* but a *transitory stage* in our development as sentient beings. Without the process of constant change in the material realm, life could not evolve. There can be no absolute finality to our development as sentient beings here in the physical universe because that would negate our natural evolutionary role in creation.

When Euro/American societies talk of *progress*, we tend to equate the term with specific perceptions of temporal flow from one point to the next, imparting some form of incremental development of knowledge that facilitates greater self, group and social awareness in relation to our being in time and space. The African consensus reality paradigm, being deeply rooted within a spiritual/multi dimensional awareness, did not (in the past) use that particular understanding of progress. For Africans the past and present had specific vibrational qualities that determined any understanding of *'future'*. The future in the African sense was rooted in a purely *holistic metaphysical* perception of the relationships that governs our multi-dimensional existence and experiences, not just our earthly one. For example, in Africa, the rainy season would come at a specific time in the future or a celebratory event would take place at such and such time in the future, but all these things depended on a range of forces that *'intelligently'* guided each moment and event toward their *'scheduled appearance'*. The future in the African sense wasn't something that would just appear out of the present moment but was already broadly *laid out* from the moment of creation and could be revealed to the individual who had expert knowledge of the workings of the **Creation Field,** (*space/time/dimensions*) and its diverse energies. There are rules and regulations that govern the understanding and dispensing of this knowledge as conscious perception of the future can throw up all sorts of ethical considerations which, if one is not careful, could upset very delicate balances inherent within the system of the Creation Field.

The future largely depends on the understanding of the many choices that we can make here in the present, informed by pertinent knowledge of the past and the *essential* ethics that bind our relationship to our *environment, community, our extended spiritual nature*, the **Creation Field** and our **Creator**. As human beings, *freewill* within the cycles of our existence also means that we can choose our own path of evolution whether positive and life affirming or negative and regressive; this ultimately ends in our spiritual salvation and higher evolution or self destruction.

Traditionally, when one consults the African systems of divination such as the *Ifa*

165

Oracle, (usually to gain some clarity about ones destiny in the world and so on), the priest or priestess leads one through a possible future outcome which is entirely dependent on personal understanding and acceptance of the divine law of creation – *Livity*. An individual's future is not so much seen but rather *'chosen'* depending on ones ethical and spiritual understanding and so on. The paradigm is vast and engaging and has to be studied in-depth to really appreciate its profound subtlety, intricacies and inherent expansive wisdom.

Within African cultures there was never the concept of projecting humanity into a *space-age, high tech future, science fiction* scenario or final *utopia* as in western cultural terms because the cultural consensus matrix of Africans determined the direction of human development - *ethical living* within the earth environment, which leads inevitably to greater spiritual *elevation* and *cosmic transcendence*. The rules of ethical living (*Livity*) are determined foremost by our perception of these principles, manifest on earth through human beings and human community. Thus when a child is born into this world, traditionally its parents are not just its biological forebears but also the entire community whose responsibility it is to teach it the precepts of ethical living, thus ensuring its *generative powers* as a living being and after death its rebirth into the world and continued development to the point of evolution when it becomes a *spiritually enlightened being,* thus joining in eternal *evolutionary communion* with The Creator. The traditional African conception of Livity that underpins human progress in any evolutionary sense can be encapsulated thus:

*In a good world, everyone has full knowledge of all things, there is joy everywhere, and because everyone has **inner power**, **good character**, and **wisdom**, life is without anxiety or fear.*

*People must continue to go to the [**spirit realms**] after death and return to Earth in a new reincarnation until our world is a good world for everyone. **Many good things of [the spirit realms] that are not now on Earth will thus be brought here in due course.***

If you undertake any evil actions, good spirits will turn their backs on you and see to it that you feel the repercussions of your evil actions when you return to Earth after your death.

*To become good, you must attain **wisdom, (Zhen)**; help those who need help, **(Shan)**, and forebear from doing anything that might harm the world's prosperity, **(Ren)**.*

[My emphasis]

The traditional African ethics of *Livity* is completely clear. Evolutionary progress for human beings has nothing really to do with how complicated we can make our societies or physical high-tech machines such as robots, computers and so on but on how we can understand the relationship between our humanity and the *Supreme Creative Energy* through a natural, holistic and harmonious synthesis of spiritual enquiry, the ethics of Livity and conscious acceptance of our roles in creation. These are the only processes through which *real* human evolution occurs.

Everyone has *'inner power'* or what we usually refer to as Soul, (as our beloved Brother, James Brown would have put it – *we got Soul!*). Inner power or Soul isn't something that technology bestows upon human beings; it's just something inherent to all life. Becoming a spiritually enlightened being is the determinative that molds pertinent concepts of the future and outlines our purpose in creation. From the higher platform of an enlightened *Ancestor* one gains access to wider perspectives of existence, including greater vision of not just the future but the past and also the present and the actual reasons behind the *design* of life itself. This multi-dimensional perception of past, present and future in relation to our spiritual being is at the very heart of how many black people, even today, (despite the mind numbing deceptions of the Babylon System) perceive human development. The negative consensus reality paradigm imposed on Africans through colonialism and slavery severely fractured this framework which sustained our development on earth and brought us *down* into the Babylon System. The confrontation with the negative aspect of the white consensus reality was one of the biggest rude awakenings Africans have ever experienced in several thousand years.

As black people now in Western countries, and indeed Africa itself, we have developed a dangerously warped view of our place in the future on earth. This issue is at the very heart of the problems we face everywhere in the world. Culturally, black societies had no concept of progress in the same way that whites do. Blacks had no need to build cities in the way that Euro/Americans do or develop material technology in the same manner because the imperative of life on earth was not perceived through the same consensus reality. Blacks had no need to think about leaving the earth in space ships to go to the moon or Mars or anywhere else. The very idea from a point of real reasoning is quite absurd given our present state of unethical development on earth.

The dynamics of future progress must first and foremost depend upon the ethical and spiritual needs of human community and our spiritual interconnectedness as human beings, not solely on individual perception. Problems occur when personal perceptions at times outweigh positive group dynamics and ethical consensus. The role of tradition outlines the path of development which is a major part of the consensus reality mechanism. The past and present determines the future *only in our perception of linear time*. Societal progress in African terms was essentially a group/community effort, not an imposition of abstract ideas by an individual or an elite few. New and innovative discoveries by an individual or group had to be ratified by the conventions that determined the well being and ethical framework that underpins the wider social cohesion, *regardless of what that discovery might be*. These points are at the heart of our understanding concerning progress and the future. Black people had (and largely still have) no desire or inherent need to create a white Euro/American style *high-tech*, *Transhumanist*, *Star Trek*, scientific utopia on earth or to *conquer* space because the consensus reality that informs the African understanding of life, its meaning and potential, dictates a more far reaching, practical and powerful perception of the future; *Justice, Peace, compassionate understanding* and *ONELOVE* for and between all human beings is the prerequisite for charting any meaningful future on earth. Nuts and bolts technology has not, and cannot bring these things to us, only the practice of the *Law of Livity*. Livity elevates the human mind and spirit to the highest heights of ethical awareness and consequently, material and spiritual well being. From the point of view of the Tradition, these are the things that promote meaningful progress and unfold the relevant future for humanity. Until these things can be attained, the future cannot be understood in its proper and beneficial context.

Within the African Tradition, time is very different to what Euro/Americans might believe. Time is an *energy form* that, by its very nature, operates as a *cyclic system* which motivates our evolutionary processes. Ethical living is the real goal of life and this can take many cycles of birth, death and rebirth in the various realms or dimensions of being to reach its goals. When one has reached an enlightened stage of development and leaves the world physically, one takes up the mantle of being a great and wise *Ancestor* – a being dedicated to the higher development of all life. To become a revered Ancestor is not a small thing but one of the principle goals of life. An Ancestor is the energetic essence of the individual that has become *spiritually purified* or enlightened to the real extended *inter-dimensional* nature of existence. In this state of being, time and space takes on very different perspectives. Enlightened Ancestors of Rastafari such as The Sublime Prophet and Teachers, H.I.M Haille Selassie I, Marcus Mosiah Garvey, Leonard Howell, Robert Hinds, Peter tosh, Bob Marley and countless others have dutifully and compassionately worked tirelessly while on earth for the *Greater Good* of all human beings, regardless of colour or culture. The reward of this is to be spiritually elevated to the platform of higher spiritual realization and greater *cosmic consciousness* and union with the **Divine Will** of **Jah Rastafari**. The Divine Will is ever present therefore our *Great Fathers and Divine Mothers* are also ever-present spiritual guiding forces in our lives on earth. There is absolutely no such thing as death in the *reality* of *Jah Rastafari*.

The Divine Will of the Creator can only be known through the ethics that defines Livity, which is the cultivation of knowledge, intellect, wisdom and consequently the exercising of *loving compassion* and dutiful regard for all sentient life trapped in the Fields of Illusions of the Babylon System, not by building spaceships to run away from the earth and to colonize Mars and so on. If we do not know what ethical living is while running around on earth destroying everything we encounter, just imagine if we meet other life forms and colonize other planets in space? Going by the past record of human behaviour, the same sad nonsense will no doubt occur all over again, only worse.

New World Order

*'The Illuminati (or **Moriah Conquering Wind** as they seem to prefer to call themselves these days) is a very secretive group of occult practitioners who have been around for thousands and thousands of years, and are using the **Jewish Kabala** (amongst other such tools) as one of their guidelines to oppress the rest of the population. It is not a boy's club or a group of adults trying to get some excitement in life; this is something much bigger and very sinister. This is an extremely well structured organization consisting of people in very high places. Those people are the super wealthy, who stand above the law. Many of them don't even appear on the list of the wealthiest people in the world - they are that secret. Their driving force is **money**, **power** and **control'**.*

Wes Penre – (Author)

*"The real menace to our Republic (Unites States of America) is the **invisible government** which, like a giant octopus, sprawls its slimy legs over our cities, states and nation. At the head is a small group of **banking houses**. This little coterie runs our government for their own selfish ends. It operates under cover of a self-created screen; seize our executive officers, legislative bodies, schools, courts, newspapers and every agency created for the public protection."*

-Former Mayor of New York, John Hylan-

The word ***Illuminati*** means enlightened ones. The despotic rulers of the world have commandeered this title in an attempt at suggesting that they are somehow more gifted in some strange ways than the average human beings. Research has shown us that this cabal is the key player in the game for global domination. They are supposedly spawned from among the thirteen wealthiest families in the world, and through their Machiavellian tactics dominate all international affairs from behind the dark curtain of global politics, economics and the military/industrial complexes. The

171

main emphasis of the Illuminati appears to be an allegiance to specific bloodlines and loyalties to specific causes that enables them to continually acquire more power by which they might eventually usher in a New World Order of human civilization on earth.

They are the real decision makers, who create the format for political policies and military invasions of various countries; Vietnam, Panama, Nicaragua, Iraq, Afghanistan and so on were all Illuminati funded conflicts that killed millions of innocent human beings. They are the *king-makers* who set up presidents, tyrants and dictators, and they are always hidden from public scrutiny through virtue of the media and various press organizations such as *Fox Television* station, *CBS*, *ABC*, the British *BBC* news network, *Newsweek magazine, Time Magazine, The Washington Post, The New York Times* and most European newspapers, (which they ultimately own and control).

They are the people that decide who will become president of the USA, and through their political maneuverings make sure that their man gets into the seat of power, (even if they have to rig an election as they did in Florida when President George W Bush supposedly won the public mandate to become president by defeating Al Gore). If by some stroke of chance their pre-selected candidate does not win through prior preparation, bribes and influences they are able to buy-off, threaten, blackmail or use whatever means necessary to get their puppet in place. *Barack Obama*, the first *'black'* president of America was chosen by the Illuminati to further their agenda, like all the other Illuminati sponsored presidents before him – Clinton, Reagan, Ford, Nixon and so on.

Obama's background provided the heady *psychological* mixture that galvanized the *emotional* support of millions of Americans to elevate him to the presidency. The psychologists and *'spin-doctors'* behind Obama created a specific strategy that blinded the population to the reality of the Illuminati plans for a new one-world government. They manipulated the *gullibility* and *sentimentality* of black People and the *guilt complexes* within the *white psyche*, using precisely measured slogans like *'change has come to America'*, and so on to appeal to the subconscious desires within people's mind; very expertly but very transparent to those who can see that *'the emperor really has no clothes on'*. Nothing has changed in America, just the same old tired lie prostituting in the final hours before dawn.

With this scenario, the candidate that wins the race to the presidency or the role of *Prime Minister* is always sanctioned by the Illuminati and their organizations. Elections are always a smoke screen; it gives people, especially in Euro/American

172

countries, the illusion that they live in a democracy, when in actual fact they really live in a *demon-cracy*.

There have been presidential campaigns in the USA financed with drug money and arms sale to despotic regimes in Africa and Asia. The Illuminati organization has always been the biggest players in the drug trade industry for hundreds of years. Men such as Prescott Bush, George Bush's grandfather and other prominent Illuminati stooges have built massive fortunes through this avenue. The *Opium Wars* (1839 - 1842 and 1856 - 1860), is a classic example of the Illuminati agenda in drug dealing over the centuries. During the 19th century, Britain, using classic Machiavellian techniques, tried to sell the *Chinese* people addictive drugs in the form of opium in order to make huge profits. (It's noted that the British did not consider selling their own people in Britain the addictive opium drug):

*David Sassoon, the **British Royal family**, and the **Rothschilds'** were implicitly involved. The Manchu Emperor orders the trade be stopped. He names the Commissioner of Canton, Lin Tse-Hsu, as leader of a campaign against opium being sold to Chinese citizens. Lin Tse-Hsu organizes the seizing of 2,000 chests of Sassoon opium and orders it to be thrown into the river. David Sassoon informs the Rothschilds' of this and they in turn **demanded** that the armed forces of Great Britain retaliate in order to protect their drug running interests.*

*Thus, the Opium Wars begin with the British Army once again fighting as **mercenaries** for **Rothschild interests**. They attack cities and blockade ports. The Chinese Army, by now decimated by 10 years of rampant opium addiction, prove no match for the British Army. The war ends in 1842 with the signing of the **Treaty of Nanking**. This includes the following provisions designed to guarantee the Rothschilds' through their puppet, David Sassoon, the right to provide an entire population with opium:*

*1) Full **legalization** of the opium trade in China.*

*2) **Compensation** to David Sassoon of £2,000,000 for the **opium dumped into the river** by Lin Tse-Hsu.*

*3) **Territorial sovereignty** for the **British Crown** over several designated offshore islands.*

This *extortion racket* by the British elite (headed by their Illuminati agents of the *Rothschild* family) gained them further territories such as *Hong Kong* which they held onto until the latter 20th century as a so-called *'British Protectorate'*. The same methods were used time and again by the British in Africa, India and anywhere across the globe where the power of their guns could frighten and bully people into submission. The same policy is pursued even today albeit in more subtle guises such as bringing *freedom* and ***demon-cracy*** to the world. When the British Prime Minister ***David Cameron*** stands up and speaks of Britain's ***moral authority***, (November 2010) it is an expression of the most appalling ***desecration*** of words imaginable.

The Illuminati are connected by bloodlines going back thousands of years in time, and they are very careful in keeping their bloodlines as 'pure' as possible from generation to generation. The only way to do so is by interbreeding. That is why you so often see such notable Illuminati families such as the Rothschilds, Rockefellers and European royalties marry their cousins and relations, for example. Their parents decide whom to marry. No one can simply become Illuminati. They preserve their bloodlines fiercely. Research by renowned author David Icke, (among many others) have clearly shown that this bloodline is directly related to the same ancient ***hybridized*** bloodline that was created and manipulated into power over many thousand years ago by the ***Nordic/Reptilian and Grey*** alien groups. The adherence to the bloodline principle by the Illuminati exposes the fact that they possess guarded and clear knowledge of their status.

According to findings these are reputed to be some of the main Illuminati Families: *'Astor, Bundy, Collins, DuPont, Freeman, Kennedy, Li (Chinese), Onassis, Rockefeller, Rothschild, Russell, van Duyn, Merovingian (European Royal Families)*

The following bloodline families are also interconnected with those above:

Reynolds, Disney, Krupp and McDonald. *In addition to these four families, there are hundreds of others that are connected to the main **13 Illuminati bloodlines**. Although significant, they are not mentioned here; they are considered less powerful and less 'pure' by the 13 Elite Bloodlines'.*

The Rothschild and Rockefeller families are among the key players in the game of control and domination. These people are generally completely cold, ruthless and without any form of human compassion and will kill, or discredit anyone who try to expose them using their control of the media – television, newspapers, magazines and the internet. The awful wars and conflicts across the world that destroy ***millions of human beings***, particularly black Africans, is a clear testament to their complete lack of any real human ***morality*** and ***empathy***.

There is also what could be termed a small offshoot ***'black bloodline'*** that spans the Caribbean, USA and Africa. During the times of slavery, there was much ***interbreeding*** between slaves and their owners, many of whom were bloodline

Illuminati *affiliates*. A significant percentage of so-called black leaders in the Caribbean and the USA are able to trace their blood lineage back to *slave owning Illuminati affiliated families*. In fact research has clearly shown that many of the ruling elite of countries like Jamaica have some relationship to the once ruling elite of slavery times. Of course the black bloodline is subsidiary to the *pure-blood white* elite Illuminati and is used merely as *local management teams* for countries in the Caribbean and some parts of African such as Liberia, Sierra Leon and Guinea and so on as part of the *'black showcasing'* agenda. According to *Fritz Springmeier*, an important researcher on the subject of the Illuminati and the Satanic/Luciferic bloodline:

*'The Satanic hierarchy and their Satanism is clearly the most **secret religion** in the world. They are a **priesthood** that rules the world through **political leaders** that they place in power. And because of their power, they have the ability to suppress a great deal of the publicity that could arise from their numerous activities. Let's just put it this way, if you were a billionaire, which several of the leading **Olympians** (King Illuminati) are, what kind of security could you afford? And what kind of clout would you have with **national governments** and **police forces** to get even **governments** to provide security for you? Remember these people own the **press**, and the **media**.*

*Don't be surprised if both of these happen to me, the author. Just know this--they can kill the body but they can not kill the soul. They also control the **CIA** and **FBI**. Many leading FBI agents have not only been **Masons** but many have been **Satanists**'.*

The main centre of the cabal is based in the City of London, (what is referred to as *the square mile – the financial district or 'heart of empire'*). From there various organizations and think-tanks protrude their invisible tentacles to manipulate the powers of finance and economics. The entire banking system is owned and managed by Illuminati proxies who are the heads of cooperations and multinational conglomerates; the oil-industry, pharmaceutical industry, arms manufacturing, food distribution and so on. The world economy thrives or tumbles into recession at their casual whim and only for their financial benefit. The *Federal Reserve*, *The Bank of England* and the *Bundesbank* are all owned, managed and run by the Illuminati and their various serpentine organizations.

The Illuminati agenda surpasses anything most people could ever dream of. In any given situation where power and control is to be gained they always sponsor both sides, whether it is a conflict such as *World War I* and *World War II* or numerous other pointless and horrific wars that kill millions of human beings. The most disturbing part of this incredible affair is the facts that this cabal of evil is also steeped in the use of what people usually refer to as the occult – *black magic*. Through virtue

175

of occult magic and what appear to be variant forms of ancient *Jewish kabalistic* magic, they have enveloped the minds of the masses in a blanket of pseudo-science and mysticism that has kept people away from investigating the reality of the Babylon System. It's well know now that the Illuminati and their related organizations such as the *Free Masons, Rosicrucians* and other secretive groups affiliated to the *Roman Catholic Church* frequently use specific rituals and ceremonies to communicate and interact with *inter-dimensional* entities in a bid to gain more power and control over human beings. Human sacrifices, blood drinking and the most abominable sexual depravities and evil are crucial parts of their operations across the world. Hundreds of thousands of children go missing every year never to be seen or heard of again; many of them often end up in secret ritual human sacrifice on the bloody alters of the Illuminati to their satanic gods and demonic entities. In Africa, Latin America, Euro/America and the Far East this has reached epidemic proportions. The British author David Icke has pioneered an incredible framework of knowledge that reveals the extent of these things.

Most poor and underprivileged Jamaican people suffering under the unending weight of poverty cannot even guess at the enormity of the global agenda for a fascist New World Order instigated by these unspeakably evil people. The local politics of the island keeps peoples minds locked into the incomprehensible merry-go-round of political infighting and pointless rhetoric by politicians who know they are being used as puppets by more ruthless powers. Jamaica is run along the same lines as a private company serviced by two different *management teams* alternately. The people are given the impression that real politics is alive and well. Nothing could be further from the truth. Here in Jamaica our country is run by policies dictated from the *United Kingdom/EU* and the *USA*. We have never been a free country and we will never be a free country. Free countries do not exist where the Illuminati is concerned.

*"We shall unleash the **Nihilists** and **Atheists**, and we shall provoke a formidable **social cataclysm** which in all its horror will show clearly to the nations the effect of **absolute atheism**, origin of savagery and of the most bloody turmoil. Then everywhere, the citizens, obliged to defend themselves against **the world minority of revolutionaries**, will exterminate those destroyers of civilization, and the multitude, **disillusioned with Christianity**, whose deistic spirit will from that moment be without a compass (**direction**), anxious for an ideal, but without knowing where to render its adoration, will receive the pure light through the universal manifestation of the pure doctrine of **Lucifer/Satan**, brought finally out in the **public view**, a manifestation which will result from the general reactionary movement which will follow the **destruction of Christianity** and **Atheism**, both **conquered** and **exterminated** at the same time".*

*-**Albert Pike, one of Euro/America's (former) chief Satanists on the plan for Illuminati world conquest-***

Since ancient times there has been an agenda by various conquerors and tyrants to consolidate and centralize political and economic power in a bid to rule the world. Thankfully due to the internet, the New World Order is on many peoples minds these days as millions of us are waking up to the reality that our personal freedoms are being eroded rapidly by ***governments***, ***big businesses*** and various ***cooperate interest groups***, internationally. Many books have been written that deals with these issues, yet mainstream media, the political establishments and academia refuses (unsurprisingly) to endorse this view as being the real state of things in our world at present. The words '***conspiracy theory***' is used by the establishment to play-down and debunk pertinent discussions on the realities of the New World Order. Important activists/freedom fighters such as ***Alex Jones (USA), David Icke (UK)*** and many, many others have helped millions of ordinary people around the world to come face to face with the extraordinary extent of this nightmare that we're all living in. I cannot stress enough how important the works of these men are to all our futures on planet earth.

Rastafarians have been fighting against the Babylon System and the New World Order for many decades, long before most people ever heard of conspiracy theories. Our ***Sublime Prophet, Marcus Mosiah Garvey*** in his great works explained clearly the need for African peoples to become acquainted with the white supremacy agenda and its ultimate aims many decades ago. His outspoken views on the methods and means by which we could become liberated from the Babylon System have formed the bedrock of the beliefs of true Rastas and resonate even more loudly and urgently now in the 21st century. History has shown us clearly that through the manipulations of the white supremacy agency, (under the guise of the CIA), plans were implemented to discredit Garvey and the UNIA movement created to free black peoples from slavery. The same treatment was meted out to *His Sublime Majesty, Haille Selassie I, King of Kings, Emperor of Ethiopia* decades later by Illuminati agents planted in Ethiopia to destroy the great works of our leader. *Malcolm X, Martin Luther King Jr.* and the revolutionary leaders of the African liberation struggles all fell as victims to the Illuminati and their evil agenda. The great African leader *Nelson Mandela* was deliberately kept in prison for twenty seven years solely as a counter weight to the hopes and aspirations of his people. He was then released at a calculated appointed time in order for the Babylon System to implement specific measures to *readjust* and *reinforce* its power base in *South Africa*. The details of these things are outlined in many volumes which I urge the reader to find the time to analyze and digest.

The concept of the New World Order as we have come to know it in our time was formulated at least two centuries ago by a secret cabal of very rich and influential white *Anglo Saxon* European males, affiliated with the *Free Masons, Rosicrucians* and various other *cults* that pervade the higher echelons of European intellectual and upper class society, (the details of which can be read on the internet and in the extensive works of the above mentioned activists/writers and their websites). Many researchers have outlined in great detail the salient contribution to the Illuminati organization by a distinctly pronounced *Jewish element* within the organization. In fact, the Jewish background of many of the high profile Illuminati leaders is one of the most telling aspects of this affair. According to the findings of *Andrew Carrington*, author of the *Synagogue of Satan*, (which can be downloaded free from the internet):

*"One major reason for the historical blackout on the role of the international bankers in political history is that the **Rothschilds are Jewish**... The Jewish members of the conspiracy have used an organization called The **Anti-Defamation League** (ADL) as an instrument to try and convince everyone that any mention of the Rothschilds and their allies is an attack on all Jews. In this way they have **stifled** almost all honest scholarship on international bankers and made the subject taboo within universities. Any individual or book exploring this subject is immediately attacked by hundreds of ADL communities all over the country. The ADL has never let the truth or logic interfere with its highly professional smear jobs... Actually, nobody has a right to be angrier at the Rothschild clique than their fellow Jews... The **Rothschild empire** helped finance **Adolf Hitler**".*

Research shows that among the principle founding members of what we now refer to as the Illuminati were *Mayer Amschel Rothschild* and *Adam Weishaupt* who resided and operated in Germany, (circa 1770). Notable historical incidents such as the *French Revolution* were definitely inspired, bankrolled and controlled by *agents* of the Illuminati organization. The rise of *Bolshevism* and the *Russian Revolution* were also key parts of the *strategic interests* of the Illuminati in its early days of consolidating its power base among the elite political and financial groups of European ruling classes. One of the key strategies of the *steering committee* of the Illuminati is the funding of *both sides* in any conflict from which they can gain control of the outcome. In all the major wars of the 20th century the Illuminati have been the instigators and the funding body that allowed millions of people to be killed only to profit financially and geopolitically from the results.

A crucial part of the Illuminati's operation throughout history was the physical and cultural enslavement of black African peoples who were used as a work force on the plantations of America and the Caribbean, (many writers usually side-step this very important issue. The white supremacy component to the conspiracy appears, at times, uncomfortable to digest by many white writers and researchers. This is indicative of the basis and strength of the mind control program that afflicts the psyche of many whites in general). In fact the *principle players* in slavery were the *exact same people* involved with the monetary/economic development of the banking/Capitalist system that runs the world. The horrifying details of the *Maafa,* (the *African Holocaust of slavery),* has always been covered up by racist Euro/American academia and political establishment.

All the principle families that have ties to the Illuminati agenda in our time invested heavily in the slavery of black Africans. For 400 years the wealth from *sugar, cotton, coffee, cocoa* and a variety of other commodities grown by black slaves on plantations in the Caribbean and the Americas (*under the most unspeakably barbaric and inhumane conditions*) enriched the white elite of Euro/America beyond their wildest dreams. Many of the elite white Europeans were funded largely by *Jewish money* and *economic clout*. Marc Lee Raphael in his volume *Jews and Judaism in the United States: A Documentary History* states the following in relation to the slave trade in America:

'Jewish merchants played a major role in the slave-trade. In fact, Jewish merchants frequently dominated'.

The advent of the *Industrial Revolution* made slavery economically unviable and so blacks were *'set free'*, (or so we were led to believe). We do know that we were never freed from slavery and that the system was merely reengineered to be more effective. The same rules still apply, only the conditions of our slavery have changed. Our *prison yard* was extended a bit further to give us the *illusion of freedom* so that we wouldn't cause too much trouble. The Illuminati found, through their testing, that mental slavery of black peoples was a far more effective means of oppression. Ultimately, the aim of the New World Order is to take complete control in the establishing of a new format for human existence on planet earth. They have harnessed the best intellects that money can buy to create the scientific and philosophical paradigm that will make their ascension to ultimate power unavoidable.

*The scientists of Babylon search for the secrets of the universe. They childishly speak of **'conquering space and time'** (as though such a thing was conceivable). They say this is science but this is a gross deception. Their real aim is conquest. Conquest brings subjugation which inevitably leads to oppression and enslavement and the end of freewill. This speaks volumes about their science; **(think of Nazi concentration camps and Guantanamo Bay, the atomic bomb, genetic engineering and Nano technology)**.*
Time and space is the creation of the Supreme.
*The Babylonian's **subconscious desires** betray them. Their desire to conquer time and space is a reflection of their real aims and ambitions – **to find a way to conquer and usurp the power of the Supreme Creator.** That is at the very heart of their agenda.*

-The Golden Path of Jah Rastafari-

What we all must come to realize (and we don't have much time to do it) is that the Illuminati faction on earth is not really concerned (ultimately) whether we are black or white. The white supremacy mind control program is a specific instrument used to manipulate the masses of whites into the Illuminati's *Final Solution*. Although the elite conspirators *'wear'* the bodies of white people, clear evidence proves conclusively that these shameless tyrants are not concerned about whites at all. White supremacy is a double edged sword that cuts both ways. The Illuminati and their proxies actually believe that they are a *chosen race* set apart from the rest of humanity. Their main concern is their personal survival and continued rule over the majority of human beings on earth. They have in the past, right now in the present and certainly in the future will continue to manipulate whites just the same as blacks to achieve their aims. If there is too much widespread resistance by the masses of people, black and white, to their plan of a micro-chipped world population, they intend to kill at least *eighty percent* of the people on earth. They believe that this would make the planet much easier to manage. There is no need to maintain a *large white population* that might sometime in the future wake up to the evils of their New World Order and create a revolution to destroy it. They cannot risk that. The intention is to keep the masses of white people *busy*; use them as buffers to keep everything off balance until the moment when they will cull them like the cattle they believe them to be. Having their advanced technology in place, the elite will be able to comfortably exist with very little worry about physical labour, energy needs and so on. They already possess the technology to create *'free energy'*. Technology is their greatest life insurance policy and they fund its development through various agencies such as *Lockheed Aerospace, Boeing, Monsanto, Pfizer pharmaceuticals* and a network of others, some not so well known in areas of high-tech surveillance, the police, the military, futuristic weapon systems such as the *Star Wars Defense Initiative, Missile shields, Echelon, HAARP* and many other such secretive devices. Around the world there are hundreds of secret *underground bases* that have been built by the Illuminati and their shadowy agencies as a means of perpetuating their rule should a cataclysm occur on earth whether natural or otherwise.

The Illuminati conspirators have for some time now possessed the technology to create disturbances in the weather patterns of the planet. This can be used as a weapon to create *famine, floods, Tsunamis* and even *earthquakes* in specific parts of the world. It is worthwhile noting also that after the terrible earthquake that claimed thousands of lives in Haiti, the country has been suddenly attacked by a horrendous bout of cholera which has so far claimed many more thousands of lives. The people of Haiti have (to the surprise of the 'international community') *accused* the *United Nations* occupying forces of *deliberately unleashing cholera on the population as a weapon of population control*. There appears to be insightful justifications for this claim by the beleaguered people of Haiti and no doubt in the near future we will learn more about this despicable act. This issue is ongoing.

There are many facets to the Babylon System's conspiracy. Look up in the sky on a sunny day and you will usually see large swathes and streams of clouds that remain there for hours. They appear quite similar to jet aircraft exhaust clouds but on closer inspection they do not disperse as jet trails do. These *chemtrails* or *contrails* are sprayed in the sky usually by military airplanes or other airplanes disguised as commercial airliners. No explanation has ever been given by governments anywhere in the world as to why this is occurring and what the effects are on human health.

 Most people these days tend to think that the space program that *NASA* controls is a complete lie. The elite use it purely for their own purpose of world domination and control. Real information concerning the space program is never released to the general public. We see *Space Shuttles*, rockets and satellites go up into space but the masses of human beings will never know the real reasons why this happens or what is *inside* these shuttles, satellites and so on. Whatever the public is told that's what they will happily believe. The images of space that are beamed back to earth are also controlled by the agencies surrounding NASA such as the NSA and the CIA and its shadowy counterparts. All information is compartmentalized and fed out to a compliant media who manipulate the public on behalf of the predatory Illuminati faction.

An increasing part of the Illuminati's strategy is the utilizing of *right wing* elements in Euro/American societies to create civil strife and turmoil among the different racial groups. Racism is one of their most tried and tested methods of manipulation (it works every time) and in the very near future will be a key instrument in the arsenal of the Babylon System to create disturbances and *'racial wars'*. In Europe this is now a reality and is presently influencing governmental policies right across the continent. Information gleaned from the *analytic mode* clearly outlines a precise strategy of progressive racial tensions that will create the necessary *problem-reaction-solution* scenario which researchers such as David Icke outlines succinctly in his work. The robotic *storm-troopers* of the New World Order are already on the march; the *British National Party, (BNP),* The *English Defense League (EDF), Combat 18, The National Front, Freedom Party (Austria), Pro-Deutschland (Germany), Sweden Democrats (Sweden), Lega Nord (Italy), Vlaams Belang (Belgium), Danish People's Party (Denmark)* and other repellent, shadowy racist groups in France, Spain, Russia, and Holland are being used now to stir the flames of hatred among human beings. The so-called far-right in Europe has made massive gains in elections and the public consciousness in recent times. In Austria and Germany, (the traditional white racist heartlands of Europe) democratically elected governments and officials are cognizant of this growing threat but are powerless to curtail the rise of the illuminati's *'cannon-fodder'*. The racists will be given the platform from which they will attempt to influence the confused white majority of Europe. This is another string in the hands of the Illuminati who are expertly playing the field by pitting various groups against each other until the bewildered masses, frightened at the disintegration of society and the very real threat of white racists gaining real political power, give their consent to the establishment of the New World Order. *Problem, Reaction Solution – Endgame.*

These developments are necessary for the New World Order brigade to implement their plans of global dictatorship.. The trick is to make the whites of Europe feel insecure and threatened by other peoples of the world, particularly Muslims, Chinese, Africans, Gypsies and so on, and they will give up their rational, critical judgment in exchange for a *totalitarian dictatorship* that will supposedly *'protect their interests'*. This happened the same way during the Nazi era and is now being used very successfully once more in the 21st century. In America the same scenario is being played out against the African Americans, the Hispanic population and the *Mexicans* by the puppet masters who are pulling the strings of the so-called *Tea Party* movement, (a rag-tag collection of racist white Americans) which aims to protect America against the harmful effects of a black president and the erosion of the *'American Dream'*. All these things are precise instruments that will enable a final surgical strike at the *heart* of human freedom before 2020.

Beneath the surface of all this is the manipulation by the predatory forces waiting to implement the final solution – *the annihilation of 'undesirable' peoples on planet earth*. The racial element extend deeper into our history here on earth than we can imagine and is clearly linked to the *hybrid breeding program* of the predatory alien manipulators who obviously will protect their *'interests'* in any way they can.

Many upgraded alien/human hybrids are now being phased into human societies rapidly. The new breed must retain its *programmed genetic qualities* and not become *'contaminated'* by other strains of what the aliens perceive as inferior models of human beings (namely the rest of us). Simple things such as the banning of smoking and the promotion of Genetically Modified foods, healthy eating and the alien/human *hybrid look* in advertising, the fashion world and the *Hollywood film* and *glamour industry,* (among many other seemingly trivial details), conditions the masses subliminally to accept the new reality when it comes; (incidentally it has been said that GM foods are being specifically created not because the system wants to make foods better or to stop hunger in the developing nations, but specifically for the hybrid alien/human *food consumption requirements of the future*). The *Codex Alimentarius* policy to ban the use of vitamins, minerals, various nutritional supplements and natural food products and to regulate the *type of foods* that we will all be allowed to consume is a very important part of this agenda.

These are but some subtle ways in which the agenda operates. It's incredibly complex and more far reaching than most of us would imagine. When society breaks down, race riots, food shortages, job shortages, financial collapse, housing shortages and so on, the wholesale lynching of Muslims, blacks and foreigners on the streets of Europe by 'enraged white mobs and government sanctioned agencies' will become an accepted phenomenon, (much like the initial persecution of the Jews in Nazi Germany). The mind control program that turned nice, ordinary peaceful Germans into unconscionable murderers is been wheeled out once more in our time for the same purpose. The *'Muslim Terror Factor'* has been primed as the effective weapon in this mind control program. Contrived and deliberately erroneous stories in the media are specifically designed to heighten *'white fear'*. Many Muslims have for some time been very aware of the attack on their religion and culture by the white supremacy mind control program and have taken decisive steps to counter this; the present situation in *Occupied Palestine, Iraq, Pakistan, Afghanistan* and *Iran* illustrates these issues. A thousand years ago Muslims were in conflict with the same force for the same reasons; the *Crusades* by white supremacists – the *Knights Templars*, the *Catholic Church* and so on. Whatever the rights and wrongs and moralities involved in the processes Muslims employ in this war to preserve their religion and culture, their aim is opposition to being overrun by ideological, political, economic and most of all military aggression of the white supremacy mind control program; (one should be in no doubt however that *some* Muslims too have their own very *unsavory agendas* brewing behind the scenes).

Whites who think they are immune to the mind control programs of the New World Order agenda will have the rudest awakening imaginable. The tyrannical group that controls the world ultimately does not care about the masses of white people in the end, only about their system of control, oppression and slavery. Anyway, according to the Illuminati, a high percentage of white peoples living now will be eliminated in order to artificially breed a new *uncontaminated*, superior white race that will act as their work force in their New World Order. The Babylon System's armies of *'jailors'* *'minders'* and *'wardens'* play out their roles as politicians, bankers, journalists, factory workers and so on without suspecting that they are mere disposable minions in this vast and seemingly incomprehensible drama.

In recent years there has been much published about these things by many researchers. The internet is full of much information, some of which is pertinent and can lead to great insight and some that's complete fabrication by *Babylon System agents* who plant disinformation to mislead people into dead end speculations. One has to be most discerning and critical about this form of knowledge.

We must not be fooled by the politics we see on TV. Endless debate about race and gender in the media is set only to confuse and alienate people. Within a few short years from now, the new World Order will be established (if there is no *real* opposition by the masses of humanity). Their evil agenda is in its final stages now. The bombing of the *Twin Towers* and the entire *9/11* scenario, *7/7* bombings in London, and the so-called *'War on Terror'* were only the beginning of its establishment. The Illuminati now believe that nothing can stop them from ascending to 'ultimate power' at this late stage, (so supremely confident are they of their plans) because the masses of people, black and white, fail to take these things seriously enough.

As per the agenda, Iran will be drawn further into open conflict with the world *Jewish power-bloc* and the formidable military might of *Euro/America,* guided by the hidden hand of the *Illuminati* faction. Natural disasters such as the recent *'floods'* in Pakistan this year will pave the way in the foreseeable future to intensify and ignite regional *political strife* and *civil war*. Should this happen, American/Nato (Euro/American military hegemony) forces will certainly have to be stationed on Pakistani soil to assist in *'protecting'* Pakistan's *nuclear arsenal*. This will obviously not be tolerated by Muslim nationalistic elements and Taliban affiliates in that country. The so-called *War on Terror* will eventually lead to a final show of strength and power by the *Illuminati armed forces* under the heading of *NATO*. Countries such as Syria, various Gulf States and Egypt will be drawn into the conflict and large swaths of the Middle

East will become embroiled in anarchy and destruction. Dramatic incidents will be created to draw *North Korea* and *China* into open hostilities with the Euro/American powers, (this will no doubt be orchestrated to seem believable, although China will become an intrinsic and important part of the New World Order agenda at a later stage). One of the requirements of the New World Order is the culling of the Chinese population. Therefore war with China is the usual way to accomplish this. The *analytic mode* clearly states that specific incidents involving *missiles* and *launchers* (mobile weapons system) somewhere along (or near) the Sino/Russian border will be instrumental in future developments. It's worth noting that the *Russian Federation* is now aligned with the *Euro/American hegemony* militarily, and eventually also politically. China's alliance with North Korea will prove significant in the events that will lead to what will be called World War III. The Illuminati will stage manage the entire events to scare the populations of the world into compliance with their agenda for a *global police state*, using the magic words *'security'*, *'terrorism'* and *protecting 'demon-cracy'*. We will watch on our TVs frantic *diplomatic missions by Euro/American politicians in an attempt to stop the world being engulfed in World War III,* (or so they will tell us). The Olympics scheduled for London in *2012* could certainly become a major turning point in the agenda also. They usually use events such as these to *highlight* the necessity for a New World Order to the populations of Europe and the world. The 2012 end-time scenario supposedly predicted by the *Mayan Calender* will become another asset in the mind control program of the Babylon System. A glut of information, whether real or disinformation, has been fed to the public and many people at times become confused as to what is pertinent data.

For some years now the Illuminati controlled media has been setting up the scenario of terrorists getting hold of a *dirty bomb – (a small atomic weapon)* and unleashing it in a major Euro/ American population centre. This situation is very likely to occur on account of its dramatic potential to frighten the world into compliance with the draconian measures that will be taken by Euro/American military forces after this event. No doubt we will be told by the news networks that the terrorists are Muslims, (most likely affiliated to so-called *Al Qaida* and conveniently, backed by *Iran*). The majority of whites will believe the propaganda, because the white supremacy mind control program is being constantly reinforced by the white *media* to ensure mass compliance of whites under the banner – protecting freedom *(slavery)* and promoting *demon-cracy.*

America will most certainly see serious symptoms of civil unrest intensifying in the years ahead culminating in a staged *civil war* between *'rebel'* states and *Federal government*. The drug wars across the borders in *Mexico* and the constant infiltration of thousands of migrant Hispanic workers into the USA are all parts of the catalyst that affect mainstream American society in many ways. The NAFTA trade agreements between The USA, Mexico and Canada that will see the merging of these nations *economically* and the abandonment of the US Dollar for a common North American currency (the *Amero*) will be the first stages in what the Illuminati hope will finally become a *political and military union* of the three countries. This scenario will closely follow the complete *collapse of the monetary systems* of the world. Debt crisis will be deliberately engineered to cause panic in the money markets. The masses will become confused and the banking elite will then remove from the public the ability and means to store any real wealth or resources by forcefully repossessing all private properties. Their real intention now is to cause the *break up of the United States of America* and a *suspension* of the constitution in order to create a *new America*; a *totalitarian dictatorship*. *Directly engineered terrorism, identity cards, bio Micro-chips,* will be freely offered to the masses in order to gain our compliance in the establishment of a New World Order. Already suffering from the fall out of Illuminati sanctioned policies such as child molestation/pedophilia and gay marriages, the Christian Churches will be *'attacked'* more directly by the Illuminati controlled media in order to create further disillusionment among the masses. This is deliberately designed to create maximum confusion among Christians and the public at large. The same treatment is being dished out to the *Islamic* faith in order to destroy its hold on Muslims. The War on Terror scenario is being used to vilify Islam and to gain the complicity of the white western world and *liberal* Muslims in its destruction.

We will then begin to see the dismantling of religions by newly formed alternatives such as *New Age movements, Humanist* and *Transhumanist* philosophies. During the next decade science will almost certainly announce the discovery of some form of intelligent *extraterrestrial life* and the *analytic mode* clearly states that contact will be established publicly with what will appear to be alien beings in spaceships. The world will finally know that alien beings really *exist* and the fallout of this will change the dynamics of human society *forever*. The most likely scenario is that the aliens will *appear* as blond haired, white skinned and blue-eyed beings. Many will be shocked, awed, bewildered and amazed at this event. It will change the nature of human perception completely and permanently. People left in a wilderness bereft of solid grounding and the knowledge that the religions were *'wrong'* in their teachings will create individual belief systems or completely abandon religious dogma and institutions. They will gravitate towards *New Age* doctrines and the *new religion* of *Transhumanism* (or *Post-Humanism* as some refer to it in some quarters) in the vain hope that if they throw their lot in with the New World Order and their *alien partners* at least they might be saved from suffering and death. The Jehovah's Witnesses and various Evangelical churches all secretly subscribe to the principles of the New World Order and many of their leaders are quietly preparing their sheep (congregations) to accept this new reality through mass indoctrination.

There will certainly be a quiet mass roundup of anyone or group that appear to be *trouble makers, dissidents* or *rebels* against the establishment of the new World Order. In fact, in the USA there are many sinister looking concentration camp styled facilities being built in several different states and millions of what appear to be black *biodegradable coffins* stacked up in purpose-built, guarded warehouses for this eventuality.

Usually when we recognize the awful truth of our situation we become fearful. This is a reflex action caused by our recognition that when the illusion of life we've been living starts to break down we seem to loose our sure footing on solid ground. Control the fear by absorbing the lessons and insights it imparts. Hold firmly onto the shining principles of the *ONE LOVE*. This can and will assist greatly in controlling your fears.

The *Illuminati* in their complete ignorance of the true nature of reality, desire to become *gods* in the literal *flesh and blood* sense, (much like ancient Roman and Greek tyrants who had a pathological preoccupation with becoming gods). This is a great part of the real meaning behind their operations across the span of thousands of years.

The philosophy of Trans-Humanism developed in the twentieth century by Euro/American thinkers is intended to replace all other forms of philosophical enquiries. It has been touted by its advocates as a new paradigm for human development which involves radically altering the human being as we know it through advanced genetic engineering, cloning and various secretive projects that involves *Nano Technology*. Euro/American scientists are presently attempting to develop the ability to *extend* life for vast periods of time, certainly hundreds of years. Their intention is to create new bodies when they are about to die or have had a damaging accident to *breed* a new *human race*; a superior model, improving on the work of nature; more intelligent, faster, stronger, more physically appealing, more resilient to diseases, and also possessing *psychic abilities* such as *telepathy* and *telekinesis*.

An interesting element to this program is that this new super elite '*white race*' will at some time in the future recognize the advantages of having a higher concentration of *melanin* in the skin, which protects bodies from ultraviolet radiation amongst other things, not to mention the light absorbing qualities that acts as a catalytic converter of light energy. There will be no more '*white*' people like there is now, (nor blacks for that matter); the Illuminati's *real concerns* goes way beyond such things as mere skin colour.

This insane group of megalomaniacs actually believes that they will carry out their plan of human genocide and world domination successfully without any effective opposition because the world remains ignorant of the awful nature of their deceptions. All these things are only a prelude to the real actors waiting in the wings of the stage, the *predators* of human beings - *Grey aliens, Reptilians, Nordics* and an array of inscrutable *inter-dimensional discarnate entities* who have been manipulating the human race on earth *through time and dimensions.*

During the last sixty years of the twentieth century the advances in genetic science rapidly changed our perceptions of ourselves as human beings. Throughout the 1990s the *Human Genome Project* was hailed one of the most important breakthroughs of science in human history. The important thing to recognize is that the research in genetic science is *controlled entirely* by white Euro/American scientists and to lesser degrees in recent years Asian nations such as South Korea, Japan and China; *cloning, stem cell research, gene therapy* and a host of *'life sciences'* projects are leading the way to an uncharted future of bewildering possibilities. The development in genetic science was not arbitrary but specifically and clandestinely *assisted* by the predatory alien groups who have channeled much technical data to the Illuminati group to allow their scientists to create the present paradigm of genetic advancement. This is absolutely crucial to the negative alien agenda on earth.

What we can discern is that within the context of the Babylon System, genetic science forms the *central* part of the aims and ambitions to create a scientific/technological utopia ruled by an autocratic elite. The Illuminati control all aspects of genetic engineering. They fund all research into the remodeling of the human being. At present they are offering out tantalizing glimpses into their New World and its possibilities to the chosen and the gullible, promising the reward of their coming utopia for compliance from those humans that might wish to resist.

One key aspect of the *'genetic rush'* that people won't read about in the media or see on television is that there appears to be a very grave problem with the *'breeding ability'* of a sizeable percentage of white peoples world wide. The fertility rate of whites seems to be *diminishing* at an alarming rate. This fact has been withheld from white peoples in general as the repercussions of such knowledge could potentially be quite catastrophic in a socio/political context. We are told that the reasons why the fertility rate of whites has rapidly declined are not presently known, albeit a range of factors have been considered, particularly a drastic change in the chemical and biological structure of the reproductive mechanisms due to processed dead foods, the ingesting of water treated with a host of chemicals such as fluoride, pollutants in the air and soil and so on. We see similar anomalies in fish in rivers that have been polluted with various chemicals. Conversely, the fertility rate of the other groups on earth who are not as *industrialized* has remained steady and a recent report from the USA,(2010), predicts that in fifty years from now the white population of America could become a *minority* group due to the steady growth of ***Hispanics*** from central and South America and African Americans. The frantic rush in the development of ***invitro-fertilization, cloning*** and other breeding programs by whites appear indicative of the dire need to promote the continuation of white breeding capacity. This is, when we analyze deeper, a deliberate and sinister ploy by the Illuminati faction to ***cull the white population of the world without them knowing that that is the real agenda***. Their plan is to ***genetically engineer and breed an entirely new race of whites to populate their new utopia***. The so-called alien breeding program is an intrinsic part of this process. Should white people find out the incredible and chillingly sinister details of these plans, then the Illuminati faction would no doubt step up its actions or change tactic to avoid ***open revolutionary confrontation*** by an aware and ***enraged white population***. There are many groups of white people in America and Europe who are now becoming aware of these issues but the Illuminati controlled media would have the general public believe them all to be *'anarchists, **ultra right-wing militia/nationalists, religious crackpots'*** and so on. In this way opposition and dissent is neutralized and they can carry out their plans while a sedate and powerless white population sit idly by in senseless stupor and watch as the light of humanity go out.

We should understand that when the UN or WHO speak of ***population reduction*** in the *'third world'* this really is designed to stimulate fear in the minds of whites of *'genetic submergence'* by other groups of humans and consequently is also used by the Illuminati led establishment to push forward their plans in the field of ***eugenics***. It must be remembered that these people care nothing in any real sense for the masses of poor white, black, Indian or Chinese people, only that we can all be used to further their agenda of world conquest and domination.

*"I saw the human being of the future, and he is **cold** and **intrepid**...He frightened me"*

-Adolf Hitler-

Transhumanism is a small but growing white Euro/American intellectual and cultural organization that completely embraces and actively promotes the use of white supremacy, science and technology as a means of transforming basic human beings into literal **superhumans** with **God-like powers and abilities**. They regard the natural human condition as unnatural. Sickness, aging and death are aspects of human nature that they believe can be eradicated completely using science. In fact the core philosophy of this movement is the expressed aim of gaining the ability to *'improve, radically alter and completely change'* human nature physically and mentally. Already, in our societies, the propagation of **plastic surgery** and **biological/genetic enhancements** is clearly designed to prime white society to accept the vast implications of the coming New World Order. This philosophy is clearly without doubt informed by the writings of eighteenth century European philosophers such as Nietzsche and the Nazis and their doctrine of **Aryanism**.

The world pop and film culture, headed by **Hollywood,** has for a very long time, been harnessed by the controllers of the Babylon System to fill our minds with these ideas so that these things will become acceptable to the masses. The prevalence of science fiction genre movies, super-hero films such as **X-Men, Spiderman, Heroes** and **Superman** and so on are indicative of this agenda. Through Hollywood, advertising and popular music/fashion and the entertainment culture that posits the notion of the perfect human body, **Transhumanist** doctrine is being constantly fed to the masses. Most people will subscribe to the philosophy of Transhumanism as a natural course of the relentless indoctrination process. No one will want to be left out.

Genetic research is certainly the most crucial area of human endeavors presently. This field of science has been touted as what is tantamount to being the *'holy grail'* of human existence. With genetic engineering it's possible to clone, reshape and remodel the physical biology of not just human beings but potentially all other life forms on the planet earth. What's being termed the *.science of Transhumanism'* has been thrown around for many years by a growing number of white academics and scientists who appear to suffer from the old disease of paranoia and megalomania. They are the end result of Darwinian scientific speculation, locked within a paradigm of existence that they believe (astonishingly) they have the ability (and worse still), the authority to enforce upon the entire world.

The Illuminati controllers believe that white people will take the *bait* and become willing slaves because the false utopian dream that they present will not be rejected by a frightened and confused white society; a high tech computerized world, physically enhanced intelligence and *comic book style human beings with super-powers*. Everyone will want to be a super-human. Those who reject these things will be left behind to quietly fade from existence.

The *'new humans'*, according to Transhumanist doctrine, will be predominantly *white* or *Aryan*. Those few Indians, Chinese, Japanese and so on who comply with the agenda will also have various minor or subordinate roles to play within specific parameters; (a small handful of black Africans will be kept alive for genetic research and slave labour purposes. As the primary template for human life-form on earth, black Africans hold much *key* genetic information. The new humans will be made with specific *genetic traits* that assist the function of the Illuminati's new utopia. They will use phrases to describe themselves such as - *'homo superior'* and *'meta-humans'*:

*The mapping of the human genome (now underway) is understood as desirable regarding two major areas: **medical applications** and **genetic engineering**.*
*Simply put, the major concept pertinent to those two areas involves deleting **undesirable genetic materials** and **inserting desirable ones**.*
*The ultimate goal, of course, is the production of the **perfect human specimen;** 'perfect' at least from the genetic point of view. The potentials of this are awesome, staggering. **One of the fall-outs is that human history will be completely redirected,** more or less in one fell swoop.*
*The potentials, however, are not yet clear regarding their details. But whatever those will turn out to be, they are inevitable, certain and unavoidable. **You see, hardly anyone will resist the engineering of the genetically perfected human... Those who do resist, or have reservations, will find themselves pissing into the wind of this great change.***

The Illuminati *bloodlines* will be the dominant force within the *gene-pool* of the *new white race* alongside their *'human/alien hybrid masters'*. This new utopia will function on advanced technology (which they already have waiting in place for when the *change* comes).

*It might be okay to contemplate the genetic engineering of **super bodies, super immune systems, super strength, even super intelligence**, but the genetic engineering of **super-powers** such as **mind-reading, telepathy, clairvoyance or PK**, well, this will be another matter, so much so that its parameters almost surely will be dealt with **in deepest secrecy**.*

We do know that human beings possess an array of sensory faculties that are mostly not used consciously. The Transhumanist scientists are aware of these and have set out to activate them artificially in their chosen subjects:

*Indeed, neurobiologists have already discovered many different kinds of **sensory receptors** [in human beings] as well as a number of receptors for which no function is recognizable so far. **Also, certain DNA-sequencing has been discovered for which no functional correlation is recognizable**.*

The future Illuminati *autocracy* will create the principle mode of civilization on earth alongside their *alien/human hybrid* extraterrestrial partners and *interdimensional handlers*. Part of the problem in understanding this reality is the fact that it sounds so much like comic book fantasy or science fiction. In the enormously important book entitled *The Threat* by *Dr. David Jacobs*, some people who have been abducted by the Grey aliens report that they have witnessed *hybrid alien children* who displayed extraordinary *super-powers* of *telekinesis* and *telepathy*. The Grey aliens have been breeding hybrids that can manipulate normal human beings in the most extraordinary ways. This speaks volumes about the future to come when human beings will have to confront this threat to our very survival. The natural abilities that humans are supposed to realize through conscious and methodical development on earth over time will be *brought forward* by genetic engineering to manifest in the hands of some of the most evil people on earth.

The *psychic super-powers* are a natural part of the *consciousness technology* of the human mind. Secretly, the mapping of the human genome by *Illuminati sponsored scientists* is geared toward the development of human super powers in selected individuals and groups of Illuminati affiliates. The development and application of genetic technology that will assist in the enhancement of human sensory faculties to *project* psychic abilities and 'super-powers' is a conscious and expressed endeavor of the new World Order conspirators.

Within the African Tradition for thousands of years human beings have employed the super-power capabilities of the human mind. On deeper analysis this is essentially what *African magic* really entails and indeed the *shamanic traditions* of the world's indigenous cultures. Through a process of initiation, meditation and various mental disciplines, a human being can *naturally* activate the super-powers of the mind and this is attested to by numerous African spiritualists and masters of mental sciences all across Africa, Jamaica and many other places. Within the Indian *Vedic* culture and *Tibetan Buddhist* tradition these things are outlined very clearly. The process of spiritual initiation is designed to separate the egotistical and negative elements who might wish to use these powers for selfish (*service-to-self*) or evil purposes. The predatory alien controllers of the Babylon System are applying these principles right now as a means to consolidate their powers on earth. The breeding of *'super-soldiers'* and armies of *'sensitives'* and *psychics* is intended to extend their power base and allow them to finally take complete control of human development and the direction of human evolution. *This is the real nature of the future being established right now, whether one chooses to believe it or not.* The future alien/human hybrid will represent the labour of thousands of years of alien genetic experimentation upon selected human bloodlines that will eventually facilitate the conjoining of extra-dimensional forces in our time/space reality.

'For we fight not flesh and blood but powers and principalities'

-The Holy Bible -

The real dark side to the Illuminati's incredible plans is what we call the *Alien* or *Extraterrestrial Agenda*. This can sometimes be the most misunderstood and confusing part of the New World Order conspiracy. Presently, there is much material emerging about this so I urge the reader to find pertinent information wherever possible. It's crucial to our survival to learn as much about these things as we can now. Forewarned is forearmed.

The alien agenda will become the most important part of the future for us all and we need to be armed with clear information. Use the Internet while it is still there. Join discussion groups and forums. Buy and read books about these topics. Analyze information and think for yourself. Above all do not be fooled by what you read or see in the media, TV, magazines and newspapers. Recently the United Nations appointed an *ambassador* who will represent humanity in the eventuality of alien beings coming to earth in the near future. This is a most telling occurrence. *Why would the United Nations spend money appointing someone to act as earth's ambassador to an alien nation when we are constantly told that aliens don't exist?*

The negative forces that the *Illuminati* represent are the guiding hands behind the destruction, suffering and horror we have all been experiencing on planet earth. The Illuminati is led by a completely evil Luciferic/Satanic energy that is attempting to subvert the natural evolutionary impulses of human beings. *This is their God* and it is this that motivates their incredible ambitions. Essentially they want to bring the world to its knees by creating a scenario predicted in the Christian Bible called *Armageddon.* They believe that if they stage manage a series of *apocalyptic events* that creates panic and mayhem on earth they will be able to assume total authority over us all and their God, Lucifer/Satan, or whatever they choose to call it will manifest on earth in some manner to reign over the world.

Many millions of people across the world over the past sixty years or so have witnessed the movements of unidentified flying objects (UFOs) in the skies. This phenomenon has been dismissed (publicly) by most governments as *mass hallucinations* or mistaken sighting of weather balloons, aircraft, flocks of birds and so on. Behind the scenes there are governmental agencies that have been studying this phenomenon and compiling masses of data on the subject of UFOs. What we can discern from decades of research is the fact that UFOs are without doubt a very real phenomenon and the governments of most developed countries are not only interested in it but are very complicit in hiding the real information about the existence of *extraterrestrial* or *alien* life-forms and the fact that they have been *'visiting'* the earth for many thousands of years. The alien question impacts dramatically upon our understanding of the Babylon System and the Illuminati agenda.

There have been hundreds of thousands of reports across the world of people being abducted by various different alien beings. These abductions almost always result in the removal of *sperm* and *egg samples* from human beings during a physical and psychological medical examination. The human beings are always tagged with some sort of tracking device implanted in the body and returned to their usual activities. The enormity of this problem cannot be understated and research has shown that perhaps in actuality many millions of people in America alone have been abducted and treated in this manner. Pertinent research has also shown that a secret human cabal (*black ops*) aligned to the Illuminati and factions of the *military complex* (MILAB) have been carrying out abductions of specific humans for similar purposes. The shadow government of the Babylon System has been carrying out secret genetic research on countless innocent human victims for at least three decades in underground facilities.

The main groups of alien beings in question are the same types that appear to have been very much involved with the genetic manipulation of the human race many thousands of years ago: the *Grey,* and the *Tall Blonds* or *Nordics* that look similar to white Europeans (particularly blond haired Scandinavians) and the *Reptilian* faction that appear to be the aligned with elements of the Grey Alien faction. To date it is estimated that over *two hundred and fifty* different alien races have been catalogued by the Euro/American secret government apparatus. It appears that a great deal of *disinformation* is dispensed out by these beings so that nobody truly know who or what they are, where they come from and what their agenda might be on earth. It is known that for several decades (in our perception of time) the alien inter-dimensionals (particularly Greys and Nordic hybrids) have been conducting a *breeding program* using abducted human beings and advanced genetic procedures. Many *abductees* have reported in recent years that the *hybrids* (alien/human) cross breeds have also been active in the abduction and experimentation on human beings. The breeding program is designed to create a race of human-looking aliens that can blend successfully into our society without anyone noticing the difference in their appearance. Research clearly shows that these hybrid alien/humans are presently *interfacing* within our societies and in the near future will take over the reigns of power on governmental levels. It is believed that there are contingents of alien/human hybrids operating secretly within several government departments in Euro/American societies. There are many influential people who are attempting to get information out to the public so that we can be aware of these things.

What is certain is that the alien agenda is integral to the operations of the *Babylon System* and we need to prepare our minds to confront this reality in whatever manner it will manifest in the very near future. When we analyze specific historical data from various cultures, we come to realize that this alien agenda is a continuation of the same principles of alien manipulation and control that the ancient *Book of Enoch* described in such vivid details and that the African Mystery Systems explains clearly. The *same* types, Nordic/Reptilian and Greys from our ancient past are still actively involved in the manipulation of humanity even today. As I have explained, *time* and dimensional structures are not what we think they are and can be manipulated by beings that possess the technology to do so.

These beings are really *inter-dimensional intelligences* that are able to manifest (mentally and physically) within the human world and affect our physical and mental nature in time and space. Some of these inter-dimensional entities can also manifest as *viral, parasitic thought forms* that *infest* the human mind and affect the consciousness faculties without manifesting in physical space/time. It must be remembered that in order to understand this phenomenon we must first become cognizant of the way in which *time* and *space* and particularly dimensional structures operate. *Frequency* is the key to understanding this. Just as you would turn the dial of your *radio* or TV from one station to another to *tune into the frequency* that the station is *broadcasting*, so we can mentally/psychically tune into the different dimensional spaces that exist all around us. Human beings can tune into many other dimensional frequencies and, using the natural consciousness faculties we possess, perceive varying different strata of reality. Certain animals such as cats and dogs are able to perceive specific frequency ranges that are inaudible to human beings. An example is when a cat might be disturbed by something that we cannot see or hear. That animal perceives something that is of a different frequency and reacts to it. In Jamaica sometimes a person might say they experience their *'head raise'* because they encountered some force or presence (such as a *duppy*) that is not visible to the naked eyes yet can be *'felt'* on a psychic level. Many people in Euro/America who experiment with drugs such as *LSD* and *MDM, Mushrooms* and so on, report being able to perceive completely different and new dimensional realities where they encounter various strange beings, environments and situations that appear quite real to their senses.

Human history shows clearly that through the ritualistic use of drugs and ritual magic, contact with inter-dimensional entities can and has been made. This is one of the secrets behind such organizations as the feared *DeLawrence* secret society in Jamaica and various unsavory lodges and so on that spiritually corrupt and enslave the minds of ignorant people in abominable evil. In fact these things have played one of the key parts in the development of human societies for a very long time and the secret agenda of the Illuminati bloodlines on earth.

Researcher Reginald Crosley describes [aspects of] Haitian *VoDou* in terms of *Quantum Physics* using physics models that are currently conventional and fashionable, saying, for example:

*'... According to some new theories developed by subatomic physicists, we may be sharing our [visible] reality with **another plane made up of invisible intangible shadow matter** or **dark matter** operating in at least **ten dimensions**.*

*The entities of the shadow world crave for the actions of ordinary reality. Thus, they enter into some connection with earthlings. **Vodouns are spiritual entities**, or **shadow-matter entities** that have had a long commerce or interaction with human beings. Some would be the shadow-matter component of human beings [which have] basic constituents...*

- *the visible body or corp-cadavre.*
- *the semedo - Gros Bon Ange - a duplicate of the person in shadow matter.*
- *the selido - Ti Bon Ange - a psychic parcel coming from Mawu, the Creator. ... At death, it returns to Mawu ... It does not receive any reward or punishment. **It is in itself a network of information.***
- *sekpoli - most likely a shadow entity, a vodoun, that enters into composite state with an individual through Fa initiation'.*

What follows might seem strange and unpalatable to some but is absolutely necessary to greater understanding of the human condition. Whether one calls oneself Rasta or not, evolving knowledge is crucial to greater insight into the situation that we find ourselves in here on earth.

I cannot speak of the beginning because in actuality there is no such thing as a beginning as we might understand it. The African Knowledge Tradition as elaborated by many priests and priestesses of the Ancient Mystery System and the *Knowledge Keepers* within the shamanic tradition tells us that we exist within a *nine* dimensional structure. There are also many other dimensional structures beyond these that can be accessed using specific forms of *'higher dimensional technologies'*.

The physical universe we know is just one very small part of wider structures, the *multi-verse*. The multi-verse is composed of many different structures of varying *'densities'* and vibrational qualities we refer to as dimensions. Some spatial and dimensional structures operate within the context of an energy array we refer to as *time,* which is crucial in the ***continuously unfolding chain reaction*** that creates what we perceive as *space*. There are other dimensional structures that use other forms of *energetics* apart from time and space to function. Time is a variable and malleable (*plastic*) medium/energy and can be manipulated as much as space and dimensional formats. It can be stopped, altered, changed and redirected in various ways. Science in the near future will demonstrate these principles clearly. There are many dimensions in existence that functions on different aspects of energy *vibrational* laws. All this is in actuality part of the most incredible, unimaginably complex *'System' which I referred to as the Creation Field*. *This aspect to our existence must not be misconstrued with the basic holographic technologies that humans have been trying to create in laboratories or the explanations offered by emerging holographic theories; this is by far a more superior and mentally challenging perspective*. Euro/American sciences such as *String Theory, Quantum Physics, Chaos Theory* and *Fractal Science* have tentatively touched on the edges of this knowledge that our African forebears knew very well and used to a high degree, *but from a very different perspective.* This is absolutely *crucial* when trying to understand the dynamics, knowledge and perception of what's really going on.

There are infinite ways and means of mental perception but not an infinity of *physical* space time. The term infinity (in the way we apply it) is a misnomer as our present *perception* of reality is constrained by a basic dualistic mode of understanding. There is not an infinity of physical realms but *infinite possibilities of 'mental movement'*. Existent nature as we know it, is in all respects a *'type'* of holographic projection that uses the technology of consciousness (unified within the matrix array of all life forms) as a medium to *'collapse down'*, *translate* and *manifest* through time, space and dimensional energies. (Incidentally, the theoretical and practical basis of the *African Ifa Oracle* system is linked to this field of knowledge in ways that are utterly remarkable).

All living creatures, big or small, are linked energetically and consciously to the process of creation, which is a continuous paradigm. Everything operates through the *unified field* of our minds and consciousness perceptions; (that's why killing is considered unethical and so forth). Our consciousness (which is really a technological apparatus of mind) is linked and *projected* as a 3D holographic sensory experience – (the physical universe in which we exist) – although we are not 3D beings in *origin*. Our consciousness is really a projection from our minds which creates the point of awareness that generates our recognition of this. Our minds are not just situated *inside* our bodies but are also at the same time *linked* energetically together with all other minds as a *unified field* – (allusion to the ONELOVE) – which transcends space time and dimensionality. This field energy (*mind*) uses biological vessels as *interfacing* mechanisms to experience the existence of our '*collective consensual experiences*' (allusions to West African Yoruba/Igbo spiritualism and ancient knowledge of creation). It's very much like an astronaut wearing a space suit to experience outer space. Our souls/ spirits are *crucial* to our ability to participate and link into this process. Without soul a being has no reality beyond the illusions of the Babylon System. Because we have souls we are really transcendent to the effects of all illusions. Soul is our key through the gateway to *eternity* – our link with The Creator. *Don't sell it.*

There are different dimensional formats in which we can use varying densities of bodies to experience them. As an example, 4D existence requires '*bodies*' that are of what we term *etheric nature* – less dense than 3D. 5D vessels are less dense than 4D vessels due to the type of vibrational quality of space time that governs that particular structure and so on. When human beings die, most of us phase *through* the etheric plane, (which is purported to be situated between our physical 3D and the 4D planes and forms the *barrier* between dimensions) and into 4D existence, while others (the spiritually elevated and so on) move into 5th, 6th and even 7th Dimensional and beyond. There are also many different levels of 4D existence just as there are many different levels or grades of living in our physical 3D universe; different planets, countries, perception of personality, being and so on. There are also -1D, -2D, -3D and -4D structures and so on. It's just that due to the multifaceted structure of these things, words and their limited meaning can at times become impediments to greater explanation. Here in Jamaica we refer to spiritual forces such as *duppy* (the spirit manifestation of a deceased person – ghost). We still hold firmly to the belief that when a person dies their spiritual *essence* live on and can affect the living in some ways; this is actually true to certain extents.

When white Europeans encountered black African spiritual cultures they poured scorn on what appeared to be superstitious belief systems, not knowing of the deep rooted knowledge of multi-dimensional space time existence that our African forebears were well acquainted with through the ancient Mystery Schools and Secret Societies of Africa. The same can be said for the animal-headed images of the Gods in our ancient Kemet/Nubia/Kushite civilizations wherein these images were used by our Ancestors with the explicit knowledge that they were not worshiping idols but accessing the mental/spiritual energetic *Creation Field* (what has been referred to as the *Demiurge* in ancient Egyptian and later Greek spiritual systems) via specific mental mediums. Our ancient ancestors were well versed in the various techniques of *spiritual technologies* that enabled them to establish successful civilizations on earth that lasted countless thousand of years. This knowledge appeared inscrutable when viewed through the prism of the white European *'consensus reality program'* and was therefore labeled *'primitivism'*. The systematic destruction of African cultures was (and still is) a *deliberate tactic* by the controllers of the *Babylon System* to subvert ancient black spiritual knowledge and replace it with their version of *'altered'* Christianity. Africans were taught by white Europeans to become afraid of their own very powerful spiritual systems, referring to the Obeah system as *black magic*, Vodou as evil and so on. *They used us to subvert and destroy our own spirituality*, our true connection to the divine principle of Creation, thus locking our minds securely into the mind controlling Babylon System. *Racism, slavery* and *colonization* were used as multiple-pronged *weapons* to attack and destroy black and indigenous spiritual cultures, which on hindsight is the conveyer of powerful ancient *'spiritual technologies'* that can assist in freeing humanity from the Babylon System and the inter-dimensional alien/demonic predators. The *Fire Meditation* expressly shows that racism was created as a tool to manipulate and control specific groups of human beings; (allusions to *biblical scriptures* that clearly explain the nature of this paradigm – the segregation of specific *gene-lines* for *breeding* and *monitoring* purposes and so on).

When Europeans analyzed *spiritual* African art they unwittingly assumed that the various styles across the continent were indicative of a primitive people, not knowing that the African artist and thing made were connected to multi-dimensional perspectives. Words like *primitive* and *abstract* were used to downplay the relevance and power of this art form. The artist Pablo Picasso was able to tap into the psychic and metaphysical energies that spiritual African art forms can naturally induce, and created a *conscious dynamic* that made him one of the western world's greatest artists. There was no guess work there. He understood what he was doing.
A sculptural form in the eyes of an African was not really an attempt at a physical likeness but a potent testament to an *'energy principle'* that bridged time, space and dimensions. Spiritual art in the African sense could really be seen as a *hybridized 4D technological apparatus* that functioned on multi-dimensions through healing, connecting with *archetypal* and *Ancestral* spiritual forces, countering evil forces, maintaining balance with the earth and its life-forms and so on; *4D techniques for 3D applications*.

Everywhere across the world indigenous cultures used these forms of what is, to all intents and purposes, multi-dimensional technologies successfully to guard against, and even in some cases, do battle with the predatory alien/demonic forces. The development of systems of *magic, rituals, initiation* and *occult* knowledge outlines this principle clearly. These systems were deliberately *subverted* by Europeans wherever they came into contact with them. The Babylon System made us believe that this knowledge was primitive and therefore inferior and could not possibly constitute *true technology*. The negative predatory forces had to institute varying aspects of the Babylon System as a counter measure to *interrupt* and *corrupt* this technology's effects on blocking them from *preying upon humans*. Unlike our present perception of nuts and bolts technology, multi-dimensional technology relies on the *mentality* and *spirituality* of the individual, group or community to *activate* it. Originally that's where the idea of *'positive'* African Magic or Voudou came into play in very ancient times, and here in Jamaica the *original* Obeah system brought to Jamaica by our learned African ancestors during the times of slavery.

Across the world the shamanic culture of the Native American nations, the Native Australian nations, Asian and South American/Amerindians explains this reality clearly. These ancient spiritual traditions were very sophisticated *instruments* and pertain to the real nature of human development and evolution. The Pyramids of Giza, Stonehenge and certain megalithic structures are all manifestations and forms of hybrid-4D technological apparatus, which I referred to as the ancient *Technomagic*. These things might sometimes appear difficult to understand outside the consensus reality in which we exist because the Babylon System mind control program *superimposed* on our consciousness faculties clouds our perception of their purpose and function.

Unfortunately the predators have tried, to varying degrees of success, to eradicate this knowledge from the world through the mind control program of *racism* and *oppression* against the various tribal cultures that preserved this technology – the more ancient branches of humanity. It's this same ancient knowledge of *spiritual technology* that the predators successfully subverted and eradicated in specific branches of *European tribal cultures* through various means of manipulation (especially on a genetic level) which saw the rise of rapid and aggressive conquest of Europe by Rome and later the Roman Catholic Church. The destruction of the ancient tribal spiritual systems (*Pagan*) - *witch burning*, the *inquisitions* and the calculated systemic oppression and *subversion and control* of women (who hold the genetic/breeding capabilities of the human species and largely the *keys* to the spiritual heart of the European tribal nations in ancient times) were all parts of the methods to divest *white peoples* of their natural, traditional spiritual heritage so that they would be easier to control. The ancient *Pagan* spiritual traditions of white European tribes were deliberately and systematically *sabotaged* and destroyed by the Babylon System and its agents such as the emperor *Charlemagne* who massacred in cold blood hundreds of thousands of European tribal peoples who refused to be subjugated and converted to the religion of the Roman Church. It's a curious fact that many churches in Britain and Europe were built on the sites of worship of the ancient spiritual systems (*ley lines* and the *geomantic earth energy-grids*) as a means of tapping into and consciously subverting the spiritual energies of the white nations of Europe.

Within the space time dimensions, life forms take seed and expand as sentient awareness. Essentially there are no separate little sparks of energy that we can call individual selves but an *energy field* that perceives and interacts with the holographic projections of the Creation Field in such a way as to simulate individuated existence. We are all together, (in *Reality*) unified energy perceiving this actuality from unique *'soul perspectives'* no matter the nature of the dimension or space time we inhabit. *Individuality* and *freedom* or *freewill* for naturally created beings exist and is very crucial and necessary determinatives to our perception and development within creation. These principles are at the very foundation of our existence and are crucial aspects of why we exist in the way that we do, albeit our understanding of the terms is not yet evolved to allow us greater functionality.

Essentially, all existence is the manifestation of energy by a source, The Creator, that is not really, or more to the point, cannot be known to human beings *objectively* because creation is an interactive structure that relies on our conscious, subjective participation. Some specific groups of alien predators cannot understand our *subjective* view of existence because they are not natural creations but artificially generated beings and forms that are purely products of material nature, no matter the formidable *intelligence* they might at times appear to exhibit. Machines can display astonishing intelligence but are not true living beings.

We refer to the source of Creation as *God* in religious or spiritual terms. As Rastafarians, we hail the Source of all existence as *Jah Rastafari, The Creator* and the *Limitless Field of Potentialities*. The Creator does not exist as a physical being as we would understand it but an energetic *presence* or *reality* that continually creates life through the *mystic agency* of the *Creation Field*. The Creation Field is multi-versal and multi-dimensional and essentially has the *potential* to be infinite in its relationship with mind in its extended form. It exists within *infinity* (as everything else does) which is the basis of what we could term *Absolute Reality*. Absolute Reality is only a working framework and does not necessarily mean what it says but can only imply by the use of human language the *inexpressible* nature of the *Supreme Being, God*; that which is the *Illimitable Power of All Creation*.

Within the dimensions of being there are countless energetic life forms that are constantly being issued into existence through the agency of the Creation Field. The Creation Field is the ground of experience for all sentient life. What we term evolution is merely a process by which beings experience sensory worlds and existences and learn and develop through a process of *consciousness extension, exploration* and *knowledge creation through the tripartite resonance wave (Ifa Wave) – time, space and dimensional formats.* It's crucial to understand that knowledge in its purest sense is also a subtle form of *energy* that nourishes us. That's why the elite has corrupted and hidden the knowledge of our true state of being. If we don't know who and what we are, we will be forever trapped in the Babylon System.

Within the context of the science of the *Creation Field* (what has been erroneously referred to as the holographic theory of space/time), the dimensions of being are separated on energetic and vibrational levels only. Specific vibrational patterns of energies create the set matrix structure for each dimension. Probably the easiest way to understand this is to use the idea of densities such as *oil* and *water*. They're both liquids but due to their different *vibrational qualities* they remain separate even if they are put together into the same container. Or perhaps something like air which is composed of several different elements such as oxygen, nitrogen, argon, carbon dioxide and other gases, but it functions as, and we perceive it as a singular thing – air. We (our minds) *'collapse'* and *'translate'* the *sub-quantum energies* of space/time into usable frameworks and reference points to navigate through our perceived reality. Because of the nature of *subtle energies* involved in this process we conceive of it as holographic, *although it (being energy form) actually has its own reality beyond our sensory perceptions*.

We live in 3D and interpenetrating our realm is 4D existence but we cannot physically see this with our eyes due to the energetic vibrational quality of each realm. With specific technology such as powerful *psychic abilities* coupled with *high quantum science* we can very much discern the nature of 4D existence. When we dream at night we actually slip into a *level* of 4D existence. We are able to behave similar to the way we do when we are awake but without our physical bodies. Sometimes when we wake up we might think how real our dreams seemed. 4D existence is similar to this in many ways but with a greater degree of conscious awareness and control over ones thoughts and actions.   If beings from 4D space time enter our 3D space time we tend to perceive them sometimes as subtle energy vibrations or emotional and psychic perturbations, ghostly apparitions and increasingly, due to our evolving perception of wider knowledge these days, as aliens in UFOs. The UFO phenomenon is very much rooted in 4D and 5D space/time, (current research indicates that it extends far *deeper* than that in space/time). Our consciousness shapes the appearance of their manifestation in our world. *These energies function on the level of archetypes, where thought and imagination have the greatest effects in relaying and manifesting the paradigm of reality that we subscribe to, according to our knowledge base. The more our knowledge base develops, the more we are able to perceive these things as a physical or outer/external reality.*

Just like we have planets on which we live in our physical 3D universe, so too there are '*spheres* or *zones of habitation*' in 4D space where various beings live and operate. Beyond that there are 5th, 6th and 7th Dimensional formats through to the 12th and so on. It's mainly from the higher dimensions (5th, 6th and 7th) that the greater part of the cosmic war is taking place. Most beings are '*created*' from specific templates and therefore experience awareness from similar points of view although this might not be apparent at first. 4D beings aspire to similar things as 3D beings or even 5D beings for that matter; it's all a matter of perspectives from which beings perceive existent nature. The 5th and 6th dimensional life-forms that appear to be running the show in our world are highly evolved, non-physical beings that have access to vast knowledge and power. They have developed the ability to function across space/time and appear as gods in their manner and aspect of power.

Much of the mythologies and spiritual teachings of human societies, specifically the ancient African/Kemetic/Egyptian, Hindu (Vedic) and the Mahayana Buddhist groups, reflect the structure and nature of the Creation Field's origins, the interdimensional manipulations of these multidimensional evolved beings and our destiny within it all. As explained in previous chapters some of the ancient 'Gods' of earth were actually warring interstellar and interdimensional beings who used *hybridized 4D technology* to interface with our 3D existence and are still affecting us as a species even today. This explains much of the anomalies that surround human existence on earth. The characteristics of ancient Gods; religion and worship/praying (which is really the *channeling* of mental/spiritual energy through multi-dimensional space/time) all point to the interaction of humans on earth with these inscrutable extraterrestrials and interdimensional 4D and 5D beings.

Human society is going through tremendous changes (and has been doing so constantly for thousands of years) on many levels because of the constant manipulation of the Babylon System by specific groups of extraterrestrials and interdimensionals and the *Illuminati* group on earth. As I have pointed out, one of the major clues to understanding this principle is *time*. Because the *technology* to manipulate or *slide* through time has been mastered by various groups of beings (some opposed to human freedom and development) we are mostly not able to perceive this reality with sufficient degrees of clarity. An '*element*' can be sent back through time to be discovered at a specific *temporal-junction*. The *cognizing* of that element then creates the *catalyst* for specific mental *shifts* and subtle changes in perception about the past in relation to what we view as the future. This creates an energy dynamic that manifests between that which is observed and the observers mentality. Time manipulation affects the Babylon System matrix in ways that create subtle changes, perturbations and alterations to any given perception paradigm; specific events and scenarios are played out in what appear as *'real time scenarios'* yet we are unaware of the subtle affects of temporal *alterations* and *adjustments* at specific *junctures* because of our *sensory deprived* states and the constant bombardment of the negative consensus reality forming *'viruses'* that affect our mental processing faculties. How many of us can remember all the details of our lives clearly? Time, in the manner we understand it, is really an energy field that operates within the context of our consciousness faculties on a quantum level. This assist us in creating *mental constructs* moment-to-moment, and like all mental constructs can be changed, altered and rechanneled and we wouldn't know the difference in our lives. This is one of the highest forms of mind control. The beings, Reptilian/Grey/Nordic alliances, who affected our ancient past and who appeared as gods to ancient human beings, possess very sophisticated and advanced *time manipulation technologies* and are able to move into and through our linear past at will, affect changes and move out again. We perceive specific changes over what appear to us as hundreds or thousands of years while for them, mere minutes, hours or days have passed. That is why the *hybrid bloodline* scenario can be easily explained and understood as a very credible and actual phenomenon. *Time is one of the great keys*.

There is a war going on that human beings have been completely unaware of. This war has been conducted by multiple predatory inter-dimensional forces ever since human beings first entered this earth space/time reality in prehistoric times. A predator hunts to find sustenance. A world so lush and teeming with sentience isn't going to go unnoticed for very long by an *advanced, intelligent, extra-dimensional, predatory life-form*. Much like we humans farm animals such as sheep, cattle and chickens for food so too are we being herded as food source by forces that lies beyond our material perceptions. *Make no mistake; the food chain here on earth does not end with human beings.* Food isn't just about physical nourishment for our bodies; various demonic entities feed on specific forms of *etheric, emotional* and *psycho-physical energy* as food; our history on earth and the occult traditions of various cultures speaks eloquently of these things. The Babylon System is the *farmyard* upon which we are all kept locked in cages, mentally and spiritually. Just as chickens, cattle and sheep cannot rationalize the mechanics of farming and the structure and purpose of an abattoir, so too we cannot rationalize the nature of our inter-dimensional predators and the true nature of our mental and spiritual prison. The negative entities that afflict the human race are very real. Our human spiritual and mythological traditions have always made these things very clear and this knowledge when understood in its proper context can expand our consciousness faculties greatly.

One of the most pronounced aspects of this is the **Grey aliens** or simply the **Greys**. Many researchers in this field of knowledge have now realized the extent of the Grey's interaction with human beings through time and the dire portent that that has for the future of the human race.

What can be deduced from the bodies of information that's been flooding out about these creatures is that the Greys are not actually living beings like humans but artificially cloned cybernetic life-forms that are pursuing a breeding program that will culminate in the **assimilation** of the human being and the **phasing out** of the human race as we know it. The Nazi ideology of the Aryan super race of the future is very much **embedded** within the paradigm of the breeding program of these predators. They have been guiding the program of racialism (among other anomalies) that informs human culture over what appear as vast periods of time.

The abduction of humans, experimentation with human sperm and eggs; the presence of hybrid **human/grey beings,** (pertinent data shows that there are a number of Grey **hybrids** operating in various fields of the secretive intelligence services such as the **CIA** and what is referred to as **Black OPs**) and the continuing hostile behaviour of Grey aliens themselves now points to inescapable and chilling facts; humanity is at war with a predatory force that intends to take control of the earth and phase out the human race in its present form, completely. The **bloodline Illuminati** faction on earth has been an intrinsic part of the agenda for thousands of years. The Greys (along with various factions of negative inter-dimensional **Nordics** and **Reptilians**) have been covertly and expertly manipulating the Illuminati hierarchy to implement the coming New World Order on earth.

The part the Nordic/Reptilians play presently is, to some degree, uncertain but what we do know is that they are among the principle groups of predators that have been manipulating human beings. The Reptilians have been very active in human affairs on earth for hundreds of thousands of years and have been instrumental in the process of enslaving humanity. The biblical book of **Genesis** and the **serpent** mythologies of various cultures such as the Mayans, Chinese, ancient Egyptians, Indians and Europeans allude clearly to the multidimensional Reptilian operations on earth. The author **David Icke** explains this scenario perfectly in his many volumes (**The Robot's Rebellion, Children of the Matrix** etc). These books, among many others, are crucial reading material in order to get a greater understanding of the situation. There are several different Nordic groups that are **positive,** enlightened beings and who have been assisting the human race in various ways over thousands of years.

The **analytic mode** of the **Fire Meditation** has clearly shown a scenario of alien beings appearing on earth openly in the **very near future** at a time when some form of biological, nuclear warfare or apocalyptic scenario has taken place. The world will come to a stand still. No airplanes will fly and humans will exhibit great fear. There are some who believe that the Illuminati will be the guiding hand behind this scenario to promote a false flag alien invasion in order to consolidate their ambitions of a one world government and a New World Order however, analysis has clearly shown the *alien* agenda as the guiding principle behind all that will occur.

The multi-pronged attack (by our inter-dimensional predators) involved attempts to split the human psyche, or fracture it, so that we develop a type of group **schizophrenia**; *thus the original God-consciousness we once used as our navigation tool became inextricably confused with the manipulations of our predators. This can be seen quite clearly in the western philosophical perspective that has overwhelmed the African spiritual and philosophical perspectives. It's there, in* **black** *and* **white**.

-The Golden Path of Jah Rastafari-

The African Knowledge Tradition clearly and unambiguously explains the multi-dimensional nature of our perceived reality and the various forces that exist in our reality paradigm. The shamanic/Obeah/Healer traditions in African cultures were *consciously created* as ways to prevent negative extra-dimensional forces from subverting human development and evolution. Through the process of continuous (mostly hereditary) secret initiations, new *'spirit warriors'* were always created to protect the environments, communities and the earth from being overrun by these negative forces. The Native American peoples also were very key instruments in this process until the white Europeans destroyed much of their ancient traditions and hence their *spiritual technologies* – (Just like the Illuminati bloodlines, there exists a *spirit-line* of *Spiritual Warriors* who incarnate on earth at specific junctures in time. We are never alone in the struggle). What we nowadays refer to as the *Rastafarian spiritual tradition* has been an important *thread* in this multi-dimensional tapestry for many thousands of years in various different guises.

According to the perspective of Rastafari, the *Rasta Fire-Warriors* are among the incarnations of this principle in our time, their purpose being to defend the Creation Field of Jah Rastafari. As The Sublime Prophet, *Peter Tosh* once explained most eloquently: *"Jah Rastafari put the Rastaman here to be the defender of the universe".* The advent of Rastafari and its musical expressions (*sound/rhythm/vibration – word/sound/power principles*) holds much vital clues in terms of the nature of the type of spiritual *warfare* that is being waged on a *multi-dimensional level*.

A high percentage of indigenous tribal populations of the earth are the descendents of remnants of the last *overt* ancient inter-dimensional wars that devastated the Early Global Civilizations of earth; Africans, Native American, indigenous South American, Polynesian and Australian Aboriginals peoples and so on.

The seriousness of the situation on earth over time warranted the tradition of secrecy among *'spirit-warrior'* initiates, as negative multi-dimensional *agents* were always able to infiltrate and impede human development, specifically through the religious establishments.

The last great battle recorded with negative inter-dimensionals occurred around the end of the last Ice Age civilization, in the time of *Enoch the Ethiopian,* (the grand father of Noah) who outlined these scenarios explicitly in the biblical *Apocryphal Book of Enoch* quoted in previous chapters. This particular book was conspicuously left out of the bible by the early church censors. A discerning read of it will make it clear why this was done; (there have been various overt and covert skirmishes with the alien predators over the past several thousand years since the time of Enoch).

It was after this time that human beings *'training manual'* in the arts of spiritual/inter-dimensional *warfare* (spiritualism, religions, holy scriptures, magic and rituals) was upgraded in order to protect our particular path of evolution on earth. Specific forms of *Ancient knowledge systems*, *esoteric/occult initiations* and *Religious scriptures* began to appear in places like Egypt, the Indus Valley civilizations and later Asia/Pacific cultures; the *Egyptian Book of the Great Awakening*, *The Bhagavad Gita*, the *Tao Te Ching* and so on. Assistance has always been given to the human race on subtle levels. At the same time the *hybridized bloodlines* embedded within the various cultures such as Sumer, Babylon, Egypt, Greece began to infiltrate and corrupt this knowledge by propagating their particular brands of philosophies and corrupt *'spiritual doctrines'*. The *priesthoods* of these ancient cultures were targeted by the hybrid bloodline for *'hostile takeover'*. The original ancient teachings were contaminated over time just as much as the bible and many other writings were later on. One of the ways of circumventing the corruption of the original spiritual teachings was to *embed* them in a secret and obscure *oral tradition* that might not be easily understood by outsiders, (which many African cultures did), thus maintaining a sense of continuity in the knowledge base. Of course this method was not entirely fool proof and some corruption naturally occurred over time for various reasons.

Various enlightened *spirit-lines* of Ancestral humans and *Fire Warriors* constantly reincarnate at specific junctions to assist our efforts on earth, (the term human is generic to a wide range of related beings across the dimensional fields; just like we have humans of different colours here on earth so too are there many different *'human soul-related'* groups inhabiting nearby star systems such as *Sirius, Vega, Orion* and *inter-dimensional space/time* and so on). Some present Ufology literature gives indications of these things, albeit there is much deception that abounds on the internet, so tread carefully. Be discerning at all times with your information.

Unknown to most of us there are contingents of enlightened human Ancestors who inhabit *zones* in the 4D and also 5D and beyond - Buddha's, Christ's, Potent Ancestors, various Avatars and so on. These human ancestral lines of spiritual beings are continuously working to avert the worse effects of the coming upheavals that the establishing of the New World Order and the alien predators will cause and to shed more light upon the dark forces aligned against our evolution. Certain *'pure-line'* Buddhists and Vedic (Hindu) are among groups of positive human related beings who are operating on the multi-dimensional level to protect human interests on earth; specific reincarnated lamas, Native American and African shamans, tulkas, gurus and so on are consciously involved on various levels. The continuous controversy about the imprisonment in China of the reincarnated Tibetan Buddhist tulka, the *Panchan Lama,* and the *Dalai Lama's* refusal to accept a Chinese *government sanctioned* replacement as a genuine Buddhist reincarnation alludes clearly to this principle. The battlefield is truly as diverse inter-dimensionally as it is here on earth spiritually and politically. A large part of the problem seems to be that not enough Euro/American *spiritualists* have reached the necessary understanding to become decisively involved on this particular level. The controllers of the Babylon System have manipulated the spiritual heritage of the Caucasoid groups into a state of apathy and ineffective philosophical pretension in an attempt at nullifying their participation. The predators have a deep interest in specific blood-lines generated by that particular group in which it appears they invested much time and energy. The British writer *Nick Kerner* dissects this rational to some degree in his books the *Song of the Greys* and *Grey Aliens and the Harvesting of Souls*:

...the new techno-colonialism of which **Professor Greenfield** *speaks, and the fact the technological progress that makes it possible springs* **almost entirely from the Euro-Caucasian genotype**, *may well suggest this is the Grey's* **prime homozygotic group**. *In fact, this group is considered by genetic anthropologists to be the most in-bred of all. Tracing its origins to Cro-Magnon man, it's one of the most homozygotic in the world.* **As I have said, it goes without saying the most heinous forms of racism also originate from this group, again confirming the hypothesis...**
It would seem the vanguard of the new **artificial intelligence revolution** *is also the vanguard of* **racism** *and disregard for the predicament of those of a different skin colour who, as Professor Greenfield points out, don't even have clean water to drink. Thus, those who are already* **de-humanized** *seem to be those promoting further* **dehumanization**.
And so it seems that the old Master Race principle of pure white non-mixed

*superiority is the biggest canard and **self delusion** that prevails in the psyche of the Homo sapiens gene base. A dangerous and deadly delusion programmed through genetic engineering by an alien roboid form to keep our genes more easily amenable for supplementation with theirs, to thus gradually give rise to a **machine man**; a form of hybrid that is artificially composed and configured to give alien roboids **the facility to multiply through a natural birthing process.***

It has been inferred that the discovery of specific types of *'**junk DNA**'* found in the **human genome** is clear evidence of the **genetic manipulation** of groups of human beings over thousands of years on earth by the ***interdimensional predators***.

The role of **Yeshua, (Jesus Christ)** and other enlightened **human-line** beings is an interesting and crucial one in this affair. Yeshua, as a prophet, appeared and taught many people the fundamental path back to God consciousness. There is actually nothing written about the man during his lifetime, and in actual fact, there is no corroborative evidence that could substantiate his existence apart from the writings of the New Testament Gospels. The Gospels were written centuries after his death by men who did not know the historical details of his life. As we have ascertained in previous chapters, the Jesus phenomenon was not a unique one at all. There were many other messiahs and saviours who shared the exact same traits and we can therefore clearly ascertain that almost the entire story of Jesus' life was made up to fit a certain paradigm by the manipulative hybrid priesthoods who controlled religion and the ancient Mystery System at that time.   Over several centuries, many scholars affiliated with and funded by the Illuminati factions and the Roman Catholic Church have sought ways to destroy his teachings. The bible has been ***deliberately*** tampered with by being edited to the point where some people nowadays doubt its authenticity. The point is that ***conceptually***, Yeshua (or the Christ Consciousness when understood in its multi-dimensional form) can be an important element in the search for a viable method of disengaging from the mind control program of the Babylon System if understood in the correct manner. His **life**, **death** and **resurrection** were clear metaphors and **_symbols_** for spiritual development for all humanity. In fact, in his time he clearly denounced his fellow Jews who held religion in thrall to their ulterior motives of greed, money, status and power and so on. Yeshua's mission was to ***reestablish*** the ancient knowledge base of God consciousness on earth, (which he did). The multi-dimensional predatory forces (manifest in our conception as the **Luciferic/Satanic** powers) observing his pathway, could not affect him ***personally*** as he had developed a superior and transcendent perception and therefore uniquely powerful. The only way the dark forces could *'**make a comeback**'* would be to ***infect*** the message of spiritual redemption that he imparted to humanity – the ***Gospels***. This, to all intents and purposes, is what happened. The church was targeted for subversion very early in its founding. Various false doctrines were inserted into the bible while relevant chapters were taken out and many different translations were made to confuse people searching for spiritual truth. The Roman Catholic Church hierarchy was subverted through this process.

In 1302, Pope Boniface VIII (1294-1303) said: *"We declare, affirm, and define as a truth necessary for salvation that every human being is subject to the Roman Pontiff."*

The Catholic Church fell under the control of men such as *Pope Leo X* (1513-21) who during his reign proclaimed that *"all human beings must be subject to the Roman Pontiff (Pope) for salvation"*.

It is also reported that after a dinner party with a few 'loose women' and his close friends he stood with his glass of wine and proposed a toast saying: *"It has served us well, this myth of Christ"*. He also sold *indulgences* and ordered that heretics be *flayed alive, boiled in oil and burned*.

Pope Pius X (1903-14), when he was Archbishop of Venice, said: *"The Pope is not only the representative of Jesus Christ, but he is Jesus Christ himself, hidden under the veil of flesh.*

Does the Pope speak? It is Jesus Christ who speaks", (as reported in the Catholic Nationale, July 13, 1895).

If we remember that the Roman Pontiffs are the legitimate *successors* to the ancient hybridized blood-line *Roman emperors* then the shocking *blasphemy* uttered by these so-called Popes is crystal clear for any Christian to comprehend. The *'hostile take over'* of the church by these unscrupulous self styled *'Vicars of Christ'* and their insidious armies of Satanists has sullied the legacy of Christianity, (as it was intended to do). The criminality and horrendous pedophile scandals that rocked the Catholic Church in recent times are clear indicators of this principle. This is all part of the process by which the negative inter-dimensional predators hope to defeat the work of beings such as the *Christ* and positive human-aligned, spiritual energies such as *Bodhisattvas* and so on. The New World Order is being established as the *final conflict* that will bring an end to the message of the Christ and 'positive' religions as a whole, and usher in a *New Age* of *Luciferic/Satanic* rule on earth. For those who are believers in the power and works of the *Christ Consciousness*, the times ahead will bring great tribulations. As Christians, Rastas or just truth seekers these issues are very relevant to the future. It is said that Yeshua stated: *"The kingdom of God is within you"*. For discerning Christians this statement need to be understood in its true and original context. The times ahead are going to be extremely tough for Christians,

Rastafarians, Muslims, Buddhists and all people who hold genuine faith in the power of human spirituality.

In Islam, schisms between the *Sunni* and *Shia* groups are being fiercely exploited by the Illuminati to create division and conflict that will enable the corruption, decay and eventual *destruction* of Islam. The Muslim faithful though, appears very tenacious in holding on to their religious beliefs therefore an array of strategies have been employed against Islam, chief of these we are all now familiar with – the so-called *Muslim Terror Threat* and so on. Unknown to many, the Rastafarian movement also has been quietly targeted for destruction by these same forces and we are presently seeing factional infighting occurring among the different '*houses*' of Rastafari – Twelve Tribes, Bobo Ashanti, Ethiopian World federation and others. Factional infighting and tribalism are ways that the adversary tries to divide and conquer any opposition. And as we know very well, a '*house divided, cannot stand*'. Any *affiliation* between Rastafarian organizations and Illuminati controlled organizations such as the *United Nations* is completely against the principles of our movement.

As explained above, the original spiritual systems were created partly as manuals of *spiritual self-defense* and in their original forms were very sophisticated spiritual technologies bequeathed to humanity. Religions and religious books are very much misunderstood because of the web of deception thrown over us by our predators and the hybridized bloodlines that hijacked the human religious institutions over thousands of years. They are essentially '*multi-dimensional tools*' that can be very useful to human beings. That's why they've *all* been tampered with, rewritten, mistranslated and *corrupted* so as to prevent us from accessing the real knowledge they were supposed to offer. When understood and used correctly spiritual doctrines in their pure form can assist in the activation of the vast powers of the human *mind/soul matrix*. The last thing our predators want is an *informed and spiritually armed human race* with developed supernatural powers and extended consciousness faculties. The *real war* is being fought on a *multi-dimensional, supernatural* battle field and if we are armed properly we really cannot be defeated. Our predators know this.

It's the *Tradition*; the ancient, sacred spiritual knowledge of humanity developed before the *Age of Intervention* that the Illuminati and their agencies tried unsuccessfully to destroy by colonizing Africa and enslaving black Africans who consciously were the *guardians* of this knowledge from prehistoric times. Africans are the oldest branch of humanity and consequently possess the largest workable *matrix of knowledge* pertaining to our inter-dimensional struggles as a race on earth. As explained, the *oral* tradition in Africa also operates as a specific application of '*spiritual, technological encryption coding*' developed over hundreds of thousands of years to guard and preserve the ancient knowledge of our past and to warn us of coming dangers. Story telling, rituals, song, drumming and dance all act as sophisticated systems of encryption coding that kept specific knowledge safe and out of the hands of *'negative forces'* while preserving it for posterity. Thus, knowledge was passed down for thousands of years safely until needed by future generations. Crucially, the structure of human DNA also acts as an information storage facility. That is one of the main reasons why the hybridized bloodlines tend to intermarry and interbreed so frequently. This allows them to access and utilize specific forms of knowledge that is encoded within their DNA. This knowledge when accessed becomes instinctive, *'as if born to it'*. Much of this knowledge can be accessed through understanding of genetic science, which is *exactly* what the Illuminati sponsored scientific organizations of Euro/America are busy researching avidly right now.

The incredible sacred/meta-physical knowledge of the Dogon, Bambara, Zulu, Yoruba, Igbo, Mande peoples of Africa (to name but a few) that researchers are only just discovering in the 21st century are all classic examples of this paradigm. The numerous wars, famines and destabilization of Africa that we see during slavery, colonialism and in our time are not accidental but by deliberate and calculated design and indicators of the real nature of this phenomenon on a *multi-dimensional level*. When we understand racism in its true extended forms the multidimensional structures of our predicament becomes clearer. The destruction of Africa and black Africans isn't just about physical war but multi-dimensional spiritual warfare that aims to completely subvert and destroy our original evolutionary paradigm on earth. Many white people tend to reject this analysis because the mind control program usually kicks into gear causing, anger, resentment and negative reactions to these things, but it's imperative for white *brothers* and *sisters* to take on board this crucial form of knowledge and not be swayed by the mind control *ego program*. We must come to the realization that we are a unity and join together for our mutual survival and constructive development as human beings here on earth. That is our true destiny.

Most Africans are completely unaware of the potency of the ancient knowledge they carry in their DNA, only certain priests, priestesses/Shaman/Obeah man/Healer and initiates who possessed and safe guarded the spiritual/mental *'trigger mechanisms'* that activates the technology would have full disclosure of this knowledge. Deciphering the information takes a great deal of training, intuition and insight into the mechanisms of the technology not as physical hardware but *'mental and spiritual applications'* that can be activated by the human *mind* and *voice* through specific sound vibrations (*spiritual chants*), acoustic rhythmic vibrations (*specific musical notes - harmonics*), mental visualizations (*meditation*), specific meditative forms (*yoga*), and specific dances (the physical articulation and activating of mental/spiritual energies). The ancient spiritual *Tradition* in African cultures encapsulates all these processes.

A very important point to mention is that early human cultural perception was not based on the fallacies of race as we know it now, but a wider conception of our common spiritual (*multi-dimensional*) heritage. Many ancient European societies were crucial in preserving the same knowledge base as their African counterparts before they were manipulated by the negative hybrid bloodlines and overtaken by the mind control program of the Babylon System. The consensus reality paradigm of ancient humans was closely related across diverse '*racial*' groups much more than we can imagine. The ancient Druidic spiritual system of Europe is basically the same spiritual system we find in ancient African, South America and Asia. A basic reflection of this is the *mythological encoding* systems that linked specific European spiritual cultures with the ancient African Tradition. Further research in the future will undoubtedly prove the connection of the European *Rune* system to the ancient African divination system of the *Ifa Oracle,* the *Chinese I-Ching* system, the *Tarot* and *Jewish Kabalistic* systems and so on; they all emerged from the same ancient African *root*. Crucial to this, there was a divergence in understanding when the *original* Oracular system was *propagated* across various cultures through migrations that took place over time and the subtle manipulations of the negative interdimensional predators. As a consequence, certain *divergent forms* of the Oracular system became *corrupted* by its use to solicit negative and demonic multidimensional powers by those seeking to control others, (what has been referred to as the *service-to-self* factions of negative interdimensional predators and their human hosts, the hybrid elite groups). The system of the *occult* and what is referred to as *black magic* developed over thousands of years as a result of this corruption of the traditional spiritual systems by corrupt hybridized bloodline priesthoods.

The first New World Order scenario we have record of transpired in ancient Atlantis, Lemuria and Africa (what is now East Africa (Ethiopia)/Sudan), Zimbabwe, South Africa (ancient Azania) and Mesopotamia (present day Iraq). (Incidentally these areas appear to be most prone to wars, civil strife and famine and so on even today). The story of Adam and Eve, the Garden of *Eden* - Eridu - (Earth) and the alien Reptilian/Nordic faction as I have stated above is indicative of this paradigm.
After thousands of years of enslavement and manipulation by various alien factions and inter-dimensionals that infested the earth, (the *Annunaki* Nordic and Reptilians crossbreeds), the so-called alien gods left abruptly due to a great cataclysm – the *flood*. But one should ask the question, how could supposedly superior races of god-

like beings who travelled across interstellar and inter-dimensional space, genetically manipulated early human beings and dominated the earth for hundreds of thousands of years be affected by a mere flood and retreat from a hard won, prized possession? The ancient Traditions outlines that these so-called god-beings were *made* to leave the earth under threat of more damaging conflict by an *alliance* of *higher hierarchy* inter-dimensional beings, (we refer to them as the *Orishas*). Recent discoveries in genetic science clearly shows that the negatives left behind their *'genetic imprint'* or *'markers'* (specific sequences of so-called *junk DNA*) in selected human *bloodlines* – specifically the *Aryan* and a *Mongoloid* group. Scientists have been trying to ascertain the origins of some genetic markers that appear out of sync with the normal functionality of our DNA. This junk or *non-coding DNA* sequences are actually functioning parts of our genetic makeup. It's in what appear to be the non-coding sequences that the genetic manipulation of the human race occurred. This was done to *'put a wedge in the door'* so to speak. DNA is a very crucial matter in this affair. It can facilitate the *condensing* of *ultra-dimensional* life-forms into fleshy bodies and especially so if the DNA can be made to *resonate* with specific *sub-quantum frequencies* that can attune to the subtle energies of *soul frequencies*. This process alludes to what humans have commonly referred to as *demonic possession* but there are subtle differences in the way these things manifest in the physical world when it comes to demonic possession and the manipulation of spiritual energies.

Over the ages, many of the offspring of these genetically *altered bloodlines* maneuvered themselves into positions of power and influence as Caesars, Kings, Queens and *blue-blood* nobilities, eventually manifesting in our time as the Illuminati blood lines of Euro/America. The *Roman Catholic* Church and *secret societies* such as the *Freemasons* that flowered in Europe were created to foster the *'incubation'* of specific bloodlines. The psychopathic nature of many ancient rulers such as Roman Caesars also possibly lends credence to the idea that some synthetic humanoids (*synthezoids*) could have been artificially created and slipped back in time to enact specific programmed routines – Nero, Alexander 'the great', Attila the Hun, Genghis Khan and so on; (they invariably claimed some kind of connection or kinship with the gods/aliens). The *Analytic Mode* clearly shows that synthetic humanoid life-forms have in the past and recent times been used by specific groups of predators to infiltrate and manipulate human society. The reality of synthetic life-forms will impact solidly upon our future in the years to come.

This is perhaps one of the most crucial points to understand: because time is malleable and can be manipulated to significant degrees by these highly advanced inter-dimensional predators, it appears as though these events happened thousands of years ago but in actuality these things are happening through *proxy* or *altered sub-stratum* of our current timeline and is then *interwoven* or *spliced* into our current mode of perception. What might seem like thousands of years ago to us is but yesterday to multidimensional beings that are able to *slide* back and forth through time and manipulate events and *timelines*. Research in the fields of *quantum mechanics*, *String Theory* and *Quantum Many Worlds Theory* substantiates these principles.

The negative alien predators use their knowledge of *occultism*, *advanced genetics* and *multi-dimensional technology* to interface with humans (specifically *multi-generationals*) who have been *imprinted* with their DNA. It appears that it's easier for them to home in and lock onto humans with whom they share corresponding genetic and soul signatures. The Grey alien abduction scenarios we hear of in our time uses this principle.

It was at this point (at the end of the Ancient Global Civilization after the *'great flood'* and the end of Atlantis) that the ancient secret societies in Africa (Sumer, the Indus Valley) began to flourish again, culminating some time later in the Mystery Schools of ancient Egypt. The huge migrations that followed these events *dispersed* some of the black African population east towards the Nile valley, South East towards what became the ancient empire of Kush/Nubia, South and to the west, what we now know as Mali, Nigeria, Senegal, and Ghana and so on. In ancient times most Africans did not inhabit the dense, dangerous rain forest belt of the continent. A thorough survey of the Sahara Desert area will certainly show that soil analysis and the level and type of *background radioactivity* is higher and more unusual than would be expected if natural desertification had occurred. The *Gobi Desert* in Mongolia is another area that was affected in similar ways in ancient times; (in fact, there are remnants of the Ancient Global Civilization such as pyramids that will be discovered in this area in the near future). A *specific strand* of the Mongoloid/Chinese groups was hybridized by the predatory Reptilian/Grey/Nordics during Atlantean times.

This paradigm of ancient colonization, exploitation and enslavement of human beings curiously mirrors the same paradigm that the negative extraterrestrial/inter-dimensional Reptilians, Nordics and Greys are using to colonize earth and enslave the human population in our present *timeline*. This is not a trivial matter and must be seen in its proper context.

The Greys are essentially a *biological type* that are genetically engineered/cloned and gestated in vats of coloured amniotic liquid very rapidly. There's definitely an alien base on the *moon* that's used by these beings and also on several other planetary bodies in our solar system, specifically Mars and Titan (a moon of Saturn). The technology to clone or breed various life-forms is old and widespread among interstellar civilizations, both positive and negative. Specific gene-lines are considered lucrative commodities and are prized for their ability to facilitate *condensation* of ultra-dimensional beings into biological vessels and to create *synthetic humanoid life-forms,* classes of *slave races* and *food sources*. It's known that some humans have been taken from the earth to be used in experiments by various extraterrestrials and inter-dimensionals over many thousands of years.

Beyond all this is another force that remains completely hidden and disguised by this vast web of deception and inter-dimensional intrigue. Very little is known at present about its structure except to say that it appears to be the *controller* of massive events that spans *timelines* and *dimensions*. Its concerns appear to be centered not just on the enslavement of human beings and other life-forms but ultimately to do with gaining access to *manipulating* the incredible multidimensional energies of the *Creation Field* itself. This vast web of manipulation and deception is the reason why the Babylon System was put in place eons ago on earth. An important key to the understanding of this alien agenda is the *human soul*. History and mythology specifically tells of devils and demons who steal the souls of human beings. This is prevalent in every culture on earth and is clearly rooted in the relationships between humans and the parasitic interdimensional demonic predators.

All across Africa one of the things that the colonial forces and Roman Catholic *'missionaries'* did on entering was to seek out the traditional holy men/shamans/healers and mystics, catalogue their knowledge, then killing them. This has been recorded throughout many communities in Africa. This suppression of *'the knowledge'* by labeling it *superstition* was deliberately done by ruthless priests and agents of the Babylon System. In recent times such notable African shaman such as *Credo Mutwa* have been attacked, threatened and robbed of some of his ancient talisman and spiritual paraphernalia by unknown shadowy figures who oppose his revelations of ancient African spiritual knowledge and his affiliation with certain progressive anti-New World Order movements.

Most black people don't know why we have been so subjugated, oppressed and vilified for hundreds of years in western societies, even though the proof that we were the first humans and the bearers of the first and most ancient civilizations on earth to date cannot be seriously disputed anymore. Black consensus reality is obviously different from white consensus reality. The two have become opposing forces (hence black and white, night and day, positive and negative and so on). This is no accident of history. Have you ever wondered who first used the term *black* people and *white* people? How was the idea of race inserted into our reality matrix? When did this happen? Who ultimately gains from the negative interaction between black and white humans? The works of eminent thinkers such as *Dr. Francis Cress Welsing* and the

Welsing Theory, Dr. Jewel Pookrum and Dr. Neely Fuller and many other important teachers gives far reaching insight into these issues and are crucial reading that helps to elucidate these points.

The above information impacts upon Rastafari culture in that part and parcel of being a Rasta is to gather and understand knowledge from all perspectives, thus arming oneself with pertinent information at all times. Encoded in our Jamaican spiritual traditions we can glean vital aspects of the ancient knowledge of our African ancestors in the ***Kumina, Revivalist, Obeah***, and ***Poco*** spiritual systems. These ancient ***encrypted*** systems of African knowledge, (which are clearly offshoots of the ancient African Mystery System), were made illegal in Jamaica by the British colonial government and black Jamaicans were told that such things were ***evil*** and of the Devil. Even today, many brain-washed Jamaicans still believe positive Obeah, Poco, Kumina and their derivatives are bad, because the mind control of the Babylon System does not want us to activate the natural abilities of our spirits and minds.

The alien inter-dimensional threat is shatteringly real and will culminate in the very near future in a New World Order fascist dictatorship on earth and the ***genocide*** and enslavement of ***billions*** of human beings. On analysis, one can deduce the signal of ***timeline manipulation*** on a scale we cannot yet fathom. This is perhaps the most confusing and disturbing aspect of this issue. The alien agenda has been hidden from the general public in our time by a calculated web of ***deception*** so intricate as to be completely invisible to those not able to use their critical and analytic judgment. It's at the very ***beating heart*** of the Babylon System and must be understood whatever ones personal persuasion might be.

The African Universe

*The incapacity of language to embrace exactly the **contours** of the **real** is often the cause of errors in philosophical, scientific or even mathematical reasoning.*

The Sublime, Cheikh Anta Diop

-Civilization or Barbarism-

Euro/American academia tells us that European civilization is the progeny of ancient Greek civilization, which itself was supposedly the zenith of human endeavors in human social development and the acquisition of knowledge that resulted in a great explosion of philosophic and scientific learning that is still today the bench mark for human civilized values and so on. Countless volumes have been written about ancient Greek achievements; the epic of the Iliad, the Greek gods of mount Olympus and their shenanigans; the glorious wars and noble deeds of mythical warriors such as Achilles, Hector, Odysseus and Perseus and so on have been drummed into the brains of most school children. We are led to believe that the Greek 'fathers' of Euro/American civilization were somehow astonishing ***intellectual supermen*** who charted and laid bare the mysteries of the heavens and earth and the length and breath of the human psyche and the soul, imparting the exhaustive secrets found through their countless volumes of discourses. The heady wine of intellectual ***romanticism*** during eighteenth century Europe stimulated writers who painted a sweetly seductive picture of the glorious Greeks and their unparallel achievements. What they did not write about however, was the real ***origins*** of Greek culture and philosophical achievements.

Conclusive evidence exists which clearly demonstrates that the ancient Greeks were at best among the keenest ***plagiarists*** in history. There are countless, highly informative and very challenging theses such as ***Black Athena*** (volumes 1 & 2) by Martin Bernal, ***Stolen Legacy,*** by George G.M James, ***Civilization Or Barbarism?*** by Cheikh Anta Diop and many others that clearly outlines the facts that recorded history supports but which present day white academia still tries to hide from the masses. Because of the overwhelming importance of this historical paradigm, it is necessary to look at some of the issues involved and their mind-blowing implications. In his thesis, ***G.M James***

223

states:

*'The term Greek philosophy is a misnomer for there really is no such philosophy in existence. The ancient Egyptians developed a very complex religious system called the **Mysteries**, which was also the first **system of salvation**. As such it regarded the human body as a prison house of the soul, which could be liberated from its bodily impediments through the disciplines of the **Arts** and **sciences** and advance from the level of mortal to that of a God'.*

It was this system of philosophical and spiritual enquiries developed in Africa by African peoples that was commandeered by the Greeks. Even to this day we can see the same Mystery System in operation in virtually all religions such as Christianity, Hinduism, Buddhism, Islam, Roman Catholicism, and the Free Masonic and Rosicrucian cults and their offshoots. G.M James further reveals:

*'This system became the basis of all ethical concepts. The Egyptian Mystery System was also a **secret order** and membership was gained by initiation and a pledge to secrecy. After nearly 5,000 years of prohibition against the Greeks they were permitted to enter Egypt for the purpose of receiving education. First through the Persian invasion then through the invasion of Alexander 'the great'...From the sixth century B.C to the death of **Aristotle** (322 B.C) the Greeks learned all they could about Egyptian culture through the Egyptian priesthood. After Alexander invaded Egypt the royal temples and libraries were **plundered and looted** and Aristotle (**Alexander's teacher**) converted the great library at Alexandria into a research centre. **The unusually large numbers of books ascribed to Aristotle has proved a physical impossibility for any single man within a lifetime'.***

Aristotle the Greek *scientist* was a student of ***Plato*,** whom we know studied under some of the most eminent priests/teachers of Egypt in his day. Plato was initiated into the *Egyptian Mysteries* and during his tutelage in Egypt he received the story of *Atlantis*. A most telling point in this affair is history's silence on Aristotle's movements during his life time. Apparently there is no documentation of him ever visiting Egypt. George G.M James further explodes the great myth of Greek philosophical genius:

*'Aristotle is said to have spent twenty years under the tutelage of Plato who is regarded as a **philosopher**, yet he graduated as the greatest of **scientists** of antiquity... Two questions might be asked;*

- *How could Plato **teach** Aristotle **science** when he himself did not study or know these things? History categorically states that Plato was a **philosopher** not a **scientist**.*

- *Why should Aristotle spend **twenty years** under a teacher from whom he could learn nothing? ...this bit of history sounds incredible. In order to avoid suspicion over the extraordinary amounts of books Aristotle is supposed to have written, history tells us that Alexander the 'great' gave him large sums of money to get the books'*

- *In order for Aristotle to **purchase** books on science they must already have been in **circulation**.*

- *If the books were in circulation before Aristotle purchased them, **and since he is not supposed to have visited Egypt at all**, then the books in question must have been in circulation among Greek philosophers, then we would expect the subject matter of such books to have been known **before Aristotle's time**, and consequently he could not have been credited either with producing them or introducing the new ideas of science.*

The venerable African philosopher, scientist and academic **Cheikh Anta Diop**, is the author of a seminal work (**Civilization or Barbarism**) that exposes the depths of this historical fraud that has been consciously perpetrated on the world. He explains:

*Plato and Eudoxus spent **thirteen years** in Egypt in Heliopolis where the **Heliopolitan cosmogony** was born which heavily inspired Plato in **Timeus** to the extent that he reproduced whole sentences from the Egyptian texts in his work word for word without citing where the material came from, as when he wrote: **"That which became has become; that which becomes is in the process of becoming..." (Timeus, 38b).***

This is where I firmly believe Plato got his inspiration. We can relate this very easily to the ancient Egyptian Mystery System which incorporates the Egyptian Book of the Great Awakening (Egyptian Book of the Dead) chapter 17, concerning the universal God Ra:

*Speak O universal Master, he says after having become. **It is I the becoming of Khepera, when I became the becoming of those who became after my becoming**, for numerous are the desires coming out of my mouth, **when earth had not yet been formed, when the sons of the earth had not yet been made...***

*Out of the **Nun** [the **primordial essence of Potentiality**] no place was found where I could stand. I found in my heart that which would be useful to me, and in the **void** that (would serve me) as a foundation, when I was alone, when I had not begotten Shu **(air, empty space)**, when I had not yet spat out Tefnut **(water)**, when no other divinity that would have been made had not yet become. **Therefore I conceived myself in my own heart and the becoming of my numerous becomings of my becomings in the***

225

*becomings of the children, and in the becomings of their children... Says my father Nun: "They have weakened my eye (**my consciousness, my attention**) behind them since the periods that have distanced them from me [meaning the periods that have passed, during the stage of the creation of the universe in potentiality]. After having been __one__ God it is __three__ Gods that I became for myself and Shu and Tefnut came out of Nun, where they were... Shu and Tefnut gave birth to Geb (**earth**) and Nut (**the celestial heavens, space**) and Geb and Nut gave birth to **Osiris**...*

All the revealed religions of the world owe their structures of philosophical enquiries to these principles outlined in the very ancient spiritual systems. The later *Vedantic* philosophy of the sub-continent of India and *Buddhist* philosophy, which came out of it, have all in very profound ways been influenced by this ancient African school of thought; the *Baghavad-gita, Upanishad* and so on in their concise rendering of a philosophical paradigm for god consciousness and spiritual development flows through this same stream. Brahman the unmade and unformed issued the demiurge that created the universe along with other Gods and so forth. In the *Tibetan Book of the Dead* and various canonical teachings of the *Mahayana* Buddhist tradition we find parallels to this when the Buddha gave his many treatise on spiritual development:

*There is, disciples, an **unbecome and unmade and an unformed**. It is not limitless space, nor is it infinite thought...It is the ending of sorrow. Because there is an unbecome there is escape for sentient beings from this state of become.*

The doctrine of the *void, personal* and *impersonal* aspects of the Creator in Buddhism and Hinduism clearly shows parallels with Greek philosophy, which in turn is an **unmistakable derivative** of much more ancient African thought and spiritual philosophy. This is a crucial point in deeper understanding of these issues. Cheikh Anta Diop explains further that:

*If we consider the Greek school of idealism, (Plato, Aristotle, the Stoics and so on), there appears to be no essential difference with [the Egyptian school], because here too we are dealing with a barely modified Egyptian philosophy: everywhere in the **Platonic cosmogony** and in **Aristotelian metaphysics**, myth peacefully coexists with concept... Things changed radically with the **development** of the Greek **materialistic school**; the principles, the laws of natural evolution became intrinsic properties of **matter**, which no longer necessitate coupling with,(even symbolically), any **concept of divinity**. Likewise any primary cause of a divine nature is **rejected**. [According to this principle then], **the world was never created by any divinity; matter has always existed.***

[My emphasis]

These are extraordinarily crucial points. Black African societies such as ancient Egypt and ancient Kush/Nubia functioned not just on a materialistic paradigm; that was clearly unthinkable given the ***multi-dimensional*** conceptual understanding of life and its ***deliberate*** creation by a conscious ***Creator***. The materialistic structure in philosophical thought emerged purely out of Greek misrepresentation (and what could be seen as obvious and calculated dishonesty on the part of some ancient philosophers), as Anta Diop explains:

*Even though this thought was the logical development of the materialistic component of Egyptian cosmogony, it sufficiently deviated from its Egyptian model to become identifiably Greek. **Atheistic materialism is a purely Greek creation**; Egypt and the rest of black Africa seemed not to know of it. As for the sociopolitical conditions of its birth, that is another story.*

*Throughout the European Middle Ages, religious spiritualism **(the Catholic Church)** tried to accommodate itself to **Greek philosophical idealism**. But at the end of the Middle Ages scholasticism lost its vigor and the **Renaissance** inaugurated the era of Democritus, Epicurus and Lucretius: Galileo, Descartes, Kant, Newton, Leibniz, Lavoisier and so on. The modern **Atomists** were strongly inspired by this school, which in its passing on of black African thought, is largely responsible for modern science, **even if one pretends not to know this**.*

The Greeks, in their rush to elevate themselves culturally, ***changed the course of history by giving birth to a new consensus reality paradigm which overturned the God-centered philosophical paradigm of the older African cultures***. The pathological obsession by ancient Greek rulers such as Alexander of Macedonia and successive generations of Roman Caesars with being worshiped as Gods is indicative of these truths. The Egyptian pharaoh's claim to being the ***Son of God*** (in a highly symbolic/political and spiritual sense) informed this particular obsession by Greek and Roman rulers and certainly later Christianity. Ultimately it's this Atheistic materialism created by the Greeks, abstracted from African spiritual thought, which is at the heart of the Euro/American consensus reality paradigm which now propels the world into the future.

This is only the beginning of real inquiry into this tremendous ***historical deception*** and manipulation that has been cleverly perpetuated on black African peoples and consequently, the entire human race. ***Stolen Legacy, Civilization or Barbarism, Black Athena*** (volumes 1 & 2), and many other valuable works (which most libraries in Europe won't stock) are only some of the numerous volumes that systematically unravels the posturing and pretentions of an ungracious and dishonest Euro/American academia. Another point to mention, which Euro/American historians always conveniently side step, is the fact that Greek philosophers in their time were systematically *persecuted* by the Athenian state *because* they were introducing *foreign ideas* into Greece and *corrupting the youth*. These foreign ideas came from ancient Africa:

'*Anaxagoras* was imprisoned and exiled; *Socrates* was executed; *Plato* was sold into slavery and *Aristotle* was indicted and exiled, while *Pythagoras* was expelled from Croton in Italy'.

Alexander, during his rampage through Egypt, stole all the books and ancient manuscripts he could find and sent them back to Greece to his teacher Aristotle to be stacked up in his academy. After the death of Aristotle, philosophy and Greek learning swiftly *atrophied* and died out completely, perhaps on account of the fact that the Greeks really did not possess the *'natural ability to advance these sciences'* as we have been led to believe by eighteenth century European romantics.

We must remember that during the initiation process of neophytes, the Egyptian teachers placed great emphasis on the *secrecy of knowledge* and the *unwritten code* of transmission of specific and crucial information, which is typical of all African societies even today. For one who wishes to claim some form of greatness and *fame* among his compatriots, writing down and publishing the Mysteries and secret doctrines as ones own work of inspiration is a very useful path.

We learn more of this historical scam from *Strabo* himself, another famous Greek scholar (58 BC – 25 AD) who went to Egypt for his training:

*[When we went to Egypt] we were shown the halls in which **Plato** and **Eudoxus** once stayed. They stayed here in Egypt for thirteen years among the priests. This is affirmed by several witnesses and writers. These priests, so profoundly knowledgeable about celestial phenomena, were at the same time mysterious people who did not talk much, and it was only after a long time and with **skillful maneuvering** that Plato and Eudoxus managed to be **initiated** into some of their theoretical speculations. But these barbarians [Plato and Eudoxus] kept the best parts to themselves. And if today the world owes them the knowledge of what fraction of a day has to be added to 365 whole days to make a complete year, the Greeks did not know the true duration of the year and many other facts of the same nature until **translators** of the Egyptian priest's papers into Greek language popularized these notions among our modern astronomers, who have continued up to the present day to draw heavily upon them as they do the same from the **Chaldean's** writings and observations.*

[My emphasis]

A damning indictment indeed from Strabo, a contemporary of Plato and Eudoxus and fellow Greek student in Egypt. In plagiarizing the ancient knowledge of African peoples the Greeks broke the *code* of knowledge transmitting and also *corrupted* the purity and form of that knowledge in the process. Consequently, from that point in history the development of a *Eurocentric* philosophical paradigm *diverged* from its original *African root* into the speculative form that Aristotle, Plato, Anaxagoras, Socrates and the others created. This divergent form of the ancient African Mystery System, later labeled *Philosophy* by Eurocentric scholars, today informs the structure of all Euro/American learning processes. The Greeks did exactly what their African teachers would have found unthinkable by abstracting s essential elements to their intellectual and spiritual progress. This, in the true sense, created a form of intellectual and spiritual *schism*. Similar schisms can be seen in the Buddhist teachings of the *Theravada* and the *Mahayana*, the *impersonalists* and the *personalists* view points of the Hindu Vedantic philosophies and also in Islam (*Sunni* and *Shia* factions) and so on.

The Greeks translated many other systems of knowledge known to us such as the Christian Bible, Jewish texts and so on, but as G.M. James concludes:

'The absurdity is easily recognized when we remember that the Greek language was used to translate several systems of teachings which the Greeks could not succeed in claiming to have invented. Such were the translation of the Hebrew Scriptures into Greek, the Septuagint, the Christian Gospels, Acts and the Epistles in Greek, (still called the Greek New Testament). It is only the unwritten philosophy of the Egyptians translated into Greek that has met with such an unhappy fate: a black African legacy stolen by the Greeks.

Almost all Euro/American classics scholars have shied away from this paradigm of history, yet none have come forward with even a plausible argument to refute these facts. Their only hope is that black people won't become interested in learning about this fraud and young whites can remain ignorant of these earthshaking historical occurrences. Space does not permit me to go further but the evidence is readily accessible for all see. Read, reason and understand. Whether we consider ourselves to be black or white it's important to know the truth for the sake of our mutual and collective development in peace, harmony and respect.

Philosophy as we know it now is purely a European invention and cannot really be related to the black African perspective because it's inherently a product of a specific cultural modality that does not inform the naturally organic development of African based cultures. Terms such as *existentialism* and *dialectic* are parts of a Eurocentric paradigm rooted in the consensus reality of Europeans, which no matter how we would like it to be different, remains so. We cannot use standard English as a way of interpreting African sacred knowledge because as we all know, that which is lost in translating holds vital clues to clear and concise understanding.

An important aspect of all this is the manner in which the knowledge system of the Ancient Global Civilization of Africa became corrupted by the infiltration of the hybridized blood-line into the Mystery schools of ancient Egypt.

*..The subject of the **Ifa Oracle** raises a lot of fundamental questions bordering on available data on its history, myth and science. And if, I think, the entire gamut of Western theories and epistemology derives from the interactive interpretations of these tripod stand of philosophical knowledge (**history, myth, science**), then we of the humanities research in Africa need to know more about the potential wisdom and relative science encapsulated in **Ifa divination**, and how this may be appropriated to the postmodern life of Africa. Historically, Ifa was not a product of traditional religious fundamentalism. Rather, it was a composite corpus of human existence whose inextricable religious resorts are found in those prescribed ritual sacrifices which are not to be viewed or read as literal scripts, but as **symbolic codes**. And as symbolic codes, they are quasi-scientific formulas delineating by every **atomic and molecular sense, the gravity, trigonometric and numeric range of Earth magnetic force energies and potential energies in measures and degrees of solution to human problems.** Thus, there is need to replace the theory of Ifa corpus in the context of [ancient] and contemporary contributions to human knowledge in **science** and **technology**. Here lies a great task for contemporary researchers in African studies.*

[My emphasis]

-Nelson Fashina, PhD, Nigeria, University of Ibadan, Ibadan-

Most of us seem not to know that there was an ancient, prehistoric *spiritual scientific system* that human beings once used. This system was developed in Africa long before the religions and sciences we know today came into existence. There was no name for it that we can recognize at present but we can trace its glowing, ambient energy across the world. Many African mystics and Wise Men and Women today can attest to this. In fact all traditional African spiritual formats are based on what has been termed the *Ancient Global Religion* and systems such as the African *Ifa Oracle* system of divination, *Obeah* and *Poco* in Jamaica, *Voudou (Voodoo)* in Haiti, *Santeria* in Brazil, Cuba and several other South American countries are all offshoots of this ancient African spiritual system.

Science as we understand it in our time is an invention by modern Europeans. There was never anything called science before then. Recent research by astute scholars such as *Laird Scranton* has thrown astonishing light on this issue. His welcomed volume entitled *The Science of the Dogon* highlights some of the most amazing facts about ancient African spiritual and scientific knowledge that are now reverberating loudly around the halls of white academia. In his thesis he dissects the scientific structure of the ancient Dogon people's spiritual system and has uncovered some of the most stunning information about the ancient African Mystery School system. Scranton postulates that the Dogon mythological symbols and concepts relating to *science* so closely follow modern scientific information that, if our purpose was to refute their basis in science, we would first need to explain in some credible way these extraordinary similarities:

The po, which is explained in terms similar to those that describe the atom.
Sene seeds, which are described in form and behavior as being similar to **protons, neutrons**, and electrons and whose 'nesting' is recognizable as an electron orbit.
The germination of the sene, whose drawn images are a match for the four types of **quantum spin particles**.
The spider of the sene whose threads weave the **266 seeds of Amma**, much as string theory tells us all matter is woven from strings.
The basic creative impulse of the gods, from whom all of these particles emerged, which is stated in terms that run parallel to the concept of the four basic **quantum forces.**

Laird Scranton goes on to explain that:

'*In many previous examples, this study has demonstrated a consistent relationship between symbols and concepts of the Dogon people and modern science. These examples show, among other things, that the Dogon myths clearly describe:*

• *The correct attributes of the unformed universe*
• *That all matter was created by the opening of the universe*
• *That spiraling galaxies of stars were formed when the universe opened*
• *That this same event was responsible for the creation of light and time*
• *The complex relationship between light and time*
• *That matter can behave like a particle or as a wave*
• *That sound travels in waves*
• *That matter is composed of fundamental components*
• *The correct counts of the elements within each component category of matter*
• *That the most basic component of matter is a thread*
• *That this fundamental thread vibrates*
• *That under some conditions threads can form membranes*
• *That threads give rise to the four fundamental quantum forces*

- *The correct attributes of these quantum forces*
- *The correct attributes of the four types of quantum spin particles*
- *The concept of the uncertainty principle*
- *That atoms are formed from smaller particles*
- *That electrons orbit atoms*
- *That component particles other than electrons make up the nucleus of an atom*
- *The correct shape of an electron orbit*
- *That electrons of one atom can be 'stolen' by other atoms to form molecular bond*
- *That light is emitted by changes in the energy level of an electron*
- *The correct electron structures of water and of copper*
- *That hydrogen atoms form pairs*
- *That sunlight is the result of the fusion of hydrogen atoms*
- *That water goes through phase transitions*
- *That the emergence of matter in the universe is related to phase transitions*
- *The correct steps in the natural water cycle*
- *That the first single cell emerged spontaneously from water*
- *That cells reproduce by mitosis to form two twin cells*
- *The correct sequence of events during sexual reproduction and growth of an embryo*
- *That female and male contributions are required for sexual reproduction*
- *That children inherit genetic characteristics from each parent*
- *That there are 22 chromosome pairs*
- *That sex is determined by the X and Y chromosomes*
- *That chromosomes move apart and spindles form during mitosis*
- *The correct shapes and attributes of chromosomes and spindles*
- *That sexual reproduction starts with the formation of germ cells*
- *That germ cells reproduce by a process unique to themselves*
- *That eggs live longer than other cells*
- *The correct configuration and attributes of DNA*

This knowledge, kept by our African ancestors has been unknown to most of us because we have been ***enslaved*** and ***brainwashed*** by the Babylon System to think of our wise progenitors as inferior peoples. The truth of this matter is astonishing beyond belief. There is very little to add to this except to say that we need to educate ourselves ***urgently*** and our children even more so in order to reach a point of realization that we must take control of our destiny on this earth. ***You will never be taught about these things in schools, colleges or universities.***

When we scrutinize the spiritual traditions of our African forebears, we can clearly see the nature of their *'spiritual scientific'* enquiries encoded in the language of what we refer to as myth and ritual. For example, the Yoruba of West Africa explains the nature of the universe and its creation as follows:

*The Realm of **Olorun**, the abobe of the Mighty Creator, **Oloddumare,** is at the center of everything there was, is and will be. All creation, **Ashe**, came forth from this center in **pots** which Oloddumare created. In each Ashe, each pot, there is his **creative force** which he uses to make and maintain **the totality of creation**. And for every **male creative force** there is a **female creative force**.*

*Now realize, before the beginning of everything there was only **Ashe, the creative force itself. It was in no pot**. There was nothing but Ashe. But one day **Ashe began to think**. And when thinking began Ashe became **Oloddumare**. And as Oloddumare thought, he thought **matter**, and so matter came to be. And the matter is called **Olorun**, the Abobe at the center of everything. But matter became a **she** as Oloddumare is a **he**, for **thinking causes a reaction in the opposite direction**. A male thinking generates a female thing; a female thinking generates a male thing. The name of the **thinking creating matter** in Olorun is **Nana Baruku**, the Grandmother of all the **divinities**. This female creator has many names: Nana Baruku, Nana Baluku, Na Na Baraclou, and Boucalou are but a few.*

The concept of Ashe as the primordial ground of being is synonymous with what is referred to as the **Primordial Creation Field** (the **Demiurge**) that issued from the **Unformed** and **Uncreated Nature**. It was in no **'pot'** meaning that it had no **boundaries** or **borders** or **dimensional format** – being infinite and so on. Ashe gave rise to thought (the **Logos**) which manifested as the primary principle of **divine** being, an extension of the creative energy. This extension gave rise to what we perceive as matter, the **Creation Field** of the Created and Formed. The relationship between thought and its **translation** into matter is explained in this poetic rendering. Each fundamental force of nature has an equal and opposite – **male** and **female** (negatively and positively charged, matter and anti-matter) energies that imparts balance to the universal continuum and so on. The deeper metaphysics of ancient African cultures are usually shrouded in secrecy and only passed through lines of initiation so that much data can only be accessed by very few initiates. What we are given in stories are only basic symbolic versions of deeper secretive knowledge:

*Nana Baruku (the **thinking creating matter**) thought, and through this process gave birth to **Mawa** and **Lissa** who are the **Cosmic Egg** and the **seed** which **fertilizes** it respectively.*

In most oral renderings of the story of creation it's this egg that gives rise to everything else.

Before there was day, before there was night, and before there was a Universe, All things lived in harmony in **Olorun**, *the Cosmic Heavens, located in the realm of* **Ikode Orun**, *the* **Giant Egg** *that sat in the center of* **Nothingness**.

The Giant **Egg**, Mawa and the seed inside the Egg, Lissa and the Great Grandmother (Nana Baruku) are called the first or **Great Divinities**, the **Irunmole**. The Irunmole includes: Olofin, Kiori, Dakuta, and **1001** other Irunmole (energies), all results of the seed and the egg. These are the primary **cosmic forces** and their **combinations** of which the early universe was formed:

Now it was the **Irunmole** *who decided they wanted to* **expand the universe**. *They went to* **Oloddumare** *and told him what they wanted. They debated the matter and decided that if the universe was to* **expand** *then something must* **bind it**. *It was thusly that the* **Oshumare** *was create; the* **Rainbow Serpent** *that* **coils around the egg**, *(which is the* **whole universe**), *binding it firm. But Oloddumare said, "Someday, Oshumare will become* **hungry** *and will begin to* **devour its own tail**. *When that happens, all that is, was and will be, will return to the center,* **uncreated as quickly as it was created**. *So be it"*.

Africans knew from very ancient times how the universe came to be from the realm of the **Unformed Nature**. The expansion of the universe, the quantum energies and the forces of gravity are all clearly implicit in these structures of ancient African spiritual thought outlined in the **symbolic language** of **metaphors** and **myths**; the relationship between **being** and **non-being**, **thing** and **thought**, **opposites** and **equilibrium** and so on. We find these ideas exactly in ancient Egypt, Kush/Nubia and much later on in the development of Greek philosophy.

In this regard we need to understand the language of the symbols and codes embedded within this form of knowledge. Ancient Africans knew very well that the universe came into being through specific processes that caused its **expansion** from some type of **quantum singularity** stimulated by a specific and orderly Creative Principle. An array of inconceivable forces came into being in the forms of **'spiritual intelligences'** and **'divinities'** and **other mysterious forces**. These **archetypal energies** manifest as byproducts of the creative process and take shape and form through the conscious awareness of human beings. These days, western scientists use words such as **quark**, **muon**, **Higgs Boson**, **gravity**, **quantum particles** and so on; the same principles, just very different mental approaches. The engaging of the extended consciousness faculties with the field energies of the quantum universe is the means by which these can be collapsed down **mentally** into **recognizable forms, shapes and structures** that we can then create *relationships* with, whether as science or myth. In science today, we recognize the *expanding universe theory* just as our ancient African ancestors did within the framework of what western academia call *myth*. In their case, the expansion had to be controlled by another force, the *Rainbow Serpent* that *coils around the universe binding it together*. This is obviously equated with the *gravitational forces* that *bind the universe* as a cohesive whole. Curiously also, the Rainbow Serpent will one day become *hungry* and the universe will be *devoured* back to its point of origin. Euro/American science is presently analyzing this very same principle through their form of *'myth'* – *science*. The *Big Crunch* hypothesis of western science alludes to these African *'myths'* precisely.

Within the African knowledge system and secret societies are clearly embedded the inquiries into some of the most fundamental aspects of modern scientific structures, laid out elegantly and poetically as symbolic myth. Sadly today, this knowledge is being quietly, carefully and calculatingly destroyed in Africa.

*The **IFA** model can be used to describe **quantum consciousness**, not only on the level of human consciousness, but also of our entire Universe, and to give us a framework within which to consider our **<u>future history</u>** and our possible fates.*

Technology is the study, development, and application of techniques and devices for a given use. Usually when we use the word technology, we invariably think of shiny machines such as computers, cellular phones, IPods, cars, rocket ships and various gadgets and devices that we use within our modern societies. Upon reflection, the system of racism that operates within the Babylon System would have us believe that black peoples of this planet have never produced real advanced technology of any significance. The great lie maintained by white racists is that blacks are inferior mentally and could never produce any form of technology on par with white technological innovations. If we analyze the history of human beings on earth, without prejudice, we can clearly understand the pattern of real advanced technological developments by black African peoples of the world going back countless thousands of years into the past. In fact, black Africans have been the first group of human beings to invent radically advanced technology. Most people don't even know that the **wheel** was invented and used in Africa by black Africans before anywhere else in the world. The clear evidence can be known by anyone who cares to research these issues.

As I have outlined in above chapters, recent and ongoing archaeological research around the **Sahara**, East and Southern Africa is at present revealing staggering evidence of what is to date the **oldest known civilizations** ever to be discovered; civilizations created and maintained by black African peoples. There are many African scholars, academics and spiritual wise men and women that have always alluded to ancient civilizations buried by the sands of the Sahara and the regions around West Africa, Zimbabwe and South Africa.

When archaeologists excavate the remains of ancient civilizations in the Sudan, Mexico, India, China or anywhere else in the world, they expect to find evidence of the technological knowledge of that particular period or culture. For instance, if the ancient black African Kushites (Nubians), Kemetic (Egyptians) or Xi (Olmecs) of Mexico built pyramids, then where is the **evidence** of the **technology** they used to

237

make these things? There are no wires, screwdrivers, bits of broken equipment buried in the ground, no metal based machines or plastics; no precision instruments that can cut the hardest materials, no cranes or bulldozers or even remnants of these things. We know that much of the technological achievements by ancient black peoples are not know or cannot even be replicated with ease using 21st century Euro/American technology.

One of the most outrageous programs of historical deception is the deliberate and systematic destruction of artifacts and sites containing irrefutable proof of ancient black civilizations that go back hundreds of thousands of years in Africa. A continuous program of *archaeological genocide* by Euro/American researchers has been instituted for centuries to destroy evidence of prehistoric black African cultures on earth. A case in point is the building of a large dam in Aswan, Sudan during the nineteen sixties that destroyed forever the remains of one of the greatest ancient black African civilizations the world had ever known; the ancient empire of *Kush/Nubia,* the forerunner to ancient Egyptian civilization. Damming the Nile caused a number of environmental and humanitarian problems. Over 60,000 people were displaced and *most* of the important archeological sites of ancient Kush/Nubia were submerged under water, forever lost to the world. There are literally countless other similar incidents that have occurred all across continental Africa and many other places around the world. More recently, the complete act of desecration, pillaging and destruction of priceless historical treasures from the museums and archaeological sites in *Iraq* during the illegal war carried out by the Euro/American hegemony highlights these issues.

The advanced *scientific/spiritual knowledge* of African peoples such as the *Igbo, Yoruba, Dogon, Bambara* and *Zulu* to name but a few is only now being analyzed by few dedicated and serious Euro/American researchers. Ninety nine percent of this knowledge will never be made public knowledge or make it into school text books and college curriculums because by the standards of white racist academia, black African peoples could not have created any form of advanced technology or civilizations. Count Volney an eighteenth European century writer and thinker, during his journey to Egypt once remarked upon bearing witness to the achievement of ancient black African peoples:

'This very black race of men whom we have subjugated ... To think that a race of black men who are today our slaves and object of our contempt is the same race to whom we owe our arts, sciences and even the very use of speech...'

Should impartial, intelligent and honest scholars choose to look at these issues, they will be confronted with the most amazing evidence that ancient African peoples of the earth were in possession of a structured method of *'scientific enquiry'* and application that parallels (and in specific cases surpasses) our present scientific knowledge even in the 21st century. The remains of ancient megalithic cultures around the world and the emerging knowledge of the *Ancient Global Civilization* of earth are clear indications of this. We can discern the roots and structure of the sciences that we are familiar with today in the ancient knowledge of African peoples; *astronomy, quantum mechanics, particle physics, string theory, genetic science* and so on. Although these words and labels stem from our modern languages the basis of these scientific enquiries are clearly embedded in ancient African spiritual and mythological traditions.

Often one would watch programs on television such as *Discovery* on the *History* channel outlining to the masses completely false knowledge and assumptions about historical development in Africa. Children watch these programs and educators use them to instill the mind control program of the Babylon System without questioning the validity of such knowledge. The Babylon System's armies of *thought police* – academics, scientists and sociologists – are employed to completely rubbish any pertinent research or findings that expose the myth of the Babylon System. In order to understand these issues, we have to take a drastic shift in our consciousness perception of what technology, spirituality and human development means from a black African perspective. This is crucial to greater understanding of our situation on planet earth.

As an example, the light absorption potential of the human body could lead to great possibilities to enhance our lives on earth. If the body has the ability to absorb light through melanin, (as have been proven) it's not so farfetched that more *natural technologies* could be created that would allow human beings to use light as a medium to create *biological quantum computer systems* that would not need any bulky physical hardware, merely one could interface *mentally* with such technologies in a way that might seem like *magic*. One could store and retrieve information using the physical body (brain/mind link) without any physical objects or attachments present. In fact, when we analyze what appears to be the nonexistence of physical ancient African technology, *aspects* of these techniques appear to have been in use by Africans since remote prehistoric times. The great wise men and women of Africa have always maintained and expressed these ideas clearly. Within the Igbo spiritual culture, an adept who assumes the title of *Dibia* (a spiritually enlightened human being) is able to transform his or her body into *'radiant light'* and move through time and space in a non-linear manner. We find the same principle in Tibetan Buddhism and Hindu spiritual philosophies in the attaining of a *rainbow body* (light body) at the moment of physical death and transformation. Incidentally, it's worth noting that most human beings once wore very little clothing in the past as the importance of light and its *'organic'* effects upon the human body was a natural part of our understanding.

The technology of consciousness deals with the natural psychic *supernormal powers* of the human *mind/spirit matrix* and their ability to extend beyond the boundaries of our gross senses to affect noticeable changes in the physical and spiritual space/time continuum. This ability, when developed through specific processes of *mental conditioning*, can radically reorganize ones understanding of space/time and relationship to the universal forces of creation. The knowledge to consciously project the powers of the mind through space/time effectively is the *highest science* that man can realize as an earthly being. In fact, in Jamaica, this ability has always been referred to strictly as science and is still held in very high regard by many, (in some cases more so than the material, *high-tech* sciences of Euro/American societies).

The untutored Europeans who first encountered African cultures assumed that the absence of physical metal based *machinery* was a consequence of black people's primitive state. *Because of the differences in the 'consensus reality matrix' that governs both cultures, the 'technological apparatus' of ancient black Africans appeared nonexistent or misconceived by whites and labeled as African black magic, Voudou, animism, fetishism, Ancestor worship* and so on. Whites when confronted with ancient African technology could not perceive it in its *multi-dimensional* format because their *'mental computers'* were disengaged from the necessary (mental/spiritual) mechanisms that would enable them to tap into the *'black/African consensus reality'* paradigm, which would reveal to them the true nature and extent of ancient African technological *perspectives* and the ways in which these manifested and were commonly used. In fact, the word *technology* had no equivalent in any African language, as technology was never conceived by Africans as something *exterior* or *separate* from a human being's body or mind.

"Africans are in bondage today because they approach spirituality through religion provided by foreign invaders and conquerors. We must stop confusing religion and spirituality. Religion is a set of rules, regulations and rituals created by humans, which were supposed to help people to grow spiritually. Due to human imperfection, religion has become corrupt, political and divisive and a tool for power struggle. **Spirituality** *is not* **theology** *or* **ideology**. *It is simply a* **Way of Life**, *pure and original as was given by the* **Most High of Creation**. *Spirituality is a network linking us to the Most High, the universe and each other. As the essence of our existence, it embodies our culture, true identity, nationhood and destiny. A people without a nation that they can really call their own, are a people without a soul. Africa is our nation and is in spiritual and physical bondage because Her leaders are turning to outside forces for solutions to African problems when everything Africa needs is within Her.* **When African righteous people come together the world will come together; this is our divine destiny!"**

-H.I.M, The Sublime, Emperor Haille Selassie I, The King of Kings -

---

Perhaps the most widely recognized form of ancient African spiritual science is the technique of **divination** practiced by traditional healers throughout Africa called the **Ifa Oracle** or **Fa** system of divination. Ifa divination is usually carried out by a **Babalawo** (an Obeah man/woman/Shaman/Healer/**Dibia**) who after many years of apprenticeship becomes recognized as an **Ifa Priest** or **Priestess.** The role of the Babalawo in Yoruba tradition is an intricate and comprehensive one. It's the Babalawo who serves as the mediator between the powerful cosmic energies (collectively known as **Orishas**, the **Higher Spiritual Hierarchies**) that supports the manifestation of time, space and dimensions in the African universe. The Ifa Oracle prescribes the social structure of Yoruba traditional customs and overall culture, as stated by the great legendary priest/prophet **Orunmila**, who it is said served as a witness to the creation of all the **universal forces**. Thus, the Yoruba oral tradition recognizes Ifa as the **word** or **law** of the Supreme Creative Energy known as **Olodumare**.

The Babalawo consults the Ifa Oracle to determine the nature of an individual's problem. He then prescribes the appropriate offerings and medicines which reflect the person's needs indicated in the **Odu** that is being consulted. To determine whether or not all the Orishas (cosmic energies) are satisfied (balanced) with the prescribed offerings, the **Obi Abata** is cast. The Obi Abata Oracle is done on a divining board called an **Opon-Ifa**. Opon-Ifa symbolizes the **universe**, (the universal energetic manifestation) and is regarded as omniscience in the ancient wisdom of the Yoruba people. It indicates the four cardinal points of the universe, the top representing the North, the bottom representing the South, the right representing the East, the left representing the West. These four cardinal points are also used to symbolize the four basic elements of nature, i.e., **Air, Earth, Fire**, and **Water;** (in contemporary sciences this also alludes to the four basic **quantum forces**).

One of the traditional ways in which Ifa Oracular divination is carried out is the utilizing of the **Koala Nut**, (in Jamaica we call it **Bissie** and it's used as one of the most important traditional medicines). According to Tradition, the Creation Field is a fixed matrix of energy which revolves around set laws. The Ifa Oracle is itself part and parcel of these laws that an individual mind/soul can access at any given point in time and space because every individual is in essence an **extension** of these energies; as above, so below, the macrocosmic and the microcosmic. The Oracle in one sense is similar to an **archive** or **blueprint** of the energies of which creation is formed. By using the technology of the multi-dimensional medium that the Oracle represents, one can literally '**peer over the event horizon**' of creation to perceive the past, or future, foreseeing individual or collective **causes** and **effects**. According to the African Tradition, *the Ifa Oracle and knowing how to use it properly is a good thing; it's a factor of reality just as electricity and the atomic bomb are. The use you put it to becomes the case. It is written, "**The wise man looks into the future and prepares for it**".*

The Ifa Oracular system is comprised of what could be termed a feedback mechanism which functions successfully where two **cardinal factors** are present. These are:

- *An enlightened consciousness* on the physical plane on one side, (psychic/healer/Obeahman/Dibia/Babawalo), who **knows** he is part of an **orchestrated reality**. With his expert knowledge of the **application** of Ifa Oracular **technology** he is able to solicit information from the spiritual (**unseen or quantum**) dimensions, from where most of the supervision of the human realm emanates. He must also be able to employ specific and required **multi-dimensional technological apparatus** which is a system based on the $2^4 = 16$ Tetragrams or Quadruples of sets containing either 1 or 2 elements such as nuts, shells, beans, calabash, metal, brass, copper, aluminum, silver, lead, iron, wood, ivory, pangolin or crocodile scales, fish or turtle bones or shells as a means with which he would communicate with the various *energies* or *forces* of the multi-dimensional planes: hence the *'technological'* array he chooses to use must have defined and specific intentions. (A bean or shell is not really a dead object but operates very much as *'nuts'* and *'bolts'* and *energy conduits* within an element of the *psycho/spiritual multidimensional machinery*). The heightened consciousness faculties become the fuel that activates this psycho/spiritual multidimensional energy array.

- A corresponding flow of energy from the higher dimensional planes directed by evoked *group thought forms*, *guardian spirits*, *Ancestors*, *God* and so on, with the aim of ensuring that the chosen medium of divination is affected correctly according to prior definitions by the evoker. The fundamental nature of the universal structures such as quantum forces is given *'personalities'* through this perception and are therefore interpreted as *divinities*, *spirits* and so on in the ancient Tradition. This method *'mentally collapse'* energy fields in a manner that allows the mind to articulate a *personal* and *subjective* connection with the vital energies of creation. (Incidentally, the Ifa Oracle, in a strange way, seems to reflect similar qualities to such things as what has been referred to as the *Looking Glass* technological system that Euro/American scientists have been trying to utilize over the past three decades or so. This system is a means of accessing *future probabilities*. The Ifa Oracular system however is based on a natural *organic* technological form and can be freely accessed by anyone).

The Ifa Oracle, in essence, is a multidimensional medium that allows human beings direct *interface* with the *database* of the Creation Field, which contains all the possibilities of past, present and future. This can be achieved on personal and subjective level as we are all expressions of the Creation Field; our DNA and biological array are *translations* of this energy form. We actually possess all the knowledge in existence within our being and we can access any form of knowledge in an instant if we learn the methods to do so.

An informative article entitled, *OBI -The Mystical Oracle of Ifa Divination* outlines some of the methods and structures of the Oracular system of divination:

In Ifa Divination, the Oracle consists of reading the positions of the principles of **light and darkness**. These two principles among Yoruba Cosmology which personify the essence of "truth" were created by the Supreme Being called Olodumare; a "truth" which changes not, and provides an explanation for the creation of all things.

In order to fully know and understand the real interpretations of the **Obi Abata** Oracle, it is essential that the reader learn by heart the recognized order of the **sixteen principal (16) Major Odus within the Ifa Corpus**.

The Sixteen Major Odus (16) offer a simple and short method of interpreting the Obi Abata within the Ifa System of divination. When a segment of the Obi Abata is facing up (open), it is regarded as a principal of "light" and is marked as - I. When a segment of the Obi Abata is facing down (closed), it is regarded as a principal of "darkness" and is marked as - II. Thus, "light" and "darkness" precede all things and are referred to as:

1.OGBE-LIGHT	2.OYEKU-DARKNESS
I	II
I	II
I	II
I	II

Ifa divination is based on the principle that 'light' must always displace 'darkness'. This system is further interpreted as a series of **binary choices** that can be interpreted to reveal information about any aspect of an individual's problems.

According to very recent research on the subject of the **Ifa Oracle** by a few interested Euro/American scientists, the incredible spiritual scientific knowledge of ancient African has thrown astonishing light on the realities behind what was considered primitive mumbo-jumbo by early European explorers in Africa:

...the **Global Early Religion** of the **Global Early Civilization** was probably similar to **Ifa**, the indigenous [spiritual system] of Africa, the place of origin of humanity. Most likely, **all human religions evolved from Ifa**, sometimes introducing special characteristics based on local/regional cultures after the breakup of the **Global Early Civilization**...

Ifa, *whose divination system is based on the same **256-dimensional** Clifford Algebra Cl(1,7) as the D4-D5-E6-E7-E8 **Vodu Physics Model**, is probably not only the source of all human religions, but also divination systems such as **I Ching** (64-dimensional), **Tarot** (78-dimenisonal), the ancient Hebrew **Urim & Tumin**, the Indian **Rig Veda** and **European geomancy** and the abstract structures of the natural physical world such as **Elementary Particle Physics, Quantum Consciousness, Cosmology** and so on...*

[*My emphasis*]

Through a rigorous process of mathematical and scientific analysis it has been found that the Ifa Oracle has clear relationships to modern *particle physics*, *quantum mechanics* and *String Theory* on a level that seems completely astonishing. Because of the earth shaking implications of this knowledge I shall outline its principle to specific lengths and details:

Ifa divination always starts with the binary choice that forms a string of binary 1s and 0s.

1   0

This is based on 8 binary choices

One way of divining is to cast a chain (*Opele Chain*) of 8 two-sided things, such as cowries or palm nuts. I will however use a binary system of 0s and 1s.

1 1 1 1 1 1 1 1

0 0 0 0 0 0 0 0

Within the Oracular system we then have the *paired combination* of binaries that is symbolizes as:

$$2 \times 2 \times 2 \times 2 \ \times 2 \times 2 \times 2 \times 2$$
$$= 2^8 = 256 \text{ possible outcomes}$$

There is only 1 outcome with no 1s (all 0s) and there are 8 different outcomes with exactly one 1. The 8 are, explicitly shown as:

1	0	0	0	0	0	0	0
0	1	0	0	0	0	0	0
0	0	1	0	0	0	0	0
0	0	0	1	0	0	0	0
0	0	0	0	1	0	0	0
0	0	0	0	0	1	0	0
0	0	0	0	0	0	1	0
0	0	0	0	0	0	0	1

Following on from this, there are 28 different outcomes with exactly two 1s: 1 1. There are 56 different outcomes with exactly three 1s: 111

And there are 70 different outcomes with exactly four 1s: 1111

There are 56 different outcomes with exactly five 1s: 11111

There are 28 different outcomes with exactly six 1s: 111111

There are 8 different outcomes with exactly seven 1s: 1111111

There is only one outcome with all eight 1s: 11111111

If we call the number of 1s in a given outcome the grade of that outcome, then we can organize the $2^8 = 256$ outcomes by grade from 0 to 8:

$1 + 8 + 28 + 56 + 70 + 56 + 28 + 8 + 1 = 256 = 2^8$

The Ifa **Opele Chain** method of divination describes the **graded structure** of the 256 $= 2^8$ outcomes. There are numerous ways in which Ifa Oracle is invoked throughout Africa, yet the underlying characteristics remain within the parameters of specific and coherent *'natural scientific laws'*. Another method is as follows which is equivalent to dividing the **8-element Opele Chain**:

1	1	1	1	1	1	1	1
0	0	0	0	0	0	0	0

Into 4 halfs

1	1	1	1
0	0	0	0

1	1	1	1
0	0	0	0

and then casting each *4-element* half separately so that each outcome is a pair of 4 binary choices. Since 4 binary choices have $2^4 = 16$ possible outcomes, a pair of 4 binary choices has 16 x 16 = 256 possible outcomes, which are the same 256 outcomes obtained by casting the whole 8-element *Opele* Chain. It is from these series of numerical calculations, applied with a precise methodology of *spiritual perception* that the African *Babalawo* (traditional priest/priestess) deciphers the intricate details of the universal forces which by Euro/American science refer to as *quantum dynamics*.

In Ifa, each of the 16 possible outcomes of 4 binary choices can be represented by Tetragrams:

1	2	3	4
0	1	1	0
0	1	0	1
0	1	0	1
0	1	1	0

5	6	7	8
0	1	0	1
0	1	1	1
1	0	1	1
1	0	1	0

9	10	11	12
0	1	1	1
0	0	0	1
0	0	1	0
1	0	1	1

13	14	15	16
0	0	0	1
1	0	1	0
0	1	0	1
0	0	1	0

The 16 *Tetragramic* forms can also be arranged in binary number sequences wherein the first line of 8 Tetragrams (0-7) is a reflection of the second line (15-8) through the central point *X* that changes 0 to 1and 1 to 0.

0	1	2	3	4	5	6	7
0	0	0	0	0	0	0	0
0	0	0	0	1	1	1	1
0	0	1	1	0	0	1	1
0	1	0	1	0	1	0	1

X

8	9	10	11	12	13	14	15
1	1	1	1	1	1	1	1
0	0	0	0	1	1	1	1
0	0	1	1	0	0	1	1
0	1	0	1	0	1	0	1

This Tetragramic method describes the 256 = 16 x 16 outcomes in terms of 16 sets of 16 outcomes. The 16 = 8 + 8 sets can be seen as two groups of 8 sets, with one group of 8 (call it <8) being a Mirror Image of the other (call it 8>).

Therefore, Ifa, through the Opele Chain Casting and Tetragramic methods of divining, gives this structure to the fundamental **256** outcomes: *1 + 8 + 28 + 56 + 70 + 56 + 28 + 8 + 1 = (<8 + 8>) x 16.*

This alludes clearly to what is called a ***physics model*** as seen below:

*In order to make a model of fundamental **particle physics**, you must describe the basic action by which a fundamental particle **moves** from an **origin** point A in **space/time** to a **destination** point B in space/time.*

```
        --B
        / /|
       / / /
      / / /
      |/ /
      A--
```

John and ***Mary Gribbin*** clarify these processes in their book ***Richard Feynman, A Life In Science*** (Dutton, Penguin, 1997, at pages 85-87):

A line A →B represents the history of a particle as it moves from A→ B.

*Every possible way in which a particle could go from A→B – every possible **'history'** must be considered. A Particle going from A→B is conceived as a sum of all of the possible **paths** that connect A→ B. Three of the possible paths are shown in the diagram above. For each possible way that a particle can go from one point to another in **space/time** there is an **amplitude** that has two parts, which can be thought of in terms of little arrows. An arrow has a certain length, and it points in a certain direction.*

Richard Feynman elucidates in his book ***QED: The Strange Theory of Light and Matter*** (Princeton, 1988, at pages 82-83, 91, 129):

*"... an event [such as going from A→B can be divided into alternative paths, each path can be divided into successive steps. The arrows for each step can be 'multiplied' by successive **shrinks** and **turns** to get an arrow for each alternative way. The arrow[s] for each [alternative] way can be 'added' to obtain a final arrow, whose square is the **probability** of an observed **physical event** (such as going from A→B).*

Another basic action is that a particle emits or absorbs another particle; the *amplitude to emit or absorb a particle is just a number that describes **the strengths of forces in Physics**. The amplitude for a real **electron** to emit or absorb a real **photon** has been a mystery ever since it was discovered, and all good theoretical physicists put this number up on their wall and worry about it. **It's one of the greatest damn mysteries of physics**. There is no theory that adequately explains the observed masses of the particles. We use the numbers in all our theories, but we don't understand them - what they are or where they come from. I believe that from a fundamental point of view, this is a very interesting and serious problem. ...".*

The Ifa (or what some have been referring to as the Voudou model of fundamental particle physics) solves the mystery of the amplitudes for particles to emit or absorb other particles, which give Force Strengths, and also solves the problem of Particle Masses.

From the following we get a concise rendering of the true implications of the magnitude of the Oracle in scientific terminologies:

The numerical structure form of the Ifa structure comes from the correspondence of the fundamental 256 outcomes with the Graded Structure and Spinor Structures of the 256-dimensional Cl(8) Clifford Algebra of 16x16 real matrices M(16,R):

1 + 8 + 28 + 56 + 70 + 56 + 28 + 8 + 1 = (<8 + 8>) x 16

$$x\,x\,x\,x\,x\,x\,x\,x\,x\,x\,x\,x\,x\,x\,x\,x$$
$$x\,x\,x\,x\,x\,x\,x\,x\,x\,x\,x\,x\,x\,x\,x\,x$$
$$x\,x\,x\,x\,x\,x\,x\,x\,x\,x\,x\,x\,x\,x\,x\,x$$
$$x\,x\,x\,x\,x\,x\,x\,x\,x\,x\,x\,x\,x\,x\,x\,x$$
$$x\,x\,x\,x\,x\,x\,x\,x\,x\,x\,x\,x\,x\,x\,x\,x$$
$$x\,x\,x\,x\,x\,x\,x\,x\,x\,x\,x\,x\,x\,x\,x\,x$$
$$x\,x\,x\,x\,x\,x\,x\,x\,x\,x\,x\,x\,x\,x\,x\,x$$
$$x\,x\,x\,x\,x\,x\,x\,x\,x\,x\,x\,x\,x\,x\,x\,x$$
$$x\,x\,x\,x\,x\,x\,x\,x\,x\,x\,x\,x\,x\,x\,x\,x$$
$$x\,x\,x\,x\,x\,x\,x\,x\,x\,x\,x\,x\,x\,x\,x\,x$$
$$x\,x\,x\,x\,x\,x\,x\,x\,x\,x\,x\,x\,x\,x\,x\,x$$
$$x\,x\,x\,x\,x\,x\,x\,x\,x\,x\,x\,x\,x\,x\,x\,x$$
$$x\,x\,x\,x\,x\,x\,x\,x\,x\,x\,x\,x\,x\,x\,x\,x$$
$$x\,x\,x\,x\,x\,x\,x\,x\,x\,x\,x\,x\,x\,x\,x\,x$$
$$x\,x\,x\,x\,x\,x\,x\,x\,x\,x\,x\,x\,x\,x\,x\,x$$
$$x\,x\,x\,x\,x\,x\,x\,x\,x\,x\,x\,x\,x\,x\,x\,x$$

*The numbers 56 + 70 + 56 + 28 + 8 + 1 and 16 also have physical interpretations, some of which are related to the **duality** between **position** and **momentum** that is related to the **Heisenberg Uncertainty Principle of Quantum Theory**. Those interpretations are:*

- *The **16**, which breaks down into 8 + 8, correspond to a set of **8 matrices** (called **Dirac gamma matrices**) that describe how **Spinor Particles** move in space/time from the point of view of position in space/time, and another set of 8 matrices (also called **Dirac gamma matrices**) that describe how Spinor Particles move in Space/time from the point of view of **momentum** in Space-time.*

- *The **56** (corresponding to outcomes with three 1s) is fixed and not dynamically active after 8-dimensional Space-time is broken into **4-dimensional Physical Space/time and 4-dimensional Internal Symmetry Space**. At very high energies where the 8-dimensional Space-time is not broken, there may be some phenomena related to the 56, but such high energies (possibly **Planck-level**) are currently beyond the reach of human experiments and observations, such as some subtle phenomena related to interactions among the **World-Lines of Possible Histories in the Quantum Many-Worlds**. Such Interactions can be described in terms of an **M-theory** with global symmetry of the exceptional **Lie algebra E7**, whose 56-dimensional representation corresponds to the 56.*

- *The **70** (corresponding to outcomes with four 1s) breaks down into 35 + 35. One 35 is fixed and not dynamically active after 8-dimensional Space/time is broken into 4-dimensional Physical Space/time and 4-dimensional Internal Symmetry Space. At very high energies where the 8-dimensional Space-time is not broken, there may be some phenomena related to that 35, but such high energies (possibly Planck-level) are currently beyond the reach of human experiments and observations, such as some subtle phenomena related to the **Higgs Scalar**.*

- *The other 35 and the 56 + 28 + 8 + 1 are dual to the 1 + 8 + 28 + 56 and the first 35, and describe in terms of momentum, the same physical phenomena that the 1 + 8 + 28 + 56 and the first 35 describe in terms of position.*

*Taken together, the 56 and 70 correspond to the **126 root vectors** of the exceptional **Lie algebra E7** that is the global symmetry group of an M-theory describing Interactions among the World-Lines of Possible Histories in the Quantum Many-Worlds.*

Of course, our Universe and its Quantum Many-Worlds is very big and one set of 256 IFA outcomes, that is, one copy of the 256-dimensional Cl(8) Clifford algebra, describes only one small part, or one Event. To describe such very big things, you need a very big Clifford algebra, say Cl(8N) where N can be as large a number as you want. What makes IFA effective for such very big things is the fact that any very big Clifford algebra Cl(8N) can be factored into N copies of the basic 256-element IFA Cl(8) Clifford algebra.

The IFA model can be used to describe Quantum Consciousness, not only on the level of human consciousness, but also of our entire Universe, and to give us a framework within which to consider our Future History and our possible Fates.

[My Emphasis]

The depth of this ancient African system of knowledge is vast and thoroughly engaging. More details of this research will be published in the very near future in a separate volume that also explains the relationships between **Reggae Music** and **Rasta Consciousness Music – Nyahbinghi** and the **4x4** beat system derived from the knowledge of **harmonics** and the **rhythmic vibrational** matrices of traditional African musical structures. This is implicit in the **Word – Sound – Power** harmonics grid of Rastafari, and so on. This also relates to the musical rhythms and spiritual systems of **Kumina**, **Poco** and **Revivalism** in Jamaica, all of which have clear correlations with the Oracular systems of Africa. Space, once again does not permit me to go further, but as usual I urge the reader to *take up the struggle* and delve into this intriguing *mystery*, wrapped in a *puzzle* and bound by an *enigma*. There are many great African scientists (most notably, the venerable and Sublime, **Chiek Anta Diop**) that have been trying to bring these things to the attention of the world but with very little success. Some of these theories can be downloaded from the internet right now - (see bibliography). It's really worth the time and effort. This ancient African system of knowledge must now be uncovered completely. It's the **heritage of all human beings** (whatever colour skin we wear) and is there to *enlighten* us, should we choose to look at it with conscious regard.

The Opon Ifa Divining Board with Koala Nuts (Bissie)

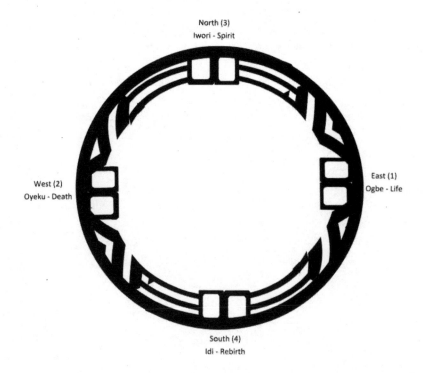

North (3)
Iwori - Spirit

West (2)
Oyeku - Death

East (1)
Ogbe - Life

South (4)
Idi - Rebirth

Sacred Geometric forms generated by the Oracle that echoes functional relationships with advanced physics models, hyperdimensional realities and Quantum Many Worlds theories.

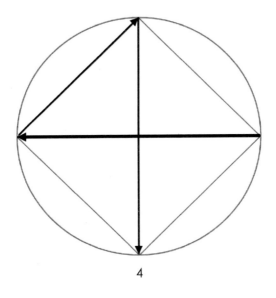

4

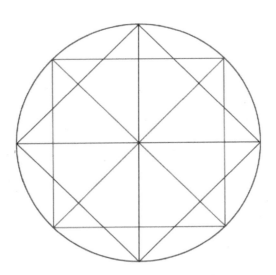

8

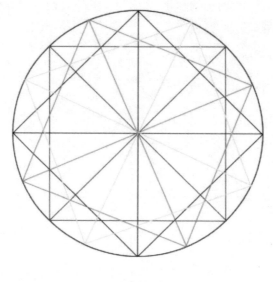

16

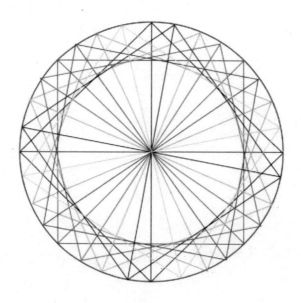

32

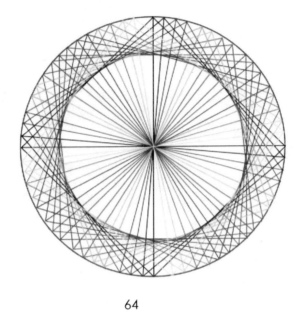

64

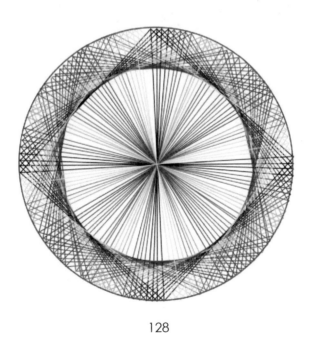

128

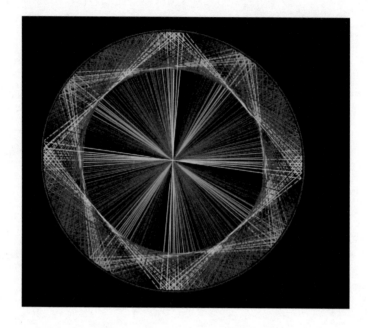

*All **256** Ifa outcomes are closely related to the **240 root vectors** of the exceptional Lie algebra E8 that is the global symmetry group of an F-theory describing Interactions among the World-Lines of <u>Possible Histories</u> in the <u>Quantum Many-Worlds</u>.*

Jah Rastafari – The Human Revolution

---

*Mind is the **Formless Nature**, the root of all things in creation. Thoughts come from mind, emotions come from thoughts, and actions come from emotions, which come from thoughts, which come from mind, which has **no form**.*

-The Golden Path of Jah Rastafari -

---

*Jamaican people are only now in this generation realizing the great gift of **Jah Rastafari** in the symbols and manifestation of His Sublime Majesty, Emperor Haille Selassie I, The Sublime Marcus Mosiah Garvey, His Sublime Grace, Father Leonard Howell, His Sublime Grace, Prince Emmanuel and all the other Great Men and Women of the Human Liberation Struggle and the Body of Rastafarian Fire Warriors on earth. In times past, the masses rejected Rasta because of ignorance and fear created by the mind control programs of the Babylon System. Many now turn to Rasta as a means to gaining deeper knowledge pertaining to their spiritual salvation. Herein the great **prophetic parable** of anciency is made revealed truth – **The stone that the builder refused in the morning shall be the head corner stone in the evening.***

-The Golden Path of Jah Rastafari -

Rastafari is about our very basic human nature as created beings. It addresses all issues that are pertinent to our development and conscious evolution as a race on earth. In reality, the terms black people and white people are essentially meaningless where Rastafari is concerned. These ways of categorizing human beings were specifically developed to polarize and compartmentalize the various groups of the species and to cause conflict and discord among us so that it would be easier to corral and control us in the Babylon System. We are essentially *one* race on this planet, no matter the various speculations by various scientists, separatists (both black and white), New Age promoters and the manipulations by predatory extra-dimensional forces. As long as we are divided by skin colour we can be controlled indefinitely. I have largely addressed the issues of the black African perspectives because it's extremely important to galvanize our emerging *consciousness expansion* with pertinent information about our past and to find the correct manner in which we can forge ways to live together in unity on our planet earth. The African perspective has not been looked at very much before by researchers of the conspiracy because of the mind control systems of academia and the media, and the various substratum of organizations that support them. Clear reasons have been given above for this. Africa isn't just about the black man, it's about the entire human race, black, white, Chinese, Indian and so on. It's the beginning of all of us. We need to become cognizant of this and begin to reshape our thinking to encompass the enormity of our potential as the human race collectively by helping each other and fostering the real virtues of human compassion and true understanding.

The teachings of Livity inherent in the traditions of Rastafari are as ancient as the universe. Throughout countless ages the Supreme Potentiality of All-Being, Jah Rastafari has been the guiding force for the evolution of all life and forms. The conscious manifestation of the energies of the Infinite Field of Potentiality continually imparts knowledge in many different guises as perceptions of divinity and spiritual teachings in diverse languages and to each human culture from their own perspectives but is completely *consistent* in the aim of liberating the minds of human beings from the shackles of ignorance and illusions.

Within the tradition of Rastafari of the present generations, the ***Golden Path of Jah Rastafari*** manifests as the ***wisdom teachings*** that clears away all obscuration and illusions so that human beings may come to realize the true nature of reality and our purpose for being within the Creation Field we designate as time, space and dimensionality. The creation of time, space and dimensions, matter and all life forms were calculated and deliberate acts by a Creative principle that could never really be approached literally in terms of a physical objective structure because physical reality is a mere reflection of the true reality that transcends the boundaries of shape and form. From this point of view, our rationalisation of physical reality must be underpinned by the knowledge of our original state of being, which ultimately transcends the senses we use to perceive the world of form. The African spiritual perspective explicitly outlines valuable principles that still very much underpin our perception of the Creator and creation even today. In fact, on closer scrutiny, (despite commonly held misconceptions) our ancient ancestors were monotheists in the real sense. One should not believe for a moment the spin delivered by Euro/American academia, whose perceptions have been skewered to misinterpret and denigrate our ancient Ancestors perspectives on these matters.

It does appear that some societies of ancient human beings utilized the concept of polytheism (the worship of many Gods) as a tool to consolidate faith. Although this might appear to be the case, (and no doubt in some societies people were, to some degrees polytheistic), the belief in a singular God was always at the heart of religious understanding in ancient cultures.

History tells us that the black Egyptian pharaoh **Akhenaton** was the first recorded individual to have postulated the idea of a unified concept of the universal God as one and not many. His monotheism positioned God as the omnipresent *'effulgence behind the power of the sun'*. This was represented by the solar disc, the *Aten* that radiated benevolence down from the heavens as slender, loving hands protruding down from the Aten solar disc. His poetic and moving rendering of the concept of God as a *singular divinity* that created, looked after and sustained his creation with love and justice precedes similar concepts that we find in the Christian bible. It appears that Akhenaton's motivation was basically to reroute the lapse in the traditions of anciency, (which in all probability occurred in Egypt during the Hyksos episode), back to the original monotheistic understanding that was always central to the ***deeper knowledge*** of the ancient Mystery System of Africa.

Some scholars and researchers have pointed to the similarities between the religion of Akhenaton and the early Jewish religion as expounded by the biblical prophet Moses. In fact, as explained above, the Jewish people had no written religious formula until Moses *'led'* them out of Egypt and created a distinct religious structure, which is still adhered to even today. The influence of ancient Egyptian religious beliefs on early Jewish spiritual culture can clearly be gleaned from the Old Testament scriptures. The prophet Moses, (having been trained in the ancient Egyptian Mystery System and thus having had access to the secret spiritual Tradition and ancient knowledge of Egypt), created a priesthood, a central place of worship (a temple in which there was a ***holy of holies,*** reminiscent of the structure of ancient Egyptian temples), and a coherent doctrine establishing the worship of one God, ***Yweh***. This new God Yweh, (El Shadei, the ***unseen*** God) was basically modelled on ***Amen***, the Unseen God of the Kushites/Nubians and the Kemetic/Egyptians). That is why Christians still to this day end their prayers by chanting ***Amen*** without really understanding what the word actually means and its ancient Egyptian/Kushite origins. Given the paradigm of the ancient global language one might add that the Sanskrit word ***Om*** and the Buddhist ***Aum*** share clear linguistic relationships with the African word, Amen.

The Jewish religious scriptures, on closer scrutiny, appear to have been derived from various sources such as the more ancient Egyptian (and to some extents ancient Sumerian) civilizations. We should remember that ***Abraham,*** the great patriarch of the Jewish nation, originally came from Ur, a city in ancient Chaldea, (ancient Mesopotamia). The peoples we refer to nowadays as ***Arabs*** and some ancient ***Jews*** are ultimately of the ***same genetic extraction***.

Certainly we can discern clear parallels between the book of ***Genesis*** and much older stories etched in clay tablets from ancient Mesopotamia. The secret teachings of Moses were an exact copy of what he had learnt studying under the priests of Egypt, but transposed in order to disguise this fact; (the same thing was done by ancient Greek philosophers as mentioned already). The Book of Genesis, Leviticus and Deuteronomy all contain the clues that link biblical literature to its Egyptian roots. The occult ***Jewish Kabala*** system is a replication of ancient Egyptian Mystery Teachings with *'other things'* added to it and so on. Diligent scholars can verify these things quite easily.

The quest to rationalise concepts of divinity appears to be mankind's oldest and most frustrating endeavour. In order to understand where Rastafari is coming from as a spiritual and earthical system we have to analyze the ancient roots of our African spiritual heritage. This might appear a daunting task as some cultures in Africa did not leave written records of their presence in ancient times. Thankfully, surprising amounts of data have been preserved through the African oral traditions of many tribes and cultures that clearly outline significant threads of knowledge that elucidates these issues. As explained in above chapters, the oral traditions of Africa (and indeed the world over) are very unique methods of using the human *consciousness faculties* as *information storage facilities* that bridge the gap between generations in unbroken continuity for thousands of years, retaining accurate information. Although some information can at times be compromised, the base of that information can also operate on the sub-conscious level. That's where specific forms of rituals, secret initiations, songs, musical instruments, dance, story telling, and mythology and so on comes into play. These *tools* were created in order to *embed* vital information in the mind and to ensure its continuity through generations. Information is *coded* and *encrypted* by these processes and can be retrieved through the same or similar rituals that elicit specific psychological and emotional responses, which helps to articulate and divulge relevant information and so on. I firmly believe also that DNA is crucial in the storage, recalling and utilizing of information on levels that we are not aware of as yet. This in its real sense is very much a part of the multi-dimensional technological apparatus that ancient black Africans have always used. There's no *exterior* computerized storage or retrieval facility, just the human consciousness faculty, DNA and the natural *brain computer* in operation. In fact the Euro/American Transhumanist vision of a future utopia outlines these principles as their eventual goal - human beings who will be able to *mentally* and *physically* affect time and space through genetic enhancement of the brain computer with artificial body implants and so on. The *genetic revolution* in Euro/American cultures alludes specifically to these procedural developments in the very near future.

Rasta advocates a purely *organic* and *natural* path to human development and evolution through the cultivation of respect and compassion for all life, the utilizing of *beneficial* and *sustainable* technological forms and the deeper understanding of the *spiritual relationships* that binds us to our common reality and most of all, our *Creator*. The future must be one of optimism beyond the negative and ultimately destructive accord of the New World Order.

*I came to realize that the darkness I feared was just an **illusion** formed by the forgetfulness of my **connection** to the very **source** of my being. My fear grew into confusion, which grew into suffering, and my suffering became despair. I recognized that I was lost and couldn't find the way back to my true self. I asked for directions but others became puzzled by my desire. No one understood where I wanted to go. I was afraid of appearing foolish and so, sank deeper under the covers of my illusions. The happy encouragement of my friends grew into the sound of sharpening blades. Then, when I saw the **Light**, my fear gripped me even tighter, because no one else could see it. But the more I looked at the Light the more it grew. And the more it grew, the less my fear became. My fear then abandoned me, unceremoniously, like a sweaty, shifty-eyed, cold footed bridegroom at the **altar of no return**.*

- The Golden Path of Jah Rastafari -

When you consciously try to free your mind from the Babylon System's mind control program you will automatically start to feel a very powerful fear of the unknown. Perhaps you will have bad dreams, nightmares, irrational fears and panic attacks. Your thoughts will become very erratic and confusing; fear of the dark and even imagining demonic entities attacking your mind and so on. You might even think that you're going insane. This is a normal reaction to your mind fighting against the mind control mechanism in place within your consciousness to reassert its position of natural freedom. This is a very important thing to understand.

The blond haired, blue-eyed white God you once believed in is not real and you might begin to feel ashamed at ever believing in it. You will certainly feel great fear at abandoning this concept because the ***indoctrination*** of the mind control program is designed to stimulate fear inside your mind when you try to break out of the ***mental prison***. You will certainly feel as though any thoughts contrary to this are the devil's work and should not be entertained. The same feelings will occur when you reject the Devil/Satan. The Euro/American God and Devil ***mind control programs*** are two of the most effect forms of mental slavery.

The prophet, Yeshua, (Jesus) did not use mind control to get you to believe in what he symbolized. In fact, if he was here right now he would be at the front of the fight against the *Satanic Illuminati*, their mind control programs and *New World Order*. Jesus did not tell people to bow down and worship him as God; **NOWHERE IN THE BIBLE DOES IT SAY THIS**. This is part of the way in which the Babylon System has mind controlled millions of human beings to make crosses, pictures and statues that they *label* as Jesus Christ and worship these as God, (even though no one knows what he looked like); *the very things he came to stop people from doing has become the standard of the religion that bear his name*. We must remember that what Yeshua came to establish, the evil force behind the Babylon System has infected with its demonic teachings of hate, avarice, lust, greed, and death. The Luciferic/Satanic force could not conquer him and what he stood for because he became a spiritually purified being. The only way it could attack him was to attempt to destroy the message of peace and the ONELOVE that he brought to the human race by *sabotaging* the instrument of religion and spirituality that he came to establish; *the Church*.

In infecting the church and its leaders with illusory and false doctrine, the Luciferic/Satanic force has turned people away from making *real enquiries* about God. Atheism has become the accepted view in many Euro/American countries these days as the New World Order fanatics become more dogmatic in their attempts to control our societies. This doctrine is in itself clearly an agenda by many shadowy Illuminati run churches and is being promoted vigorously by its adherents and disciples.

The Illuminati's real plan is to destroy not just Christianity but all human religious and spiritual institutions. We see this occurring in the attempts at hijacking and subversion of *Tibetan Buddhist* spiritual culture and the present attack on *Islam* and *Muslim* cultures. And it's the same reasons why the British colonial government that once ruled Jamaica, attempted to destroy *Rastafari* several decades ago. If we are cut off from the divine energy then we will be at the mercy of the Luciferic/Satanic force that is behind the subversion of humanity's spiritual evolution. All the negative characteristics that we at times exhibit, give it energy to grow bigger and more powerful.

Over many decades we have seen the growth and promotion of pseudo-religious organizations such as *Mormons, Scientology, Jehovah's Witness* and various rag-tag *Evangelical* movements around the world shamelessly swindling poor people out of the little money they are able to scrape together to feed their malnourished and ill-educated children. These mind control organizations (under the guise of religion) are leading billions of human beings into spiritual and mental enslavement, exactly as they were deigned to do by the *Babylon System mind control program*. In fact these

265

days in *Jamaica* we can clearly see a prevalence of *Mormonism* rearing its unholy head from the ghettos to the suburbs of Kingston, Spanish Town and other places. Alarmingly, it's quite usual to see small groups of young white males in white shirt and black trousers cycling or walking around Jamaica trying to **brainwash black people** into joining their sinister little *cult*. They always target the poor and vulnerable in society. I recently noticed that they have been collecting all sorts of personal data about people and their communities in *Kingston* and *Spanish Town* and other places. Mormonism is another one of those insidious little pseudo-religious mind control outfits that is being used to enslave and kill black people. It is worthwhile reading some information on *Joseph Smith*, the founder of Mormonism (who was a high ranking *freemason*) and his hallucinations and the methods he used to form his *cult* of Mormonism. I refer the reader once more to the books of *David Icke* and many other researchers who have clearly explained the sinister and evil nature of this cult and its deep satanic *connections*.

*Everything has **power** – the power of life given by the **Supreme, Jah Rastafari**. Power is life and life is far more than mere **flesh** and **blood**. When you are told that **'power corrupts and absolute power corrupts absolutely'**, that is a **mind control doctrine** designed to overthrow truth. Without power we cannot exist; we would be **power-less**. If we give up our power we relinquish the gift of God. We dishonour the gift of our Creator and the struggles of our Ancestors by allowing our power to be taken from us. Power is the God-given gift of life and **absolute power** is the province of our **Creator, Jah Rastafari**, the **Supreme Emanation of All-Being**. There is no corruption in this, only perfection.*

- The Golden Path of Jah Rastafari -

The Babylon System is real only in the sense that it's a measurable phenomenon (like all illusions) and as a consequence, its effects in our lives and the world at large can be analyzed, understood and transformed. It functions on the same principles of an extremely advanced interactive *mental hologram* that interfaces with the human brain computer and its sensory faculties, specifically the ego consciousness, thus stimulating a *'perceived'* coherent structure in what appears to our senses as an *'exterior world view'* superimposed over the naturally created material world. This is not just an isolated phenomenon but part and parcel of more extended structures that encompass the *time/space continuum* in which we exist wherein mind uses consciousness to interact within the Creation Field. These things despite current trends in Euro/American scientific thinking are not new but ancient philosophies which many ancient peoples knew about hundreds of thousands of years ago and applied scientifically and spiritually in their daily lives on earth. The African knowledge Tradition has always been the vehicle to this understanding.

It is absolutely crucial that knowledge of these things now become central to our development and affect a spiritual dynamic in the world, and especially for the new generation being born in the twenty first century and beyond. The old paradigm of *'knowledge creation and gathering'* has shifted and we must shift with it or be swept away in the dust of time. In the end it's up to the individual and through a process of realization, the collective masses of humanity can be inspired to rise up and throw off the yoke of oppression and tyranny which characterizes the painful events we call human history upon planet earth.

From the point of view of Rastafari, this is an extremely important thing in walking the *Golden Path of Jah Rastafari*. There cannot be real freedom on earth if even one human being is living in slavery, whether mentally or physically. Even the *'Devil in Hell'* must one day, in eternity, be brought to see the error in the rejection of truth and be offered the gift of redemption. Beings exhibit evil tendencies because they do not know the truth of reality. All the negative propensities that we exhibit such as greed, anger, lust, envy and so on are ultimately derived from our lack of knowledge of truth. When we embrace truth then all negative and unhelpful things disappear. The Satanic energy basically exists because we give it shape and form through our negative behavioral patterns and mental projections. That is why we are the ones who ultimately can change the nature of the Babylon System. We are keeping it going by our refusal to let go of it.

All too often we are capable of great sentiments like love, kindness and heroism and at the same time stoic cynicism and apathy can insinuate into our thinking to cloud judgment of our real purpose here on earth. There are times when it appears as though the *'Rasta Movement'* as a whole seem to have fallen victim to the manifold illusions of the Babylon System. Many Rastas living in Babylon have fallen under the seductive spells of the very enemy we came into this world to defeat. Not all Rasta organizations are living up to the creed of Livity. Apathy, appalling ignorance and a denial of truth characterizes parts of the movement of Rastafari at present in the twenty first century. One is sometimes asked by interested parties, "Where are the Rasta Elders full of earthy wisdom, foresight and compassion? Where are the *Rasta Warriors of Light* standing on the *Battlefield of Truth*? Where are the *Rasta Temples of Light and Understanding* built to edify humanity and extol the manifold splendor of our creator Jah Rastafari? Where are the institutions that teach Peace, Unity and ONELOVE as the only virtues that humanity can use as vehicles to progressive evolution? Where is the congregation of enlightened preaching and so on? Here in Jamaica and across the world there are hundreds and thousands of men and women who wear the dreadlocks of Rastafari and the *Red, Gold* and *Green* standard espousing elements of doctrine that purports cognizance of Rastafari. Indeed, some of the many singers and musicians from Jamaica and other countries such as the UK, USA, Africa, France, Germany, Japan, Sweden and so on who make *'Rasta Music'* are wholly negligent in their attitude to the faith of Rastafari because they appear not to really believe in even the most basic precepts of the *Laws of Livity*. Rastafari in some quarters has become a statement of fashion and the end point of a joke in some circles because some of those who call themselves Rasta are indeed mere superficial *products* of the Babylon System, which we are here to counter and eradicate. Even within the ranks of the Brethren we are beset with the stifling stench of illusions, ignorance, foolishness, sloveness, hypocrisy and debauchery that at times beggars belief.

The youth of future generations who will chose to walk the Golden Path depend on Rastafari *Elders* and *teachers* for clear and concise direction through the turmoil of the Babylon System. Unfortunately, some Rastafarian Elders never bothered to educate themselves to any real degree. Intellectual development is a necessary, and indeed, vital part of the transmission of knowledge and so must be cultivated assiduously. Within the ranks of the Brethren intellectualism is at times frowned upon by some who are quite ignorant about a great many things. Some, being absolutely misguided, believe that brute force and ignorance can win the day. We cannot have development in Rastafari as a pertinent and relevant spiritual culture and evolutionary force unless its tenets can be established and dispensed to those who come seeking Rastafari in an intelligent and enlightened manner. And by that I don't necessarily mean a written creed but a rigorous and uncompromising analysis of our roles as guardians and promoters of natural human developmental processes. The future generations of Rastafari must be guided by Elders who are proficient in learning and immersed in the wellspring of the divine compassion that is the ONELOVE of Jah Rastafari. If Rastafari is to become relevant to human beings who chose to use it as a vehicle to earthical and spiritual development then it must metamorphose into what it was intended to be. Some have tried to hijack and steer the movement in various directions but it has always resisted being controlled and remains a natural and expressive vehicle for human freedom.

On the whole there are many stalwart Brethren such as *The Most Honorable Prophet, Rasta Elder, Mutabaruka* who has been pushing home the thrust of the faith to open the eyes of the masses of humanity to the dire consequences of the mind control programs of the Babylon System.

The Babylon System cannot be defeated with wishful thinking, ignorant bluster or clouds of pungent Ganja smoke but with *firm and unswerving dedication to the development of our minds, the evolutionary expansion of our consciousness faculties and complete, unswerving conviction to the DIVINE principles of the ONELOVE of JAH RASTAFARI.* Being a Rasta means that one must take up the mantle of the *Rasta Fire Warrior* on behalf of humanity and *all* sentient beings in creation. There cannot be any discrimination in this fact whatsoever.

The road to redemption must be traveled by all beings, whatever their persuasion in this life; whether they know it or not. In life when you really think about it, it's incredible that we know so little yet believe we know so much. Too often many of us, grown pompous with pride and the negative qualities of the *ego*, walk headlong into very great ignorance and illusion and drag others along with us. The *Eternal Body of Truth* that is *Jah Rastafari* is beyond all contradictions and heresy. Once a complete and conscious effort is made to understand the *Golden Path* everything else takes care of itself. The Babylon System *must* and *will* fall; *in that there is absolutely no doubt*, it's really just a question of *time* and *space*.

The Babylon System was created as a mental prison to trap sentient beings in order for demonic interdimensional life-forms to feed from our energies. It's *superimposed* over the original energy matrix that the mind of sentient beings use to *navigate* through our three dimensional experiences. We use the matrix medium to experience sensory worlds and existences and to *delve into varied scenarios and possibilities of being*.

The problem begins when sentient beings lose their sense of *navigation* and get carried away, becoming *lost* in sensory tastes, pleasures and worlds that, in reality, have no *substance* in terms of defining our real evolutionary progress, but only fantastic creations of the *ego* sensory faculty. *Religions and spiritual systems are primarily navigational tools; our compasses and points of reference in existent nature.* The mind, having its origins in the *Infinite Field of Potentiality,* can *imagine* anything into being. We become trapped like flies in amber because we don't understand this process of imagination and its implications in the continuous process of creation. It's like going into a theatre or cinema and watching a play or movie. At some point during the performance we begin to get absorbed by what we see on stage. The problem though is that we become so absorbed in what we are viewing that we completely immerse ourselves in it and become a part of it, forgetting ourselves completely in the process. Behind the stage are the play writers, directors and a host of other details that creates the play but whom we are not cognizant of. What we refer to as *mind* is a part of the actual *projector* of phenomenon and everything that our senses record is basically a projection or *type* of hologram created by the wondrous nature of mind and its actions within the *Creation Field*. When we can learn to understand this principle of existent nature and its causes and effects, then we are able to manipulate the energies that are inherent in it successfully and consciously in order to create *harmony, peace* and *compassion* among our fellow sentient beings in the world. We can utilize this structure to gain higher understanding, (as we're supposed to do), not to get trapped in it. All our striving to acquire money, fame and worldly possessions is completely futile if we do not understand these issues.

The mental/spiritual energies that created the matrix for the *Babylon System* have been manipulated consciously by selfish and evil beings in order to gain what they perceive as power over others. This however can easily be changed once we recognize what's really happening and make a concerted effort to stop it from continuing, once and for all, by genuinely reaching out to each other in soulful *ONELOVE* until there's a point of *critical mass* wherein the *majority* of human beings can *wake up, stand firm* and say, *"It's time for real changes. We've had enough of this nightmare!"*

*"Discipline of the **mind** is a basic ingredient of genuine **morality** and therefore of **spiritual strength**. Spiritual power is the eternal guide, in this life and the life after. Led forward by spiritual power, man can reach the summit destined for him by the **Great Creator**".*

-H.I.M, The Sublime, Emperor Haille Selassie I, The King of Kings -

Around the world many different cultures refer to the Creator in a variety of ways. For instance Rastas in general refer to the Creator of all life as Jah Rastafari, the Supreme Potency of All –Being, The Maker, The Giver of All Life, The Father, The Supreme Personality of All-Being from which all things come into being and so on. Muslims refer to the Creator as Allah, The Merciful, The Beneficent, and The Lord of All and so on. Christians generally use similar adjectives. Invariably all other societies have a name and manner of approach towards comprehension of the divine creator of all things. Even though we are really speaking about the same concept we all have different methods of understanding what the Creator is. It's not a bad thing for humans to use various different ways to connect with the divine. It's part of our evolutionary process, and a necessary one when we really think about it in the correct manner. Ultimately the Creator is the Creator in whatever language we chose to use. God in the real sense transcends all our conceptions of gender, race and indeed religion itself, but because of our limited method of thinking and erroneous mental conceptions, we ascribe shape, form and characteristics to the Creator to make it easier for us to approach. There are some Afro-Centric Rastas who erroneously maintain that God is some sort of **black super-being**. This is really an exercise in ignorance because God has no **body** or **skin** like human beings do, therefore how could *'he'* be black? The Holy Bible states that God created man in his own image. The word *image* is the root word for *imagination, imagine* and so on. If we dissect the meaning ascribe to these words we realize that *'image'* does not mean exact likeness but has to do with the subtle perceptive faculty we label imagination and its operation as a sensory faculty. God created man in or through the process of *divine imagination*. We have to be brave and rigorous when confronting these things.

272

Having said that, the most important thing to remember is the fact that The Creator is beyond all erroneous human definition, yet is defined in the very fact of human's existence in time and space. There are numerous other types of living beings in the universe who are very similar to us and also very different from us. These beings, albeit being labeled as *'aliens'*, in the final analysis, are also the creation of the *Field of Infinite Potentiality,* we designate *Jah Rastafari*. The Creator is all pervading, omniscient and immanent in creation, as the embodiment of its creation and there are no boundaries or borders to the manifestation of the *Supreme Energy*.

The fight for freedom, justice and civil rights gave birth to Rastafari as a recognizable *symbol* of the eternal struggle of life to develop and evolve along the path of its own natural accord. From humble beginnings Rastafari has propagated itself across the world, eliciting devotion from diverse peoples, its adherents ceaselessly proclaiming the *gospel* of peace and ONELOVE of *Jah Rastafari,* the *Eternal Lord of Potentiality, Shatterer of Illusions* and *The Unifying Grace*. The Rastafarian struggle is essentially the struggle of the *entire human race* for redemption and salvation from the interminable rounds of ignorance, intolerance, hate, war, sickness and suffering that afflicts us all in the Babylon System. Wherever there's injustice, intolerance, hate, enslavement of people and a breakdown in the natural spiritual morality and development of human beings, Rasta is always born into the world to counter and defeat these detriments to human evolution. Rasta is not a religion in the sense of the mind control religious structure as some people might believe. The concept of religion as practiced by most churchical establishments is anathema to the real conscious development and evolution of human beings. It creates suffocating limitations around the mind, heart and soul. There has never been a *pure* religion in the histories that have been recorded by Euro/American civilizations. Religions as we know them today are parts of the *Babylon System* of oppression and division that characterizes some of the worst excesses of our civilizations on earth. The Golden Path of Jah Rastafari is a *natural* spiritual system that allows human beings to navigate their way out of the Babylon System and back to a holistic and beneficial way of perceiving our roles as loving, creative sentient beings in creation.

For Rastafarians, *Jah Rastafari* is the *Supreme Potentiality* of *All-Being,* the manifestation of the entire creation and also the embodiment of the created within it. The Creator *suffuses* creation; every cell of all living and non-living things and every atom and sub-atomic particle that gives rise to energetic dynamism and every *mathematical equation* that the scientist of Babylon might decipher and ascribe to the workings of phenomenon. Without The Creator nothing could exist as it does. In *reality* it's irrelevant what name a being calls the Creator because The Creator transcends such things as labels, names and categories. We use these terms knowingly, only as rational reference points for the mind/soul to locate its position, purpose and functionality within the Creation Field.

The subversion of all the ancient religions and even the more modern ones is a method by which the controllers of the Babylon System have enslaved humanity. As said before, it's not that religion is wrong or unworkable; it's just that the paradigm we use to understand it needs to shift to encompass the evolution of mind/soul/ spirit in existent nature. New religions and cults are constantly created using the same old paradigm of manipulation and control, some of which we have looked at in this volume. We do not need any new religions or sciences; we have everything here on earth that we can utilize to develop ourselves, we just have to come to a point of realization of these things. We must become conscious of the fact that there is a creative power, (whatever we consider that to be) which has brought the entire multi-verse and its attendant structures into being. The refusal to consider this properly and wander off into meaningless abstractions is indeed a wanton act of intellectual recklessness and willful disregard for truth.

Even if we didn't exist, Jah Rastafari would still be because without us the expressive force of creation would be redirected in other ways and forms. Creation is *Limitless Potentiality* and we are but *one* form of expression of this miraculous power. Our potential as sentient beings is also infinite in reality. We can develop and evolve in any way we consciously choose to.

Within the paradigm f Rastafari, the way for us as human beings to develop and maximize our potential is by a clear understanding of the eternal principles of ONELOVE, which is the very reason for our being here on earth and the very purpose of our evolution as sentient beings. When we say the word ONELOVE, it might sound quite simple but as soon as we begin to apply our minds to its incredible implications our understanding begin to broaden and widen in some truly remarkable ways. *ONELOVE doesn't make us afraid; it doesn't leave us hungry and alone. It doesn't make us angry nor does it create wars. It fills our hearts and souls with pleasure and abundance. It expands our consciousness. It enhances our being and elevates us to the highest point of realization of our true potential as human beings. ONELOVE is the compass that shows us our real position in relation to each other, the whole of existence and our Sublime Creator.*

Creating peaceful environments in our societies on earth isn't really such a hard job. It's just that we've never really tried to do so before, consciously and in the correct manner. We've talked about it very much. Individuals and small groups of people have attempted to do it but have always fallen short of the goal due to the many temptations presented by our *ego sensory faculty*. The Babylon System does not permit us to live and function in peaceful situations; that would be detrimental to its continuation. It plays on our fears, egos and wayward emotions, to stimulate negativity and fear. We don't have to go out and plant bombs and attack the institutions of the system; that would only create greater negativity and trap us in the spiraling descent to hellish modes of existence. We just have to stand up with true realization and walk away from it in the opposite direction, calmly and securely in the knowledge that if we don't give it our consent it cannot function. We can live without *money* or *micro-chips* in our bodies. We have choices; we just need to educate ourselves to understand the choices open to us so that we can create the most viable solutions to our problems.

Some of the choices we can make that would change our lives from the Babylon System mode are quite simple yet very effective. For instance, if our lives are very difficult in a particular place then we can get up, pack up our children and our stuff, sell whatever possessions we want to and move to somewhere else that is more favorable to our development. Many people are doing this right now. There are places in the world such as some areas in South America, Africa, and Asia, and in Europe where we can buy land, build our own homes and grow our own food, thus cutting our *dependency* upon the Babylon System. We can gather *equipment* and accumulate resources that allow us greater freedoms in our personal day to day lives. We can *link* very easily with other like minded progressive people around the world through the internet and find out how to join groups and foundations that are genuinely trying to make a difference to the way we are living in the Babylon System - (Bearing in mind to avoid negative cults and ego-maniacs that are natural offshoots of the Babylon System's mind control programs).

- If you have the resources to do so then leave cities and countries that are preventing you from developing naturally as a free human being.

- Join communities that are involved in natural sustainable developments but not religious/cultish/racist/sectarian structures. Be free to express yourself in the way that's natural to you and your development with the understanding that you have to respect the natural rights of others just the same as they must respect yours.

- Learn how to build your own home and environment in harmonious surroundings.

- If you have money then buy land and structure your life naturally away from the turmoil of cities.

- Learn how to grow the food that you consume. Any community can grow its own food and not be dependent on supermarkets to buy from. Learning to grow food should be a requirement for all children in schools. If you control your food supply then you control important aspects of your existence. If your enemy controls your food and water then you are in a most precarious position.

- Teach your children the basic skills of how to live in natural environments.

- If you are in a community then there should be a community school where the community decides how and what the children learn individually and collectively. The role of compassionate ONELOVE and real human understanding must be the basis of any educational process.

- Link with other like minded people. When people see something real happening they will gravitate towards what you're doing and those who are really interested will join together.

- On no account should MONEY be involved in the new life that you're now living. There are numerous ways to live successfully and happily without that burden. We have to create a system that does not use money. This is really not so difficult to do; we just have to apply our minds to the methodology. If we share experiences and ideas we can easily live in communities that value people and their skills and not pieces of paper with ink printed on them. Before there was a system of money in existence people lived happy and contented lives on earth. We have to recreate this paradigm. Skills can easily be traded within a community without the exchange of money. If everyone develops their natural human abilities within a community then that natural ability can be offered to the greater good and development of that community. Everyone can share the benefits of a harmonious situation where skills are developed and used for the benefit of that community and so on.

- The pursuit of human freedom and human individuality is essential to our development collectively. Therefore respecting and upholding the natural rights of human beings must be at the forefront of our development in any social setting.

We can take back control of our lives into our own hands without firing a bullet at our oppressors. We just have to make up our minds and walk away from it all. Just imagine if nobody voted in all the pointless elections that are held; what would happen? Who could govern us? The politicians would all be running around in even more confusion like headless chickens. If we all stayed home for one week and not go to work or buy products from shops and supermarkets, the Babylon System would collapse in three days. If we all grew and shared our own food, we wouldn't have to eat Babylon's unwholesome genetically modified foods. Supermarkets would have to reassess their mandate.

We can educate our children instead of giving them to the Babylon System every day to be brainwashed. *Human beings living, working and sharing collectively need only work three to four hours a day*, the rest of time could easily be spent on personal development and leisure. The division of labour could mean that everyone do what they do best. If one has a particular skill or leaning then one should be encouraged to use that for personal development and also the *Greater Good* of all others as well. These are just some of the ways we can harness our collective power and expose the inherent weakness of the Babylon System. The balance of power lies with the majority of the people in any given society; if we all woke up from this dreadful nightmare we can all become free, instantly. And when we do, we must then learn, like the slaves in Jamaica after slavery ended, to create new lives for ourselves without the illusions of the Babylon system. In leaving Babylon, we have to become pioneers on a new frontier of life. We must have our wits about us though in this newly discovered world we can rightly call *freedom.*

Freedom means that we have to take full <u>responsibility</u> for all our thoughts and actions in the world and the <u>consequences</u> of them.

We all know that freedom means that the rights of the individual must be respected and protected, but freedom doesn't mean that *absolutely anything goes*. In Livity, there are natural rules and guidelines that assist human beings to live and develop productively and harmoniously on a socially beneficial level. Justice, tolerance and the natural rights of each individual must be tempered with the philosophical ideals of the *Greater Good* of the community and the world. A doctor is just as important as a dustman and a tool maker is just as important as a dress maker and a fisher man is equal to a lawyer. Everyone is equal and valid on the same level. No one is more important than anyone else, even though the job that each individual does is different. This principle is a crucial part of Rasta Livity. There is no distinction between people on account of the jobs they do, only the state of mind that each individual cultivates. If we can begin to function on this level then we are almost there.

Ultimately Rastafari represents the challenge to humanity to rise above the negative accord of the Babylon System and *throw off the yoke of mental and physical oppression* (whatever colour of skin or culture we subscribe to). We must form pressure groups and agitate the debate wherever we can. Approach conscious people in positions of power and stimulate their interests in a new paradigm of living for the masses. The agenda must include:

- Stimulating ways to dismantle the power structure of lies and deceit that act as governments, banks and public institutions.

- Getting rid of the bureaucratic regimes that disenfranchise 90% of the populations of our planet.

- Finding real ways to create harmony between people whatever racial background we come from.

- Finding ways to create true unity among the diverse sections of humanity by creating a new paradigm for existing together as a unified whole. It's crucial to respect differences in human beings, whatever they may be and to utilize those differences to enhance the whole.

- Utilization of beneficial technology to clean up the mess we have created and to assist people in diverse places to begin the process of social renewal and mental rejuvenation.

- Allowing all peoples free access to health care and education and developing technologies. A healthy and educated population is one of the main goals of Rastafari.

- Making a real effort to tackle the problems of environmental damage to the planet earth.

- Getting rid of weapons of mass destruction.

As human beings we can become unified while retaining our basic differences of culture, ethnicity and so on. We can't all look and function in the same way because our natural evolutionary pathway dictates the *necessity* for differences to exist as part of the *imperative* for constant change, growth, learning and development. The fact that we are so varied is one of the greatest assets of the human race. We must come to a point of recognition of this and implement changes in our societies that enable all human beings to live in peace, security and mutual beneficial situations.

---

*Beyond the fields of illusions that entrap the unwary soul in the fantasies of life, there exists the omnipresent reality that is **eternal** and **forever**; of which there was never a beginning and of which there could never be an end. It is the transcendent, **Limitless Field of Potentiality,** the **Supreme embodiment of Unity**, the **Supreme Personality of All-Being** and the **Perfect Light** that is The **ONELOVE** we Rastas refer to in **word** as Jah Rastafari.*

*Jah Rastafari is the Primordial Originator, The Fashioner and the Giver of all life and forms, the maker and the generator of the First Shining, The Supreme Unity from which all multiplicity is born into material existence; beyond concepts and duality, the purity of the pure, without flaws or contradiction and beyond sin and redemption. If the Supreme Potentiality of All-being was not, then all that exist could not be. But since Jah Rastafari is the Supreme Lord of Unfathomable Fields and the wielder of the sublime force of infinite mysteries, whose glory and divine majestic manifests continually, moment to moment, all that exist rejoices in the **Perfect Light** of life.*

-The Golden Path of Jah Rastafari –

Because the natural state of human beings is Rasta, we do not need to recruit or persuade people to locks their hair, listen to Reggae Music and label themselves Rasta. In fact, dreadlocked hair is not even a prerequisite to being Rasta. The very *'Ground of Being'* is Rasta, which means that just being a *conscious* human being with *soul, love* and *divine purpose* is itself being Rasta. Rasta is about consciousness of whom and what we are as sentient beings in creation and our recognition of our eternal relationship to the Supreme Creative energy of all existence. It must be stated here *clearly* that I am not advocating that Rasta, (in terms of spiritual consciousness), is the only way for us to develop as human beings, (that would be completely impractical to our evolutionary *prime-directive* as change and the exploration of constantly evolving ideas and structures are crucial elements in the human developmental process). There is no one way for human beings to evolve. Rasta is basically one of the ways that is relevant, and just as valid as any other pertinent form. The teachings of Rastafari, although universal and can be applied in all cases, is cognizant of the fact that we are all individuals with unique needs and this is one of the joys of being human in the world we share. Our individuality, from the point of view of our personal experiences as living beings, is absolutely vital and very necessary to our development and evolution. The true culture of Rastafari has been able to avoid the doctrinarian and dogmatic views of religious institutions purely on the basis that the human race is made up of individuals who each have a mind that sees from a unique point of view. Real freedom dictates that each point of view must be respected and taken into consideration. Because we have to use words to navigate through our perception of existence, we constantly make tremendous mistakes in our dealings with each other on a daily basis. The **Golden Path of Jah Rastafari** teaches us that:

One must always be careful of the traps and snares of words, even the words **Rastaman, Rastawoman, Golden Path, Jah Rastafari** *and* **God**. *Words only allude to conceptions and ideals that arise from our minds; they cannot define the true nature of reality. Words ultimately are products of our misconceptions of reality... There is no known language, human or otherwise that could explain what reality is. In* **reality**, *no words can explain what Jah Rastafari is, not even the words* **Jah Rastafari**.

When we look at our world today, it appears as though all the people who say that they follow the various religions are fighting and killing each other daily. Some Muslims, Christians, Hindus, Buddhists, (and even **Atheists** and **Transhumanists**, who follow what is really a religion – **an idea can also become a God**), are constantly at war to promote their ideology or brand of truth. Rastas have never joined in this religious or spiritual confusion. We have never killed in the name of religion or politics. We've never gone to war to promote the truths that we adhere to. We've never exploited our fellow human beings in the name of Jah Rastafari. We have never contended to be superior to any other beings or to even know the ultimate truth of the universe and so on. In fact, when we look at it, Rastas do not recruit followers or charge money to teach meditation and spiritual enlightenment or such things. People just seem to gravitate towards Rasta of their own **freewill**, not through fear and doubt and anxiety. Spirituality is supposed to be like that, free, open and spacious with room for everybody to breathe and develop **organically** of their own freewill.

Rasta is universal. It teaches peace, humility, simplicity, joyful ONELOVE and compassion and knowing acceptance of life for all living beings, whatever they might be, and is celebratory in the fact that all existence is the constant and eternal creation of the **Supreme Power**, the **Limitless Field of Potentiality**, and the **Eternal Body of Truth, Jah Rastafari**. Rasta has never claimed a monopoly on the Absolute Truth, as various religions profess. We do believe however, that through perfect **Livity** and the exercising of respect and **loving-compassion** for each other, Our Mother Earth and all sentient life forms, and by developing and attuning our minds to our **Creator,** the

Eternal Giver of Life, we can lead productive and evolutionary lives right here on earth. Livity is our compass to find our direction through the Creation Field as soul/spirit is our linkage point to the Divine Will of Our Creator. Without Livity nothing in our lives on earth can make real sense.

How then can human beings live progressively? As Rastas, we subscribe to the universal principles and ***Laws of Livity*** embedded in the divine expression of the ONELOVE. Only with Livity can we navigate through the turmoil of our lives and throw off the suffocating bonds of slavery and illusions that the Babylon System has inflicted upon us. Livity is the ***earthical***, philosophical and spiritually scientific method that empowers our minds with the flexibility to move through existence successfully. The prophet, Yeshua, in his ministry roughly two thousand years ago, elaborated some of the most important aspects and rules to developing right Livity; Love, cultivating human compassion, kind regard for other sentient beings, physical and spiritual cleanliness, peaceful outlook, mental, physical and spiritual sobriety which imparts a disciplined attitude to life and so on. These laws are not exclusive to Christianity but Islam, Buddhism, Hinduism and in fact all spiritual systems of the world. They have always been inherent in the foundation principles of Rastafari.

Throughout, I have used various symbols and points of references that appear to stand outside what is believed to be conventional Rasta thinking. For some, this might appear challenging and for others, utter heresy, but what we have to really understand (and this can categorically be proven by anyone who care to do so) is that these ideas are not new but gleaned from the ancient root of our spiritual legacy bequeathed to us by our ancient earthly Ancestors and spiritually enlightened predecessors. We're all going through a major period of transition at present and whether one agrees with this paradigm or not, it's vital that we at least understand these things.

*We **Rastafarians** of Jamaica have been persecuted and abused, even by some of our own fellow kinsmen. We have suffered for the sake of righteousness and truth. We have suffered the worst that the **Babylon System** can offer and still **we stand firm like unconquerable 'lions of the field'**. Still we fight **'the great evil'**. Still, we praise the majesty of our **Omnipotent Creator**. Still, we praise the divine grace of the Prophets. It is the way of true faith, to know that one walks through illusion while standing firm and fearless in the All-loving reality that is **Jah Rastafari**.*

-The Golden Path of Jah Rastafari -

I have outlined above some principles that express the expansive nature of Jah Rastafari as the Creator of existent nature and all life and forms, the *Limitless Field of Potentiality*. Because of the nature of words this might appear as though I am expressing that the Creator is something like a nebulous, wispy entity floating around in an inconceivable state somewhere. This can sometimes be the most troubling aspect of any inquiry into a clear understanding of what Jah Rastafari is. Although being the *Creator* of existent nature and the *Eternal Maintainer* of all things, yet Jah Rastafari is immanent within creation as the *Supreme Personality of All-Being*. Now that's probably a lot to say, some would no doubt think. How is that possible and by what qualification can a person assert these things without *concrete proof*? All religions in some way allude to the idea that the Creator has a specific *personality* which is exhibited throughout creation and can be understood and known by human beings and other sentient life forms in space, time and dimensions. I approach this issue from the premise that no human being alive has ever *seen* the Creator physically, and even though the Bible asserts that various Jewish patriarchs of the Old Testament saw, walked with, talked with and one (Jacob) even wrestled physically with the Creator of the entire universe we have no physical proof that these things were real events. In fact, basic common sense would lead us to see that these things did not happen in the manner we are told. These days if anyone said that they saw, sat with and talked to God, they would be given sedatives, taken to a mental institution and be labeled schizophrenic.

The various religions categorically state that the Creator at times can take human form and manifest on earth: Krishna, Jesus and so on. According to the *Vedantic* teachings an aspect of the Creator, **Krishna,** lived on earth, ate food, had friends and lovers and taught human beings God-consciousness and so on *while at the same time* upholding the universe and all reality. The story of Jesus Christ is well known by almost everybody.

The Creator of existent nature, (in our present mode of ignorance), is a very misunderstood element because we have never been really *trained* to understand its magnitude. The problem here is in our lack of understanding of the manner in which the Creator can manifest aspects of *spiritual energies and personalities* in space and time *through* the collective mind/soul consciousness of human beings. Because Jah Rastafari exists on levels far beyond our present mode of comprehension, the way in which the Creator actively participates in creation is by *operating through our minds and souls* and our active *consciousness faculties* to substantiate its *presence*. Unfortunately, human beings have a tendency to misinterpret this dynamic relationship between the Creator and the created because the means by which this process occurs is outside our present mode of erroneous perception such as *logic, reason, objectivity, science, religion* and *dualism*. How is it possible for human beings to use words and five sense perceptions to decode the behaviour of something that is as magnificently transcendent as the *Creator*? Another crucial part of this is that as human beings we tend to want a separate, personal form of existence that is divorced from the Creator. Most of our problems stem from the fact that we feel alienated from our Creator because we have been trained to use our minds to create separation from the very thing that is the essence of our being. This specific problem is stimulated by the *Babylon System* of mis-education concerning religion, spirituality and our human and divine natures.

Our faulty perception, which is derived from our *'fall'* into the Babylon System of mental oppression and spiritual illusions, is the reason why we feel limited in all that we aspire to. As an example, if I hold in my hand a nice juicy apple I know that it's an apple because my conditioned senses recognizes it as such. And if I hold up another hand that has nothing in it, of course my senses tells me that there's nothing in my hand. The thing is, as human beings we use words to navigate our sensual perceptions of existent nature. The word *apple* denotes something specific to our senses and the word *nothing* denotes another specific thing. The point is that the word *nothing* is used to specify *something that does not exist according to the laws of our physical senses of perceptions*. In using the word nothing, that ultimately implies to the mind *something*. Mind which is the *analyzer* of phenomenon has to be *tricked* into rationalizing a pathway through this conundrum. We have to use that word because many of us are incapable of comprehending *nothing* in its wordless form as an *ideogram or indeed as nothing*. It confuses our senses. Similarly, when I use the term the *Formless Nature* in relation to *Jah Rastafari, the Eternal Field of Potentiality from which all life and forms continually spring*, it might be difficult to understand how anything can be formless and yet have *Supreme Potency*. The gross senses that we use are *conditioned senses* which are governed by the phenomenal states in which we exist. The true reality behind this illusion that we all live in is not based on conditioned senses or material being alone but on much higher, more subtle and *transcendent laws*. When we approach the Creator, our *conditioned senses* can only take us so far because the Creator is a truly *Superior Presence* that functions through superior states beyond conditioned existences. *Superior Being* does not mean *physical being with arms and legs and comic book super-powers* and so on but we have to use the language format we know to try to allude to something that *transcends* language itself. In order to understand the Creator on the real level that is necessary for enlightened existence we have to *elevate our minds* to a real level of understanding ourselves as human beings in the world. This means that we have to create ethical systems based on pure Livity. Livity is the blue print or the guide book to understanding our relationship with our Creator, Jah Rastafari and with each other as sentient beings. For Jah Rastafari who created all reality, anything is possible, *even manifesting in a fleshy body* if that is the paradigm for greater understanding. This is perhaps one of the greatest contentious issues that human beings on earth have been wrestling with for many thousands of years. Because of our conditioned reflexes, (very much like the Pavlov Dog experiment mentioned earlier) when we think of God we always try to think of something like a physical being that relates to our physical nature, but with super powers or magical abilities. This is because of the mind controlling effects of the Babylon System conditioning, which also reflects us back into our ancient past and its associations with the predatory alien forces (gods) that inserted themselves into our reality matrix by manipulating our perception of this form of knowledge. This *conditioning* therefore locks our minds into a *collective consensus* that makes us approach the *concept* of The Creator in terms relative to our physical being and the devious manipulations of our interdimensional alien predators.

The great religious books of the world all allude to the nature and personality of The Creator in some detail. Firstly we need to use critical analysis and our natural intelligence factor to understand the nature of the universal Creator of all life and forms. The Holy Koran, the Holy Bible, the Vedas/Bhagavad- gita and some other spiritual systems all expound various ways in which human beings can reach understanding of the personal aspect of the multiversal Creator. Within the African Mystery Systems the same rules applies. God is God in whatever language or culture we use to reach this understanding, and our various different ways of connecting to the divine can still be valid tools in assisting us with greater clarity as we continually evolve. We might not understand the reasons for this now due to the confusion of our historical past, but our future evolutionary path will ultimately make it all very clear.

"Our deepest fear is not that we are inadequate. Our deepest fear is that we are ***powerful beyond measure****. It's our **light**, not our darkness that most frightens us.* ***Your playing small doesn't help the world".***

-Nelson Mandela-

Jah Rastafari is the Supreme Creative Energy that has given rise to, maintains and upholds all existence. This is the main principle which is the guiding force behind Rastafari. From this tenet of our faith all things flow into being; mind, soul, spirit, matter, energy and life in abundance. As we have ascertained through virtue of the analytic mode of the Fire Meditation upon these things, the fullness of life on earth is realized; respect for all sentient beings, the phenomenon of material nature, the intelligence faculties that motivates life through its evolutionary processes and the joyous knowledge that propels us along the ***Golden Path*** to the ***higher heights*** of ***Za-Yan***. Without understanding these concepts and applying them studiously, a Rasta can become hopelessly lost in the quagmire of sensory gratification, abstract fantasies; mind numbing illusions, cowardly behaviour and death and rebirth in confusion and ignorance.

The Rastafarian tradition some people are acquainted with hails our Sublime Emperor, His Imperial Majesty, Haille Selassie I of Ethiopia as the incarnation of the divine on earth, Jesus Christ returned and so forth. The very name used by Rastafarians to hail the glory of the Supreme, Jah Rastafari, was indeed inspired from the titles of his Sublime Majesty. The words Jah Rastafari is in turn gleaned from the ancient languages of north eastern Africa, as used specifically by the ancient peoples of Kush/Nubia and Egypt. The ancient Kushites and Ethiopians are related peoples who used variations of an ancient language that stretched back into ancient times. The linguistic relationship of ancient Egypt, Kush/Nubia and Ethiopia is very is clear.

The word ***Ra*** in the ***Ancient Egyptian*** language implies the ***creative*** Godhead. ***P'ta*** or ***P'tah*** means the Godhead of wisdom, and ***Fari*** means the ***establishment*** of God's dwelling on earth, later applied to the ruler as ***pharaoh*** or ***Fari***. The word ***Jah*** as used in the Old Testament Bible is also related to the ancient African root word ***Ra***. When we analyze these things we should remember (as explained in above chapters) that the prophet Moses created the religion of the Jewish people after taking them out of Egypt. The canon and practice of Jewish faith is clearly taken from ancient African Mystery Teachings which can be proven historically. All Christians end their prayers

285

with the word *Amen* which is really an invocation of the ancient African God *Amun* or *Amen*, (said by the Egyptians and Kushites to be the most sacred and hidden name of God). In fact, within secret lodges and fraternities such as the *Delaurence* in Jamaica, the word Jah is often used in various invocations and so forth.

The word *Ras* in *Ethiopian* Amharic language means head/ruler), *Ta fari* means '*one who inspires awe*'. There are also many Latin words that have been borrowed from African languages such as *Rex* which means king and has its root in *Ra/Re*, the Egyptian (Sun) God who was instructed by the *Nun* (the primordial creative energy) to fashion the universe. Words such as *royal* are derivatives of this. The etymology of the Indian/*Sanskrit* word *Raja* which means *king/royal* is also rooted in the African conception of the sun god Ra/Re and consequently relates to the word *Jah*. There are many Indian/Sanskrit words that have their roots in ancient African languages due to the influences of earlier migrations of African peoples into the Indian sub-continent in very ancient times. This is only the smallest part of the linguistic relationships between many cultures that is rooted in the *ancient global language* system that once spread outward from Africa and stretched across the world through the *ancient global African civilization* that once existed on earth. Space does not permit me to go further but I urge the reader to research these things methodically. The rewards will be profound and most enlightening. Usually, some scholars, researchers and academics in general, arrogantly dismiss the vast bodies of research into these hidden aspects of human history by trying to marginalize and denigrate this emerging knowledge as *Afro-centric wishful thinking*. Yet consistently, they all fail to adequately refute or explain away the clear anomalies that stalk the pristine pages of their model of history.

Thus the using of the *term* Jah Rastafari as a means of solidifying Rasta faith is not new or surprising but merely an echo of the manner and methods that our ancient African forefathers applied to spiritual learning and development, from very remote times. We are but carriers and conveyors of traditions that have benefited human beings in greater understanding and awareness for countless thousands of years on earth.

This issue is still very contentious among some Rastas. There are those who hail Our Sublime Emperor not as God incarnate but as a divinely inspired, enlightened *emanation*, born into the world as a human being as a means of conveying essential spiritual and ethical inspiration to us in our struggles against the forces of evil and chaos. The Rasta movement in its founding days was largely centered on the believed divinity of Our Sublime Emperor. Time has furnished this generation of Rastafarians with greater insight into the cycles of knowledge that assists in the development of a rationale that outweighs certain aspects of this particular thinking. The main emphasis in our understanding is the reality of the *Supreme Power* that gave rise to all existence, *Jah Rastafari*.

Our esteem Rastafarian Elders and Ancestors, through their selfless sacrifices and unswerving faith in Jah Rastafari, paved the way forward for future generations of adherents to analyze and clarify the tenets of Rastafarian faith for themselves. The steadfast dedication to our faith has *expanded* the frontiers of our consciousness to embrace truth wherever it is found. Who can say that God has a name, or that God has the likeness of man? Who has ever seen or touched God? And how can anyone say that His Sublime Majesty, Haille Selassie I is God? These are some of the issues that some Rastafarians have had to wrestle with over time. There are all kinds of speculations about ancient prophecies and the connection to divine bloodlines and so forth that apparently justifies the divinity of His Sublime Majesty. Sadly, some brethren are still struggling to expand their consciousness beyond things that ultimately will have no relevance to the Rasta movement of the future. Many young people at times become disheartened after trying to find some reality in Rasta because some brethren and indeed Elders, are still locked in the paradigm of Old Testament *reasoning* and cannot seem to go beyond certain basic conundrums and false interpretations of scriptures.

 The founding paradigm of Rastafari in the early twentieth century was necessary for many reasons. The deeper *metaphysical* and *philosophical* enquiries that is needed in order to clarify the truth of Rastafari is vital, especially right now at a time when the world is heading very swiftly towards the biggest change the human race will ever experience for thousands of years. The Christian Bible was indeed a *necessary tool* in shaping our philosophical stance when approaching our spiritual nature, but we need to understand that *real knowledge is a living, progressive evolutionary energy that takes no prisoners*. Ignorance is a mere pretender to the throne of greatness and must eventually fall, like the walls of Jericho when the light of righteousness and truth is called to shine. As a species, we are evolving moment by moment, (and I don't mean evolution as the scientists of the Babylon System would have us believe). True evolution encompasses the *minds, consciousness, souls and spirits* of sentient beings and not the temporary material flesh which we inhabit.

Life is the inspiration of Jah Rastafari, our Eternal Creator, and being the *Lord of Limitless Inspirations,* is revealed through the inspiring struggles of our people in Jamaica for four hundred years through the dark and terrible oppression of slavery. The proud emblems and *symbols* of Jamaican culture crystallized the pathway to this realization; in the tenacious and clever fighting spirits of our brave, fearless and indefatigable *Maroon Warriors* who defeated at every turn the colonial forces of an oppressive British empire; our great and powerful *Warrior/Priestess Nanni* who devised the means to our many victories; our brave and sublime national heroes, *Paul

Bogle, Sam Sharpe, George William Gordon, Marcus Mosiah Garvey, Brother Leonard Howell, Prince Emanuel, Alexander Bedward and countless other great *heroes of the struggle*, many whose names we cannot recount but who furnished us with the inspiration to understand that *our freedom is a <u>divine right</u>, and can never be bartered, given up, sold or held to ransom by the powers of evil.* Our struggles for freedom in Jamaica became the *vehicle* through which Jah Rastafari was revealed to the world as a potent dynamic energy that is here to dispel the dark oppressive illusions of the Babylon System. Our faith in the immutable Laws of Livity enabled our Sublime Ancestors operating in the spiritual dimensions to employ the necessary *'spiritual tools and assistance'* that helped us in the activation of our *'positive spiritual energies'* here on earth and thus, the revelation of Rastafari in Jamaica. It's this dynamic that truly shifted our people out of the slavery mode and onto the *Golden Path of Jah Rastafari*. And it's the *same energy* that stimulated our Sublime predecessors such as Marcus Garvey and Brother Howell who ignited the freedom movements in Africa, South America and the USA to create and galvanize the *Civil Rights Movement* and the greater African Liberation struggles of the twentieth century. Rasta allows human beings unimpeded access to personal articulation of the methods and means of defining our own path of evolution – mentally, physically and spiritually. *It places power and responsibility for our thoughts and actions into our own hands*. The most important tenet or commandment of Rastafari must therefore be: *"The greatest sin is allowing yourself to be oppressed by another man, physically, mentally and/or spiritually"*.

Although Rastafari arose in Jamaica, this is merely incidental to a greater process. Rasta concerns the whole human race and the universe which we are all a part of; there is no limit to Rasta. The *ghettoized* version of our faith that some people (and the mind controlled media in particular) are used to is but purely circumstantial and does not reflect the magnitude and depth of the movement. There is really nothing ghetto about Rasta. Rasta is the extension of an ancient spiritual tradition that can be traced back many thousands of years through human history and cultures. In the past, the Babylon System sought to marginalize the movement in order to eradicate its growth and influences. These days we find Rastas in all strata of society wherever we go in the world, (albeit some are still confused as to the exact practical application of faith) yet the shining symbol of freedom that Rasta represents is at the heart of the quest by humanity to find our way out of the corruption of the Babylon System to true human *freedom*.

In spending much time among various brethren, I have come to reach my particular understanding of these issues. I would not be so vain and foolish to say that I know the ultimate truth or that I have some special insight into the workings of Rastafari more than others. What I am saying is that my faith as a Rastaman, however I conceive it to be, is the most serious and important thing for me. It's the sole reason why I live and draw the breath of life and cannot be compromised by fallacies or inadequacies born of the illusions of the Babylon System. Jah Rastafari has given us all the tools we need to reach full understanding of reality. Although we exist within the debilitating illusions of the Babylon System, we are still extraordinarily powerful beings and cannot really be held prisoners once realization dawns in our minds.

Our spiritual growth and liberation must be watered by the conviction of our *souls* to rise to the higher purposes of life that our Sublime Creator intended for us. The negative vibrations of the Babylon System have tainted our view of what spirituality really means. We must now seek the *Golden Path* of spiritual renewal that can galvanize our efforts to seek freedom from the destructive mind control programs. Spiritual renewal can take diverse forms and different methods can be applied. Whatever one's faith in terms of religious persuasion, the same rules can apply. In the Christian religion, baptism is used as a visible tool to reaffirm the convictions of a person who chooses to follow the path of God-consciousness through belief in Yeshua (Jesus Christ). Many people these days use some form of ceremony or ritual to do this. Essentially, whatever way is conducive to greater spiritual understanding for an individual is valid as long as the goal is reached; as long as the mind can be freed from the destructive illusions of the Babylon System. For us as Rastafarians and Fire Warriors, the All-Embracing Divine Energy of the ONELOVE that is Jah Rastafari, is the real antidote to all our mental and spiritual sickness.

*It's only through the conscious application of Compassionate **ONELOVE** in our lives that we human beings can **positively evolve**; nothing else.*

-The Golden Path of Jah Rastafari-

As our knowledge base increases, our *consciousness expands* with our continuous evolution in the dimensions of being and our appreciation of this fact becomes more joyous. As our awareness expands we discover new tools hidden away inside our mental/spiritual *'toolbox'*. By cultivating a desire to know and live the truth that our life experiences have to offer we can activate the dormant abilities of our minds to perceive new ways of thinking, feeling and being in this reality. With expanded consciousness the workings of Jah Rastafari becomes more revealed to us in some very remarkable ways. There is no force in this process, just the constant dynamic energy of the ONELOVE operating naturally towards its goals. Jah Rastafari transcends beginnings and endings. When we can free our minds from the constraints of irrational fears, anger, petty jealousies, hate, unreasoned prejudices we can then start to reach some meaningful understanding of what life really mean for us as human beings.

The future is not something that is set in stone. We can activate our true potential to create any kind of future we want. The point is, knowing what our real purpose and motivations are so that we can generate a viable and productive future for ourselves and each other. The *science-fiction* high-tech New World Order future world that the Babylon System is attempting to create on earth is a transparently fraudulent view of human progress and is purely designed to subvert our true evolutionary potential in the cosmos. Without real *justice* there can be no human *equality* and without that, there can be no *peace*. The precepts of Livity clearly explain the path of human development on earth and if these are followed we can all have a viable and sustainable future that's beneficial for all of us. Peace, Compassionate Love and Unity are the things that must replace war, hate and selfishness on earth. We use the words very much in our daily lives but how many of us ever experience peace, compassionate love and unity, whether for a short time or prolong periods? These things are not possible unless we throw off the yoke of oppression that the Babylon

System has instilled in our minds and start to create clear and conscious ways to build the pathway to peace, compassionate love and unity.

If we truly believe that God is love, then when we feel love or when we're in love, we're actually *experiencing* the *divine energy* of God. And conversely, when we fall out of love and we're not feeling all the beautiful things that love brings to us, we feel alone, fearful and dejected. Love hasn't gone away because God is ever-present; it's just that we're not *feeling* God anymore because we have become so absorbed with our own self pity that we've turned our attention away from the connection to love and therefore our connection to God. We've put restrictions on our *feeling* the love, thus we've put limitations on our comprehension of what God is. We most times confuse real love with a poor imitation that ends up being our own fragmented, *egotistical* perception of love. Real love isn't a concoction of *chemicals* swimming around in our brains and bodies that make us feel *'emotionally high'*, as some neuro-scientists try to make us believe. Love is the very foundation of our being. Most times when we think we are in love it's actually our ego that is fooling us to think so.

Love and selfishness are opposing forces. Love is about giving and expressing our divine nature freely and fully without expecting anything back in return. And the wonderful thing about love is that it's one of those *special energies* that, when released, bounces all over the place before hitting its target, absorbs more energy and comes right back to you even more powerful, (especially when you're not even looking for it to return). Many of us are very unfamiliar with what true love is and so express selfishness and believe we're giving love because of our confused states of mind. But we can easily work ourselves back to real love and the centre of our being if we really desire to do so, through first cultivating peace within our own minds and souls.

If we apply our minds to solve the problems that affect our lives in the right way, we can find great fulfillment in life. We have the tools to affect and change the very nature of the world we live in, in any way we want. It's not really about belief but the activating of the very natural power of the mind and its attendant consciousness faculties through remembering our connection to the very *source* of all life.

One of the most astonishing parts of our *'consciousness toolkit'* is the ability to *imaginatively* participate in creation. That's part and parcel of our natural freewill as human beings; to be able to use our minds to imagine that anything is possible and to activate that with the power of our conscious freewill. By the term imagine, I don't mean wishful thinking but active and dynamic usage of the powers of intellect, natural intelligence and cognition to affect changes in the world. If we can't imagine something then it cannot exist in our perception of reality, materially or spiritually. Some of us can't imagine what Jah Rastafari is because even though Jah Rastafari is the totality of reality and the Superior energy of all things, it's very difficult to imagine something that transcends our mundane experience. But we can *experience* Jah Rastafari by actually learning the fundamental precepts of the ONELOVE and by genuinely exercising the *Law of Livity* in our lives. *In this way the Creator can manifest in our hearts, souls and minds as a living, breathing presence that suffuses our being with loving energy, magnifying our souls and imparting true wisdom and understanding of its eternal and sublime reality.*

The Babylon System has robbed us of our will to resist the poisonous illusions that it injects into our veins from birth to death. It has dulled our senses and impaired our natural intelligence factor so that we perceive ourselves as less than what we really are. We experience this daily in our lives. We can't seem to meet the demands that the Babylon System makes on us. Most of us can't pay our bills, or find jobs that are fulfilling. The adverse economic conditions that are used to keep us working like donkeys are not getting any better, (and indeed can't get any better because that's how it was designed to operate). We are ill educated and socially ill equipped to function as naturally productive individuals because the system was designed to make us that way. The predatory forces that keep us caged on this farmyard don't want us to escape and assert our divine right to our freedom and humanity. One of the clues that will help us to awaken from this *'narcotic spiritual slumber'* is the ability to activate our wondrous imaginative faculty.

By being able to activate our imagination we can project ourselves into a future world that is based on peace, love and unity instead of the present bent of division, control and enslavement.

This future world is not some imaginary dream-world to be created through the impotence of fear and subdued minds but one of clarity, brave vision and strident hope. It's not a world of cowardice, weakness and compromise but one of firm positive conviction, strength and resolve. *Peace* and *love* can only come from *mental strength* and *spiritual vitality* that is at the heart of compassionate understanding.

I can only show you where you will find the **key***. Only* **you** *can open the door.*

-The Golden Path of Jah Rastafari –

I once gave a talk about the Babylon System somewhere in London, and at the end of it a young brother asked me, ***"Yeah, I hear what you're saying, but what do I do now?"***
I was slightly startled because his question was unexpected and I am not in the business of telling people what to do with their lives. Part of my mission is merely to transmit information. What happens thereafter is up to the individual. However, the conversation that ensued between us allowed me to think very deeply about the role that each individual might play in the fight to free the minds of fellow human beings trapped in the terrible mind control programs of the ***Babylon Shit-stem***.

Within the tradition of Rastafari we are all leaders. Although there are several different groups, there is mostly no centrally organized core, and indeed, if anyone tried to do so they most probably would be frowned at. There are no sheep or followers; that is the model of the Babylon System and its mind control programs. *We must learn to lead our own minds to freedom. **Personal responsibility** is the key in this situation we find ourselves.* That's what this is all about in the end, strange as it might seem. This ***training ground***, earth, can at times seem harsh and unforgiving but when we adjust our perspective of where we are, and the reasons why we're here, we begin to see things very differently.

As you begin to wake up from the mind control program of the Babylon System, your desire for ***freedom of personal self expression*** will ***magnify*** and you will gradually begin to gravitate towards things that ***hint*** strongly at the direction you need to take in your life. Coincidences will occur at times, (bearing in mind that coincidences are specific ***conscious energy vibrations*** that can stimulate the powers of your ***intuition***). The ***law of attraction*** is a part of the ***Laws of Livity*** and anything we ***consciously*** want to happen can happen.
If you're black, white, Chinese, Indian, Amerindian, South American, Spanish, Greek, French, Japanese, PNP, Labourite, Democrat or Republican, rich or poor, good or

bad, heterosexual, gay, bisexual, non-sexual, whatever you consider yourself to be, it's all the same – **ONELOVE**. There is no *hate* in **ONELOVE**. The innate diversity of humanity is an intrinsic par t of our evolutionary process and we must find ways to understand this dynamic, positively. Jah Rastafari is the Creator and who can go against the will of the Creator? We must not deplete our energies fighting each other through politricks, economics, sexism, religion-ism, racism or any ism that is created by the Babylon System. There's no division in reality except in the illusions of the Babylon System. Its mind control programs divided us, categorized us into various *things* and put us into little *boxes*. That's one of the crucial keys that will open the doors of our prison. We can free ourselves from those little boxes at anytime we consciously choose to do so. You chose to read this book. You've reached this far in reading it because there is a strong desire in you to find out more, not necessarily about the contents of this book, but actually about *the state of your own mind*. Your desire to open your mind to different ways of seeing and greater possibilities in life is the key to gaining the necessary insights that will enable your path to freedom and that of others. Stick with it because everything is riding on you doing so – *literally.*

It's important that we use the methods of *positive action* and not just *reaction* to the mind control aspects of the Babylon System. When reaction is necessary (which is not often) it must be gauged with specific actions that *create harmonious balance inside our minds and souls – always*. It's in the ability to have a balanced multi-dimensional perspective that the basis for any success in gaining our freedom, whether as a group or individually, will be actualized.

The New World Order will almost certainly become a *'perceived reality'* for most humans in a very short space of time. That's inevitably. In order for us to make real changes we must not concern ourselves too much with all the confusing details of coming events. Although the situation is extremely dire, *we can make time*. Always remember we do have the power to change things at any moment we choose. Right now, our *clear focus* must be the work of *disabling* the negative mind control programs in ourselves and assisting others to do the same through conscious acts of *Livity* and the all embracing positive energy of the *ONELOVE*. That is an essential key. We must also prepare ourselves for the worst case when the economic system collapses very soon. Those who can move out to spaces where a self-sufficient life style can be structured should consider doing so very soon.

Crucially, the Babylon System's mind control programs have specific *flaws* that can be exploited quite easily, (once you realize what those are). The Illuminati and their alien multidimensional handlers know this. That's why they have formulated plans for mass physical control (CCTV cameras everywhere) and *mass extermination of populations*.

Our preparation for real change to the negativity of what is to come must encompass rapid *insight* into the *powers* of the *human mind* and ways in which we can use those to negate the worst effects of the negative mind programs that disable us and to work purposefully and tirelessly to readjust the *mass perspective of humanity*. Our objective (which we *must* attain at all cost) is our human freedom, which inevitably will lead to a point of return to balance that stimulates soulful harmony with creation, our true destiny and our Creator. *Make no mistake; the Creator of this universe is absolutely real and always present, whether we choose to believe it or not.*

Useful points are: we need to be cognizant of specific details in our past history that can induce the necessary *inspiration* which can add to our understanding as we *focus our energies* on the path of mental development and spiritual *renewal*. This can assist in the *critical mass* syndrome wherein vast amounts of people become *rapidly aware* of what's really going on and make conscious and dramatic changes in their lives; the present *Wikileaks* phenomenon instigated by *Julian Asange* and others, points in the right direction.

Another very important key is that as black people *we must never in any circumstances return negativity and hate with more of the same when confronted by racism* and the Babylon System. We cannot defeat evil with evil or fight fire with fire, but only with the all embracing compassion of the ONELOVE can we truly overcome. (It might sound strange but it actually works, and very much on the multidimensional level of *spirit/soul*). That does not mean that we should not be vigilant or firm in our thoughts and actions to challenge and eradicate the negativity of the Babylon System's racist mind control programs. When we have to defend ourselves from attack in any form, commonsense has to rule the day. *The preservation of life* must be the first law of any engagement. *You must always seek to preserve your life, and the lives of others at any cost.*

As white people we must begin to let go of the mind control program of *race* and all its negative baggage that has so hampered our collective development. The greatest threat to the Illuminati and the Babylon System is black and white people (and indeed all other branches of humanity) really coming together in mutual, soulful love and respect; standing together in unity. That is one of the principle goals of Rastafari.

The more people become aware that they have been lied to the more they become distrustful of the Babylon System. But apathy can grow if there's no added stimulation to open the awareness to *greater insights*. That's what's happening to many people right now. Important lessons imparted by noted figures such as Nanni, Paul Bogle,

Marcus Garvey, Brother Howell, Nelson Mandela, Mahatma Gandhi, Martin Luther King, William Wilberforce, Henry Thornton, Malcolm X, Sojourner Truth, Prophet Mohamed, Mother Theresa, Buddha and many others are invaluable tools to galvanize the mind in its intentions, aims and actions. *We have been through this before, faced overwhelming odds, walked barefoot through the fires of oppression and survived. And more than that, triumphed.*

Overt and visible confrontation to gain our freedom from the Babylon System is not a realistic option presently; this is a very different scenario being played out in our time. The Babylon System thrives on overt confrontation which it always uses to uphold its doctrine of subversion, manipulation, obedience and control; Problem – Reaction – Solution. This must be avoided when necessary. The *multi-dimensional perspective* is the key that will allow success in this endeavor. Some tools that worked in the past have become blunt beyond repair and so new tools have to be *crafted* from our *'multi-dimensional tool box'*. The *Civil Rights Movement* of the recent past (in the form that it took then) cannot create the necessary vital forces that could affect real changes now in our societies, on account of the *upgrading* of the Babylon System's mind control programs to counter this type of eventuality. So, we must quickly *upgrade* our consciousness faculties as well. One of the principle ways in which black peoples countered slavery and colonialism and fought against them successfully was the utilization of specific *spiritual tools*, (the multi-dimensional spiritual methodology – **learn what those are*), that created massive waves of *positive, conscious energy vibrations* that assisted in lowering the negative vibrations of the Babylon System in specific areas of confrontation. (*Think! - 4D techniques for 3D application*).

Due to the lowering of planetary and life-promoting vibrational energy fields by the Babylon System's continuous bombardment of the planet with various negative energies, such as microwave radiation and the *HAARP* array, the human *emotional body* has become *desensitized* to certain emotional frequencies, so it's important to understand how to galvanize your *energy body* and to stimulate your *psycho/spiritual nervous system*. Research this and understand the methods and tools that are involved in these processes; *this is invaluable*. Specific *meditational forms, (Fire meditation), spirit-work, yoga, dietary factors* must all be a part of the process of physical and spiritual cleansing and *higher mental development*. But lessons have been learnt that have enabled the Babylon System to anticipate certain scenarios and counter them effectively. Always be mindful of your goals and the methods you're using to achieve them. Make sure that *truth, love* and *compassion* are the primary tools of engagement in freeing your mind, *always.*

Not everyone will understand. Many who are unable to move beyond personal desires for material gain – *service-to-self attitudes* and the need to *control* – will inevitably fall by the way side or remain as hapless victims of the Babylon System until *more powerful stimulus* is developed to assist their freedom. Understanding of the real situation will be mostly *instinctive* at this stage because of the growing desire for personal freedom.

When you reach the point of no return you will know; you will begin to understand the *awesome responsibility* that's in your hands. The *Creator* put you here for a specific purpose, even if you don't know exactly what that purpose is (or even if you're not really sure whether the Creator is real or not); you know there's a purpose to you being here, right now on earth. You feel as though it has something to do with positive aims – *the actual positive evolution of our species here on earth*. That's a very big *responsibility*, and you've got something to do with it in some way that you're probably not sure about yet.

You know who you are and what you were *born* in this world to do. Maybe you cannot articulate it in words or perhaps it's elusive when you look at it in your mind, but *you know what you feel*, and it's that *feeling* that is at the *core* of your being, which speaks silently and persistently to you all the time. You always search for some kind of understanding in others; even to find that *special someone* whom you can unburden all this onto and who (you hope) might give you the reassurances you need to live and make sense of the world. There are times when things make complete sense without you even thinking deeply about them. You want to cry and smile and laugh all at the same time when the realization comes to your mind. *You know that you know*, but you don't know *how* you know. You just know that this isn't it. This life that you've been struggling to make sense of; this can't be all there is. *And it's exactly this <u>sense of knowing</u> that now opens up your great potential as a conscious evolutionary human being.* This is how the mind opens up and creates *new spaces* of perceptions – it's called *<u>consciousness expansion</u>*. The more you think about these things and their implications, the more you will realize that you have the ability to assist this process positively and powerfully. If irrational fear comes to your mind when you're engaged in the mental cleansing process, don't worry, it's just the mind control program trying to stop you from freeing your mind. Be firm and strong in your resolve to free your mind, your efforts will definitely *attract* positive energies to you that can assist in the process. The *Law of Attraction* works because it is an intrinsic aspect of the *Laws of Livity*. Just hold these aims at the centre of your consciousness in all that you do daily – going to college or work, sitting on a bus, talking to friends and family, when you're alone in your private space and so on. *Feel your consciousness expand when you think about these issues and how you can help*.

One of the keys is the expansion of consciousness to touch and stimulate others who are feeling the same *vibrational energy* as you. I'm talking about the process of *chain-reaction* that eventually creates the *critical mass* that's needed to open people's minds and effect change. To bring about any change in the world you have to *know* that you are *relevant* to the situation here on earth. Absolutely everything you do has consequences to the larger whole. You become part of the problem because you've been sitting down too long, unsure of what your purpose is in the grand scheme of things. You are also, crucially, a part of the *solution* because of the amazing inherent power within you. Just by being a living, breathing human being indicates what your purpose is. What you lack is the knowledge to put it all together. You first have to get yourself off the *fence* that you've been sitting on while watching the world slip past you. Are you familiar with the old African American spiritual song **WE SHALL OVERCOME** that was used so powerfully and effectively in the various protest marches during the Civil Rights era in America? Then you already know what I mean. Check it out on YouTube. *Feel the vibrations*. This is another of the crucial keys.

Did you know that you have within your mind and soul extraordinary powers that could prevent all the things that are scheduled to happen from happening? And did you know that you can activate naturally the *powers* of your human *mind/soul matrix* to affect anything you want it to affect? It's not a mystery it's just that this knowledge has been kept *top secret* from you and ridiculed so that no one will activate these remarkable powers. *Imagine if you learned the exact methods* that can *activate* these powers within you and use them, to stop the New World Order from occurring. When you consciously direct your thoughts, especially if there is more than one person doing this, the effects can be dramatic. Try it; bring a small group of friends together and concentrate positively and consciously on a subject and see what happens. Exchange views afterwards and proceed again. Check out websites that have relevant information about these issues such as *Remote Viewing* and developing the psychic powers of the human mind. Surprise and inspire yourself but always make sure your intentions are *positive and life affirming*.

It's important to remember *The Teachings*; familiarize yourself with the great psalms, parables and wisdom, *The Ifa Oracle, The Tao Te Ching, The Egyptian Book of the Great Awakening*, the *Baghavad Gita, Upanishad*, the Holy Koran, the Holy Bible, the great spiritual teachings of the *Buddha* and many other relevant authentic teachings of spiritual worth. The many speeches of HIM, The Sublime, Haille Selassie I, The Philosophies and Opinions of Marcus Mosiah Garvey, the Autobiography of the Sublime, Malcolm X, the works of The Sublime Martin Luther King Jr, the Sublime Mahatma Gandhi are some of the excellent books and knowledge that can assist to develop and enhance consciousness awareness when read with the *right intent*. There are many more. ***Search and you will find. Knock and the door will be open unto you***. Real authentic spiritual knowledge is a vital tool to galvanize the spiritual nature of human beings. Be discerning; you don't have to subscribe to erroneous and misinterpreted doctrine to find the true *spiritual vibration*. Avoid all so-called *New Age* related Illuminati sponsored demonic teachings as these are specifically created to destroy real inquiry into God-consciousness and to trap the mind and soul of human beings in the sensory experiences of the Babylon System. Learn how to *pray* and *meditate* with *clarity* and *faith*. The power of prayer and conscious meditation are invaluable keys to bolstering *strength* and *courage* in adversities.

Things are going to get harder in the Babylon System, make no mistake about that. The forces of control have started to lock down the doors of our mental and spiritual prison before more of us become aware of what is really going on. The most important thing is not to be fearful. Hold firm to your convictions. You will be free.

You must remember that you have absolute power over time and space. ***There can be no barriers to your freedom.*** You must constantly remember that you're not alone in this. There are billions of us who feel this vibration on earth and elsewhere. ***Help is always here***, just use your mind and expand your consciousness outwards to receive the help and it will appear visibly in your life. Above all be discerning by using and trusting your *intuition*. Practice using your intuition as often as you can in any situation. This will strengthen your perceptive faculties so that you become *in-tune* with your inner feelings. ***Learn to trust your inner instincts*** and practice using them in all situations.

Balance and *harmony* at all times are vital keys. In all that you do, try to maintain a balanced point of view. Balance leads to harmony. Your consciousness will certainly expand and the power of *intent* will become more pronounced as you proceed on this new path in your life. Personal responsibility is of the utmost importance. You have to trust yourself, your instincts, your thoughts, your feelings and your mind. You are no longer a *victim* of the Babylon System; denial of fundamental truths will only prolong your state of victimhood.

"Yeah, but what do I do?"

Well, *doing* is a tricky thing. We often think that doing means a purely physical movement or action that result in something physical happening in the exterior world. We can do a great deal by not even moving our bodies but applying the consciousness faculties of mind to affect changes on many levels, not just the physical. Every action starts with a thought. If you focus your thoughts consciously, actions can occur on levels that will *'knock you off your feet'* (literally).

Just be who you are. Express *naturally* the person that's inside your body, (despite the disapproval of others or the Babylon System). You will be attracted to *truth vibrations* wherever they appear because that is what you're giving out. Remember the law of attraction – *like attracts like*. The power of thought is a mighty tool that can effect dramatic changes in any way, if directed methodically and *consciously*.

It might not seem like it sometimes but there are many others just like you in the world, all waiting to meet each other. Get up; dust yourself off, stand tall. Stand strong in your mind and soul; be flexible when you walk out into the storm, and know that you will not fall or be defeated because you are the manifest *Will of the Creator*. Open your mind to life's possibilities by cultivating *calmness* and *observance* as you walk the *Golden Path* to freedom.

You've been tricked, hoodwinked and bamboozled so many times but that's alright because you're now waking up from the dark dream. Use the *power of thought* and effect the changes in your life that you so much desire. Don't be confused though. It's not about wishful thinking but *active focus* of your *mental powers* upon a particular thought form, action or state of being. If you want to be free, then use your *imagination* coupled with focused *thought energy* and you will be astonished at the results. See your life in your mind as you want it to be – *use your imagination* – and create the *outward actions* that will take you towards your goals. Close your eyes and visualize your future in your mind. Behind you is the fading illusion of the Babylon System going out of existence. All that you can now see is the shining *Golden Path* of freedom in-front of you. Don't be afraid to reach out into the dark because ultimately, *you are the light*, and wherever the light goes, whatever it touches, *darkness* must *move* out of its way.

Although the *adversary (symbolically manifest as the negative ego sense faculty)* is waging a war against you, you're not fighting *its* battle. With *expanded consciousness*, you can now make up the rules of engagement to suit any scenario. You have the power to do that. The Babylon System is built with *force* and *control*; *Za-Yan* is built on **PEACE** and the all embracing power of the **ONELOVE**. There's no greater power in the whole of creation.

When things get hot and you can't seem to handle it, just remember to be *still*. Chant the *mantra* of empowerment and renewal:

'Stillness is the key to infinity'.

I don't mean sitting down in a state of inaction but a *reflective quietness* as you *observe* everything around you and the movement of thought forms that occurs inside your mind. You might get angry at a situation or feel sad because of certain things; or you might feel afraid in the course of whatever you do. Just remember; slow down, stop and *mentally* take yourself *out* of the picture, then *observe* what's going on. You are the *controller* of all that's happening to you by the way you *see* and *react* to situations. Stillness of mind quietens your chaotic thoughts so that you can formulate right response or action to a given scenario.

Another very powerful mental mantra that can assist you in being fearless in any situation is as follows:

Mind is the Formless Nature, The root of all things in creation. Thoughts come from mind, emotions come from thoughts and actions come from emotions, which comes from thoughts, which comes from mind, which has no form.

Thus, you see the chain that binds your perception to the world of materialism and immaterialism and how to dismantle its power over your eternal, wondrous mind.

There's a real universe out there that we've never seen before and which no one ever told us about or prepared us to embrace; a place of hope and possibilities, of deep vision, peace and real love; of extraordinary worlds where life has the remarkable potential to expand in the most amazing ways and directions. There is a thing called *choice* and there is a thing called *duty*. And there is also a thing called *destiny*. With the power of your natural intelligence you become aware of the choices you can make. Using the balance of truth you perform your duty, after which choice as we understand it in human terms, no longer exist. Understanding your duty, with truth and conviction as the driving force leads you inexorably to the road of destiny. When you understand the nature of truth, you have no choice but to perform your duty. *Saving the human race from destruction isn't a matter of choice*. This is perhaps the greatest test that you will face in this time and space and which will define the nature of your very existence and future development as a *cosmic human being*. The human revolution is **NOW**! *It's happening inside your mind, heart and soul.*

*...And I saw another mighty angel coming down from heaven, having great power and authority, and the earth was lit up with his glory. And he cried mightily with a strong voice, saying "**Babylon the great is fallen and has become the habitation of devils and the hold of every foul spirit, and a cage of every unclean and hateful bird. For all the nations have drunk of the wine of the wrath of her fornication, and the kings of the earth have committed fornication with her**".*
*And I heard another voice saying "**Come out of her my people, so that you do not partake of her sins, and receive not her plagues**"...*

- The Book of Revelations (The Holy Bible) –

The earth at present is going through very obvious changes. Humanity as a whole is inextricably linked to those changes. Many of us are aware of these facts. No matter who we are or where we live, we will at some time be affected by these changes.

Our existence here has been an incredible experience to say the least. Sometimes it seems the greatest wonder that the human race has survived all the wars, plagues, genocides, hatred, killings, massacres and general opposition to our continued existence. Perhaps the reason why we have survived the great trauma is our capacity to balance these horrendous things with their opposites; peace, life affirming attitudes, love and compassion and so on. Our entire existence on earth appears to be one long balancing act. Despite the horrors that have plagued us for countless eons, we seem to have **'stuck with it'** tenaciously, the collective hope being that there has to be (some how) some kind of meaning to life. There has been dark days and dark ages, (for some, too many), but the generations come and go and we are still here, still clinging to the same hope that there has to be some real meaning to the entire process of human beings living, suffering dying and being reborn again into the same unending cycle.

We yearn for a better way; for salvation and for heaven. We've been *fighting* to get into heaven ever since we developed conception of it, but heaven seem denied to us at every turn except in our wishful thinking. Perhaps there is no heaven we might often wonder, or the way to it is so concealed that it would take the very end of the universe and time to get there.

Despite all this, everything is changing but many of us haven't realized that the change is taking place. Some of us are still waiting for a messiah or a rapture to spirit us away in a cocoon of light and unconscious bliss. Many of us are still furiously holding on to the past. We end up holding onto the things that blind us to the wondrous reality of which we are an integral part. And some of us have been so wounded, so broken hearted, down trodden and shattered with the fatigue of living in the illusions of the Babylon System that we have become cold and vitrified like obsidian; unyielding and unmoved by anything but the fear of being alone in a dark uncaring existence.

At the time of his presidential campaign and election to power, Barack Obama, the first *'black'* president of the USA touted the *'change'* rhetoric incessantly. One of the remarkable things about that whole affair is the fact of how the masses of Americans (and everyone else in the world) were *hypnotized* by the incredible stage performances and speeches of the presidential contender; the flashing lights, the euphoria, the messianic fervor and the swooning masses of emotional citizens all culminated in one of the biggest mass hypnotism ever televised. Indeed more than a year after the lights and music has died down, what has really changed for the ordinary citizens of America and an expectant world? Nothing at all. The wars continue; the monetary and economic problems merely escalate. Hunger, homelessness, depravity and the usual list of evils that plague our societies continue regardless. The Obama *deception* is another hallmark of the real powers behind the scenes that continue to manipulate and control us.

Nevertheless, we are evolving in ways we are not cognizant of. Our view of ourselves and our reality is changing rapidly but many of us stubbornly refuse to accept this fact. We cannot accept it because we've been fighting for so long that all we know is *the battle*. Our mothers and fathers were born on the battle-field. We too were born on the battlefield and our children are born on that same battle-field. When the enslavement of Black Africans ended in the nineteenth century in Jamaica, some former slaves were unable to believe or even accept that slavery had ended. Many wandered around in a complete daze, not knowing what to do or even how to start piecing a new life together because all they ever knew was slavery and the monotonous but reliable routine of the *whip*, the *slave master* and the endless *toil*. Some former slaves (despite being told officially that slavery had ended) still returned to the cotton fields and the sugar cane plantations promptly on time and waited for instructions because they were so conditioned to operate in that consensus reality. The bewilderment of former slaves was real and very frightening when they were told that they were free to just *go and take charge of their own lives*. We are collectively as the human race at this very strange and important junction right now. The controllers of the Babylon System are very aware of this and that is why they are busy trying to stop us from gaining our freedom by installing more draconian measures upon the world through the form of a New World Order.

How do we reach a point of acceptance of this fact now? One might ask, "How has the world changed without me knowing about it"? The real point to this is the knowing. Knowledge isn't just information that we absorb; it's a dynamic energy; a conscious recognition of the real potential that life has to offer. We are coming to the point of realization that all we've been fighting is ourselves. We never like change. It usually means that the comforts and complacencies that order our lives must be overtaken by the stark urgency of our greater *spiritual evolution*.

Some observations that can assist our understanding of what's happening is that in Euro/American societies since the 1960s, there has been a growing movement among white people to come to terms with their spiritual nature existentially. This is very apparent in the explosion of the *Flower Power Movement* and the *Hippie Generation* when many whites suddenly, (after the devastation of another world war) came to the realization of the abject futility of their government's perspective on human development. The great *'spiritual resurgence'* that blazed across white society during those times did not really affect black people in the same way as we were busy fighting for our *Civil Rights* from the oppressive racist Babylon System. Blacks were never interested in following oriental gurus because we were always aware that our needs transcended those boundaries. For black people the world over, spirituality was never divorced from the basic necessities of everyday life and our constant attempts to free ourselves from the destructive forces of the white supremacy mind control program. While disaffected whites struggled for spiritual freedom through Indian mystics, Chaos theories and quantum science, most blacks were busy struggling for basic earthly freedoms. While white society was entranced by the spell of *New Ageism*, we were busy trying to piece together the remnants of our children in ghettoes flushed with drugs flown from South America and the Far East and deposited in our neighborhoods with the explicit assistance of racist agencies such as the *CIA*. While white society was entranced by *UFOs* and little grey aliens, Aryan star-men and the escapism of cyber space, black African peoples were dying like flies on the unforgiving alter of racial hatred and oppression. The Old Negro spirituals, gospel music, Reggae music and the deep rooted connection to our strong spiritual culture kept black people alive, fighting, struggling with the sure knowledge that the Creator would deliver us from oppression, whatever form that took, whether through the Christian church or the power of Rastafari. The unique perspective by which we as black people interact in existence has always been the key to our survival, but many of us have been brainwashed by the Babylon System to reject the very thing that give our lives real strength, power and meaning. Many white peoples in general have been so brainwashed for so long that the newest superficial trend created by the illusory Babylon System suddenly acquires something of monumental stature right before their eyes. Sadly, a certain arrogance is born in the minds of those who have been brainwashed to believe in their self superiority when confronted with basic and simple truths, for the mind control programs of the Babylon System leads one to think that *'nothing can be that simple'*. So Euro/American society end up searching for answers in *complexity* and complexity itself then becomes *'a God of its own design'*. The more Euro/American scientists search for the complex mathematical equations that will at last yield up the secrets of the universe, the more they are astonished by the simplicity of nature. Unfortunately, complexity always ends up being its own reward.

The parasitic tendency of many of the religious movements that we have been subjected to has sucked the *'spiritual blood'* out of so many innocent people. We find the prevalent and distasteful phenomenon of Christian *crusades*, lecherous and lying preachers and pastors that brainwash masses of people while shamelessly fleecing them of their money and earthly possessions.

It's full time that as human beings we begin to see the *'elephant hiding in the living room'*. We must resurrect the *sacred spirit of the human race* once more, in any way we can, boldly. True Rastafarians across the world are in a position to extend the hand of peace, unity and ONELOVE as never before. We have to go beyond the petty prejudices that have so hampered our development on earth. For us, Rastafari is just *one* part of the *delivery system* that can send the All-Powerful *fire* of the ONELOVE straight to the cold heart of the Babylon System. In the *Eternal Body of Truth that is Jah Rastafari* there is no such thing as *races*, therefore there can be no racism. *Truth cannot be divided.*

Illusions can be so very comfortable, like a soft warm bed, a delicious plate of food, a gorgeous sunset or a beautiful love affair; all must end in *time*. And it's this fact that all illusions have a *sell-by date* that makes us frightened, angry, afraid, and resentful because we've never been prepared for the end of the illusion. Life holds out so much promise of excitement and suddenly we have to die and there are no real explanations that can seem to satisfy and reassure us that it was all worth while and that there's a tangible meaning to it all.

The role of the Babylon System is to keep the great lie going indefinitely. The universe, all the stars and galaxies, the dimensions of being, our sun, our planet earth and our human bodies all have a sell-by date attached to them. It's supposed to be that way because that's part of the *experience matrix* of our existence that manifest through the Creation Field. The love affair with the sensuous world and body has its limits and that scares us very much. But when we take onboard the things I have been trying to outline (maybe not very well, but hopefully they might be understood) change is the most fundamental part of our existence. Without change nothing can happen. It's one of the most important laws of *Livity* that we can really observe in the world.

Many of us don't know that a major change is taking place because all we are aware of is the same old day to day living. The same old drudgery of getting up in the morning, sending the children to school, going to work (if we have a job), wondering where the next meal is going to come from, defending ourselves against the tyranny of the Babylon System, quarrelling with our neighbors, lusting after unattainable sense objects, wanting, grasping, holding on to hopeless dreams and futile fantasies, feeling depressed because life offered so much with one hand and ended up betraying us with the other hand and so on. For those of us who are in these situations (which is most of us if we are to be really honest about it) we believe there is no change; quite preposterous to even think so. Yet if we just take the time, just a small amount of time to just stop, sit down for a moment and try to let our senses be quiet for as long as we can, we might be able to perceive something changing; *our state of mind is changing*. That's the key to understanding what change is. When our state of mind changes then everything else has to change because everything exists *relative* to our perceptions. Our perceptions relate to our consciousness and our consciousness comes from our minds. And it is this relationship between mind, consciousness and matter, thing and thought that must become the vital lessons that are taught to our children in schools which we must now create. This is the knowledge that will define the future for the human race for the next thousand years and beyond. It isn't new knowledge, just not remembered.

For us to see the change we have to begin with ourselves. Change is not something that's actual it's something that's always *potential*. When a change occurs it's no longer change but a recognized state of *being*; a perceived reality. And we can perceive any reality we chose at any time we chose to. There are times when we can't see or detect the changes with our physical senses but it's happening nonetheless. Cosmic changes occur on such vast scales that we are usually unaware of such things, but they happen, all the time. *What we lack is the knowledge of the ability to perceive and understand change in its real sense*. The Babylon System has tricked us into believing that we have no power to change anything by feeding us the mind control drug of apathy and self delusion.

The change that is taking place presently has affected our *consciousness perception* of what we really are. There are some of us who can't see the change because we might be looking in the wrong direction. We have to try to look in our hearts, souls and minds to see the change. We have to start to open our inner consciousness and look honestly at the things we are thinking about and the reasons why we're thinking about them. After that we then reach a point where the desire for real change in our lives converges with the knowledge that it's vital we become empowered by the processes involved with the change. Some people these days (especially in Euro/American societies) have been touting the *holographic theory* of reality as the latest new or most important trend in knowledge. These types of knowledge can scare many people into believing that life is a meaningless cyclic conundrum and that all we strive for is futile. That's part of the reason why so many theories such as Atheism and Transhumanism have become so fashionable and respected by many people in Euro/American societies. We are not just powerless beings trapped in a hologram. The irrational fear that there's no God and therefore man can then assert power over the material universe is a clear reflection of the mind control programming of the Babylon System that has created an imbalance in our ego sensory faculty.

There are those who are trying to stop the change by creating more rigid structures and institutions in which to enslave us even deeper into the Babylon System; the *white supremacist power-bloc*, racist politicians and warmongering military/ industrial complexes, the pharmaceutical industries that put profit before human health and unscrupulous *elements* within the scientific community that hide the truth from the masses. These structures must be transformed before we can move forward. They are among the greatest detriments to the survival of our species on earth. These statements might sound rather strong but in the light of the truth of the conspiracy to defraud us of our true human potential, there can be no compromise in our understanding of these issues. The New World Order is designed to drive us deeper into the illusions of the Babylon System. It's a way to lower our *spiritual vibrational capacity* so that we function as mindless *biological robots* to be used for whatever purposes the Babylon System decides. Even as the true knowledge is dawning inside the minds of many people, the Babylon System is furiously trying to extinguish it. But we know it cannot prevent us from becoming free because all that it represents is illusory. We just have to really know that, and as Rastas, and more importantly human beings, persevere on the *Golden Path* to true freedom.

The human evolutionary changes we are presently witnessing is taking place because, from the point of view of Rasta, Jah Rastafari, the Limitless Field of Potentiality, The Supreme Creator of all life and forms is being revealed more and more to human beings who desire freedom from the Babylon System of oppression, selfishness, hate, and all unprogressive qualities. This is nothing extraordinary in a sense but a natural occurrence that's stimulated by our growing, *soulful desire to develop and evolve in a spiritually-organic manner*. The thing is that Jah Rastafari does not function by *force* but a gradual incremental development in the awareness that there is an astonishingly beautiful reality beyond the Babylon System. Jah Rastafari does not impose restraints on human beings but only bestow constant knowledge, guidance and the ability to realize Compassionate ONELOVE. The great thing about our humanity is that we have been endowed with *freewill* to think, feel and function on our own volition and to pursue lives that reflects the sublime power, presence and grace of Our Creator. This ultimately imparts the most astounding joy and sense of well being in knowing that we are not just bags of flesh animated by accident, but glorious beings, reflections of the

Illimitable Power of our Creator.

Part of the problem in our lack of understanding concerning these things is that the *ego aspect* within our consciousness faculties can so easily be affected negatively by the Babylon System's mind control programs so that we fail to see these truths clearly. Some people try in vain to intellectualize The Creator out of their lives because they have been so conditioned to think in what is an abstracted manner by the Babylon System of mis-education. But even if one stops believing in God by becoming an atheist, *that cannot stop God from existing*; it simply means that one does not believe in God.

There's absolutely nothing abstract about Jah Rastafari, only the fact that we have not been trained adequately to understand the reality of our Creator. Jah Rastafari is actually the completeness of reality and can be perfectly understood. It's the ONELOVE that's Beginless, Endless and the Foundation of our being in creation. In fact, it's *our perceptions* that are abstract because we can only perceive a very small part of the greater whole. An ant, being so small, cannot rationalize the actions of a human being completely, but a human can very easily study and deduce the functions of an ant. Can you imagine if Jah Rastafari were to appear in completeness, physically. The entire universe, although being so phenomenally large, wouldn't be big enough to contain that single *manifestation* of *Supreme Power*.

Jah Rastafari is the Supreme Controller of all energies and can function on any level within and beyond our perceptions. All the tools that we can use to understand the Supreme is within our reach, we just have to open our minds, hearts and souls and use them and we can then very easily come to great understanding of our life's real purpose in the world.

We must remember that no matter what happens *we cannot really die*; that it's only the physical body that dies. We know that the body is only a temporary *vessel* for mind and its attendant structures such as the *spirit/soul*. The purported teachings of the prophet, Yeshua (Jesus), explained to us the nature of life and death and reincarnation on all the different levels of being. His *death* and *resurrection* were really *symbols*; lessons imparted to us, telling us that we cannot really die. Death as we understand it philosophically is a *creation* of the *Babylon System* to put fear into our minds so that we comply with its evil designs. *The Golden Path of Jah Rastafari* is *eternal*, because life is eternal. We are eternal because we are all equally and without distinction, expressions of *Jah Rastafari*. And *Jah Rastafari is the wellspring of Eternity – the ONELOVE of All Creation, without beginning or end.*

We now know that life on earth is just one form of physical expression and that there are many different forms of physical expressions throughout space and time and in many different dimensions of being. One of the great spiritual teachers and prophets to humanity, Yeshua (Jesus) taught us that:

"In my Father's House there are many mansions".

There are many mansions of being in eternity, not just the earth or this universe. There are myriad worlds teeming with life just like ours, and many more universes similar and very different to ours. There are many different types of black, white, Indian and Chinese people similar to us (and *related* to us also) living on many worlds similar to the earth in this universe. As the future progresses these things will certainly manifest physically into our conscious waking lives. There is a future of hope and possibility which we must all embrace without fear.

The struggles by our Great and Sublime Rastafarian Ancestors and Elders, H.I.M Haille Selassie I, Leonard Percival Howell, Marcus Mosiah Garvey, Robert Hinds, Prince Emanuel, Peter Tosh, Bob Marley, Joseph Hill and so many, many other great Rastamen and Rastawomen, have lit the way to truth and freedom, not just for Rastafarians on earth but for humanity in its entirety. Essentially, Rastafarians are servants of humanity in all that we do. That's our job because in serving the greater good and conscious, positive evolution of life, we are serving the Divine Will of our Sublime Creator, Jah Rastafari.

With the power of the ONELOVE we can dismantle the Babylon System on earth. We can overcome the predatory, negative forces that seek to put out the light of our human progress. We can transform our world into a paradise where all human beings are able to fulfill their true potential for spiritual development and evolution to greater heights of being. That is our duty; our holy and sacred mission here in creation as *Rastafarians*.

More Light, More Power, More Love, More Fire

Jah Rastafari

When I was a small boy growing up, the world appeared incredible and beautiful to innocent eyes. There was hope, joy, but above all an unshakable optimism that generated a defined sense of purpose and mission as a human being in the world. Innocence or ignorance? I prefer to view it as a child at play in the most delightful garden, completely unaware of the silent, venomous snake hidden in the shadows of the undergrowth.

If we really want to find truth we can, but sometimes when the truth appears, if we're not prepared to confront it head on in all its uncompromising details, it can completely blow our minds. It's not easy to accept the unacceptable, yet in the final analysis, truth cannot be denied. There are specific aspects of this book that might appear hypothetical to some but I firmly believe in the overall paradigm that I have outlined here.

Our entire existence as human beings on planet earth is threatened with subversion by a very small, *nihilistic* group of entities labeled the *Illuminati* who have become insane with the lust for power, domination and control. This small group is directly influenced by consciously *'negative forces'* that exist within the boundaries of the multidimensional structure in which we live. This scenario is clarified by our prevailing religious and spiritual structures, mythological and the growing knowledge of the conspiracy that elucidates the very nature of the Babylon System.

I have (hopefully) given just a very brief overview of this paradigm. Some people will find these things unpalatable for various reasons. The demonic-alien agenda is rapidly advancing to its conclusive stages and therein lays our predicament. Most people are not ready to confront the unthinkable; that the human race has become the victim of an elaborate deception that traverses time, space and dimensions. It's up to each individual to find information and educate themselves as quickly as possible, *making this the absolute priority in life*. With information comes knowledge and with knowledge comes choice. The future is not one of blind childish optimism but of stark and chilling realism. Knowing the truth isn't always comfortable but whatever happens, it's vital that we know. The *inter-dimensional alien predators*, *Greys*, *Reptilians*, *Nordics and their hierarchy of extra-dimensional handlers* represents the most clear and present danger to the entire human race and cannot be trusted whatsoever, no matter the spin by many in the *Ufo circles* and the present *disclosure projects* in the USA. The near future will reveal the true extent of the predicament that the human race faces. It's certain that the predatory are an inter-dimensional intelligence allied with various other negative/demonic forces that intends to

310

overthrow human beings and establish themselves on earth as our overlords. It has been ascertained that these creatures have definitely influenced our *racial* past in terms of genetic manipulations and other methods we are not presently aware of. How that was achieved is still in the realms of conjecture at this moment however *'time manipulation'* is a major key to understanding this principle. Crucially, the predators have manipulated specific groups of humans for some thousands of years therefore it's in the realm of possibility that their ***breeding program*** has been going on over this vast period of time. There are areas of research that has proved incredibly challenging because of the very nature of the subject matter. It's now becoming obvious to those who have developed enquiring minds that the human race has been *'tampered with'* genetically over its long history on earth, not just by the Greys, Nordics and Reptilians but others as well. No doubt the earth has long been seen as a great ***genetic treasure trove*** by various interstellar and inter-dimensional alien factions.

There is a glaringly obvious undercurrent (for want of a better word) of ***racism*** within the context of this phenomenon that almost no researcher has had the guts to admit or clarify. The UFO phenomenon is predominantly seen from the point of view of white Euro/American people's interaction with aliens. We are led to believe that black people seem to have had very little involvement (except in a few isolated cases). However my extensive research into this phenomenon has shown that black Africans were the ***first*** and (perhaps most significant group) to have been influenced by this alien agenda many thousands of years ago going back into human prehistory. Certainly the genesis of human beings on earth is interwoven within the alien agenda in ways that might appear absolutely shocking to most of us. The African tradition speaks of contingents of ***Reptilian*** beings who came to earth in prehistoric times and interacted with human beings in ***Africa***. The work of the great African mystic/shaman ***Credo Mutwa*** and the author, ***David Icke,*** is very relevant to this story and needs to be analyzed deeply.

It's imperative to understand that the problem of racism that hampers our humanity is a carefully crafted weapon to disable our progress as a species. One noted researcher, British author, ***Nigel Kerner*** has gone out on a limb in this regard and has theorized certain very uncomfortable aspects of the alien agenda on earth. My own research over many years has pointed to this scenario being extremely relevant to deeper understanding of the alien phenomenon. He contends, as do I, that specific groups of ***elite*** Caucasian (***Aryan***) people have been manipulated into the interdimensional alien agenda for reasons that deal with the future development of the entire human race. This, in a very strange way, appears to be the ***roots*** of what we have come to regard as racism on earth. Nigel Kerner states:

'Could it be that some of us have been programmed by alien experimenters to keep the

experimental group separate in order to preserve the integrity of the experiment? *Could racism be a sure sign of alien genetic interception;* an interception for their purposes and in their interests and not ours? If so, the new **techno-colonialism** and the fact that the technological progress that makes it possible springs almost entirely from the **Euro-Caucasian genotype**, may well suggest this is their **prime homozygotic group**. In fact, this group is considered by genetic anthropologists to be the most **in-bred** of all. Tracing its origins to **Cro-Magnon** man, it is one of the most homozygotic in the world. As I have said, it goes without saying **the most heinous forms of racism also originate from this group**, again confirming the hypothesis. I believe the northern **Mongoloid genotype** may also be the latest experimental hotbed for the **Greys** in this regard'.

These might appear very unsettling assertions to say the least but when we analyze historical data concerning the genesis of northern European racial groups many perplexing things become visible. The incredible **amnesic barrier** that prevents human beings from tracing a precise linear path of our evolution as a species on earth speaks volumes about the program of alien deception carried out over thousands of years and definitely alludes to what I firmly believe to be **temporal alterations** and **adjustments** on levels we cannot presently comprehend. The **manipulation of time**, as I've always maintained, is one of the key factors that must be considered in this equation. Some ancient Aryan groups that dominated the Mediterranean, I believe, were specific parts of the breeding program. We do know from biblical scriptures that the **'God'**, Jehovah or Yahweh who led Moses and the Israelites from Egypt, was very particular about the **genetic homogeneity** of **'his chosen people'**. Sex, breeding and the singular belief in these processes essentially form the core of **Jewish** faith. In fact, the ancient Jews committed some of the most horrendous **'ethnic cleansing'** against all the other peoples they encountered in their quest to conquer a territory in which they could establish themselves as a nation; a land **'promised'** to them by their **'God'** who clearly sanctioned the callous slaughter and cruel **genocide** of men, women and children who were not genetically related to them. The details of this can be read by anyone and reasoned out to the chilling point.

Throughout the millennia, the Jews have kept to this formula, even to this present day. The tragedy of the Jewish holocaust during World War II might also be part of the great puzzle. Is it possible that the **Aryanism** of Hitler and his Nazis and their quest to exterminate all Jews have correlations with the alien agenda and the breeding programs in some elusive manner? It's also possible that factions of **Greys** and **Nordics** influenced (directly or indirectly) specific interactions between different genetic groups on earth (for example, Jews and Aryans, blacks and whites) for specific reasons that we don't know? The more we delve into history and its potential ramifications the more we see elusive patterns merging into uncomfortable pictures.

These things touch on some of the interesting points that Nigel Kerner takes up in his work:

*And so it seems that the old **Master race** principle of pure white non-mixed superiority is the biggest canard and self delusion that prevails in the psyche of the Homo Sapiens gene base. A dangerous and deadly delusion programmed through genetic engineering by an alien roboid form [Greys]to keep our genes more easily amenable for supplementation with theirs, to thus gradually give rise to a **machine man**; a form of hybrid that is artificially composed and configured to give alien [Greys]**the facility to multiply through a natural birthing process.***

This is exactly what the alien/human hybrid breeding program seems to be all about in our present linear timeline. The problems we face with racism in human societies could very well have been engineered by our inter-dimensional predators as a measure to isolate specific groups of humans as e*xperimental breeding material*.

Could it be that this enigma has some form of relationship to a drastic shift of the human *psyche* and our '*collective unconscious*' that somehow has to find avenues of expression in terms of the racial *confrontation between the black and the white* on the physical plane? Black and white in colour theory produces *Grey*, and we now, coincidentally, use the term openly to describe the Grey alien beings who appear to be a type of expression that operates on multi-dimensional levels where time and space follows completely different rules than those we presently understand. The relationship between Diamonic realities as explained by writer *Patrick Harpur*, (*Diamonic Reality*) and our perception of ourselves as a human species certainly has some relevance to the *physical manifestation* of aliens that we curiously label Grey, Reptilians and Nordics. It has been reported that some factions of Greys have expressed that they are indeed *humans* from a *timeline* that is approximately *45, 000 years in the future*. They are referred to by *Dan Burrisch* as the T45s who have gone through extraordinarily traumatic physical and mental transformations over many thousands of years.

Genetic scientists assert the model of a gradual development and mutation of the Africoid race into the various branches of colours that we are now familiar with. What we do find is that the Caucasoid branch of the human family appears to have developed into its recognizable form *only* in Europe. The development of white European culture is shrouded in a mysterious fog. Antediluvian artifacts and other paraphernalia such as writing are extremely scarce in comparison to other cultures. When we scrutinize the historical data of social development of early human beings (i.e. 40,000 BC to 12,000 B.C) we are faced with very obvious and *mysterious gaps* along the way that no one has been able to clarify as yet. The sudden appearance of

Aryan peoples from the Caucasus regions onto the world stage does not seem to be substantiated by current models of human evolutionary theories. At what point did European people become *white*? What were the **genetic dynamics** that created this paradigm? What are the indicators of the transitional stages of this process? How could whites have survived something as ferocious as an Ice Age in Europe without firm cultural/social infrastructures? Look at all the social problems we have nowadays in our modern societies when just a few inches of snow falls. A great deal of nonsense has been written about this issue but no one has ever seriously tackled these enigmas. The rise from complete obscurity of the elusive Aryan peoples of Europe is still one of the greatest mysteries on earth. Virtually nothing is known about them before they were supposed to have emerged in Northern India some 1700BC or thereabouts. No one seems to know very much about them at all, yet European cultural perception seems to be locked into identifying with this very enigmatic small group of ancient whites. These people were supposed to have invaded India from Europe, conquering the indigenous *dark skinned* population and eventually becoming the *high caste* rulers of India. When we analyze the data concerning this supposed great Indo-European nation that conquered India thousands of years ago, we are faced with an almost blank wall. The amnesia that seems to over shadow the beginnings of Greek civilization also seem to fit into this enigma. White Euro/American archaeologists have woven an intricately detailed tapestry of blatantly falsified information that gives completely (and deliberately) misleading data concerning these issues. Unless you are a diligent and passionate scholar you will totally miss countless crucial details and anomalies that completely overturn this paradigm. The manner in which small groups of *nomadic, war-like, illiterate barbarians* created the Indus Valley civilizations and wrote the *Vedas, Upanishad, Bhagavad-Gita* and various Indian holy books has never been *realistically* explained by any historian at all:

*The **Aryans** built no cities, no states, no granaries, and used no writing. Instead they were a **warlike** people that organized themselves in small individual tribal, kinship units, the **Jana**. The Jana was ruled over by a war-chief. These tribes spread quickly over northern India and the Deccan **in a process that we still do not yet understand**...*

The likely explanation that can elucidate the emergence of the small group designated as the Aryan type so suddenly is the deliberate intervention and *genetic manipulation* of that group by an *'outside agency'*. We can also detect very similar procedures in the historical development of the Jewish nation. The sudden emergence of the Mongoloid racial groups might also be an intricate part of this puzzle.

Certainly, the prodigious advances made in technology by whites over the centuries appear to follow a linear process but on deeper analysis can be seen to have been *'prodded'* along to suit more far reaching agendas. The vast and *sudden increase* of technological development by Euro/American nations over the last three hundred years is therefore, in this view, indicative of this process of subtle and *direct intervention* in human development by outside agencies.

We do know that the new *alien/human hybrids* now in production are being secretly integrated into human society. They are indistinct in phenotype (appearance) from normal looking Caucasian humans. British author, Nigel Kerner, states further:

It's my theory that the Greys have, through the millennia, been configuring a certain genus of humanity who is specially designed for their own purposes. This particular type of human being will do their bidding with the planet tacitly and by default. These are the colonialists of whom Professor Susan Greenfield speaks along with any notions they might have of racial purity or superiority.

It would seem the vanguard of the new artificial intelligence revolution is also the vanguard of racism and disregard for the predicament of those of a different skin colour who don't even have clean water to drink. Thus, those who are already dehumanized seem to be the ones promoting further dehumanization.

We must always keep in mind that *time* is not what we think it is and can be altered by beings that have the knowledge and expertise to do so. The human race, in the final analysis, is at war with a force so insidious, manipulative and inscrutable that all the systems of logic and reasoning we are familiar with seem to pale into insignificance. But this is the crucial point; we have to dig deeper into our *'mental tool box'* to find the proper responses to this invasion of our humanity.

The Reptilian/Grey/Nordic extraterrestrial alliance (and their 5th and 6th dimensional handlers) have, over the years, (unwittingly or otherwise) exposed certain aspects of their ultimate agenda to some *abductees* and going by this and analysis of their behavioral patterns we have gleaned crucially important parts of the agenda. There will certainly be global cataclysm and devastation such as huge tectonic plate movements causing massive earthquakes and displacement of millions of people. There will be massive volcanic eruptions and unprecedented violent hurricanes and weather disturbances that will claim the lives of many millions of human beings. According to very reliable sources the World War III scenario will almost certainly become a devastating reality; (the Iran/North Korea/China/Afghanistan situation is the warm up to this event). It's also possible that there might be an asteroid or meteor impact that would cause great damage to the earth. Any combinations of these scenarios are possible. These incidents will cause global panic as theories about the earth shifting poles or orbit becomes widespread. Our technological advances in communications will be used to consolidate the stark fear of what is happening. All these things will psychologically impact upon the human race dramatically and allow the *predatory alien-demons* to appear publicly, holding out the hand of friendship and offers of help in our moment of weakness. We do know that many abductees have been trained, programmed and implanted with cybernetic devices by the Greys to assist their efforts *'from the inside'* when the time comes for the takeover. The demons will not appear themselves on account of the terror they undoubtedly strike in the hearts of human beings by their physical appearance. The human/alien hybrids will be the *presentable side* to their agenda. Of course the hybrids will appear as *super intelligent*, *handsome* and *beautiful aliens* from some far away planet or the other, who saw our plight and have come to help us. Other aspects of this scenario will include the using of our *religious structures* to imply that they are our ancient *Gods* returned with beneficence, or angelic beings from heaven or the fourth dimension and so on. That is essentially the bait which the aliens firmly believe will lure humanity into their cold hands. It's important to remember that the Illuminati faction on earth is merely a tool to facilitate the New World Order so that the alien-demonic takeover can be as smooth as possible. The forces of the New World Order will provide the necessary logistics such as *intelligence, storm-troopers* and *armies* to quell any dissent by humans opposed to alien invasion and takeover and to implement policies of *ethnic cleansing* across the earth. The political organization of the New World Order will be headed by the alien/human hybrids who will act as management teams. Nigel Kerner alludes to this strongly when he asks:

*Are we being conned by a conspiracy controlled by a **small hidden powerful cartel of** **alien sponsored genotypes within governments**; a cartel that [goes beyond] presidents and prime ministers? What a chilling thought this is!*

The predators, being so meticulous and efficient, would certainly not want to expend unnecessary energy in having to deal with cleaning up any mess that might accrue as a result of their conquest.

Despite the nature of the situation we must *never* at any point give in to despair. We do have more than a fighting chance. The fact that these entities have had to hide in the shadows for so long while they manipulate us is a clear sign that (in some very strange way) they probably also *fear* us. We need to always remember that they are in fact not really more intelligent than us at all; they just *use* their intelligence in very different ways than we do. *They would like to become like us*; to feel like us and to have *access* to the divine *spiritual energy* that we are naturally connected to. Being a human being is a very precious thing. We are actually *portals* through which the divine energy of the *Creator* expresses itself in creation. We cannot be disconnected from our *Source* because in reality, we and the *Source* are *always **and forever a***

unified whole.

It's also important to recognize that there are many very positive and truly benign beings in our universe that are completely aware of the situation on earth. Some of these beings have also been interacting with humanity throughout our history, assisting our development through spiritual guidance and imparting consciousness transforming knowledge. The African spiritual traditions elaborate extensively on these issues. We always must remember this and be open to the positive vibrations whenever it manifests. Positive beings do not use force or manipulation to coerce us into liaisons with them; they always follow the code of ***service-to-others*** not the ***service-to-self*** mode of interaction. Within the larger spiritual realms, the higher hierarchies of positive forces are always working to assist our evolution positively.

We have to find ways to approach these issues consciously and most importantly, without fear. There are millions of us, black and white, that now know about the alien-demonic infestation of our humanity and we must now call upon the divine powers that are at our command and rid ourselves and our world of this threat to our existence by coming together and linking our minds, hearts and souls to the eternal principle of the ONELOVE. One does not necessarily have to subscribe to any particular system of religion or ideology, but merely to embrace our divine Creator, our commonality as loving human beings and the conscious hope of a better tomorrow for all.

ONELOVE

African Rock Art: Tasili N'Ajjer - *http://www.met museum.org/toah/hi/te_index.asp*

African skeletons in China: *(see: K.C. Chang, The archaeology of ancient China, (Yale University Press: New Haven,1977) p.76)*

A History of the African-Olmecs, *pub. by www.AuthorHouse.com essay by http://community.webtv.net/pabarton nubianem@webtv.net*

Ancient Nubian Civilization: *Ta-Nefer Ankh, www.kemetway.com*

Ancient Man and His First Civilizations:
http://realhistory.com/world_history/ancient/victory_ stelae_of_piye.htm

Anta Diop, Cheikh: *African Origin of Civilization - Myth or Reality (1974)*
Anta Diop, Cheikh: *Civilization Or Barbarism, (Lawrence Hill Books, 1981)*
Barton, Paul: *Black Civilizations Of Ancient America (Muu-Lan), Mexico (Xi),*
http://www.*raceandhistory.com*

Black Civilizations of Ancient America,
http://www.raceandhistory.com/historicalviews/ancientamerica.htm

Bernal Martin: *Black Athena, Vol 1, The Afro-asiatic Roots of Classical Civilization, (1987) Rutgers University Press*
Black Athena: Afro-Asiatic Roots of Classical Civilization: The Archaeological and Documentary Evidence Vol 2, *(1991)*

Carlson, D. and Van Gerven, D.P: *Diffusion, biological determinism and bio-cultural adaptation in the Nubian corridor, American Anthropologist, 81, 561-580. (1979)*

Cremo, Michael & Richard L. Thompson: *Forbidden Archaeology, (1993)*
Cress Welsing, Francis: *The Isis Papers: The Keys to the Colours (1991)*

Deem, Rich: *When Junk DNA Isn't Junk,*
http://www.godandscience.org/evolution/junkdna.

Desplagnes, M: *Deux nouveau cranes humains de cites lacustres. L'Anthropologie, 17, 134-137.* (1906)

Diehl, R. A., & Coe, M.D: *Olmec Archaeology. Ritual and Rulership, (pp.11-25). The Art Museum: Princeton University Press. (1995).*

Draper Robert: *(article) The Black Pharaohs, (National Geographic, February 2008)*

Fuller Jr, Neely: *The United Independent Compensatory Code/System/Concept: A Textbook/Workbook for Thought, Speech, and/or Action for Victims of Racism (White Supremacy), 1971*

Feynman, Richard, *QED: The Strange Theory of Light and Matter, (Princeton, 1988, pages 82-83, 91, 129): (relate to VoDou Physics/IFA et al).*

Garvey, Amy Jacques, *The Philosophies and Opinions of Marcus Mosiah Garvey (1925)*

Gribbin, John & Gribbin, Mary: *Richard Feynman, A Life In Science (Dutton, Penguin,(1997), at pages 85-87)*

Hislop, Alexander: *The Two Babylons - (1919), p. 105*
Hitchcock, Andrew Carrington: *The Synagogue of Satan*
Howell,
Icke, David: *The Robot's Rebellion,* (1994),The Biggest Secret, (1999), *Children of the Matrix (2001), et al.) Bridge of Love Publishers*

Ifa, (Global Early Religion/Global Early Civilization), *http://Valdostamuseum.org/hamsmith/vodouFa.html#vodou#vodou*

Junk DNA, *http://www.crystallinks.com/genetics.html*

Keita,S.O.Y: *Studies and comments on ancient Egyptian biological relationships, History in Africa, 20, 129-131.* (1993)

Keita,S.O.Y.& Kittles,R.A. (1997). *The persistence of racial thinking and the myth of racial divergence, American Anthropologist, 99 (3), 534-544.*

Jacobs, David: *The Threat: Revealing the Secret Alien Agenda.* (1998). *(Simon &*

Schuster),

James G.M: *Stolen Legacy*, (1954)

Keleher, Terry: *Applied Research Center at UC Berkeley, For the Race and Public Policy Conference, (2004)*

(Kwang-chih Chang, 'Prehistoric and early historic culture horizons and traditions in South China'. Current Anthropology, 5 (1964) pp.359-375:375).

Kerner, Nigel: *Song of the Greys, (1999),*
Grey Aliens and the Harvesting of Souls (2010)

Lower Nubia in the late Third Millennium B.C: *The Arrival of the "C-Group" and the Kingdoms of Wawat, Irtjet, and Setju, http://www.edc.org/copyright.html*

Massey, Gerald: *Ancient Egypt, The Light of the World, (1907)*

MacGaffey,W: *Concepts of race in Northeast Africa. In J.D. Fage and R.A. Oliver, Papers in African Prehistory (pp.99-115), Cambridge University Press. (1970)*

Nubian Civilization
Verses National Geographic Society Racist Pathology –
http://kemetway.com/index.html

Petrie, W.M. Flinders: *A History of Egypt - Part Three, (1896), p. 308*

Petrie, W.M. Flinders *The Making of Egypt, (1939), p. 125*

Reuss, Christoph: *How the IMF Destroys Countries, (2001),*
http://www.suntimes.com/ebert/ebert_reviews/2001/10/102601.html
http://www.huffingtonpost.com/social/winningticket/the-imf-destroys-iceland_b_276193_30256242.html

Runes, Dagobert D, *Despotism – A Pictorial History, Philosophical Library Inc (1963,) USA*

Swann, Ingo: *Human versus ET Superpowers*
www.biomindsuperpowers.com/Pages/humanvsET1.html -

The Global African Community, (History Notes), *A Brief Note on the African Presence in Early Central Asia, Runoko Rashidi - Global African Presence,* *http://www.cwo.com/~lucumi/runoko.html*

The Pioneer Fund Inc, *http://www.pioneerfund.org/founders.html*

Umeh, John: *After God is Dibia (volumes 1 & 2) Published by Karnak House, (1998)*

Van Sertima, Ivan: *They Came Before Columbus (New York: Random House, 1976).*

Winters Clyde: *The Nubians and Olmecs,* *http://homepages.luc.edu/~cwinter/ortiz1.htm*

Wiercinski, A: (1972). *Inter-and-Intrapopulational racial differentiation of Tlatilco, Cerro de Las Mesas, Teothuacan, Monte Alban and Yucatan Maya. XXXIX Congreso International de Americanistas, Lima 1970, Vol. 1,* pp.231-252.
Wiercinski, A. & Jairazbhoy, R.A: *The New Diffusionist, 5 (18), 5.* (1975).
Winters, C.A: (1977). *The influence of the Mnade scripts on American ancient writing systems. Bulletin de l'IFAN, t.39, Ser.B ,Number 2,* *405-431.*
Winters, C.A: (1979). *Manding writing in the New World-Part 1, Journal of African Civilization, 1 (1), 81-97.*
Winters, C.A: (1980). Appendix B: *The Jade Celts of LaVenta. In A. von Wuthenau, Unexpected faces in Ancient America (pp. 235-237). 2nd Edition. Mexico.*
Winters, C.A: (December 1981/ January 1982). *Mexico's Black heritage,The Black Collegian,76-82.*
Winters,C.A: (1983). *"The ancient Manding script". In Blacks in Science:ancient and modern, (ed.) by I. Sertima, (pp. 208-214), London: Transaction Books.*
Winters, C.A: (1984a). *Blacks in ancient America.Colorlines, 3(2), 27-28.*
Winters, C.A: (1984b). *Africans found first American Civilization, African Monitor, 1, 16-18.*
Winters, C.A: (1987). *The Harappan script, Journal of Tamil Studies, no.30,*
Winters, C.A: (1987b). *The Harappan writing of the Copper Tablets, Journal of Indian History, 62, .*
Winters, C.A: (1989). *A grammar of Dravido-Harappan Writing, Journal of Tamil Studies, 35, 53-71.*
Winters, C.A: (1990). *The Dravidian language and the Harappan script,*

Archiv Orientalni, 58, 301-309.

Winters, C.A: (1991). *The Proto-Sahara. In The Dravidian encyclopaedia (Vol. 1, pp. 553-556). Trivandrum, India: International School of Dravidian Linguistics.*

Winters, C.A: (1994). *Afrocentrism: A valid frame of reference, Journal of Black Studies, 25 (2), 170-190.*

Winters, C.A: (1996). *Foundations of the Afrocentric ancient history curriculum, The Negro Educational Review, 47 (3-4), 214-217.*

Winters, C.A. *The decipherment of Olmec Writing. Paper presented at the 74th meeting of the Central States Anthropological Society, Milwaukee, Wis, (1997, April)*

Yoruba Religion: cosmology and mythology, *http://www.mythome.org/mythhome.htm*

Yoruban Religion: *Cosmology and Mythology -*

http://www.mythome.org/mythhome.htm - Untangle Incorporated (2001)

Whitfield, John: Olmec Writing System Found, *Nature.com (http://www.nature.com/nsu/021202/021202-13.html)*

African Rock Art: Tasili N'Ajer: *http://www.metmuseum.org/toah/hd/tas/hd_tass.htm#ixzz186wvO0jn*

VoDou Physics and 130 GeV Truth Quark, *http://www.valdostamuseum.org/hamsmithd4d5e6hist http://www.valdostamuseum.org/hamsmith/sets2quarks4.html#sub3*

160,000-year-old fossilized skulls uncovered in Ethiopia are oldest anatomically modern humans: *http://www.berkeley.edu/news/media/releases/2003/06/11_oldest-humans.shtml*

Williams, Bruce Beyer: *The A-Group Royal Cemetery at Qustul, Cemetery L, The University of Chicago Oriental Institute Nubian Expedition, (1986)*

Lindsay, Robert: *The Birth of the Caucasian Race, http:/www./robertlindsay.wordpress.com*

Rensberger, B: *Black kings of ancient America, Science Digest, pg. 74-77 and 122. (September, 1988).*

S. A. Tishkoff, A. J. Pakstis, M. Stoneking, J. R. Kidd, G. Destro-Bisol, A. Sanjantila, R.-b. Lu, A. S. Deinard, G. Sirugo, T. Jenkins, K. K. Kidd, and A. G. Clark – *Short Tandem-Repeat Polymorphism/Alu Haplotype Variation at the PLAT Locus: Implications for Modern Human Origins* –
http:// www.ncbi.nlm.nih.gov/pmc/journals/203/&rct=j&sa=x&eiQFaTtfzNNSFhQfA 3fwi&ved=0CCIQ6QUoADAA&q=Tandem-Repeat+Polymorphism/Alu+Haplotype+Variations&usg=AFQjCNHOS4nrTFip

Genetics Research: *(Tishkoff et al. 1996a, 1998b), DM (Tishkoff et al. 1998a; S. A. Tishkoff, A. G. Clark, and T. Jenkins, unpublished data), DRD2 (Kidd et al. 1998), and PAH (Kidd et al. 2000) loci*

Sanger, Margaret *(Margaret Sanger, An Autobiography*, 1938)

The Yoruba People:
http://www.uiowa.edu/~africart/toc/history/giblinstate.html#yoruba

Uan Muhuggiag: Ancient Black Mummy,
http://www.time.com/time/magazine/article/0,9171,865145,00.html

Underhill,P.A.,Jin,L., Zemans,R., Oefner,J and Cavalli-Sforza,L.L.(1996, January). *A pre-Columbian Y chromosome-specific transition and its implications for human evolutionary history, Proceedings of the National Academy of Science USA,93, 196-200.*

Von Wuthenau, Alexander. *Unexplained Faces in Ancient America, 2nd Edition, Mexico (1980).*

Wiercinski,A. *(1972). Inter-and Intrapopulational Racial Differentiation of Tlatilco, Cerro de Las Mesas, Teothuacan, Monte Alban and Yucatan Maya, XXXIX Congreso Intern. de Americanistas, Lima 1970 ,Vol.1, 231-252.*

Wiercinski,A. *(1972b). An anthropological study on the origin of "Olmecs", Swiatowit 33, 143-174.*

Blessed Love:

Yicks
Akushla
Lee
Jenny
Don
Bev
Enrico
Amanda
Errol. P
Dominic
Elim Latif Tanveer
Ayesha
Kashif
Faisal

Further details

Ordering:

To order this book please visit listed websites:

www.jahlovepublishing.com

www.jahlove.co.uk

www.zayan-files.com

The author can be contacted and comments posted by e-mailed to:

tchandela@yahoo.co.uk *or*

info@jahlove.co.uk

The following working title is currently under production:

The Book of Livity

Any information or material that would be useful in my continuing research can be sent to me at the above email addresses and will be gratefully received. Please let me know the source so I can credit it. ***<u>Confidentiality is assured at all times</u>***.